America Project Making of, George Washington Paschal

# The Constitution of the United States defined and carefully annotated

America Project Making of, George Washington Paschal

**The Constitution of the United States defined and carefully annotated**

ISBN/EAN: 9783337056780

Printed in Europe, USA, Canada, Australia, Japan

Cover: Foto ©Suzi / pixelio.de

More available books at **www.hansebooks.com**

# THE CONSTITUTION

OF THE

# UNITED STATES

DEFINED AND CAREFULLY ANNOTATED.

BY

## GEORGE W. PASCHAL,

OF THE BAR OF THE SUPREME COURT OF THE UNITED STATES: AUTHOR OF "PASCHAL'S
ANNOTATED DIGEST," "A TREATISE ON CHARITABLE USES," ETC., ETC.

———————

WASHINGTON, D. C.:
W. H. & O. H. MORRISON, LAW BOOKSELLERS,
PUBLISHERS, IMPORTERS, AND STATIONERS.
1868.

TO THE

# PEOPLE OF THE UNITED STATES,

### THIS WORK

#### IS RESPECTFULLY DEDICATED BY ONE

#### WHOSE MOTTO THROUGH LIFE HAS BEEN

## "The Constitution and the Union."

## GEORGE W. PASCHAL,

OF TEXAS.

NEW YORK, 1868.

# PREFACE.

---

THE Editor offers no apology for presenting to the public an annotated copy of the Constitution of the United States. All men have fully realized the maxim, "that the next best thing to knowledge is to know where to find it." If, therefore, my book shall serve as a guide to useful and important information, a good work will have been accomplished. But it is believed that something better than the mere collection of copious references has been attained. The best definitions of every word and phrase have been given, upon the very highest authorities. The utility of such a success, if success it be, cannot be over-estimated.

The roots of the Constitution of the United States may be said to have been laid in the great principles of the English Constitution, which divided government into three separate departments, and which, from time to time, secured the absolute and subordinate rights of every subject, upon the firm basis of Magna Charta and the Petitions and Bills of Rights, and other guaranties of liberty. These principles were transplanted by our ancestors into the American colonies. They were proclaimed in the Declaration of Independence, which, in this edition, precedes the great work of our fathers; and they were re-incorporated into all the State Constitutions pending the Revolution. Therefore, the division of the powers of government into three departments—legislative, executive, and judicial—was the formation of a structure upon established models.

From the days of the promulgation of the Constitution of the United States to the present hour, it has been a subject of constant discussion. All that was preserved of the debates of the wise men of the Convention which modeled it, and of the State Conventions which ratified it; all that was said by the writers, such as the authors of the Federalist, and the press of that day, has been republished, and forms a popular portion of our current literature.

Rawle, Sergeant, Story, Baldwin, Duane, John Adams, and Farrar, have written their commentaries upon the Constitution; Curtis his excellent history of it; Calhoun his essay, giving the peculiar views of his school upon concurrent powers; Chancellor Kent devoted the best book in his great work to its elucidation; all our reports of judicial precedents abound with interpretations of it; the published opinions of learned Attorney-Generals have guided cabinets; the debates of all deliberative bodies are interspersed with closely studied or loosely expressed ideas in regard to it; every political editor and orator become its expos-

itors ; it is taught in all our law schools and many of
our colleges, and forms a chapter in the studies of all
candidates for the bar ; all officers are sworn to support
it ; every soldier and sailor in the late war took a like
oath as a condition of enlistment ; all amnestied and
pardoned rebels have been required to take oaths to
support and defend the Constitution and the Union
thereunder ; and, in those States which resisted it, no
one is admitted to be registered as a voter, without
taking the most solemn oath to the like effect ; every
naturalized foreigner is required to swear allegiance to
it ; the oaths thus administered, as the ligament or tie of
allegiance, are naturally binding upon every native-
born citizen in the country. And now, although the
sacred instrument has been published in every revision
of laws in the United States, in the Manuals of Congress, and by tens of thousands in that excellent *vade-
mecum* by Mr. Hickey, we hazard nothing in saying
that the Constitution is not conveniently accessible to
one in one hundred of the people whose duty it is to
read it. It is not even a book in all our public libra-
ries ; it is not in one house in fifty ; it is nowhere on
the catalogue of school-books ; and it is not taught in
one school in a thousand. •There is a kind of popular
fallacy that everybody understands the Constitution of
his country, when, truth to confess, comparatively few
have ever read it at all, and still fewer have studied it
carefully. And if the tenure of office depended upon
the ability to stand a careful examination upon it,

there would be enough vacancies to satisfy whole armies of "*outs*," who, in turn, could not take the oath to support it, were the previous test of ability to give all its features applied.

It is in no spirit of disparagement that we make this admission. Perhaps the same remark is applicable, to a greater or less extent, to every civilized people. There is too great a disposition among men to take essential things for granted. And yet when the philosophical historian comes to review the downfall of republics and empires, he is forced to the conclusion that the loss of liberty is more the result of ignorance of the fundamental principles of government than of apathy in defending them. The most exciting political contests which have divided this nation have been the results of political dogmas founded in willful or actual ignorance of the cardinal principles of the Constitution. A recurrence to "Americans shall rule America;" the "repeal of the naturalization laws," as a means of lessening suffrage; religious tests; "squatter sovereignty," and its opposite, need only be cited in illustration. Yet these were harmless polemics compared to the heresy of that peculiar school of "State sovereignty," which taught that the States had, in fact, *surrendered* nothing, but had only *delegated* certain powers, in trust, to a common agent; and that any State could, at any time, for any cause, or no cause, resume the delegated powers, and again peaceably take its place among the nations of the earth.

In such a book as I have prepared, and designed, as it is, for general use, and put forward to meet the wants of the millions, it is not intended to advocate or condemn any doctrine in an offensive manner. My own views of the government were formed after an examination of all the lights accessible to me, from 1830 to 1834. The doctrines of Nullification, or the right of a State to nullify, declare void, and resist a single law of the United States, and yet, as to all other laws, to be in harmony with the Union, were then the issues. From my Southern stand-point, I was compelled to examine the doctrines with all the prejudices of intelligent surroundings and motives of interest in favor of the Southern view. Opposition to a protective tariff; State pride; the apprehensions upon the subject of negro slavery, which the Missouri restriction had left, and the incipiency of abolitionism foreshadowed, naturally inclined all ardent young men to embrace the doctrines of the Virginia and Kentucky Resolutions, and the inviting school of "States Rights." But, on the other hand, we had the most prominent author of these reports and resolutions, and, indeed, the chief architect of the Constitution itself (Mr. MADISON), telling us that "Nullification and Secession had the same poisonous root." And we had the weight and power of GENERAL JACKSON's name and his iron will, standing upon the doctrines of that great expounder, DANIEL WEBSTER. I was obliged to take my position as a lawyer, as well as a lover of my country, with those who held that

the Constitution had created a government, not a mere
agency or compact; an enduring union, not a league
dissoluble at the pleasure of any State; a government
of limited powers, to be sure, but yet having all the
inherent powers necessary to protect, defend, and perpetuate the Union. These views have been greatly
strengthened by a life-long study of the principles and
practical workings of the government. And they carried along my convictions, that, as a citizen of the
United States, I owed my first and paramount allegiance to the nation, and not to the State of Georgia,
where I was born, and came to the bar, nor to the States
of Arkansas and Texas, where I afterward chanced to
reside, and which have been the theaters of the little
which has marked my unambitious public career; nor
yet to New York, where now I exercise my profession.

I can most simply illustrate these views by the example of Texas. That Republic, from 1836 to 1846, was
independent and sovereign. It possessed the powers
of national taxation, commerce, coining money, granting patents, punishing piracies, enforcing admiralty,
declaring war, raising and supporting armies and
navies, making treaties, forming alliances and confederations, being represented by ministers abroad, and
changing the republic to a dynasty, with princes and
orders of nobility. In fact, Texas had the lawful right
to do all that free, independent, and sovereign States
may do. But by annexation these people became citizens of the United States. As a government, they sur-

rendered or merged every vestige of nationality. They lost these rights to regulate commerce; to coin money and prescribe tenders; to declare war and make peace; to naturalize foreigners; to decitizenize any citizen of the United States, and to exercise every enumerated and non-enumerated national power. In consideration of this surrender of power, all Texans, of whatever nationality, became citizens of the United States, entitled to all the benefits, privileges, immunities, protection, and blessings of the Union. And, when compared to the previous impoverished State of Texas, these blessings were incalculable.

With these convictions, both as to principle and policy, I could never view the ordinances of secession in any other light than as revolution—resistance to lawfully constituted authority, without any appreciable justification. In anticipation of the mad, because excited effort, I prepared a treatise upon the doctrines of secession. But the crash was so sudden, that it smothered my effort before it reached the public eye. None shaken in my views, with the commencement of the terrible civil war, the fearful consequences of which I publicly foretold, not in any spirit of prophecy, but because they were the legitimate fruits of the efforts to sever such a government, I sat down to compile the "ANNOTATED DIGEST" upon the laws of Texas, and the Spanish laws, upon which many land-titles within half the area of the Union rested. I selected a provincial work, because long years of practice had forced me to

collect the materials. The Constitution of the United
States formed a single chapter; and because FREDERICK
W. BRIGHTLEY, Esq., had kindly permitted me to use
his exhaustive notes, my annotations were not the most
labored chapter in the book. I did little more than
add to his very accurate references, bringing the notes
down to 1865, re-arrange, number, and "cross-note"
them, so as to connect the subjects with other kindred
matter in my own digest. Yet I have received so many
high testimonials of the convenience of arrangement
and the great value and accuracy of the references, that
I have determined to put forth this little volume upon
the same plan of the "Annotated Digest," with the
commendations and approval of which I have had so
many reasons to be proud.

Upon the suggestions of some popular school-men,
the plan of authoritative definitions and side questions
has been adopted. While then the work will be an
exhaustive reference-book for the lawyer, the judge,
the statesman, the publicist, the editor, and the political writer (who should always have such a work upon
their tables), it is hoped that it may also prove a popular text-book for all our schools; or, if this fond anticipation shall fail, I trust that some more experienced
hand may be led to prepare a text-book which may
become as popular in its appropriate place as was ever
Webster's spelling-book.

Let us remember that we have four millions of freemen
who have been constitutionally made citizens of the

United States, in whose behalf the fundamental charter has been amended, few of whom can yet read the instrument which guaranteed their liberties, in common with others of their fellow-citizens. We have three hundred thousand lovers of liberty coming every year to our shores; and we have millions of native-born children, in rural districts and in cities, to whom the Constitution is not accessible. The course of safety, and of the preservation and perpetuation of liberty, would demand that Congress should adopt some well-arranged Manual upon the Constitution, and distribute it among the people. None occurs to the author as better than that which defines every phrase, and points to every higher authority which has discussed it, and which has an index so copious that none can be misled.

I beg all readers to believe that the political bias hereinbefore expressed has had no influence in the preparation of the notes. They have been given, honestly, as they were found in the authorities. If any light has been overlooked, it has been accidental, and the omission will be repaired in the future editions.

There are some great facts which the strongest prejudices cannot overlook. The efforts to establish the doctrines of secession in the name of State sovereignty have tested the strength of the Union; and whether doubtful powers have been rightfully or wrongfully exercised, they have been so exercised as to become estoppels upon the whole people. The Southern school started upon the theory that the " common de-

fense and general welfare" guaranties must be stricken
out of the Constitution. And while they retained the
great landmarks, and almost the identical language,
the idea of national internal improvements and protective tariffs was forbidden ; slavery was attempted to
be perpetuated ; and our "Rights in the Territories"
were so clearly defined, that the people thereof could
not protect themselves by their own wholesome legislation. But a single year of war found the anti-in-
ternal improvement States-Rights Government making
railroads, and in possession of all the railroads and
other means of transportation in the States, enforcing
general conscription, impressments, martial law, and
almost subsidizing the States which had confederated
themselves. And as to "new States," Kentucky and
Missouri were represented at Richmond, while the governments thereof were firm to the Union. In a word, the
plea of NECESSITY afforded an excuse for every exercise
of power. So, in the efforts to put down the rebellion,
the military power was pushed far beyond the most
ulterior centralizing ideas, and every obstacle which
stood in the way of preserving the life of the nation
was easily removed. West Virginia was admitted as
a State of the Union, upon the same principle that Kentucky and Missouri were admitted as States of "the
Confederate States of America ;" that is, because the
minority, who acknowledged their allegiance to the
central Government, were recognized as the lawful
State governments. It has thus become established,

that the powers to suppress insurrection and to crush rebellion, and the obligation to guarantee a republican form of government, carry along the right to recognize none but the State government in harmony with the Union as a lawfully existing State. Such is the clear theory of President Johnson's proclamations, setting aside State governments and appointing new magistracies; such the theory of Congress in passing the reconstruction laws; and such were the precedents in Richmond, which are binding upon the " engineers hoist by their own petards."

Therefore, the doctrines of "States Rights" seem to be narrowed down to the practical theory, that when all State officials cease to acknowledge the Constitution of the United States, and the laws and treaties made in pursuance thereof, as the "supreme law of the land," and the great mass of the people sustain them in rebellion, they so far lose their positions as States, as to leave the *means* of restoration to the law-making power of the Union, after amendments forming conditions of security shall have been superadded. Such are always the fruits of unsuccessful revolution.

These things are said in the interest of no partisan view. I would only exhort all men, and all children, to consider the Constitution of the United States as perpetual; to carefully study its every word and phrase, and the spirit and intention of every clause. And, above all, never to engage in its discussion without a clear comprehension of every word employed in regard to it ; and to trust no man nor journalist as an expounder who misquotes its language, and shows a real or willful ignorance of its provisions. Such teachers are the blind leading the blind.

The Constitution has created no authoritative expounder. Every exposition has, at last, to come to the test of popular opinion. How important, then, that the public judgment shall be enlightened. As the war has stricken human slavery out of the Constitution, we all, in some sort, stand upon a new era in regard to the protective principles and the guaranties of liberty which it contains. And yet it is the order of the human mind, under all dispensations, to consult precedents ; to allow them always to be persuasive, and generally controlling. In this light every citation in this little book has its value.

The Editor does not claim perfection even in references, or the extent of research. And as it is intended to keep the work up as long as new editions are demanded, he would be very thankful for any suggestion of errors or omissions. The effort is an experiment. All who will weigh the great problem of liberty, will acknowledge the importance of educating every mind in the true principles of our government. This can only be done by precept upon precept, line upon line, here a little and there a little. If the zeal and anxiety of the Editor is great, let his apology be, that he has suffered keenly from the intolerance growing out of ignorance of the true principles of constitutional liberty, and the reckless depravity in regard to their preservation. His moral duty, in the direction of enlightenment, is therefore great.

GEO. W. PASCHAL, of Texas.

*No. 26 Exchange Place, New York.*

# TABLE OF CONTENTS.

*Articles, Sections, Clauses, Pages, and Numbers, of Notes of the Constitution of the United States, Unnoted and Annotated.*

xxii                    CONTENTS.

# TABLE OF AUTHORITIES CITED AND ABBREVIATIONS USED.

Ab. on Ship............Abbot on Shipping.
Adams................John Adams' Defense of the American Constitution.
Adams Rom. Ant.......Adams' Roman Antiquities.
Allen.................Allen's (Mass.) Reports.
Ala..................Alabama Reports.
Am. Almanac..........American Almanac.
Am. Almanac Rep.......American Almanac Repository.
Am. Jur..............American Jurist.
Am. Lead. C..........American Leading Cases.
Am. L. J.............American Law Journal.
Am. L. R.............American Law Register,
And. Rev. L..........Andrew's Revenue Laws.
Ang. on Tidewaters....Angel on Tidewaters.
Ang. and Ames........Angel and Ames on Corporations.
Archbold's Law of Bankruptcy.
Ash.–Ashm............Ashmead's Reports.
Bacon's Ab...........Bacon's Abridgment.
Bailey...............Bailey's Reports.
Bald. C. C...........Baldwin's Circuit Court Reports. *(?)*
Barb.................Barbour's Reports. *(?)*
Barnes...............Barnes' Cases of Practice.
Barr.................Barr's Pennsylvania State Reports.
Bates................Attorney-General, Edward Bates.
Benton's Debates......Benton's Condensed Congressional Debates.
Benton's Thirty Years in the Senate.
Bing.................Bingham's Reports. *(English)*
Binn.................Binney's Reports.
Bevan................Bevan's Reports. *(Beavan)*
Bioren and Duane's Laws of the United States.
Bishop on Cr. L.......Bishop on Criminal Law.
Black................Black's Reports.
Blackf...............Blackford's Reports.
Bl.–Bl. Com..........Blackstone's Commentaries.
Blackwood............Blackwood's Reports.
Blatch...............Blatchford's Reports.
Blount's Trial.
Breese...............Breese's Reports.
Brightly.............Brightly's Reports.
Brightly's Dig........Brightly's Digest of Laws of U. S.
Brock................Brockenborough's Reports. *(Va.)*
Burr's Trial.

Burr.-Bur.............Burrow's Reports.  (English)
Bynkershoek...........Bynkershoek on War.
Caine ................Caine's Cases in Error. (N. Y.)
Calhoun's Essay on Government.
Cal....................California Reports.
Call...................Call's Reports.
Camp...................Campbell's Reports.
Carth .................Carthew's Reports.
Casey .................Casey's Pennsylvania State Reports.
Chase's Trial.
Chev. ................Cheve's Reports.
Ch. Pl................Chitty's Pleadings.
Cicero pro Sulla........Cicero's Oration for Sulla.
Clark & Finnell........Clark and Finnelly's Reports. (             end.
Cl. & Hall.............Clark and Hall's Reports.
Cobb...................Cobb on Slavery.
Cobbett's Parliamentary History.
Coke...................Coke's Reports. (English)
Co. Litt...............Coke on Littleton. (Va )
Coldwell...............Coldwell's Reports. (Va )
Comst ......  ........Comstock's Reports. (N. Y.
Com. Dig..............Comyn's Digest.  Eng
Cond..................Peters's Condensed Reports.  (U. S.  ,
Conn. ................Connecticut Reports. (N. Y.)
Cow...................Cowen's Reports. (N. Y.)
Crabbe...............Crabbe's Reports.
Cr...................Cranch's Reports. (U. S.
Cr. C. C..............Cranch's Circuit Court Reports.
Curt. C. C............Curtis' Circuit Court Reports.
Curt. Com............Curtis' Commentaries.
Curt. Hist............Curtis' History of the Constitution.
Curtis' Law of Patents.
Cush..................Cushing's Reports. (Mass.)
Dall..................Dallas' Reports. (U. S. & P.)
Daveis ...............Daveis' Reports.
De Lolme..............De Lolme's Works. (N. Y.
Den..................Denio's Reports. (N. Y.)
Dev..................Devereux's Reports. (N. C.)
Dev. & Bat...........Devereux and Battle's Reports.
Doug.................Douglass's Reports.
Duane................Duane's American Law. (N. Y.)
Duer.................Duer's Reports. (N. Y.)
Duval...............Judge Thomas H. Duval.
Duvall..............Duvall's Reports.
Dyer.................Dyer's Reports.
East ................East's Report's. (Eng
Elliot's Deb..........Elliot's Debates.
Eng. L. and Eq........English Law and Equity.
Farrar...............Farrar on the Constitution.
Federalist.
Finch ...............Finch's Reports.
Fort.................Fortescue's Reports.

Ga..................Georgia Reports.
Gill.................Gillman's Reports.
Gr...................Greene's Reports.
Gray................Gray's Reports.
Greenlf. Ev...........Greenleaf's Evidence.
H. & McH............Harris and McHenry's Reports.
Hagg............ .....Haggard's Reports.
Hale P. C........ .....Hale's Pleas of the Crown.
Hall L. J.............Hall's Law Journal.
Hall's Journal..........Hall's Journal of Jurisprudence.
Halleck..............Halleck's International Law.
Halst...............Halsted's Reports.
Hare ............ ...Hare's Reports.
Harg................Hargrave's State Trials.
Harp ................Harper's Reports.
Harring.—Harrington...Harrington's Reports.
Hawk................Hawk's Reports.
Hawkins.............Hawkins's Pleas of the Crown.
Hayw...............Hayward's Reports.
Hemphill's Report on Internal Improvements.
Hemp ................Hempstead's Reports.
Hickey's Const........Hickey's Constitution.
Hill.................Hill's N. Y. Reports.
Hough's Convention Manual of State Constitutions.
How.... .............Howard's Reports.
Humph.............Humphrey's Reports.
Hutch.'s Hist..........Hutching's History of New England.
Ill. R................Illinois Reports.
Ind. Rep..............Indiana Reports.
Ing. on *Hab. Corp*......Ingersoll on *Habeas Corpus*.
Ired ................Iredell's Reports.
Jefferson's Manual.
Jeff. Corresp..........Jefferson's Correspondence.
Johns... .............Johnson's Reports.
Johns. Ch............Johnson's Chancery Reports.
Journal of Convention.
Journal of the Senate.
Journal of the House.
Kent.—Kent's Com.....Kent's Commentaries.
Kentucky Resolutions.
Kern.—Kernan........Kernan's Reports.
Kirby................Kirby's Reports.
Law Mag.............Law Magazine.
Legal Int.............Legal Intelligencer.
Legaré ..............Attorney-General Legaré.
Leigh ...............Leigh's Reports.
Lewis, Commissioner of Internal Revenue.
Lieber...............Lieber's Encyclopedia Americana.
Litt ................Littell's Reports.
Littleton .............Coke on Littleton.
Lloyd's Debates.
Lord King's Life of Locke.

M. and Sel............Maule and Selwyn's Reports. *(English)*
Mackeld's Civ. L.......Mackeld's Civil Law.
*Magna Charta.*
Marshall's Life of Washington.
Mas.—Mas. C. C........Mason's Circuit Court Reports. *(U.S.)*
Mass................Massachusetts Reports.
McAllister............McAllister's Reports. *(Cal. Ci. Ct.)*
McLean .............McLean's Reports.
Md.................Maryland Reports.
Meigs...............Meigs's Reports.
Met................Metcalf's Reports.
Miles...............Miles's Reports.
Minn...............Minnesota Reports.
Miss...............Mississippi Reports.
Mo ................Missouri Reports.
Monr...............Monroe's Reports.
Mont.—Montesq.......Montesquieu's Spirit of Laws.
Moore Privy Council...Moore's Privy Council Reports.
Mumf...............Mumford's Reports.
N. H.. ............New Hampshire Reports.
N. Y. *Herald.*         New York *Herald.*
N. Y. Reports.          New York Reports.
O. Bridge Reports .....Sir Oliver Bridge's Reports.
O..................Ohio Reports.
Op.................Opinions of the Attorney-General.
Paige ..............Paige's Reports. *(N.)*
Paine ..............Paine's Reports.
Paschal's Annotated Digest of the Laws of Texas.
Peake...............Peake's Cases.
Penn...............Pennington's Reports.
Penn. L. J..........Pennsylvania Law Journal.
Penn. State.........Pennsylvania State Reports. *(U.S. S.C.)*
Pet................Peters's Reports.
Pet. C. C...........Peters's Circuit Court Reports.
Phila. R............Philadelphia Reports.
Philadelphia *Ledger.*
Phillimore...........Phillimore's International Law.
Pick ...............Pickering's Reports. *(Mass.)*
Pitk...............Pitkin's History of the United States.
Pittsburg L. J.......Pittsburg Legal Journal.
Port...............Porter's Reports.
Puffendorf..........Puffendorf's Works.
Randolph. .........Randolph's Reports.
Rawle .............Rawle's Reports.
Rawle's Const........Rawle on the Constitution.
Rich...............Richardson's Reports. *Eng.*
Salkeld............Salkeld's Reports. *Eng.*
Sandf..............Sandford's Reports *(N.Y.)*
S. C...............Same Case. *(Ills.)*
Scam...............Scammon's Reports.
Sedgwick on Statutory and Constitutional Law.
Seld ..............Selden's Reports. *(N.Y.)*

Senate Journal.
Serg. Const............Sergeant on the Constitution. *(Penna.)*
S. & R ................Sergeant and Rawle's Reports.
Shep. ................Shepley's Reports.
Shepherd.............Shepherd's Touchstone.
Smith.................Smith's (Penn.) Reports.
Smith's Leading Cases
Smith's Wealth of Nations.
So. Car...............South Carolina Reports.
Speed........... ....Attorney-General, James Speed.
Spelman...............Spelman's Works.
Stanbery ............Attorney-General, Henry Stanbery
Stewart ..............Stewart's Reports.
Stanton ..............Attorney-General, Edwin Stanton.
Story ................Story's Reports.
Story's Confl. of L......Story's Conflict of Laws.
Story's Const..........Story on the Constitution.
Story on Cont.........Story on Contracts.
Strange...............Strange's Reports.
Sumner's ............Sumner's Reports.
Taylor's Civil Law.
Tex..................Texas Reports.
Thatcher Cr. C........Thatcher's Criminal Cases.
Tomlin's Law Dic.......Tomlin's Law Dictionary.
Tucker's Black. App.....Tucker's Blackstone, Appendix.
Vallandigham's Trial.
Vattel's Law of Nations.
Verm. R.—Vt. R.......Vermont Reports.
Vern.................Vernon's Reports.
Ves..................Vesey's Reports.
Vesey, Jr.............Vesey, Jr.'s, Reports.
Virginia Resolutions and Report.
Walker...............Walker's Report.
Wall.................Wallace's Reports.
Wall., Jr.............Wallace, Jr.'s, Reports.
Wash. C. C...........Washington Circuit Court Reports
Watts '...............Watts Reports.
Webster's Dic.........Webster's Dictionary.
Webster's Speeches.
Wend................Wendell's Reports.
Western Leg. Obsr......Western Legal Observer.
Wharton La...........Wharton's Criminal Law.
Wharton on Homicides.
Wh.—Wheat..........Wheaton's Reports.
Wheaton's Life of Pinckney.
Wheat. Int. L..........Wheaton's International Law.
Wheeler's Law of Slavery.
Whiting..............Whiting on the War Power.
Wil. M. C............Wilcock on Municipal Corporations.
Wils. Law Lect. ......Wilson's Law Lectures.
Will.................Wills's Reports.
Wirt................Attorney-General, William Wirt.

# THE DECLARATION OF INDEPENDENCE.

## *A Declaration by the Representatives of the United States of America, in Congress assembled.*

WHEN, in the course of human events, it becomes necessary for one people to dissolve the political bands which have connected them with another, and to assume, among the powers of the earth, the separate and equal station to which the laws of nature and of nature's God entitle them, a decent respect to the opinions of mankind requires that they should declare the causes which impel them to the separation.

We hold these truths to be self-evident, that all men are created equal; that they are endowed by their Creator with certain unalienable rights; that among these, are life, liberty, and the pursuit of happiness. That, to secure these rights, governments are instituted among men, deriving their just powers from the consent of the governed; that whenever any form of government becomes destructive of these ends, it is the right of the people to alter or to abolish it, and to institute a new government, laying its foundation on such principles, and organizing its powers in such

1

form, as to them shall seem most likely to effect their safety and happiness. Prudence, indeed, will dictate that governments long established, should not be changed for light and transient causes ; and, accordingly, all experience hath shown, that mankind are more disposed to suffer, while evils are sufferable, than to right themselves by abolishing the forms to which they are accustomed. But, when a long train of abuses and usurpations, pursuing invariably the same object, evinces a design to reduce them under absolute despotism, it is their right, it is their duty, to throw off such government, and to provide new guards for their future security. Such has been the patient sufferance of these colonies, and such is now the necessity which constrains them to alter their former systems of government. The history of the present king of Great Britain is a history of repeated injuries and usurpations, all having, in direct object, the establishment of an absolute tyranny over these States. To prove this, let facts be submitted to a candid world :

He has refused his assent to laws the most wholesome and necessary for the public good.

He has forbidden his Governors to pass laws of immediate and pressing importance, unless suspended in their operation till his assent should be obtained ; and, when so suspended, he has utterly neglected to attend to them.

He has refused to pass other laws for the accommodation of large districts of people, unless those people would relinquish the right of representation in the legislature ; a right inestimable to them, and formidable to tyrants only.

He has called together legislative bodies at places unusual, uncomfortable, and distant from the depository of their public records, for the sole purpose of fatiguing them into compliance with his measures.

He has dissolved representative houses repeatedly, for opposing, with manly firmness, his invasions on the rights of the people.

He has refused, for a long time after such dissolutions, to cause others to be elected ; whereby the legislative powers, incapable of annihilation, have returned to the people at large for their exercise ; the State remaining, in the mean time, exposed to all the danger of invasion from without, and convulsions within.

He has endeavored to prevent the population of these States; for that purpose, obstructing the laws for naturalization of foreigners ; refusing to pass others to encourage their migration hither, and raising the conditions of new appropriations of lands.

He has obstructed the administration of justice, by refusing his assent to laws for establishing judiciary powers.

He has made judges dependent on his will alone, for the tenure of their offices, and the amount and payment of their salaries.

He has erected a multitude of new offices, and sent

hither swarms of officers to harass our people, and eat out their substance.

He has kept among us, in times of peace, standing armies, without the consent of our legislature.

He has affected to render the military independent of, and superior to, the civil power.

He has combined, with others, to subject us to a jurisdiction foreign to our constitution, and unacknowledged by our laws; giving his assent to their acts of pretended legislation:

For quartering large bodies of armed troops among us:

For protecting them, by a mock trial, from punishment, for any murders which they should commit on the inhabitants of these States:

For cutting off our trade with all parts of the world:

For imposing taxes on us without our consent:

For depriving us, in many cases, of the benefits of trial by jury:

For transporting us beyond the seas to be tried for pretended offenses:

For abolishing the free system of English laws in a neighboring province, establishing therein an arbitrary government, and enlarging its boundaries, so as to render it at once an example and fit instrument for introducing the same absolute rule into these colonies:

For taking away our charters, abolishing our most valuable laws, and altering, fundamentally, the powers of our governments:

For suspending our own legislatures, and declaring themselves invested with power to legislate for us in all cases whatsoever.

He has abdicated government here, by declaring us out of his protection, and waging war against us.

He has plundered our seas, ravaged our coasts, burnt our towns, and destroyed the lives of our people.

He is, at this time, transporting large armies of foreign mercenaries to complete the works of death, desolation, and tyranny, already begun, with circumstances of cruelty and perfidy scarcely paralleled in the most barbarous ages, and totally unworthy the head of a civilized nation.

He has constrained our fellow-citizens, taken captive on the high seas, to bear arms against their country, to become the executioners of their friends and brethren, or to fall themselves by their hands.

He has excited domestic insurrection amongst us, and has endeavored to bring on the inhabitants of our frontiers, the merciless Indian savages, whose known rule of warfare is an undistinguished destruction of all ages, sexes, and conditions.

In every stage of these oppressions, we have petitioned for redress, in the most humble terms; our repeated petitions have been answered only by repeated injury. A prince, whose character is thus marked by every act which may define a tyrant, is unfit to be the ruler of a free people.

Nor have we been wanting in attention to our British brethren. We have warned them, from time to time, of attempts made by their legislature to extend an unwarrantable jurisdiction over us. We have reminded them of the circumstances of our emigration and settlement here. We have appealed to their native justice and magnanimity, and we have conjured them, by the ties of our common kindred, to disavow these usurpations, which would inevitably interrupt our connections and correspondence. They, too, have been deaf to the voice of justice and consanguinity. We must, therefore, acquiesce in the necessity, which denounces our separation, and hold them, as we hold the rest of mankind, enemies in war, in peace, friends.

We, therefore, the representatives of the UNITED STATES OF AMERICA, in GENERAL CONGRESS assembled, appealing to the Supreme Judge of the World for the rectitude of our intentions, do, in the name, and by the authority of the good people of these colonies, solemnly publish and declare, That these United Colonies are, and of right ought to be, FREE AND INDEPENDENT STATES; that they are absolved from all allegiance to the British crown, and that all political connection between them and the State of Great Britain, is, and ought to be, totally dissolved; and that, as *FREE AND INDEPENDENT STATES*, they have full power to levy war, conclude peace, contract alliances, establish commerce, and to do all other acts and things which INDEPENDENT

STATES may of right do. And for the support of this declaration, with a firm reliance on the protection of Divine Providence, we mutually pledge to each other, our lives, our fortunes, and our sacred honor

The foregoing declaration was, by order of Congress, engrossed, and signed by the following members:—

JOHN HANCOCK.

*New Hampshire.*
Josiah Bartlett,
William Whipple,
Matthew Thornton.
*Massachusetts Bay.*
Samuel Adams,
John Adams,
Robert Treat Paine,
Elbridge Gerry.
*Rhode Island.*
Stephen Hopkins,
William Ellery.
*Connecticut.*
Roger Sherman,
Samuel Huntington,
William Williams,
Oliver Wolcott.
*New York.*
William Floyd,
Philip Livingston,
Francis Lewis,
Lewis Morris.
*New Jersey.*
Richard Stockton,
John Witherspoon,
Francis Hopkinson,

John Hart,
Abraham Clark.
*Pennsylvania.*
Robert Morris,
Benjamin Rush,
Benjamin Franklin,
John Morton,
George Clymer,
James Smith,
George Taylor,
James Wilson,
George Ross.
*Delaware.*
Cæsar Rodney,
George Read,
Thomas M'Kean.
*Maryland.*
Samuel Chase,
William Paca,
Thomas Stone,
Charles Carroll, of Carrollton.
*Virginia.*
George Wythe,
Richard Henry Lee,
Thomas Jefferson,
Benjamin Harrison,

*Virginia.*
Thomas Nelson, Jr.,
Francis Lightfoot Lee,
Carter Braxton.

*North Carolina.*
William Hooper,
Joseph Hewes,
John Penn.

*South Carolina.*
Edward Rutledge,
Thomas Heyward, Jr.,
Thomas Lynch, Jr.,
Arthur Middleton.

*Georgia.*
Button Gwinnett,
Lyman Hall,
George Walton.

*Resolved,* That copies of the Declaration be sent to the several assemblies, conventions, and committees, or councils of safety, and to the several commanding officers of the continental troops; that it be proclaimed in each of the United States, and at the head of the army.

---

## ARTICLES OF CONFEDERATION AND PERPETUAL UNION BETWEEN THE STATES.

The following have been critically compared with the original Articles of Confederation in the Department of State, and found to conform minutely to them in text, letter, and punctuation. It may therefore be relied upon as a true copy.

TO ALL TO WHOM THESE PRESENTS SHALL COME, WE THE UNDERSIGNED DELEGATES OF THE STATES AFFIXED TO OUR NAMES, SEND GREETING.—Whereas the Delegates of the United States of America in Congress assembled did on the 15th day of November in the Year of our Lord 1777, and in the Second Year of the Independence of

America agree to certain articles of Confederation and perpetual Union between the States of New Hampshire, Massachusetts-bay, Rhode-island and Providence Plantations, Connecticut, New-York, New-Jersey, Pennsylvania, Delaware, Maryland, Virginia, North-Carolina, South-Carolina, and Georgia, in the words following, viz.

"ARTICLES OF CONFEDERATION AND PERPETUAL UNION BETWEEN THE STATES OF NEW HAMPSHIRE, MASSACHUSETTS-BAY, RHODE-ISLAND AND PROVIDENCE PLANTATIONS, CONNECTICUT, NEW-YORK, NEW-JERSEY, PENNSYLVANIA, DELAWARE, MARYLAND, VIRGINIA, NORTH-CAROLINA, SOUTH-CAROLINA, AND GEORGIA.

ARTICLE I. The Stile of this confederacy shall be "The United States of America."

ARTICLE II. Each state retains its sovereignty, freedom and independence, and every Power, Jurisdiction and right, which is not by this confederation expressly delegated to the united states, in congress assembled.

ARTICLE III. The said states hereby severally enter into a firm league of friendship with each other, for their common defence, the security of their Liberties, and their mutual and general welfare, binding themselves to assist each other, against all force offered to, or attacks made upon them, or any of them, on account of religion, sovereignty, trade, or any other pretence whatever.

1*

ARTICLE IV. The better to secure and perpetuate mutual friendship and intercourse among the people of the different states in this union, the free inhabitants of each of these states, paupers, vagabonds, and fugitives from Justice excepted, shall be entitled to all privileges and immunities of free citizens in the several states; and the people of each state shall have free ingress and regress to and from any other state, and shall enjoy therein all the privileges of trade and commerce, subject to the same duties, impositions and restrictions as the inhabitants thereof respectively, provided that such restriction shall not extend so far as to prevent the removal of property imported into any state, to any other state of which the Owner is an inhabitant; provided also that no imposition, duties or restriction shall be laid by any state, on the property of the united states, or either of them.

If any person guilty of, or charged with treason, felony, or other high misdemeanor in any state, shall flee from Justice, and be found in any of the united states, he shall upon demand of the Governor or executive power, of the state from which he fled, be delivered up and removed to the state having jurisdiction of his offence.

Full faith and credit shall be given in each of these states to the records, acts and judicial proceedings of the courts and magistrates of every other state.

ARTICLE V. For the more convenient management of the general interest of the united states, delegates shall be annually appointed in such manner as the legislature of each state shall direct, to meet in congress on the first Monday in November, in every year, with a power reserved to each state, to recal its delegates, or any of them, at any time within the year, and to send others in their stead, for the remainder of the Year.

No state shall be represented in congress by less than two, nor by more than seven members; and no person shall be capable of being a delegate for more than three years in any term of six years; nor shall any person, being a delegate, be capable of holding any office under the united states, for which he, or another for his benefit receives any salary, fees or emolument of any kind.

Each state shall maintain its own delegates in any meeting of the states, and while they act as members of the committee of the states.

In determining questions in the united states, in congress assembled, each state shall have one vote.

Freedom of speech and debate in congress shall not be impeached or questioned in any Court, or place out of congress, and the members of congress shall be protected in their persons from arrests and imprisonments, during the time of their going to and from, and attendance on congress, except for treason, felony, or breach of the peace.

ARTICLE VI. No state without the Consent of the united states in congress assembled, shall send any embassy to, or receive any embassy from, or enter into any conference, agreement, alliance or treaty with any King prince or state; nor shall any person holding any office of profit or trust under the united states, or any of them, accept of any present, emolument, office or title of any kind whatever from any king, prince or foreign state; nor shall the united states in congress assembled, or any of them, grant any title of nobility.

No two or more states shall enter into any treaty,

confederation or alliance whatever between them, without the consent of the united states in congress assembled, specifying accurately the purposes for which the same is to be entered into, and how long it shall continue.

No state shall lay any imposts or duties, which may interfere with any stipulations in treaties, entered into by the united states in congress assembled, with any king, prince or state, in pursuance of any treaties already proposed by congress, to the courts of France and Spain.

No vessels of war shall be kept up in time of peace by any state, except such number only, as shall be deemed necessary by the united states in congress assembled, for the defence of such state, or its trade; nor shall any body of forces be kept up by any state, in time of peace, except such number only, as in the judgment of the united states, in congress assembled, shall be deemed requisite to garrison the forts necessary for the defence of such state; but every state shall always keep up a well regulated and disciplined militia, sufficiently armed and accoutred, and shall provide and have constantly ready for use, in public stores, a due number of field pieces and tents, and a proper quantity of arms, ammunition and camp equipage.

No state shall engage in any war without the consent of the united states in congress assembled, unless such state be actually invaded by enemies, or shall have received certain advice of a resolution being formed by some nation of Indians to invade such state, and the danger is so imminent as not to admit of a delay, till the united states in congress assembled can be consulted : nor shall any state grant commissions to any ships or vessels of war, nor letters of marque or reprisal, except it be after a declaration of war by the united states in congress assembled, and then only against the kingdom or state and the subjects thereof, against which war has been so declared, and under such regulations as shall be established by the united states in congress assembled, unless such state be infested by pirates, in which case vessels of war may be fitted out for that occasion, and kept so long as the danger shall continue, or until the united states in congress assembled shall determine otherwise.

ARTICLE VII. When land-forces are raised by any state for the common defence, all officers of or under the rank of colonel, shall be appointed by the legislature of each state respectively by whom such forces shall be raised, or in such manner as such state shall direct, and all vacancies shall be filled up by the state which first made the appointment.

ARTICLE VIII. All charges of war, and all other expenses that shall be incurred for the common defence or general welfare, and allowed by the united states in congress assembled, shall be defrayed out of a common treasury, which shall be supplied by the several states, in proportion to the value of all land within each state, granted to or surveyed for any Person, as such land and the buildings and improvements thereon shall be estimated according to such mode as the united states in congress assembled, shall from time to time, direct and appoint. The taxes for paying that proportion shall be laid and levied by the authority and direction of the legislatures of the several states within the time greed upon by the united states in congress assembled.

ARTICLE IX. The united states in congress assembled, shall have the sole and exclusive right and power of determining on peace and war, except in the cases mentioned in the sixth article—of sending and receiving ambassadors—entering into treaties and alliances, provided that no treaty of commerce shall be made whereby the legislative power of the respective states shall be restrained from imposing such imposts and duties on foreigners, as their own people are subjected to, or from prohibiting the exportation or importation of any species of goods or commodities whatsoever—of establishing rules for deciding in all cases, what captures on land or water shall be legal, and in what manner prizes taken by land or naval forces in the service of the united states shall be divided or appropriated—of granting letters of marque and reprisal in times of peace—appointing courts for the trial of piracies and felonies committed on the high seas and establishing courts for receiving and determining finally appeals in all cases of captures, provided that no member of congress shall be appointed a judge of any of the said courts.

The united states in congress assembled shall also be the last resort on appeal in all disputes and differences now subsisting or that hereafter may arise between two or more states concerning boundary, jurisdiction or any other cause whatever; which authority shall always be exercised in the manner following. Whenever the legislative or executive authority or lawful agent of any state in controversy with another shall present a petition to congress, stating the matter in question and praying for a hearing, notice thereof shall be given by order of congress to the legislative or executive author-

ity of the other state in controversy, and a day assigned
for the appearance of the parties by their lawful agents,
who shall then be directed to appoint by joint consent,
commissioners or judges to constitute a court for hearing and determining the matter in question : but if they
cannot agree, congress shall name three persons out of
each of the united states, and from the list of such persons each party shall alternately strike out one, the
petitioners beginning, until the number shall be reduced
to thirteen ; and from that number not less than seven,
nor more than nine names as congress shall direct, shall
in the presence of congress be drawn out by lot, and
the persons whose names shall be so drawn or any five
of them, shall be commissioners or judges, to hear and
finally determine the controversy, so always as a major
part of the judges who shall hear the cause shall agree
in the determination : and if either party shall neglect
to attend at the day appointed, without showing reasons, which congress shall judge sufficient, or being
present shall refuse to strike, the congress shall proceed
to nominate three persons out of each state, and the
secretary of congress shall strike in behalf of such
party absent or refusing ; and the judgment and sentence of the court to be appointed, in the manner before
prescribed, shall be final and conclusive ; and if any
of the parties shall refuse to submit to the authority of
such court, or to appear or defend their claim or cause,
the court shall nevertheless proceed to pronounce sentence, or judgment, which shall in like manner be final
and decisive, the judgment or sentence and other proceedings being in either case transmitted to congress,
and lodged among the acts of congress for the security
of the parties concerned : provided that every commis-

sioner, before he sits in judgment, shall take an oath to be administered by one of the judges of the supreme or superior court of the state, where the cause shall be tried, " well and truly to hear and determine the matter in question, according to the best of his judgment, without favour, affection or hope of reward :" provided also that no state shall be deprived of territory for the benefit of the united states.

All controversies concerning the private right of soil claimed under different grants of two or more states, whose jurisdictions as they may respect such lands, and the states which passed such grants are adjusted, the said grants or either of them being at the same time claimed to have originated antecedent to such settlement of jurisdiction, shall on the petition of either party to the congress of the united states, be finally determined as near as may be in the same manner as is before prescribed for deciding disputes respecting territorial jurisdiction between different states.

The united states in congress assembled shall also have the sole and exclusive right and power of regulating the alloy and value of coin struck by their own authority, or by that of the respective states—fixing the standard of weights and measures throughout the United States—regulating the trade and managing all affairs with the Indians, not members of any of the states, provided that the legislative right of any state within its own limits be not infringed or violated—establishing or regulating post-offices from one state to another, throughout all the united states, and exacting such postage on the papers passing thro' the same as may be requisite to defray the expenses of the said office—appointing all officers of the land forces, in the service of the united states, excepting regimental officers—appointing all the officers of the naval forces, and commissioning all officers whatever in the service of the united states—making rules for the government and regulation of the said land and naval forces, and directing their operations.

The united states in congress assembled shall have authority to appoint a committee, to sit in the recess of congress, to be denominated " A Committee of the States," and to consist of one delegate from each state ; and to appoint such other committees and civil officers as may be necessary for managing the general affairs of the united states under their direction—to appoint one of their number to preside, provided that no person be allowed to serve in the office of president more than one year in any term of three years; to ascertain the necessary sums of Money to be raised for the service of the united states, and to appropriate and apply the same for defraying the public expenses—to borrow money, or emit bills on the credit of the united states, transmitting every half year to the respective states an account of the sums of money so borrowed or emitted,— to build and equip a navy—to agree upon the number of land forces, and to make requisitions from each state for its quota, in proportion to the number of white inhabitants in such state ; which requisition shall be binding, and thereupon the legislature of each state shall appoint the regimental officers, raise the men and cloath, arm and equip them in a soldier like manner, at the expense of the united states; and the officers and men so cloathed, armed and equipped shall march to the place appointed, and within the time agreed on by the united states in congress assembled : But if the united states in congress assembled shall, on consideration of circumstances judge proper that any state should not raise men, or should raise a smaller number than its quota, and that any other state should raise a greater number of men than the quota thereof, such extra number shall be raised, officered, cloathed, armed and equipped in the same manner as the quota of such state, unless the legislature of such state shall judge that such extra number cannot be safely spared out of the same, in which case they shall raise, officer, cloath, arm and equip as many of such extra number as they judge can be safely spared. And the officers and men so cloathed, armed and equipped, shall march to the place appointed, and within the time agreed on by the united states in congress assembled.

The united states in congress assembled shall never engage in a war, nor grant letters of marque and reprisal in time of peace, nor enter into any treaties or alliances, nor coin money, nor regulate the value thereof, nor ascertain the sums and expenses necessary for the defence and welfare of the united states, or any of them, nor emit bills, nor borrow money on the credit of the united states, nor appropriate money, nor agree upon the number of vessels of war, to be built or purchased, or the number of land or sea forces to be raised, nor appoint a commander in chief of the army or navy, unless nine states assent to the same: nor shall a question on any other point, except for adjourning from day to day be determined, unless by the votes of a majority of the united states in congress assembled.

The Congress of the united states shall have power to adjourn to any time within the year, and to any place within the united states, so that no period of adjournment be for a longer duration than the space of six months, and shall publish the Journal of their proceedings monthly, except such parts thereof relating to treaties, alliances or military operations, as in their judgment require secrecy; and the yeas and nays of the delegates of each state on any question shall be entered on the Journal, when it is desired by any delegate; and the delegates of a state, or any of them, at his or their request shall be furnished with a transcript of the said Journal, except such parts as are above excepted, to lay before the legislatures of the several states.

ARTICLE X. The committee of the states, or any nine of them, shall be authorized to execute, in the recess of congress, such of the powers of congress as the united states in congress assembled, by the consent of nine states, shall from time to time think expedient to vest them with; provided that no power be delegated to the said committee, for the exercise of which, by the articles of confederation, the voice of nine states in the congress of the united states assembled is requisite.

ARTICLE XI. Canada acceding to this confederation, and joining in the measures of the united states, shall be admitted into, and entitled to all the advantages of this union: but no other colony shall be admitted into the same, unless such admission be agreed to by nine states.

ARTICLE XII. All bills of credit emitted, monies borrowed and debts contracted by, or under the authority of congress, before the assembling of the united states, in pursuance of the present confederation, shall be deemed and considered as a charge against the united

states, for payment and satisfaction whereof the said
united states, and the public faith are hereby solemnly
pledged.

ARTICLE XIII. Every state shall abide by the
determinations of the united states in congress assembled, on all questions which by this confederation is
submitted to them. And the Articles of this confederation shall be inviolably observed by every state, and
the union shall be perpetual ; nor shall any alteration
at any time hereafter be made in any of them ; unless
such alteration be agreed to in a congress of the united
states, and be afterwards confirmed by the legislatures
of every state.

*And Whereas* it hath pleased the Great Governor of
the World to incline the hearts of the legislatures we
respectively represent in congress, to approve of, and
to authorize us to ratify the said articles of confederation and perpetual union. Know Ye that we the undersigned delegates, by virtue of the power and authority
to us given for that purpose, do by these presents, in
the name and in behalf of our respective constituents,
fully and entirely ratify and confirm each and every of
the said articles of confederation and perpetual union,
and all and singular the matters and things therein contained : And we do further solemnly plight and engage
the faith of our respective constituents, that they shall
abide by the determinations of the united states in congress assembled, on all questions, which by the said
confederation are submitted to them. And that the
articles thereof shall be inviolably observed by the
states we respectively represent, and that the union
shall be perpetual. In witness whereof we have hereunto set our hands in Congress. Done at Philadelphia

in the state of Pennsylvania the 9th Day of July in the Year of our Lord, 1778, and in the 3d year of the Independence of America.

| | | |
|---|---|---|
| Josiah Bartlett, | John Wentworth, jun. August 8th, 1778, | On the part and behalf of the state of New Hampshire. |
| John Hancock, Samuel Adams, Elbridge Gerry, | Francis Dana, James Lovell, Samuel Holten, | On the part and behalf of the state of Massachusetts Bay. |
| William Ellery, Henry Marchant, | John Collins, | On the part and behalf of the State of Rhode-Island and Providence Plantations. |
| Roger Sherman, Samuel Huntington, Oliver Wolcott, | Titus Hosmer, Andrew Adam, | On the part and behalf of the state of Connecticut. |
| Jas. Duane, Fras Lewis, | William Duer, Gouvr Morris, | On the part and behalf of the state of New. York. |
| Jno Witherspoon, | Nathl Scudder, | On the part and behalf of the state of New-Jersey, Nov. 26th, 1778. |
| Robt Morris, Daniel Roberdeau, Jona Bayard Smith, | William Clingan, Joseph Reed, 22d July, 1778, | On the part and behalf of the state of Pennsylvania. |
| Tho. M'Kean, Feb. 12, 1779, Nicholas Van Dyke, John Dickinson, May 5, 1779, | | On the part and behalf of the state of Delaware. |
| John Hanson, March 1st, 1781, | Daniel Carroll, March 1st, 1781, | On the part and behalf of the state of Maryland. |
| Richard Henry Lee, John Banister, Thomas Adams, | Jno Harvie, Francis Lightfoot Lee, | On the part and behalf of the state of Virginia. |
| John Penn, July 21st, 1778, | Corns Harnett, Jno Williams, | On the part and behalf of the state of North. Carolina. |
| Henry Laurens, William Henry Drayton, Jno Matthews, | Richd Hutson, Thos. Heyward, jun. | On the part and behalf of the state of South-Carolina. |
| Jno Walton, 24th July, 1778, | Edwd Telfair, Edwd Langworthy, | On the part and behalf of the state of Georgia |

# CONSTITUTION

# UNITED STATES OF AMERICA.

WE the People of the United States, in order to form
a more perfect Union, establish Justice, insure domes
tic Tranquillity, provide for the common defence,
promote the general Welfare, and secure the Blessings of Liberty to ourselves and our Posterity, do
ordain and establish this CONSTITUTION for the United
States of America,

## ARTICLE. I.

SECTION. 1. All legislative Powers herein granted
shall be vested in a Congress of the United States,
which shall consist of a Senate and House of Representatives.

SECTION. 2. 'The House of Representatives shall
be composed of Members chosen every second Year by
the People of the several States, and the Electors in each
State shall have the Qualifications requisite for Electors
of the most numerous Branch of the State Legislature.

$^2$No Person shall be a Representative who shall not have attained to the Age of twenty five Years, and been seven Years a Citizen of the United States, and who shall not, when elected, be an Inhabitant of that State in which he shall be chosen.

$^3$Representatives and direct Taxes shall be apportioned among the several States which may be included within this Union, according to their respective Numbers, which shall be determined by adding to the whole Number of free Persons, including those bound to Service for a Term of Years, and excluding Indians not taxed, three fifths of all other Persons. The actual Enumeration shall be made within three Years after the first Meeting of the Congress of the United States, and within every subsequent Term of ten Years, in such Manner as they shall by Law direct. The Number of Representatives shall not exceed one for every thirty Thousand, but each State shall have at Least one Representative; and until such enumeration shall be made, the State of New Hampshire shall be entitled to chuse three, Massachusetts eight, Rhode-Island and Providence Plantations one, Connecticut five, New-York six, New Jersey four, Pennsylvania eight, Delaware one, Maryland six, Virginia ten, North Carolina five, South Carolina five, and Georgia three.

$^4$When vacancies happen in the Representation from any State, the Executive Authority thereof shall issue Writs of Election to fill such Vacancies.

$^5$The House of Representatives shall chuse their

Speaker and other Officers ; and shall have the sole Power of Impeachment.

SECTION. 3.   ¹ The Senate of the United States shall be composed of two Senators from each State, chosen by the Legislature thereof, for six Years; and each Senator shall have one vote.

² Immediately after they shall be assembled in Consequence of the first Election, they shall be divided as equally as may be into three Classes.   The Seats of the Senators of the first Class shall be vacated at the Expiration of the second Year, of the second Class at the Expiration of the fourth Year, and of the third class at the Expiration of the sixth Year, so that one-third may be chosen every second Year ; and if Vacancies happen by Resignation, or otherwise, during the Recess of the Legislature of any State, the Executive thereof may make temporary Appointments until the next Meeting of the Legislature, which shall then fill such Vacancies.

³ No Person shall be a Senator who shall not have attained to the Age of thirty Years, and been nine Years a Citizen of the United States, and who shall not, when elected, be an Inhabitant of that State for which he shall be chosen.

⁴ The Vice President of the United States shall be President of the Senate, but shall have no Vote, unless they be equally divided.

⁵ The Senate shall chuse their other Officers, and also a President pro tempore, in the Absence of the Vice

President, or when he shall exercise the Office of President of the United States.

'The Senate shall have the sole Power to try all Impeachments. When sitting for that Purpose, they shall be on Oath or Affirmation. When the President of the United States is tried, the Chief Justice shall preside : And no Person shall be convicted without the Concurrence of two thirds of the Members present.

'Judgment in Cases of Impeachment shall not extend further than to removal from Office, and Disqualification to hold and enjoy any Office of honour, Trust or Profit under the United States : but the Party convicted shall nevertheless be liable and subject to Indictment, Trial, Judgment and Punishment, according to Law.

SECTION. 4. 'The Times, Places and Manner of holding Elections for Senators and Representatives, shall be prescribed in each State by the Legislature thereof; but the Congress may at any time by Law make or alter such Regulations, except as to the places of chusing Senators.

²The Congress shall assemble at least once in every Year, and such Meeting shall be on the first Monday in December, unless they shall by Law appoint a different Day.

SECTION. 5. ¹Each House shall be the Judge of the Elections, Returns and Qualifications of its own Members, and a Majority of each shall constitute a Quorum

2

to Business; but a smaller Number may adjourn from day to day, and may be authorized to compel the Attendance of absent Members, in such Manner, and under such Penalties as each House may provide.

² Each House may determine the Rules of its Proceedings, punish its Members for disorderly Behaviour, and, with the Concurrence of two thirds, expel a Member.

³ Each House shall keep a Journal of its Proceedings, and from time to time publish the same, excepting such Parts as may in their Judgment require Secrecy ; and the Yeas and Nays of the Members of either House on any question shall, at the Desire of one fifth of those Present, be entered on the Journal.

⁴ Neither House, during the Session of Congress, shall, without the Consent of the other, adjourn for more than three days, nor to any other Place than that in which the two Houses shall be sitting.

SECTION. 6. ¹ The Senators and Representatives shall receive a Compensation for their Services, to be ascertained by Law, and paid out of the Treasury of the United States. They shall in all Cases, except Treason, Felony and Breach of the Peace, be privileged from Arrest during their Attendance at the Session of their respective Houses, and in going to and returning from the same; and for any Speech or Debate in either House, they shall not be questioned in any other Place.

[2] No Senator or Representative shall, during the Time for which he was elected, be appointed to any civil Office under the. Authority of the United States, which shall have been created, or the Emoluments whereof shall have been encreased during such time ; and no Person holding any Office under the United States, shall be a Member of either House during his Continuance in Office.

SECTION. 7.  [1] All Bills for raising Revenue shall originate in the House of Representatives ; but the Senate may propose or concur with Amendments as on other Bills.

[2] Every Bill which shall have passed the House of Representatives and the Senate, shall, before it become a Law, be presented to the President of the United States ; If he approve he shall sign it, but if not he shall return it, with his Objections to that House in which it shall have originated, who shall enter the Objections at large on their Journal, and proceed to reconsider it.  If after such Reconsideration two thirds of that House shall agree to pass the Bill, it shall be sent, together with the Objections, to the other House, by which it shall likewise be reconsidered, and if approved by two thirds of that House, it shall become a Law.  But in all such Cases the Votes of both Houses shall be determined by yeas and Nays, and the Names of the Persons voting for and against the Bill shall be entered on the Journal of each House respectively.   If

any Bill shall not be returned by the President within ten Days (Sundays excepted) after it shall have been presented to him, the Same shall be a law, in like Manner as if he had signed it, unless the Congress by their Adjournment prevent its Return, in which Case it shall not be a Law.

⁹Every Order, Resolution, or Vote to which the Concurrence of the Senate and House of Representatives may be necessary (except on a question of Adjournment) shall be presented to the President of the United States; and before the Same shall take Effect, shall be approved by him, or being disapproved by him, shall be repassed by two thirds of the Senate and House of Representatives, according to the Rules and Limitations prescribed in the Case of a Bill.

SECTION. 8. The Congress shall have Power

¹To lay and collect Taxes, Duties, Imposts and Excises; to pay the Debts and provide for the common Defence and general Welfare of the United States; but all Duties, Imposts and Excises shall be uniform throughout the United States;

²To borrow Money on the credit of the United States;

³To regulate Commerce with foreign Nations, and among the several States, and with the Indian Tribes;

⁴To establish an uniform Rule of Naturalization, and uniform Laws on the subject of Bankruptcies throughout the United States;

⁵ To coin Money, regulate the Value thereof, and of foreign Coin, and fix the Standard of Weights and Measures;

⁶ To provide for the Punishment of counterfeiting the Securities and current Coin of the United States;

⁷ To establish Post Offices and post Roads;

⁸ To promote the progress of Science and useful Arts, by securing for limited Times to Authors and Inventors the exclusive Right to their respective Writings and Discoveries;

⁹ To constitute Tribunals inferior to the supreme Court;

¹⁰ To define and punish Piracies and Felonies committed on the high Seas, and Offences against the Law of Nations;

¹¹ To declare War, grant Letters of Marque and Reprisal, and make Rules concerning Captures on Land and Water;

¹² To raise and support Armies, but no Appropriation of Money to that Use shall be for a longer Term than two Years;

¹³ To provide and maintain a Navy;

¹⁴ To make Rules for the Government and Regulation of the land and naval Forces;

¹⁵ To provide for calling forth the Militia to execute the Laws of the Union, suppress Insurrections and repel Invasions;

¹⁶ To provide for organizing, arming, and disciplining, the Militia, and for governing such Part of them as may

be employed in the Service of the United States, reserving to the States respectively, the Appointment of the Officers, and the Authority of training the Militia according to the Discipline prescribed by Congress;

"To exercise exclusive Legislation in all Cases whatsoever, over such District (not exceeding ten Miles square) as may, by Cession of particular States, and the Acceptance of Congress, become the Seat of the Government of the United States, and to exercise like Authority over all Places purchased by the Consent of the Legislature of the State in which the Same shall be, for the Erection of Forts, Magazines, Arsenals, Dock-Yards, and other needful Buildings;—And

"To make all Laws which shall be necessary and proper for carrying into Execution the foregoing Powers, and all other Powers vested by this Constitution in the Government of the United States, or in any Department or Officer thereof.

Section. 9.  ¹The Migration or Importation of such Persons as any of the States now existing shall think proper to admit, shall not be prohibited by the Congress prior to the Year one thousand eight hundred and eight, but a Tax or Duty may be imposed on such Importation, not exceeding ten dollars for each Person.

²The Privilege of the Writ of Habeas Corpus shall not be suspended, unless when in Cases of Rebellion or Invasion the public Safety may require it.

'No Bill of Attainder or ex post facto Law shall be passed.

'No Capitation, or other direct, Tax shall be laid, unless in Proportion to the Census or Enumeration herein before directed to be taken.

'No Tax or Duty shall be laid on Articles exported from any State.

'No Preference shall be given by any Regulation of Commerce or Revenue to the Ports of one State over those of another: nor shall Vessels bound to, or from, one State, be obliged to enter, clear, or pay Duties in another.

'No Money shall be drawn from the Treasury, but in Consequence of Appropriations made by Law; and a regular Statement and Account of the Receipts and Expenditures of all public Money shall be published from time to time.

'No Title of Nobility shall be granted by the United States: And no Person holding any Office of Profit or Trust under them, shall, without the Consent of the Congress, accept of any present, Emolument, Office, or Title, of any kind whatever, from any King, Prince, or foreign State.

SECTION. 10. 'No State shall enter into any Treaty, Alliance, or Confederation; grant Letters of Marque and Reprisal; coin Money; emit Bills of Credit; make any Thing but gold and silver Coin a Tender in Payment of Debts; pass any Bill of Attainder, ex post

facto Law, or Law impairing the Obligation of Contracts, or grant any Title of Nobility.

²No State shall, without the consent of the Congress,
lay any Imposts or Duties on Imports or Exports, except what may be absolutely necessary for executing
it's inspection Laws: and the net Produce of all Duties
and Imposts, laid by any State on Imports or Exports,
shall be for the Use of the Treasury of the United
States; and all such Laws shall be subject to the Revision and Controul of the Congress.

³No State shall, without the Consent of Congress,
lay any Duty of Tonnage, keep Troops, or Ships of
War in time of Peace, enter into any Agreement or
Compact with another State, or with a foreign Power,
or engage in War, unless actually invaded, or in such
imminent Danger as will not admit of Delay.


## ARTICLE. II.

SECTION. 1. ¹The executive Power shall be vested
in a President of the United States of America. He
shall hold his Office during the Term of four Years,
and, together with the Vice President, chosen for the
same Term, be elected, as follows

²Each State shall appoint, in such Manner as the
Legislature thereof may direct, a Number of Electors, equal to the whole Number of Senators and
Representatives to which the State may be entitled
in the Congress: but no Senator or Representative,

or Person holding an Office of Trust or Profit under the United States, shall be appointed an Elector.

The Electors shall meet in their respective States, and vote by Ballot for two Persons, of whom one at least shall not be an Inhabitant of the same State with themselves. And they shall make a List of all the Persons voted for, and of the Number of Votes for each ; which List they shall sign and certify, and transmit sealed to the Seat of the Government of the United States, directed to the President of the Senate. The President of the Senate shall, in the Presence of the Senate and House of Representatives, open all the Certificates, and the Votes shall then be counted. The Person having the greatest Number of Votes shall be the President, if such Number be a Majority of the whole Number of Electors appointed ; and if there be more than one who have such Majority, and have an equal Number of Votes, then the House of Representatives shall immediately chuse by Ballot one of them for President ; and if no Person have a Majority, then from the five highest on the List the said House shall in like Manner chuse the President. But in chusing the President, the Votes shall be taken by States, the Representation from each State having one Vote ; A Quorum for this Purpose shall consist of a Member or Members from twothirds of the States, and a Majority of all the States shall be necessary to a Choice. In every Case, after the Choice of the President, the Person having the greatest Number of Votes

1\*

of the Electors shall be the Vice President. But if there should remain two or more who have equal Votes, the Senate shall chuse from them by Ballot the Vice President.

⁸ The Congress may determine the Time of chusing the Electors, and the Day on which they shall give their Votes; which Day shall be the same throughout the United States.

⁴ No Person except a natural born Citizen, or a Citizen of the United States, at the time of the Adoption of this Constitution, shall be eligible to the Office of President; neither shall any Person be eligible to that Office who shall not have attained to the Age of thirty five Years, and been fourteen Years a Resident within the United States.

⁵ In Case of the Removal of the President from Office, or of his Death, Resignation, or Inability to discharge the Powers and Duties of the said Office, the same shall devolve on the Vice President, and the Congress may by Law provide for the Case of Removal, Death, Resignation, or Inability, both of the President and Vice President, declaring what Officer shall then act as President, and such Officer shall act accordingly, until the Disability be removed, or a President shall be elected.

⁶ The President shall, at stated Times, receive for his Services, a Compensation, which shall neither be encreased nor diminished during the Period for which he shall have been elected, and he shall not receive

within that Period any other Emolument from the United States, or any of them.

' Before he enter on the Execution of his Office, he shall take the following Oath or Affirmation :—

"I do solemnly swear (or affirm) that I will faithfully "execute the Office of President of the United States, "and will to the best of my Ability, preserve, pro- "tect and defend the Constitution of the United States."

SECTION. 2. 'The President shall be Commander in Chief of the Army and Navy of the United States, and of the Militia of the several States, when called into the actual Service of the United States ; he may require the Opinion, in writing, of the principal Officer in each of the executive Departments, upon any Subject relating to the Duties of their respective Offices, and he shall have Power to grant Reprieves and Pardons for Offences against the United States, except in Cases of Impeachment.

² He shall have Power, by and with the Advice and Consent of the Senate, to make Treaties, provided two thirds of the Senators present concur ; and he shall nominate, and by and with the Advice and Consent of the Senate, shall appoint Ambassadors, other public Ministers and Consuls, Judges of the supreme Court, and all other Officers of the United States, whose Appointments are not herein otherwise provided for, and which shall be established by Law : but the Con- gress may by Law vest the Appointment of such infe-

rior Officers, as they think proper, in the President alone, in the Courts of Law, or in the Heads of Departments.

'The President shall have Power to fill up all Vacancies that may happen during the Recess of the Senate, by granting Commissions which shall expire at the End of their next Session.

Section. 3.   He shall from time to time give to the Congress Information of the State of the Union, and recommend to their Consideration such Measures as he shall judge necessary and expedient ; he may, on extraordinary Occasions, convene both Houses, or either of them, and in Case of Disagreement between them, with Respect to the Time of Adjournment, he may adjourn them to such Time as he shall think proper ; he shall receive Ambassadors and other public Ministers ; he shall take Care that the Laws be faithfully executed, and shall Commission all the officers of the United States.

Section. 4.   The President, Vice President and all civil Officers of the United States, shall be removed from Office on Impeachment for, and Conviction of, Treason, Bribery, or other high Crimes and Misdemeanors.

## ARTICLE III.

Section. 1.   The judicial Power of the United States, shall be vested in one supreme Court, and in such inferior Courts as the Congress may from time to time ordain and establish. The Judges, both of the supreme and inferior Courts, shall hold their Offices during good Behavior, and shall, at stated Times, receive for their Services, a Compensation, which shall not be diminished during their Continuance in Office.

SECTION. 2. ¹The judicial Power shall extend to all Cases, in Law and Equity, arising under this Constitution, the Laws of the United States, and Treaties made, or which shall be made, under their Authority; —to all Cases affecting Ambassadors, other public Ministers, and Consuls;—to all Cases of admiralty and maritime Jurisdiction;—to Controversies to which the United States shall be a Party;—to Controversies between two or more States;—between a State and Citizens of another State;—between Citizens of different States,—between Citizens of the same State claiming Lands under Grants of different States, and between a State, or the Citizens thereof, and foreign States, Citizens or Subjects.

²In all Cases affecting Ambassadors, other public Ministers and Consuls, and those in which a State shall be Party, the supreme Court shall have original Jurisdiction. In all the other Cases before mentioned, the supreme Court shall have appellate Jurisdiction, both as to Law and Fact, with such Exceptions, and under such Regulations as the Congress shall make.

³ The Trial of all Crimes, except in Cases of Impeach-

ment, shall be by Jury; and such Trial shall be held
in the State where the said Crimes shall have been
committed; but when not committed within any State,
the Trial shall be at such Place or Places as the Congress may by Law have directed.

SECTION. 3. ¹Treason against the United States,
shall consist only in levying War against them, or in
adhering to their Enemies, giving them Aid and Comfort. No Person shall be convicted of Treason unless
on the Testimony of two Witnesses to the same overt
Act, or on Confession in open Court.

²The Congress shall have Power to declare the
Punishment of Treason, but no Attainder of Treason
shall work Corruption of Blood, or Forfeiture except
during the Life of the Person attainted.

## ARTICLE. IV.

SECTION. 1. Full Faith and Credit shall be given
in each State to the public Acts, Records, and judicial
Proceedings of every other State. And the Congress
may by general Laws prescribe the Manner in which
such Acts, Records and Proceedings shall be proved,
and the Effect thereof.

SECTION. 2. ¹The Citizens of each State shall be
entitled to all Privileges and Immunities of Citizens in
the several States.

²A Person charged in any State with Treason,
Felony, or other Crime, who shall flee from Justice,

and be found in another State, shall on Demand of the executive Authority of the State from which he fled, be delivered up, to be removed to the State having Jurisdiction of the Crime.

' No Person held to Service or Labour in one State, under the Laws thereof, escaping into another, shall, in Consequence of any Law or Regulation therein, be discharged from such Service or Labour, but shall be delivered up on Claim of the Party to whom such Service or Labour may be due.

SECTION. 3. ' New States may be admitted by the Congress into this Union ; but no new State shall be formed or erected within the Jurisdiction of any other State ; nor any State be formed by the Junction of two or more States, or Parts of States, without the Consent of the Legislatures of the States concerned as well as of the Congress.

' The Congress shall have Power to dispose of and make all needful Rules and Regulations respecting the Territory or other Property belonging to the United States ; and nothing in this Constitution shall be so construed as to Prejudice any Claims of the United States, or of any particular State.

SECTION. 4. The United States shall guarantee to every State in this Union a Republican Form of Government, and shall protect each of them against Invasion, and on Application of the Legislature, or of the Executive (when the Legislature cannot be convened) against domestic Violence.

## ARTICLE. V.

The Congress, whenever two thirds of both Houses shall deem it necessary, shall propose Amendments to this Constitution, or, on the Application of the Legislatures of two-thirds of the several States, shall call a Convention for proposing Amendments, which, in either Case, shall be valid to all Intents and Purposes, as Part of this Constitution, when ratified by the Legislatures of three fourths of the several States, or by Conventions in three fourths thereof, as the one or the other Mode of Ratification may be proposed by the Congress ; Provided that no Amendment which may be made prior to the Year one thousand eight hundred and eight shall in any Manner affect the first and fourth Clauses in the Ninth Section of the first Article ; and that no State, without its Consent, shall be deprived of its equal Suffrage in the Senate.

## ARTICLE. VI.

[1] All Debts contracted and Engagements entered into, before the Adoption of this Constitution, shall be as valid against the United States under this Constitution, as under the Confederation.

[2] This Constitution, and the Laws of the United States which shall be made in Pursuance thereof ; and all Treaties made, or which shall be made, under the

authority of the United States, shall be the supreme Law of the Land ; and the Judges in every State shall be bound thereby, any Thing in the Constitution or Laws of any State to the Contrary notwithstanding.

² The Senators and Representatives before mentioned, and the Members of the several State Legislatures, and all executive and judicial Officers, both of the United States and of the several States, shall be bound by Oath or Affirmation, to support this Constitution ; but no religious Test shall ever be required as a Qualification to any Office or public Trust under the United States.

## ARTICLE. VII.

The Ratification of the Conventions of nine States, shall be sufficient for the Establishment of this Constitution between the States so ratifying the Same.

Done in Convention by the Unanimous Consent of the States present the Seventeenth Day of September in the Year of our Lord one thousand seven hundred and Eighty seven and of the Independance of the United States of America the Twelfth. In witness whereof We have hereunto subscribed our Names,

GEO WASHINGTON—
*Presidt and deputy from Virginia*

NEW HAMPSHIRE.

| John Langdon, | Nicholas Gilman. |
|---|---|
| | MASSACHUSETTS. |
| Nathaniel Gorham, | Rufus King. |

## CONNECTICUT.

Wm. Saml. Johnson,        Roger Sherman.

## NEW YORK.

Alexander Hamilton.

## NEW JERSEY.

Wil: Livingston,        David Brearley,
Wm. Paterson,        Jona. Dayton.

## PENNSYLVANIA.

B. Franklin,        Thomas Mifflin,
Robt. Morris,        Geo: Clymer,
Tho: Fitzsimons,        Jared Ingersoll,
James Wilson,        Gouv: Morris.

## DELAWARE.

Geo: Read,        Gunning Bedford, Jun'r,
John Dickinson,        Richard Bassett,
Jaco: Broom.

## MARYLAND.

James M'Henry        Dan: of St. Thos. Jenifer,
Danl. Carroll.

## VIRGINIA.

John Blair,        James Madison, Jr.,

## NORTH CAROLINA.

Wm. Blount        Rich'd Dobbs Spaight,
Hu. Williamson.

## SOUTH CAROLINA.

J. Rutledge,        Charles Cotesworth Pinckney,
Charles Pinckney,        Pierce Butler.

## GEORGIA.

WILLIAM FEW,                    ABR. BALDWIN.

Attest:          WILLIAM JACKSON, *Secretary*.

---

# ARTICLES

### IN ADDITION TO, AND AMENDMENT OF

## THE CONSTITUTION

### OF THE

# UNITED STATES OF AMERICA,

*Proposed by Congress, and ratified by the Legislatures of the several States, pursuant to the fifth article of the original Constitution.*

### (ARTICLE 1.)

Congress shall make no law respecting an establishment of religion, or prohibiting the free exercise thereof; or abridging the freedom of speech, or of the press ; or the right of the people peaceably to assemble, and to petition the Government for a redress of grievances.

### (ARTICLE 2.)

A well regulated Militia, being necessary to the security of a free State, the right of the people to keep and bear Arms, shall not be infringed.

## (ARTICLE III.)

No Soldier shall, in time of peace be quartered in any house, without the consent of the Owner, nor in time of war, but in a manner to be prescribed by law.

## (ARTICLE IV.)

The right of the people to be secure in their persons, houses, papers, and effects, against unreasonable searches and seizures, shall not be violated, and no Warrants shall issue, but upon probable cause, supported by Oath or affirmation, and particularly describing the place to be searched, and the persons or things to be seized.

## (ARTICLE V.)

No person shall be held to answer for a capital, or otherwise infamous crime, unless on a presentment or indictment of a Grand Jury, except in cases arising in the land or naval forces, or in the Militia, when in actual service in time of War or public danger ; nor shall any person be subject for the same offence to be twice put in jeopardy of life or limb; nor shall be compelled in any Criminal Case to be a witness against himself, nor be deprived of life, liberty, or property, without due process of law ; nor shall private property be taken for public use, without just compensation.

## (ARTICLE VI.)

In all criminal prosecutions, the accused shall enjoy

the right to a speedy and public trial, by an impartial jury of the State and district wherein the crime shall have been committed, which district shall have been previously ascertained by law, and to be informed of the nature and cause of the accusation; to be confronted with the witnesses against him; to have Compulsory process for obtaining Witnesses in his favour, and to have the Assistance of Counsel for his defence.

### (ARTICLE VII.)

In Suits at common law, where the value in controversy shall exceed twenty dollars, the right of trial by jury shall be preserved, and no fact tried by a jury shall be otherwise re-examined in any Court of the United States, than according to the rules of the common law.

### (ARTICLE VIII.)

Excessive bail shall not be required, nor excessive fines imposed, nor cruel and unusual punishments inflicted.

### (ARTICLE IX.)

The enumeration in the Constitution, of certain rights, shall not be construed to deny or disparage others retained by the people.

### (ARTICLE X.)

The powers not delegated to the United States by the

Constitution, nor prohibited by it to the States, are reserved to the States respectively, or to the people.

## ARTICLE XI.

The Judicial power of the United States shall not be construed to extend to any suit in law or equity, commenced or prosecuted against one of the United States by Citizens of another State, or by Citizens or Subjects of any Foreign State.

## ARTICLE XII.

¹ The Electors shall meet in their respective states, and vote by ballot for President and Vice President, one of whom, at least, shall not be an inhabitant of the same state with themselves; they shall name in their ballots the person voted for as President, and in distinct ballots the person voted for as Vice-President, and they shall make distinct lists of all persons voted for as President, and of all persons voted for as Vice-President, and of the number of votes for each, which lists they shall sign and certify, and transmit sealed to the seat of the government of the United States, directed to the President of the Senate;—The President of the Senate shall, in presence of the Senate and House of Representatives, open all the certificates and the votes shall then be counted;—The person having the greatest number of votes for President, shall be the President, if such number be a majority of the whole number of Electors appointed; and if no person have such majority, then from the persons having the highest numbers not ex-

ceeding three on the list of those voted for as President, the House of Representatives shall choose immediately, by ballot, the President.   But in choosing the President, the votes shall be taken by states, the representation from each state having one vote ; a quorum for this purpose shall consist of a member or members from two-thirds of the states, and a majority of all the states shall be necessary to a choice.   And if the House of Representatives shall not choose a President whenever the right of choice shall devolve upon them, before the fourth day of March next following, then the Vice-President shall act as President, as in the case of the death or other constitutional disability of the President.  ' The person having the greatest number of votes as Vice-President, shall be the Vice-President, if such number be a majority of the whole number of Electors appointed, and if no person have a majority, then from the two highest numbers on the list, the Senate shall choose the Vice-President ; a quorum for the purpose shall consist of two-thirds of the whole number of Senators, and a majority of the whole number shall be necessary to a choice.  ' But no person constitutionally ineligible to the office of President shall be eligible to that of Vice-President of the United States.

NOTE.—1. The Editor has availed himself of the foregoing copies of the original Constitution and Amendments found in the valuable work of Mr. W. Hickey, who obtained the certificate of the Secretary of State that they were "correct, in *text, letter*, and *punctuation*," except as to "the small figures designating the clauses," called by printers "superior figures," which were "added merely for convenience of reference."   The certificate is by JAMES BUCHANAN, Secretary of State, and dated July 20th, 1846.

## AMENDMENT OF 1ST FEBRUARY, 1865.

## ARTICLE XIII.

1. Neither slavery nor involuntary servitude, except as a punishment for crime, whereof the party shall have been duly convicted, shall exist within the United States, or any place subject to their jurisdiction.

2. Congress shall have power to enforce this article by appropriate legislation.

## ARTICLE XIV.

*[Not yet ratified by twenty-seven States.]*

SECTION 1. All persons born or naturalized in the United States, and subject to the jurisdiction thereof, are citizens of the United States and of the State wherein they reside. No State shall make or enforce any law which shall abridge the privileges or immunities of citizens of the United States; nor shall any State deprive any person of life, liberty, or property, without due process of law, nor deny to any person within its jurisdiction the equal protection of the laws.

SECTION 2. Representatives shall be apportioned among the several States according to their respective numbers, counting the whole number of persons in each State, excluding Indians not taxed. But when the right to vote at any election for the choice of electors for President and Vice-President of the United States, Representatives in Congress, the executive and judicial officers of a State, or the members of the legislature thereof, is denied to any of the male inhabitants of such State, being twenty-one years of age, and citizens of the United States, or in any way abridged, except for participation in rebellion or other crime, the basis of representation therein shall be reduced in the proportion which the number of such male citizens shall bear to the whole number of male citizens twenty-one years of age in such State.

SECTION. 3. No person shall be a senator or representative in Congress, or elector of President and Vice-President, or hold any office, civil or military, under the United States, or under any State, who, having previously taken an oath, as a member of Congress, or as an offier of the United States, or as a member of any State legislature, or as an executive or judicial officer of any State, to support the Constitution of the United States, shall have engaged in insurrection or rebellion against the same, or given aid or comfort to the enemies thereof. But Congress may, by a vote of two-thirds of each house, remove such disability.

SECTION 4. The validity of the public debt of the United States, authorized by law, including debts incurred for payment of pensions and bounties for services in suppressing insurrection or rebellion, shall not be questioned. But neither the United States nor any State shall assume or pay any debt or obligation incurred in aid of insurrection or rebellion against the

United States, or any claim for the loss or emancipation of any slave; but all such debts, obligations, and claims shall be held illegal and void.

SECTION 5. The Congress shall have power to enforce, by appropriate legislation, the provisions of this article.

## ARTICLE XV.

Section I. The right of citizens of United States to vote shall not be denie abridged by the United States, or by any on account of race, color, or previous con tion of servitude.

Section 2. The Congress shall have to enforce this article by appropriate l lation.

# DIRECTIONS FOR READING THE ANNOTATED CONSTITUTION.

1. Every noun will be found in the index, with reference to article, section, clause, and pages where found.

2. The text is in "long primer," or the larger type, and the notes in " brevier," or the smaller type.

3. The notes are numbered consecutively, and they stand between the texts in the order of the words and phrases defined and expounded.

4. The marginal numbers refer to other notes having relation to the same subjects-matter.

5. The abbreviations of authorities will be found after the " Table of Contents."

6. The citations in (parenthesis) show that they have been quoted in the case, or by the author to whom they are credited.

7. The definitions are all upon the highest authorities, and are usually the first remark in the note.

8. The interrogations (?) in the margin are for the use of teachers.

9. The figures in [17.] are not in the Constitution as filed in the State Department, but are inserted for convenience, because the general mode of printing the Constitution is with these enumerations.

# THE CONSTITUTION

OF THE

# UNITED STATES OF AMERICA.

———◆———

What is the
Constitution
and its his-
tory?

4

**2.** Let it be remembered : 1. That it is a government; 2. That it is the supreme law of the land. Farrar's Const. § 1–4. And the laws of the Union can be enforced by its own authority, on all persons and subjects-matter, over which jurisdiction was granted to any department or officer of the Government of the United States. Rhode Island v. Massachusetts, 12 Pet. 657, 729. It is not a league, but a government. Gibbons v. Ogden, 9 Wheat. 187. For a history of the thirteen colonies, until the formation of the Constitution of the United States, see Story's Commentaries on the Constitution, vol. 1; Johnson v. McIntosh, 8 Wh. 543–573; Curtis's Hist. of the Const. chap. 1, Book 1, §. 1–197; 1 Kent's Com. 11th Ed., sec. 10 and notes. See Stearns v. United States, 2 Paine, 300.

Went into
operation
when?

**3.** This Constitution went into operation on the first Wednesday (4th day) of March, 1789. Owings v. Speed, 5 Wheat. 420; 1 Kent's Com. 219.

Did it create
a new gov-
ernment?

**4.** The new government was not a mere change in dynasty, as in a form of government, leaving the nation or sovereignty the same, and clothed with all the rights, and bound by all the obligations of the preceding one; but it was a new political body, a new nation, then, for the first time, taking its place in the family of nations. Scott v. Sandford, 19 How. 397.

Mutations?

According to Mr. Duane, the Constitution of the United States has passed through three forms: 1. The revolutionary; 2. The confederate; 3. The constitutional; and the first and the third proceeded equally from the people in their original capacity. 1 Kent's Com., 11th Ed., 212, note a.

Was it a
mere
compact?

The Constitution is not a mere compact among the States; but it is a government agreed to by the people of the United States. 1 Story's Const., 3d edition, § 344–365, and notes; 3 Elliot's De-

bates, 286, 287, 288, and notes; Webster's Speeches, 410; Farrar's   6
Const. § 5-38. And whether it be formed by compact between the
States, or in any other manner, its character is the same. President
Jackson's Proclamation, 10th Dec. 1833; Story's Const., 3d Ed.,
p. 727. When adopted it was of complete obligation, and bound Its obliga-
the State sovereignties. McCulloch v. Maryland, 4 Wh. 404; tion?
Chisholm v. Georgia, 2 Dall. 471; Cohens v. Virginia, 6 Wh. 414;
Metropolitan Bank v. Van Dyck, 27 N. Y. Rep. 409. For a clear   2
exposition of the government, see Scott v. Sandford, 19 How. 396;
Ableman v. Booth, 21 How. 506.

WE, THE PEOPLE OF THE UNITED STATES, in order to Preamble.
form a more perfect union, establish justice, insure
domestic tranquillity, provide for the common defense, 5-13.
promote the general welfare, and secure the blessings
of liberty to ourselves and our posterity, do ordain
and establish this Constitution for the United States
of America.

**5.** The preamble in the Constitution is constantly referred to by What is the
statesmen and jurists, to aid them in the exposition of its pro- use of the
visions. Chisholm v. Georgia, 2 Dall. 475; Brown v. Maryland, preamble?
12 Wh. 455-6; 1 Story's Const. chap. 4, § 5, *et seq.* It is the essence and epitome of the whole instrument by which the government is ordained and created, and its purposes, authority, and
duty established. Farrar's Const. § 5.

It was one of the last clauses incorporated in the Constitution. Its history?
Farrar, § 6. It was adopted after various other forms had been
proposed and rejected. Farrar, § 6-12; 2 Curtis's Hist. of the Constitution, chap. xii. 372-376.

(1.) To form a more perfect union; (2.) to establish justice; What are its
(3.) to insure domestic tranquillity; (4.) to provide for the com- divisions?
mon defense; (5.) to promote the general welfare; (6.) to secure
the blessings of liberty to themselves and posterity. (Chisholm
v. Georgia, 2 Dallas, 419; 2 Cond. 635, 671.) Story's Const. § 463;
Farrar, § 15-17.

The differences of opinion of the Southern States Rights or Cal- How dif-
houn school, as they have been called, may be seen in the pre- fered the
amble to the Constitution formed at Montgomery, Alabama, in Southern
March, 1861. school?

"We, the people of the Confederate States, each State acting in The Confed-
its sovereign and independent character, in order to form a federal erate States?
government, establish justice, insure domestic tranquillity, and secure the blessings of liberty to ourselves and our posterity—looking
to the favor and guidance of Almighty God—do ordain and establish this Constitution for the Confederate States of America." It
will thus be seen that a " Federal Government" was substituted
for a " more perfect union," which may be no great difference, as
" government" carries the idea of perpetuity; for although "each

State acted in its sovereign capacity," the instrument was submitted to conventions of the people for ratification. This was the South Carolina form, offered by Mr. Rutledge in the Federal Convention. Farrar, § 8. It was at first so adorted, but afterwards changed. 2 Curtis, 373. The fourth and fifth objects, "general welfare and common defense," were also omitted, although the latter was retained in the first clause of section viii. of art. i., and all the war-powers were retained. Paschal's Annotated Digest, pp. 86, 88, notes 216, 217.

*79, 80.*

The parenthetical—"looking to the favor of Almighty God"—however piously uttered, met no response from the true Preserver of liberty. The actions of the Secessionists, more than any declaration in their Constitution, showed their belief in the right of each State to retire from the Union.

**6.** "WE THE PEOPLE." The Constitution was ordained and established, not by the States in their sovereign capacities, but, emphatically, by the *people* of the United States. Martin v. Hunter's Lessee, 1 Wh. 324; Banks v. Greenleaf, 6 Call, 277. It required not the affirmance of, nor could it be negatived by, the State governments. McCulloch v. Maryland, 4 Wheat. 316, 404, 405. Cohens v. Virginia, 6 Wheat. 264, 413, 414; 1 Kent's Com., Lect. 10, p. 217; Farrar's Const. § 1–60; Rhode Island v. Massachusetts, 12 Wheat. 657, 720. The true doctrine would seem to be, that the Constitution was adopted by the people of the several States, which had been previously confederated under the name of the United States, acting through the delegates by whom they were respectively represented in the convention which formed the Constitution. Baldwin's Constitutional Views, 29–42. And see Worcester v. Georgia, 6 Pet. 569, where it is said by Mr. Justice McLean to have been formed " by a combined power exercised by the people through their delegates, limited in their sanctions to the respective States." And see Farrar, § 1–60. See Barron v. Mayor of Baltimore, 7 Pet. 243.

*By whom ordained and established?*

The Constitution resulted neither from the decision of a majority of the people of the Union, nor from that of a majority of the States. 1 Story's Const., § 360; Ware v. Hylton, 3 Dallas, 199; Chisholm v. Georgia, 3 Dall. 419; 2 Cond. 668, 671; 2 Elliot's Debates, 47; The Federalist, Nos. 22, 33, 39.

*Was it by majorities?*

The words, "WE THE PEOPLE OF THE UNITED STATES" and "CITIZENS" are synonymous terms, and mean the same thing. Scott v. Sanford, 19 How. 404. They are "the people of the several States;" "citizens of the United States;" "citizens of each State;" "numbers," "free persons," and "other persons." Farrar, § 30–38.

*What means "we the people"?*

*16, 17, 24, 46, 169, 220.*

The language is, "WE THE PEOPLE," instead of "We the States." Patrick Henry, 2 Elliot's Debates, 47; and see 1 Elliot's Debates, 91, 92, 110; 1 Story's Const. § 348, note 1 of 3d ed.

And for a full exposition of the action of the people, see Story's Const., § 362–365, note 4 of 3d edition; 1 Webster's Speeches, 1830, p. 431; 4 Elliot's Debates, 326; Madison's Letter in the North American Review, October, 1830, p. 537, 548. For the forms of ratification by the State Conventions, see Hickey's Const., chap. 2, pp. 129–192.

Negroes, whether slaves or free, were not included in the terms "people," or "citizens of the United States." Scott v. Sandford, 19 How. 404–5. The case of Legrand v. Darnell, 2 Pet. 664, does not conflict with this view. Id. 423–4. But the States may confer all the rights of citizenship upon an alien, or any other person, so far as that State is concerned; this, however, does not make him a citizen of the United States. Id. 405–406. *Were the Negroes people? 220 93*

But a man is not incapacitated to be a citizen of the United States by the sole fact that he is colored or of African descent, and not a white man. Opinion of Attorney-General Bates, of 29th Nov., 1862, in which the whole subject of citizenship is discussed. *Can the States confer citizenship? 220*

There is no authoritative definition of the phrase "citizen of the United States." Id.

But the question was put to rest by the Civil Rights Bill, in the following words:— *Declared citizens by the Civil Rights Bill?*

"Be it enacted, &c., That all persons born in the United States, and not subject to any foreign power, excluding Indians not taxed, are hereby declared to be citizens of the United States." 14 St. p. 27, § 1; Paschal's Annotated Digest, Art. 5382. *275*

There can be no doubt of the power of Congress to pass this act. Smith v. Moody, 26 Ind. 307.

**7.** "In order to form a more perfect Union." That it should not, like the Confederation, be a mere treaty, operating by requisitions on the States; and that the people, for whose benefit it was framed, ought to have the sole and exclusive right to ratify, amend, and control its provisions. (2 Elliot's Debates, (Virginia) 47, 61, 131, 57, 97, 98; 3 Id. (North Carolina) 134, 145; 1 Id. (Masachusetts,) 72, 110.) 1 Story's Const. § 464, 469–480, and notes to third edition; Federalist, Nos. 13, 14, 51. *How a more perfect Union?*

The Government which preceded were "Articles of Confederation and Perpetual Union between the States." Ante, p. 9; Story's Const. § 229; Public Journals of Cong., by Way and Gideon, vol. i.; 1 Bioren and Duane, Laws of U. S. 6; Hickey's Const. 483. *How was the Union to be more perfect?*

It was intended to make the Union stronger, by giving it a well-balanced representative Legislature, an Executive, and a Judiciary, with guaranties for the enforcement of law; these provisions carried along the idea of a "more perfect" and "perpetual union." See 2 Curtis's History of the Constitution. *14, 165, 195.*

**8.** To establish Justice.—Justice is the constant and ardent desire to render to every one that which is his own. Justinian; Burrill's Law Dic., Justice. It was probably used here in reference to the judicial power, as there was neither executive nor judiciary under the Articles of Confederation.—Ed. Justice is law. 9 Op. 481 (Black). The objects to be attained may be found in the jurisdiction given in the judicial power, and in the extradition obligations, as well as in the general powers of legis- *What is justice? 7 How attained?*

196, 198, 210, lation on specified subjects, and the inhibitions upon the States.
224, 225.  Story's Const. § 482–489; 2 Kent's Com. 333–4.

How insure      **9.** To INSURE DOMESTIC TRANQUILLITY.—This, doubtless, means
domestic   peace among and between the States.  And it was sought to be
tranquillity? attained by the equality of representation, actual and proportionate;
the power to regulate commerce among the States; the inhibitions
upon them; the jurisdiction of the Supreme Court over controver-
21, 89, 161, sies between them; the guaranties of the rights of the citizens in
162, 220, 223, each; the rendition of criminals and persons held to service; the
238. guaranties of republican forms of government, and against domestic strife; and the national power of legislating over all irritating
subjects.  See Story's Const. § 490–494; the Federalist, Nos. 9,
10, 41.

What is the     **10.** To PROVIDE FOR THE COMMON DEFENSE.—This means the
common   defense of the nation against all enemies, foreign and domestic.
defense?   The end was intended to be attained by giving the power to
How
attained?   Congress to declare war; to provide for armies and navies · grant
letters of marque and reprisal; forts and arsenals; for arming and
disciplining the militia; making treaties the supreme law; making
117, 123, 130, the President the commander-in-chief of the army and navy, and
175, 238, 240. of the militia when in actual service.  Federalist, Nos. 24, 25, 41;
Ex parte Coupland, 26 Tex. 386; Paschal's Annotated Digest, notes
218, p. 88–90; Story's Const. §§ 494, 495; Farrar, § 95.

What is the     **11.** To PROMOTE THE GENERAL WELFARE.—This, doubtless,
general wel- means the general and equal advantages to all the people and the
fare?   States, arising from the grants of power contained in the Consti-
79, 80.   tution, as well as the inhibitions upon Congress and the States, and
the guaranties in the Constitution.

Without claiming this as a warrant for the exercise of doubtful
87, 110, 220, implied powers, we may point to the regulation of commerce, the
221. coining of money; post-offices and post-roads; the acquisition and
extent of territory; the patents and copy-rights, and the general
protection of the citizen everywhere, as vast blessings, the true
value of which no one can comprehend.—ED.  See Story's Const.
497–506.

The words "common defense and general welfare" were not inserted until 4th Sept., 1787.  "Safety" seems to be the first object.
3, 4. (Jay, Federalist, Nos. 3, 4), Farrar, § 101.  The same words occur in
80. the first clause of section 7.  See criticisms upon them.  Id.

**12.** To SECURE THE BLESSINGS OF LIBERTY TO OURSELVES AND
OUR POSTERITY.

What is      Civil liberty means the natural liberty of every one to pursue
liberty?   his own happiness, except so far as he is restrained by the laws of
the land.  Burrill's Law Dictionary, CIVIL LIBERTY; Co. Litt. 116,
b; 1 Bl. Com. 125; note 5; 2 Kent's Com. 26.

This was doubtless the liberty intended to be secured and trans-
How   mitted to posterity in perpetuity.  The object has been sought to
attained?   be more permanently secured by the amendments incorporating

the great principles of *Magna Charta;* the reservation of powers
to the States; the destruction of negro slavery, which became
dangerous to liberty, and the guaranties to the citizen in all the 246.
Amendments.   Story's Const.  § 17, 507–517; 1 Elliot's Debates, 245-275.
278, 296, 297, 332; 2 Id., 47, 96, 136; 3 Id., 243, 257, 294.   The
Federalist, everywhere.   See Farrar, §§ 34, 104–122.

**13.** "OF THE UNITED STATES OF AMERICA."—Mr. Calhoun, in his What is
essay on Government and in his speeches, contended, that this meant by
meant "States united"—that is, a league or compact—and not a States of
government.   But the true definition doubtless is, the union of America?
States under all the restrictions contained in the Constitution.  "The
Government of the United States."   Cohens v. Virginia, 6 Wheat. 2, 4, 6.
264.   The United States is a government, and consequently a body
politic and corporate, capable of attaining the objects for which it Is it a corpo-
was created, by the means which are necessary for their attain- ration?
ment.   United States v. Maurice, 2 Brock. 109.   And, to the ex- 2, 4, 138.
tent of its limited powers, it is supreme.   See the Dred Scott decision, and Abelman v. Booth.   Through the instrumentality of the
proper department to which the delegated powers are confided, it 2, 4.
may enter into contracts not prohibited by law, and appropriate
to the just exercise of those powers.   United States v. Tingey, 5
Pet. 128.   As a corporation, it has capacity to sue by its corporate
title.   Dixon v. United States, 1 Brock. 177; Dugan v. United
States, 3 Wh. 181.   It may compromise a suit, and receive real Can it com-
and other property in discharge of the debt, in trust, and sell the promise
same.   United States v. Lane's Administrators, 3 McLean, 365; suits?
Neilson v. Lagow, 12 How. 107–8.   The above decisions quoted
and approved.   Dikes v. Miller, 25 Tex. (1860;) and held, that,
upon the same principle, the owner of land may file a release
in the general land-office, and divest himself of the right to
recover.  Id.; Paschal's Annotated Digest, note 4.   Absolute What was
sovereignty, and complete supremacy in the exercise of all govern- intended?
mental powers confided to the National Government, were intended to be secured; and it is believed that such intention was
accomplished.   Metropolitan Bank v. Van Dyck, 27 N. Y. Rep. 407.
The powers of the General Government and of the States, al- Distinguish
though both exist, and are exercised within the same territorial the powers?
limits, are yet separate and distinct sovereignties, acting separately
and independently of each other within their respective spheres. 71.
And the sphere of action appropriated to the United States is as
far beyond judicial process issued by a State Judge or a State 138.
Court, as if the line of division were traced by landmarks and monu-
ments visible to the naked eye. (Ableman v. Booth, 21 How. 506,
516); Metropolitan Bank v. Dan Dyck, 27 N. Y. R. 411.   See
also Story's Const. § 413; The People v. New York Central Railroad Company, 24 N. Y. 485, 486; Newell v. the People, 3 Seld.
93; Gibons v. Ogden, 9 Wheat. 188; Martin v. Hunter, 1 Wheat.
304, 326, 327; McCulloch v. Maryland, 4 Wheat. 416, for the rules
of interpretation as to the powers hereinafter granted.

3*

## ARTICLE I.

Where is the legislative power?

SEC. I.—All legislative powers herein granted, shall be vested in a Congress of the United States, which shall consist of a senate and house of representatives.

What is legislative power?

**14.** LEGISLATIVE POWER is the law-making power or supreme power, wherein, according to Blackstone, resides the sovereignty, or at least the exercise of sovereignty, of the State. 1 Bl. Com. 49.

Why a Congress?

**15.** CONGRESS.—An assembly of persons; an assembly of envoys, commissioners, or deputies. An assembly of representatives from different governments to concert measures for their common good, or to adjust their mutual concerns. Webster. Here it is the National Legislature. 1 Kent's Com. 221; Burrill's Law Dic., CONGRESS.

The word was doubtless transferred from the Articles of Confederation, where each State expressly retains its sovereignty, freedom, and independence, and every power, jurisdiction, and right which is not by this Confederation expressly delegated to the United States in Congress assembled. The government was only "a firm league of friendship." Art. 2, ante, p. 9.

Is this wise?

The wisdom of this division of legislative power into two branches has been vindicated by our wisest statesmen. Story's Const. chap. viii. § 545–570; 1 Kent's Com. 208–210; The Federalist, No. 22; De Lolme on the Constitution of England, B. 2, chap. iii.; Randolph's Letter, 3 Amer. Museum, 62, 66; Adams's Defense of American Constitutions, 105, 106, 121, 284, 286; 2 Pitk. Hist. 294, 305, 316; Paley's Moral Philosophy, b. 6, ch. vii.; Wilson's Law Lect. 393–405.

In regular logical consecutive order the Senate should be first defined, but it is not. [ED.]

Of what is the house of representatives?

SEC. II.—[1.] The house of representatives shall be composed of members chosen every second year by the people of the several States; and the electors in each State shall have the qualifications requisite for electors of the most numerous branch of the State legislature.

Why by the people of the several States?

**16.** The House simply means the popular branch. By THE PEOPLE is meant the wise principle of direct representation and responsibility. (The Federalist, Nos. 40–52; 1 Wilson's Law Lect. 429–433; 2 Id. 124–128; 1 Tucker's Blacks. Com., App. 28; Paley's Moral Philosophy, b. 6, ch. 6); Story's Const. § 571–576; Curtis's Hist. of the Const. 148.

What people?

"THE PEOPLE" are that portion of the citizens of the United

States who are the resident inhabitants of particular States. Aliens are excluded. Farrar, § 24–38. This accords with Mr. Calhoun's *24-38.* speech upon the admission of Michigan. But it is not sustained by practice, and was denied in the speeches by Mr. Stephens and others on the admission of Minnesota. Properly, "THE PEOPLE" *6, 21-25, 220.* here really mean the qualified voters. But here Mr. Farrar contends that Congress may prescribe the qualifications. Farrar, § 124 –141. Mr. Farrar admits the practice to be contrary to his theory, but insists that an alien is not an inhabitant. (College v. Gove, 5 Pick. 373); Farrar, § 133. It will be observed that the elec- *Who are* tions are by "the people of the several States." But what *electors?* people shall vote? They are the "electors of the most numerous branch of the State legislature." There was then very little uniformity as to these voters. 2. Elliot's Debates, 38; 2 Wilson's Law Lecture, 128–131; Federalist, No. 52 to 54; Story's Const. chap. 9, § 570, *et seq.* 2 Curtis's Hist. of the Const. 198. Time has only lessened the uniformity, for many of the States allow unnaturalized aliens to vote. See the constitu- *Is a negro* tions of Illinois, Indiana, and Michigan, and the congressional *one of the* debate upon suffrage, 1865–66. In the Dred Scott case the sub- *people?* ject was fully discussed, and it was said that, while congress possessed the exclusive power of naturalization, a negro could *220.* not be made a citizen of the United States; that a State could confer the right of suffrage on an alien, or any one else, but it *May he be a* could not thereby make them citizens of the United States. *voter?* Scott v. Sandford, 19 How. 404–414.

The Constitution of the Confederate States, which showed the *What of the* Southern mind as to proper amendments, interpolated the words *Confederate* "*shall be citizens of the Confederate States.*" And to the section was *tion?* added a clause, "*but no person of foreign birth, not a citizen of the Confederate States, shall be allowed to vote for any officer, civil or political, State or federal.*" Paschal's Annotated Digest, p. 86.

This proved the willingness to make suffrage a matter of na- *6, 220.* tional legislation, and the determination to avoid participation in the elections by persons who were not national citizens.

Mr. Farrar has only followed these extreme views. The ques- *What is the* tion of limited suffrage, and the motives which influenced the *reason of the* Convention to leave the power with the States, will be found in the *rule?* following authorities: 1 Blacks. Com. 171, 172, 463, 464; Montesquieu's Spirit of Laws, b. 11. chap. vi.; Paley's Moral Philosophy, b. 11, chap. vi.; Locke on Government, p. 2, §§ 149, 227; Adams's Amer. Const., letter vi. pp. 263, 440; Jefferson's Notes on Virginia, 191; Story's. Const. 576–587; Curtis's Hist. of the Const. 187, 194, 200.

QUALIFICATIONS.—The word as here used is hardly within any *What means* of the ordinary significations. Webster's Dic., QUALIFICATION. *qualifica-* *tions?*
There was this logic and consistency in the rule adopted: 1. Those who indirectly elect the senators and the president and *19, 35, 46,* vice-president, directly elect the representatives in Congress. *167.* 2. The National Constitution could not well fix a rule as to voters for Congress without also extending it to all elections. 3. Any

28, 233.　absolute abuse of the rights of electors, such as transferring the choice to other magistrates, or to a particular profession, would be subject to the guaranty of a republican form of government.

What are the qualifications as now defined by the States?

**17.** The following are the "QUALIFICATIONS" for electors in the different States at the present time: In all the States, males twenty-one years of age.

Alabama?

ALABAMA.—White citizens of the United States; residence in the State one year, and in the county three months. Soldiers, seamen, and marines of the United States, and persons infamous for crime excluded. Const. of 30th Sept., 1865. Hough, New York Convention Manual, 82. See new Constitution of 1867.

Arkansas?

ARKANSAS.—White citizens of the United States; six months residence; soldiers, seamen, and marines in time of peace excluded. Constitution of 1864–'5. Id. 85.

California?

CALIFORNIA.—White citizens of the United States and of Mexico, who shall have elected to become citizens of the United States under the treaty of the 30th May, 1848. Indians may be qualified by two-thirds of the legislature.—Constitution of 13th October, 1849. Id. 96, 97.

Connecticut?

CONNECTICUT.—Every white male citizen of the United States; one year's residence; freehold of the yearly value of six dollars; good moral character; able to read any article of the Constitution, or any section of the statutes of the State. Amendments of October, 1845, and October, 1855. Id. 115.

Delaware?

DELAWARE.—Free white citizens of the United States; one year's residence; having paid a county tax within two years, which had been assessed at least six months before the election; no tax if between twenty-one and twenty-two years old; no person in the military, naval, or marine service of the United States shall be considered as acquiring a residence in this State by being stationed in any garrison, barrack, or military or naval place or station within this State; and no idiot or insane person, or pauper or person convicted of any crime deemed by law felony, shall enjoy the right of an elector. Constitution of 2d December, 1831. Id. 121.

Florida?

FLORIDA.—Citizens of the United States, with one year's residence. Officers, soldiers, and marines of the army and navy do not thereby acquire residence. The legislature may exclude persons convicted of infamous crimes. Constitution of 7th November, 1865. Id. 135.

Georgia?

GEORGIA.—Free white male citizens of this State and of the United States; have paid all taxes required of them, and which they have had an opportunity of paying, for one year preceding the election; two years' residence in the State and one year in the county. Constitution of 7th Nov., 1865. Id. 149.

Illinois?

ILLINOIS.—White male citizens. Residence one year; *inhabitants* of one year's residence at the adoption of the Constitution. Constitution of 31st August, 1847. Id. 169.

INDIANA.—White male citizens of the United States; six months Indiana? residence; if of foreign birth, one year's residence in tho United States and six months in this State; and shall have declared his intention to become a citizen of the United States, conformably to the laws on the subject of naturalization. No soldier, seaman, or marine of the United States, or of their allies, shall bo deemed to have acquired a residence in the State in consequence of having been within the same; nor shall any such soldier, seaman, or marine have the right to vote. No negro or mulatto shall have the right to vote. Const. of 10th Feb., 1865. Id. 171.

IOWA.—White male citizens of tho United States; six months Iowa? residence in the State and sixty days in the county. Persons in the military, naval, or marine service of tho United States; idiots, insane, or convicted of infamous crimes excluded. Const. of the 5th March, 1857. Id. 184.

KANSAS.—Citizens of the United States; or persons of foreign Kansas? birth who shall have declared their intentions to become citizens, conformably to the laws of the United States on the subject of naturalization; six months residence in the State, and thirty days in the township. No person under guardianship, *non compos mentis*, or insane, or any person convicted of treason or felony, unless restored to civil rights, nor any soldier, seaman, or marine shall be allowed to vote. Const. of 29th July, 1859. Id. 202.

KENTUCKY.—Free white male citizens; residence two years in Kentucky? the State, or one year in the county, town, or city in which he offers to vote, and sixty days in the precinct. Const. of 11th June, 1850. Id. 210.

LOUISIANA.—White male citizens of the United States; residence Louisiana? in the State twelve months, and three months in the parish. Const. of Sept., 1854. Id. 227.

MAINE.—Male citizens of the United States, excepting pau- Maine? pers, persons under guardianship, and Indians not taxed; established residence three months. Persons in the military, naval, or marine service of the United States or this State, and students not deemed to have acquired residence. Const. of 29th Oct., 1819. Id. 240.

MARYLAND.—White male citizens of the United States; resi- Maryland? dence one year in the State and six months in the county. Const. of 1867 (and so of 1864). Id. 250.

MASSACHUSETTS.—Male citizens (excepting persons or paupers Massachu- under guardianship); residence in the State one year; in the town setts? or district six months; having paid all required taxes. Const. of 1780, as amended. Id. 294. Amendment, Art. XX. No person shall have the right to vote, or be eligible to office, under this Commonwealth, who shall not be able to read the Constitution in the English language and write his name; *Provided, however*, that the provisions of this amendment shall not apply to any person prevented by physical disability from complying with its requisitions, nor to any person who now has the right to vote, nor to any person who shall be sixty years of age or upward at the time this amendment takes effect. Id. 298. By amendment XXVI., of 1850, persons of foreign birth not allowed to vote until two years after naturalization. Id. 300.

**Michigan?**

MICHIGAN.—Every white male citizen; every white male inhabitant residing in the State on the 24th day of June, 1835; every white male inhabitant on the first day of January, 1850, who has declared his intention to become a citizen of the United States, pursuant to the laws thereof, six months preceding an election, or who has resided in this State two years and six months, and declared his intention as aforesaid; and every civilized male inhabitant of Indian descent, a native of the United States and not a member of any Indian tribe, shall be an elector and entitled to vote. Residence three months in the State. Const. of 1850. Id. 307. Persons absent in the actual military service of the United States not disqualified. Presence in such service is not residence. Id. 308.

**Minnesota?**

MINNESOTA.—1. White citizens of the United States; 2. White persons of foreign birth who shall have declared their intention to become citizens; 3. Persons mixed with white and Indian blood, who have adopted the customs and habits of civilization; 4. Persons of Indian blood residing in this State who have adopted the language, customs, and habits of civilization, after an examination before any district court of the State, &c., and pronounced capable of citizenship, residence one year in the United States and four months in the State before the election. Const. of 1857–8. Id. 325.

**Mississippi?**

MISSISSIPPI.—Free white male citizens of the United States; one year's residence in the State, four months in the county or town. Const. 1832 as amended in 1865. Id. 336.

**Missouri?**

MISSOURI.—White male citizens of the United States, and every white male person of foreign birth who may have declared his intention to become a citizen of the United States, according to law, not less than one year nor more than five years before he offers to vote; residence one year in the State and sixty days in the county, city, or town. The disqualification of all who participated in or sympathized with the rebellion is most searching and comprehensive. After 1876, new voters must be able to read and write or be disabled therefrom by physical disability. Const. of 1865. 348–351.

143.

**Nebraska?**

NEBRASKA.—1. White male citizens of the United States; 2. White persons of foreign birth who shall have declared their intention to become citizens, conformably to the laws of the United States on the subject of naturalization. Const. of 1867. Id. 371.

By the act of admission agreed to by the legislature, the right is not restricted to whites.

This State was admitted March, 1867, as the 37th State.

**Nevada?**

NEVADA.—Every white male citizen of the United States; residence six months in the State and thirty days in the county; persons convicted of treason or felony and not restored to civil rights,

or who, after arriving at the age of eighteen years, shall have voluntarily borne arms against the United States, or held civil or military
office under the so-called Confederate States, unless an amnesty be
granted to such person by the Federal Government, excluded; also
idiots and insane persons.  Const. of 1864.  Id. 380, 381.

NEW HAMPSHIRE.—Every male inhabitant of each town, and
parish with town privileges, and places unincorporated, excepting
paupers, and persons excused from paying taxes at their own request.  Const. of 1792.  Id. 403.  *(margin: New Hampshire?)*

NEW JERSEY.—White male citizens of the United States; residence one year in the State and five months in the county; officers,
soldiers, and marines of the United States do not acquire residence;
paupers, idiots, and insane persons and persons infamous excluded.
Const. of 1844.  Id. 413.  *(margin: New Jersey?)*

NEW YORK.—Male citizens who shall have been such ten days;
residence in the State one year, and in the county four months.
Men of color, unless citizens of this State for three years, and for
one year seized of a freehold of the value of two hundred and
fifty dollars, on which they shall have paid a tax, excluded.  Absence in military service does not exclude.  Const. of 1846, as
amended in 1863.  Id. 49, 50.  *(margin: New York?)*

NORTH CAROLINA.—Every free white man—being a native or
naturalized citizen of the United States, and who has been an inhabitant of this State for twelve months immediately preceding
the day of election, and shall have paid all taxes.  Amendment of
11th December, 1856, ratified 10th September, 1857.  Id. 431.  *(margin: North Carolina?)*

OHIO.—Free white male citizens of the United States; residence
one year in the State.  Soldiers, marines, idiots, and insane persons excluded.  Mulattoes in a certain degree are excluded.
Const. of 1851.  Id. 438.  *(margin: Ohio?)*

OREGON.—White male citizens of the United States, and white
males of foreign birth who shall have declared their intention; residence one year as to foreigners and six months as to citizens.
Sailors, soldiers, idiots, insane, Chinamen, and negroes excluded.
Const. of 1857.  Id. 449.  *(margin: Oregon?)*

PENNSYLVANIA.—Freemen; residence one year; must have paid
taxes within two years; white freemen, citizens of the United
States, between twenty-one and twenty-two years of age, not
obliged to have paid taxes; if absent in the military service of the
United States, electors not to lose the right to vote.  Const. of
1838, as amended in 1857 and 1864. Id. 472.  *(margin: Pennsylvania?)*

RHODE ISLAND.—Male citizens of the United States; residence
one year; real estate in the State of the value of one hundred and
thirty-four dollars, or which brings a clear rental of seven dollars
per annum.  Soldiers, marines, &c., do not thereby acquire a residence; paupers, lunatics, or persons *non compos mentis*, and Narra-
ganset Indians, specially excluded.  Const. of 1842.  Id. 474, 475.
Soldiers absent in actual military service allowed to vote. Id. 481.  *(margin: Rhode Island?)*

**South Carolina?**    SOUTH CAROLINA.—Free white men; residence two years in the State and six months in the district; immigrants from Europe with like residence who have declared their intention to be naturalized; paupers, soldiers, and marines specially excluded. Const. of 1865. Id. 486.

**Tennessee?**    TENNESSEE.—White men, citizens of the United States (certain blacks included under previous constitution); residence one year. Const. of 1839. Id. 495.

By the amendment of 1866, § 9, the qualifications of voters and the limitation of the elective franchise may be determined by the General Assembly which shall first assemble under the amended constitution. Id. 504. The General Assembly extended the right of suffrage to the blacks, and excluded certain classes of those engaged in the rebellion.

**Texas?**    TEXAS.—Every free male person, who shall be a citizen of the United States (Indians not taxed, Africans, and descendants of Africans excepted); residence one year in the State and six months in the county. Const. of 1866. Id. 507. The words, "or who is, at the time of the adoption of the Constitution by the Congress of the United States, a citizen of Texas," were in the Constitution of 1845, but were omitted from the revision. Paschal's Annotated Digest, 51, 932.

**Vermont?**    VERMONT.—Freemen of the State, who are natural born citizens of Vermont or some one of the United States, or naturalized. Const. of 1793 as amended. New York Convention Manual, by Hough, 523, 529.

**Virginia?**    VIRGINIA.—White male citizens of the Commonwealth; residence one year in the State and six months in the county. Must have paid the previous year's assessment of taxes. Const. of 1864. Id. 533, 545.

**West Virginia?**    WEST VIRGINIA.—White male citizens of the State; residence one year. Paupers, convicts of treason, felony, or bribery in election, persons who have given aid to the rebellion, unless he has volunteered into the military and naval service of the United States and been honorably discharged therefrom, excluded. Const. 1861–3, as amended 24th May, 1866. Id. 547, 548.

**Wisconsin?**    WISCONSIN.—1. Citizens of the United States. 2. Persons of foreign birth who shall have declared their intention to become citizens, conformably to the laws of the United States on the subject of naturalization. (The word "white" was stricken out by amendment.)

3. Persons of Indian blood who have once been declared by law of Congress to be citizens of the United States, any subsequent law of Congress to the contrary notwithstanding.

4. Civilized persons of Indian descent, not members of any tribe. Const. of 1848. Id. 561, 562.

**Is there any uniformity?**    It will thus be seen that the only uniformity is, that electors in all the States require the qualification of being *males over twenty-*

*one years of age*, and of residence longer or shorter. The general rule is, "*white citizens of the United States;*" but negroes or persons of African descent are electors in all New England except Connecticut; in Nebraska, Tennessee, Wisconsin, and by construction, perhaps, in other States; persons in the military and naval service are excluded in some States, and idiots, lunatics, and persons *non compos mentis* in others.

In Oregon, Chinamen are excluded. In all the late fifteen slave States, except Tennessee, persons of African descent are excluded. In Indiana, Michigan, Wisconsin, Oregon, and South Carolina, unnaturalized persons of longer or shorter residence who have declared their intention are voters; while in Massachusetts the naturalized are excluded until two years after naturalization. In a few of the northwestern States Indians are allowed to vote. The qualification of freeholder or tax-payer is required in a few States; and the benefit of clergy or the power to read and write is required in two States. Disqualification for infamous offenses exists in a few States. So that in fact there is no uniformity except as to sex and age, and less than there was at the formation of the federal Constitution. The qualifications in no two States were exactly alike. Story's Court., § 637; The Federalist, No. 54. As to the free persons of African descent, while they were only half a million, the majority of whom resided in the slave States, "*de minimis non curat lex,*" seems to have been the maxim. But now that they are one-eighth of the whole population, and constitute a majority of "citizens of the United States" in several States, whatever may have been our habits of thought, the statesman and the philosopher is obliged to face the question, and to consider the propriety of a uniform rule for electors.

*What is the only uniformity?*

*24.*

*Why the necessity of a uniform rule?*

*220.*

**18.** But citizenship of the United States, or of a State, does not of itself give the right to vote; nor, *e converso*, does the want of it prevent a State from conferring the right of suffrage. Scott v. Sandford, 19 How. 422.

*Is citizenship suffrage?*

The right of suffrage is the right to choose officers of the government; and it does not carry along the right of citizenship. Bates on Citizenship, 4, 5. Our laws make no provision for the loss or deprivation of citizenship. Id.

*What is the right of suffrage?*

*30.*

The word CITIZEN is not mentioned in this clause, and its idea is excluded in the QUALIFICATIONS for suffrage in all the State constitutions. Id. 5, 6.

*Does this section exclude the idea of citizen?*

American citizenship does not necessarily depend upon nor coëxist with the legal capacity to hold office or the right of suffrage, either or both of them.

*Does citizenship depend upon suffrage?*

No person in the United States did ever exercise the right of suffrage in virtue of the naked, unassisted fact of citizenship. Id.

*93.*

There is a distinction between political *rights* and political *powers*. The former belong to all citizens alike, and cohere in the very name and nature of citizenship. The latter (voting and holding office) does not belong to all citizens alike, nor to any citizen merely in virtue of citizenship. His *power* always depends upon extraneous facts and superadded qualifications; which facts and

*What is the distinction between political rights and powers?*

*19, 35, 63, 169,*

**170.** qualifications are common to both citizens and aliens. Bates on Citizenship.

What are the qualifications of representatives.

[2.] No person shall be a representative who shall not have attained to the age of twenty-five years, and been seven years a citizen of the United States, and who shall not, when elected, be an inhabitant of that State in which he shall be chosen.

What persons?

46.

Representative?

**19.** " PERSON " is here undefined, but it is supposed to mean males. A representative is one chosen by the qualified voters, at the time prescribed by the States or Congress, in the manner prescribed by law, and having the qualifications of age, citizenship, and inhabitancy or domiciliation.

Citizen of the United States?

220

Who are citizens?

The Constitution having fixed the qualifications of members, no *additional* qualifications can rightfully be required by the States. Barney v. McCreery, Cl. & Hall, 176: Story's Const. § 624–629; Federalist, No. 52. But if a country be conquered, purchased, or annexed, and the inhabitants thus incorporated by such revolutions, as the purchase of Louisiana and the annexation of Texas, and the conquest and cession of California, the inhabitants become national citizens, and are eligible to office, not as naturalized people, according to uniform rule, but as denizens of the acquired soil, whether native born or naturalized. It was so held in the case of Mr. Levy [Yulee], of Florida, upon a contest in the House of Representatives of the United States. Mr. Clark of Louisiana, and Senator Porter, of that State, as well as all the European inhabitants of Louisiana, Florida, Texas, California, New Mexico, Arizona, and Walrussia, and all born upon those Territories, owed their naturalization to the law of conquest, purchase, or annexation. Native inhabitants have been admitted as delegates from New Mexico, under the general description of citizenship. The object was to exclude aliens. Story's Const. § 612–629. See Farrar, § 256–281.

6. 17, 24, 35, 44, 220.

Yet " PERSON " and " CITIZEN " in this sentence cannot have the same comprehensive meaning of " PEOPLE " or " ELECTORS " in the preamble, and in Art. 1, § 1, clause 1. From necessity it must have a limitation beyond what is defined in the clause.

Who is an inhabitant when elected?

22, 23, 44, 46.

**20.** AN INHABITANT OF A STATE is one who is *bona fide* " a member of the State, subject to all the requisitions of its laws, and entitled to all the privileges and advantages which they confer." Bailey's Case, Cl. & Hall, 411. A person residing in the District of Columbia, though in the employment of the general government, is not an inhabitant of a State, so as to be eligible to a seat in congress. Id. But a citizen of the United States, residing as a public minister at a foreign court, does not lose his character of inhabitant of that State of which he is a citizen, so as to be disqualified for election to congress. Id.: Forsyth's Case, Id. 497. See Ramsay v. Smith, Cl. & Hall, 123. Key's Case, Cl. & Hall, 224.

[3.] Representatives and direct taxes shall be appor- What is tho
tioned among the several States which may be included ment of re-
within this Union, according to their respective num- tives and
bers; which shall be determined by adding to the direct taxes?
whole number of free persons, including those bound
to service for a term of years, and excluding Indians
not taxed, three-fifths of all other persons. The actual
enumeration shall be made within three years after the Census?
first meeting of the Congress of the United States, and
within every subsequent term of ten years, in such
manner as they shall by law direct. The number of Number of
representatives shall not exceed one for every thirty tives?
thousand, but each State shall have at least one representative; and, until such enumeration shall be made,
the State of New Hampshire shall be entitled to choose
three, Massachusetts eight, Rhode Island and Providence Plantations one, Connecticut five, New York
six, New Jersey four, Pennsylvania eight, Delaware
one, Maryland six, Virginia ten, North Carolina five,
South Carolina five, and Georgia three.

**21.** REPRESENTATIVES.—As to the reasons for the rule, see Give facts of
Story's Const. § 630–689. Notes to third edition; 1 Elliot's Representa-
Debates, 212, 213; 2 Pitk. Hist. 233–248.               tives and numbers.
As the population has increased, the ratio, or "numbers" necessary to elect a representative, has been increased, so as not to make
the body too large. They have stood through each decade as
follows:—1790—43,000. 1 St. 253; 1800—33,000. 2 St. 128; 1810
—35,000. Act of 21 Dec., 1811, ch. 9; 1820—40,000. 3 St. 651;
1830—47,700. 4 St. 516; 1840—70,000. 5 St. 491; 1850—93,420.
Rep. population divided by 233, 9 St. 432, 433; 1860—126,823. 12
St. 353; 2 Brightly's Dig. 84. Obtained by dividing by 241, giving        168.
to Ohio, Kentucky, Illinois, Iowa, Minnesota, Vermont, and Rhode
Island, each an additional member.

**22.** DIRECT TAXES, perhaps, mean, in the stricter sense, a rate What are
imposed by government upon individuals (polls), lands, houses, direct taxes?
horses, cattle, possessions, and occupations, as distinguished from
customs, duties, imposts, and excises. Webster. See Burrill's
Law Dic., TAX.

In the case of Hylton v. The United States the question was 72–77, 144.
much discussed; but no authoritative conclusion seemed to be

**163, 164.** settled. The general impression seemed to be, that a tax on real estate, such as the war tax of 1862, might be intended.

See the subject discussed. Story's Const. § 955–957.

Only four direct taxes have been laid: In 1798, 1813, 1815, 1861 Story's Const. § 642; 2. Brightly's Dig. 407; Internal Revenue pamphlets everywhere. The Internal Revenue tax is supposed to come under a different classification.

**On personals?** A tax on carriages is not a direct tax. There are three kinds of taxes: duties, imposts, and excises, which are to be laid by the rule of *uniformity;* and capitation and direct taxes on land, which

**What by uniformity, and what by apportionment?** are to be laid by the rule of *apportionment.* Hylton v. the United States, 3 Dallas, 171. License Tax Cases, 5 Wall. 477. The better opinion seemed to be, that the direct taxes were a capitation or poll tax, or a tax on land. Hylton v. United States, 3 Dall. 171; 1 Kent's Com. 255, 256. This does not preclude the right to

**144.** impose a direct tax in the District of Columbia (and the Territories) in proportion to the census directed to be taken by the Constitution. Loughborough v. Blake, 5 Wh. 317; 1 Kent's Com. 256.

**How apportioned?** **23.** APPORTIONED.—Proportion and ratio are equivalent words; and it is the definition of proportion *among numbers,* that they have a *ratio common to all—a common divisor.* (Jefferson in 1792.) Story's Const. 3d Ed. § 683, note 2; which note also contains Mr. Webster's report on fractional numbers, in 1832. These two opposite views exhaust the whole argument. See Farrar, § 131–141. In these he discusses "free persons," and "all other persons." The

**17, 18, 144, 220.** practice has been to exclude from the "numbers" none except two-fifths of the slaves, thus counting the three-fifths the "all other persons." That is, five slaves were only equal to three "free persons," whether colored or aliens. See Story's Const. § 630–689, 3d Ed., and the voluminous notes, which exhaust the whole subject.

**What are numbers?** **24.** NUMBERS.—The meaning of the word "numbers" is, that two-fifths of all the slaves were excluded; but the free negroes, and all other persons, except tribes of Indians, were enumerated. The

**144, 23.** total numbers by the eighth census (1860) were:—

In the free States and Territories—whites............18,936,579
"       "       "       free colored....... 237,218
In the slave States—whites........................ 8,039,000
"       "       slaves...................... 3,950,000
"       "       free colored.............. 251,000
Deduct two-fifths of slave population............... 1,580,000
Leaving a representative slave population of......... 2,370,000
Total free population in the States, District of Columbia, and Territories .............................27,463,797
Total slave population............................. 3,961,129
Ratio of representatives............................. 127,381

The apportionment of representation under the census of 1860 was as follows: Alabama 6, Arkansas 3, California 3, Connecticut 4, Delaware 1, Florida 1, Georgia 7, Illinois 14, Indiana 11, Iowa

6, Kentucky 9, Louisiana 5, Maine 5, Maryland 5, Massachusetts What was 10, Michigan 6, Minnesota 2, Mississippi 5, Missouri 9, New Hamp-apportionshire 3, New Jersey 5, New York 31, North Carolina 7, Ohio 19, 1860? Oregon 1, Pennsylvania 24, Rhode Island 2, South Carolina 4, Tennessee 8, Texas 4, Vermont 3, Virginia 11, Wisconsin 6. The territories of Kansas, Nebraska, and Nevada have since been 168 admitted as States, each with 1 representative; Colorado has been organized under an enabling act, and will be admitted with 1 representative; Virginia has been divided, and West Virginia has 3 representatives, leaving Virginia 8.

### NUMBERS OF THE STATES AND TERRITORIES, &c.—1860.

| STATES. | CENSUS OF 1860. | | | | RATIO OF INCREASE FROM 1850 TO 1860. | | | |
|---|---|---|---|---|---|---|---|---|
| | White. | Free colored. | Slave. | Total. | White. | Free colored. | Slave. | Total. |
| Alabama | 526,431 | 2,690 | 435,080 | 964,201 | 23.43 | 18.76 | 27.18 | 24.96 |
| Arkansas | 324,191 | 144 | 111,115 | 435,430 | 99.58 | 81.25 | 135.91 | 107.46 |
| California | 361,353 | 4,086 | | 379,994 | 294.34 | 324.74 | | 310.27 |
| Connecticut | 451,520 | 8,627 | | 460,147 | 24.35 | 12.14 | | 42.10 |
| Delaware | 90,589 | 19,829 | 1,798 | 112,216 | 27.28 | 9.72 | 21.49 | 22.60 |
| Florida | 77,748 | 932 | 61,745 | 140,425 | 64.70 | | 57.07 | 60.59 |
| Georgia | 591,588 | 2,500 | 462,198 | 1,057,286 | 13.42 | 19.41 | 21.10 | 16.67 |
| Illinois | 1,704,323 | 7,628 | | 1,711,951 | 101.45 | 40.32 | | 101.06 |
| Indiana | 1,339,000 | 11,428 | | 1,350,428 | 37.63 | 1.47 | | 36.63 |
| Iowa | 673,844 | 1,069 | | 674,913 | 251.13 | 251.53 | | 251.14 |
| Kansas | 106,579 | 625 | 2 | 107,206 | | | | |
| Kentucky | 919,517 | 10,684 | 225,483 | 1,155,684 | 20.76 | 6.72 | 6.87 | 17.54 |
| Louisiana | 357,629 | 18,647 | 331,726 | 708,002 | 39.98 | 8.78 | 35.50 | 36.74 |
| Maine | 626,952 | 1,327 | | 628,279 | 7.76 | 2.14 | | 7.74 |
| Maryland | 515,918 | 83,942 | 87,189 | 687,049 | 23.14 | 12.35 | 3.527 | 17.84 |
| Massachusetts | 1,221,464 | 9,602 | | 1,231,066 | 23.95 | 5.93 | | 23.70 |
| Michigan | 742,314 | 6,799 | | 749,113 | 87.69 | 163.22 | | 88.34 |
| Minnesota | 171,864 | 259 | | 172,123 | 2,775.06 | 709.38 | | 2,760.87 |
| Mississippi | 353,901 | 773 | 436,631 | 791,305 | 19.68 | 16.88 | 40.90 | 30.47 |
| Missouri | 1,063,509 | 3,572 | 114,931 | 1,182,012 | 79.84 | 36.44 | 31.47 | 73.30 |
| New Hampshire | 325,579 | 494 | | 326,073 | 2.56 | 5.00 | | 7.55 |
| New Jersey | 646,699 | 25,318 | 18 | 672,035 | 28.92 | 6.33 | 92.37 | 37.27 |
| New York | 3,831,530 | 49,005 | | 3,880,535 | 25.70 | 0.13 | | 25.29 |
| North Carolina | 631,100 | 30,463 | 331,059 | 992,622 | 14.12 | 10.92 | 14.73 | 14.90 |
| Ohio | 2,302,838 | 36,673 | | 2,339,511 | 17.79 | 41.12 | | 18.14 |
| Oregon | 52,317 | 128 | | 52,465 | 299.92 | 38.16 | | 294.65 |
| Pennsylvania | 2,849,266 | 56,849 | | 2,906,115 | 26.18 | 6.01 | | 25.71 |
| Rhode Island | 170,668 | 3,952 | | 174,620 | 16.62 | 7.68 | | 18.35 |
| South Carolina | 291,388 | 9,914 | 402,406 | 703,708 | 6.13 | 10.65 | 4.53 | 5.27 |
| Tennessee | 826,782 | 7,300 | 275,719 | 1,109,801 | 9.24 | 13.67 | 15.14 | 10.68 |
| Texas | 421,294 | 355 | 182,566 | 604,215 | 173.51 | 10.38 | 213.89 | 184.22 |
| Vermont | 314,389 | 709 | | 315,098 | 0.31 | 1.25 | | 0.31 |
| Virginia | 1,047,411 | 58,042 | 490,865 | 1,596,318 | 17.06 | 6.83 | 3.83 | 12.29 |
| Wisconsin | 774,710 | 1,171 | | 775,881 | 154.20 | 8.44 | | 154.06 |
| | 26,706,425 | 476,556 | 3,950,531 | 31,148,047 | 37.37 | 12.30 | 23.44 | 35.04 |
| **TERRITORIES.** | | | | | | | | |
| Colorado | 34,231 | 46 | | 34,277 a7,261 | | | | |
| Nakota | 2,576 | | | 2,576 | | | | |
| Debraska | 28,759 | 67 | 15 | 28,841 | | | | |
| Nevada | 6,812 | 45 | | 6,847 a10,507 | | | | |
| New Mexico | 82,924 | 85 | | 83,069 | 34.73 | | | 51.94 |
| Utah | 40,214 | 30 | 29 | 40,273 a426 | 254.18 | | 11.53 | 253.89 |
| Washington | 11,138 | 30 | | 11,168 | | | | |
| District of Columbia | 60,764 | 11,131 | 3,185 | 75,080 | 60.15 | 10.66 | 13.627 | 45.76 |
| | 26,973,843 | 487,970 | 3,953,760 | 31,443,322 | 37.97 | 12.33 | 23.39 | 35.59 |

a Indiana.

[Preliminary report on the eighth census, page 131.]

*The following table, showing the population of the States at the different decades, from 1790 to 1860, has been prepared by the editor with great care; and, as the numbers are taken from the census reports, he feels confident that it is correct :—*

| STATES. | 1790. | 1800. | 1810. | 1820. | 1830. | 1840. | 1850. | 1860. |
|---|---|---|---|---|---|---|---|---|
| Alabama | .... ... | ......... | 20,845 | 127,901 | 309,527 | 590,756 | 771,623 | 964,201 |
| Arkansas | ......... | ......... | .... .... | 14,213 | 30,388 | 97,574 | 209,897 | 435,450 |
| California | ......... | ......... | ......... | ......... | ......... | ......... | 92,597 | 379,964 |
| Connecticut | 238,141 | 251,002 | 262,042 | 275,202 | 297,675 | 309,978 | 370,792 | 460,147 |
| Delaware | 59,096 | 64,273 | 72,674 | 72,749 | 76,748 | 78,085 | 91,532 | 112,216 |
| Florida | ......... | ......... | ......... | ......... | 34,730 | 54,477 | 87,445 | 140,425 |
| Georgia | 82,548 | 162,101 | 252,433 | 340,987 | 516,823 | 691,392 | 906,185 | 1,057,286 |
| Illinois | ......... | ......... | 12,282 | 55,211 | 157,445 | 476,183 | 851,470 | 1,711,951 |
| Indiana | ......... | 4,875 | 24,520 | 147,178 | 343,031 | 685,866 | 988,416 | 1,350,428 |
| Iowa | ......... | ......... | ......... | ......... | ......... | 43,112 | 192,214 | 674,913 |
| Kansas | ......... | ......... | ......... | ......... | ......... | ......... | ......... | 107,206 |
| Kentucky | 73,677 | 220,955 | 406,511 | 564,317 | 687,917 | 779,828 | 982,405 | 1,155,684 |
| Louisiana | ......... | ......... | 76,556 | 153,407 | 215,739 | 352,411 | 517,762 | 708,002 |
| Maine | 96,540 | 151,719 | 228,705 | 298,335 | 399,455 | 501,793 | 583,169 | 628,279 |
| Maryland | 319,728 | 341,548 | 380,546 | 407,350 | 447,040 | 470,017 | 583,034 | 687,049 |
| Massachusetts | 378,717 | 422,245 | 472,040 | 523,281 | 610,408 | 737,699 | 994,514 | 1,231,066 |
| Michigan | ......... | ......... | 4,762 | 8,896 | 31,639 | 212,267 | 397,654 | 749,113 |
| Minnesota | ......... | ......... | ......... | ......... | ......... | ......... | 6,077 | 172,123 |
| Mississippi | ......... | 8,850 | 40,352 | 75,448 | 136,621 | 375,651 | 606,526 | 791,305 |
| Missouri | ......... | ......... | 20,845 | 66,586 | 140,455 | 383,702 | 642,044 | 1,182,612 |
| New Hampshire | 141,899 | 183,762 | 214,360 | 244,161 | 269,328 | 284,574 | 317,976 | 326,073 |
| New Jersey | 184,139 | 211,949 | 245,555 | 277,575 | 320,823 | 373,306 | 489,555 | 632,035 |
| New York | 340,120 | 586,756 | 959,049 | 1,372,812 | 1,918,608 | 2,428,921 | 3,097,394 | 3,880,735 |
| North Carolina | 393,751 | 478,103 | 555,500 | 638,829 | 737,981 | 753,419 | 869,039 | 992,622 |
| Ohio | ......... | 45,365 | 237,760 | 581,434 | 937,903 | 1,519,467 | 1,980,329 | 2,339,511 |
| Oregon | ......... | ......... | ......... | ......... | ......... | ......... | 13,294 | 52,465 |
| Pennsylvania | 434,373 | 602,361 | 810,091 | 1,049,458 | 1,348,233 | 1,724,033 | 2,311,786 | 2,906,115 |
| Rhode Island | 69,110 | 69,122 | 77,031 | 83,059 | 97,199 | 108,830 | 147,545 | 174,620 |
| South Carolina | 249,073 | 345,591 | 415,115 | 502,741 | 581,185 | 594,398 | 668,507 | 703,708 |
| Tennessee | 35,791 | 105,602 | 261,727 | 422,813 | 681,904 | 879,210 | 1,002,717 | 1,109,801 |
| Texas | ......... | ......... | ......... | ......... | ......... | ......... | 212,592 | 604,215 |
| Vermont | 85,416 | 154,465 | 217,713 | 225,764 | 280,652 | 291,948 | 314,120 | 315,098 |
| Virginia | 748,308 | 880,200 | 974,622 | 1,065,379 | 1,211,405 | 1,239,797 | 1,421,661 | 1,596,318 |
| Wisconsin | ......... | ......... | ......... | ......... | ......... | 30,945 | 305,391 | 775,881 |
| **Total** | 3,922,827 | 5,291,832 | 7,215,791 | 9,605,192 | 12,826,186 | 17,025,741 | 23,067,262 | 31,148,847 |

**TERRITORIES.**

| | 1790. | 1800. | 1810. | 1820. | 1830. | 1840. | 1850. | 1860. |
|---|---|---|---|---|---|---|---|---|
| Colorado | ......... | ......... | ......... | ......... | ......... | ......... | ......... | 36,523 |
| Dakota | ......... | ......... | ......... | ......... | ......... | ......... | ......... | 2,576 |
| Nebraska | ......... | ......... | ......... | ......... | ......... | ......... | ......... | 28,841 |
| Nevada | ......... | ......... | ......... | ......... | ......... | ......... | ......... | 17,364 |
| New Mexico | ......... | ......... | ......... | ......... | ......... | ......... | 61,547 | 83,009 |
| Utah | ......... | ......... | ......... | ......... | ......... | ......... | 11,380 | 40,699 |
| Washington | ......... | ......... | ......... | ......... | ......... | ......... | ......... | 11,169 |
| District of Columbia | ......... | 14,093 | 24,023 | 33,039 | 39,834 | 43,712 | 51,687 | 75,080 |
| **Total** | 3,922,827 | 5,305,925 | 7,239,814 | 9,638,131 | 12,866,020 | 17,069,453 | 23,191,876 | 31,443,322 |

And see Story's Const., § 644, note 1 of 3d Ed., Preliminary report on the eighth census, pages 5 and 131.

Table showing the number of the Inhabitants of the States and Territories at each Census from 1790 to 1860, inclusive, and the number of Whites, Free Colored, and Slaves, respectively, together with the rate of increase of each class during the several decennial terms and for the whole period.

| Aggregate population. | 1790. | 1800. | Rate per cent. of increase. | 1810. | Rate per cent. of increase. | 1820. | Rate per cent. of increase. | 1830. | Rate per cent. of increase. | 1840. | Rate per cent. of increase. | 1850. | Rate per cent. of increase. | 1860. | Rate per cent. of increase. | Rate per cent. of increase from 1790 to 1860. |
|---|---|---|---|---|---|---|---|---|---|---|---|---|---|---|---|---|
| Total population...... | 3,929,827 | 5,305,925 | 35.02 | 7,239,814 | 36.45 | 9,638,131 | 33.13 | 12,866,020 | 33.49 | 17,069,453 | 32.67 | 23,191,876 | 35.57 | 31,443,322 | 35.59 | 700.16 |
| Total white population | 3,172,464 | 4,304,489 | 35.68 | 5,862,004 | 36.18 | 7,861,937 | 34.11 | 10,537,378 | 34.03 | 14,195,695 | 34.72 | 19,553,114 | 37.74 | 27,978,843 | 37.97 | 750.30 |
| Total free colored pop. | 59,466 | 108,395 | 82.28 | 186,446 | 72.00 | 233,524 | 25.23 | 319,599 | 36.87 | 386,303 | 20.57 | 434,449 | 12.46 | 457,970 | 12.88 | 720.65 |
| Total free population.. | 3,231,930 | 4,412,584 | 36.54 | 6,048,450 | 37.06 | 8,095,461 | 33.84 | 10,856,977 | 34.11 | 14,581,998 | 34.31 | 19,987,563 | 37.07 | 26,461,818 | 37.40 | 747.06 |
| Total slave population. | 697,897 | 893,041 | 27.97 | 1,191,364 | 33.40 | 1,538,088 | 28.70 | 2,009,043 | 30.61 | 2,487,455 | 23.81 | 3,204,313 | 28.82 | 3,953,760 | 23.39 | 466.53 |
| Total col'd population. | 757,363 | 1,001,436 | 32.23 | 1,377,810 | 37.55 | 1,771,562 | 28.55 | 2,328,642 | 31.45 | 2,873,758 | 18.41 | 3,638,762 | 26.62 | 4,441,730 | 22.07 | 496.48 |

*Total population in 1860, including Indian tribes.*

Total population of the States and Territories.............................................. 31,443,322
White population of Indian Territory west of Arkansas........ ............... 1,988
Free colored population of Indian Territory west of Arkansas................ 404
Slave population of Indian Territory west of Arkansas........ ............... 7,369
Population of Indian tribes (according to table on page 186)...... 294,431
　　　　　　　　　　　　　　　　　　　　　　　　　　　　　　　　　　　 31,747,514

Preliminary report on the eighth census.　Page 124.

How are vacancies filled?

[4.] When vacancies happen in the representation from any State, the executive authority thereof shall issue writs of election to fill such vacancies.

Upon what does the executive act?

**25.** The executive of a State may receive the resignation of a member, and issue writs for a new election, without waiting to be informed by the house that a vacancy exists. Mercer's Case, Cl. & Hall, 44; Edwards's Case, Id. 92; Newton's Case, February, 1847.

Colonel Yell had not resigned; but had become a colonel of volunteers in the army in the war against Mexico, in 1846. The governor assumed that the two offices were incompatible: and, after a resolution by the Arkansas legislature to that effect, he issued a proclamation for an election to fill the vacancy. Thomas C. Newton was returned, and the house refused to consider the question of vacancy.

How are vacancies created?

Vacancies, therefore, may be created by death, resignation, removal, or accepting incompatible offices. See Paschal's Annotated Digest, note 200; Powell v. Wilson, 16 Tex. 60; The People v. Carrique, 2 Hill 93; Biencourt v. Parker, 27 Tex. 562.

62, 151.

The acceptance of an incompatible office is an absolute determination of the original office. (Rex v. Trelawney, 3 Burr. 1616; Millwood v. Thatcher, 2 Tr. Rep. 87; Wilcock on Municipal Corporation, 240, 617; Angel & Ames on Corporations, 255;) Biencourt v. Parker, 27 Tex. 562.

Power of choosing officers, and of impeachment.

[5.] The House of Representatives shall choose their Speaker and other officers, and shall have the sole power of impeachment.

What is the Speaker?

**26.** The SPEAKER is the presiding officer of the House of Representatives, who is elected at the meeting of the first session of each Congress, and before there can be any organization. At the opening of the 34th and the 36th Congresses, there being three political parties represented, there were very great delays, as will be seen in the table. The Speaker has the appointment of all standing committees; and he becomes President of the United States in the absence of the Vice-President, and of the presiding officer of the Senate.

The Speakers have been:—

| Congress. | Session. | Names of Speakers. | Election, or commencement of service. | Termination of service. | States of which they were representatives. |
|---|---|---|---|---|---|
| 1 | 1 | Fred. A. Muhlenberg......... | April 1, 1789 | Mar. 3, 1791 | Pennsylvania. |
| 2 | 1 | Jonathan Trumbull.......... | Oct. 24, 1791 | Mar. 2, 1793 | Connecticut. |
| 3 | 1 | Fred. A. Muhlenberg......... | Dec. 2, 1793 | Mar. 3, 1795 | Pennsylvania. |
| 4 | 1 | Jonathan Dayton........... | Dec. 7, 1795 | Mar. 3, 1797 | New Jersey. |
| 5 | 1 | Jonathan Dayton..... ...... | May 15, 1797 | Mar. 3, 1799 | do. |
| 6 | 1 | Theodore Sedgwick......... | Dec. 2, 1799 | Mar. 3, 1801 | Massachusetts. |
| 7 | 1 | Nathaniel Macon........ ... | Dec. 7, 1801 | Mar. 3, 1803 | N. Carolina. |
| 8 | 1 | Nathaniel Macon........... | Oct. 17, 1803 | Mar. 3, 1805 | do. |
| 9 | 1 | Nathaniel Macon........... | Dec. 2, 1805 | Mar. 3, 1807 | do. |
| 10 | 1 | Joseph B. Varnum......... | Oct. 26, 1807 | Mar. 3, 1809 | Massachusetts. |
| 11 | 1 | Joseph B. Varnum.... ..... | May 22, 1809 | Mar. 3, 1811 | do. |
| 12 | 1 | Henry Clay................. | Nov. 4, 1811 | Mar. 3, 1813 | Kentucky. |
| 13 | 1 | Henry Clay................. | May 24, 1813 | Jan. 19, 1814 | do. |
| 13 | 2 | Langdon Cheves........... | Jan. 19, 1814 | Mar. 2, 1815 | S. Carolina. |
| 14 | 1 | Henry Clay................. | Dec. 4, 1815 | Mar. 3, 1817 | Kentucky. |
| 15 | 1 | Henry Clay....... ...... | Dec. 1, 1817 | Mar. 3, 1819 | do. |
| 16 | 1 | Henry Clay................. | Dec. 6, 1819 | Nov. 13, 1820 | do. |
| 16 | 2 | John W. Taylor............. | Nov. 15, 1820 | Mar. 3, 1821 | New York. |
| 17 | 1 | Philip P. Barbour..... ..... | Dec. 3, 1821 | Mar. 3, 1823 | Virginia. |
| 18 | 1 | Henry Clay................. | Dec. 1, 1823 | Mar. 3, 1825 | Kentucky. |
| 19 | 1 | John W. Taylor............. | Dec. 5, 1825 | Mar. 3, 1827 | New York. |
| 20 | 1 | Andrew Stevenson.......... | Dec. 3, 1827 | Mar. 3, 1829 | Virginia. |
| 21 | 1 | Andrew Stevenson.......... | Dec. 7, 1829 | Mar. 3, 1831 | do. |
| 22 | 1 | Andrew Stevenson.......... | Dec. 5, 1831 | Mar. 2, 1833 | do. |
| 23 | 1 | Andrew Stevenson.......... | Dec. 2, 1833 | June 2, 1834 | do. |
| 23 | 1 | John Bell................. | June 2, 1834 | Mar. 3, 1835 | Tennessee. |
| 24 | 1 | James K. Polk........ | Dec. 7, 1835 | Mar. 3, 1837 | do. |
| 25 | 1 | James K. Polk........ | Sept. 4, 1837 | Mar. 3, 1839 | do. |
| 26 | 1 | Robert M. T. Hunter......... | Dec. 16, 1839 | Mar. 3, 1841 | Virginia. |
| 27 | 1 | John White................ | May 31, 1841 | Mar. 3, 1843 | Kentucky. |
| 28 | 1 | John W. Jones........... | Dec. 4, 1843 | Mar. 3, 1845 | Virginia. |
| 29 | 1 | John W. Davis............... | Dec. 1, 1845 | Mar. 3, 1847 | Indiana. |
| 30 | 1 | Robert C. Winthrop.......... | Dec. 6, 1847 | Mar. 3, 1849 | Massachusetts. |
| 31 | 1 | Howell Cobb................ | Dec. 22, 1849 | Mar. 3, 1851 | Georgia. |
| 32 | 1 | Linn Boyd................. | Dec. 1, 1851 | Mar. 3, 1853 | Kentucky. |
| 33 | 1 | Linn Boyd................. | Dec. 5, 1853 | Mar. 3, 1855 | do. |
| 34 | 1 | Nathaniel P Banks ......... | Feb. 2, 1856 | Mar. 3, 1857 | Massachusetts. |
| 35 | 1 | James L. Orr................ | Dec. 7, 1857 | Mar. 3, 1859 | S. Carolina. |
| 36 | 1 | William Pennington.......... | Feb. 1, 1860 | Mar. 3, 1861 | New Jersey. |
| 37 | 1 | Galusha A. Grow... ......... | July 4, 1861 | Mar. 3, 1863 | Pennsylvania. |
| 38 | 1 | Schuyler Colfax........... | Dec. 7, 1863 | Mar. 3, 1865 | Indiana. |
| 39 | 1 | Schuyler Colfax............. | Dec. 4, 1865 | Mar. 3, 1867 | do. |
| 40 | 1 | Schuyler Colfax............. | Mar. 6, 1867 | | do. |

The names of Speakers, *pro tem.,* who served temporarily, for one or more
days, have been omitted.    The delays of elections in the 34th and 36th Congresses were caused by political contests.

**27.** IMPEACHMENT.—We must look to the common law for the What is impeachment? definition of impeachment. William Wirt, Peck's Trial, 499; James Buchanan, Peck's Trial, 437, 438.    And see 1 Chase's
Trial, 47, 48; 2 Id. 9-18; 4 Elliot's Debates, 262.    It is
designed as a method of national inquest into the conduct of
public men.    Story on the Const. § 689.    To exhibit articles of 89, 191-194.
accusation against a public officer before a competent tribunal.
Burrill's Law Dic. 'IMPEACHMENT.    It is a presentment by

the House of Commons, the most solemn grand inquest of the whole kingdom, to the House of Lords, the most high and supreme court of criminal jurisdiction of the kingdom. (2 Hale's Pl. of Cr. 150; 4 Blacks. Com. 259; 2 Wilson's Law. Lect. 165, 166; 2 Woodeson's Lect. 40, p. 596.) Story's Const. § 688. The objects, openness, and dignity of the proceeding. (Rawle, Const. 69, 137, 225, 236; 2 Elliott's Debates, 43–46.) Story's Const. §§ 688–9.

*Pickering's Case?* Judge Pickering was impeached, tried, convicted, and removed in his absence, and without counsel. His offense was, that he was deprived of reason. Farrar, § 169. The judgment was removal

*193, 194.* from office. Story's Const. § 803, note 1. For an enumeration of
*194* the impeachable crimes at common law, see 2 Woodeson's Lect. 40, p. 202; Com. Dig. L. 28–42; Story's Const. § 799–803.

*How and by whom are senators chosen?* SEC. III.—[1.] **The senate of the United States shall be composed of two senators from each state, chosen by the legislature thereof, for six years; and each sen-**
*Vote?* **ator shall have one vote.**

*What are the objects?* **28.** Consider the nature of the representation; the mode of appointment; the number of senators; their term of service; and their qualifications. 1 Story's Const. § 691. It makes the States
*Why two for each state?* equal in the senate. This result was obtained as a compromise, without which the Convention must have been dissolved. Curtis's Hist. of the Const. 41, 48, 100, 105, 106; 1 Story's Const. § 690–700; 2 Pitkin's Hist. 233, 245, 247, 248; 4 Elliot's Debates, 74–92; Id. 99–101; Id. 107, 108, 112–127; 2 Id. 233, 245; Luther Martin's Letter in 4 Elliot's debates, 1–45. The election by the
*Why elected by the Legislature?* legislature was mainly to secure the coöperation of the State with the federal government. (The Federalist, Nos. 27, 62; 1 Kent's Com. Lect. 11, p. 211.) Story's Const. § 704.

*How elected?*
*30.* It was not fully settled whether the elections should be by joint or concurrent vote, until the act of Congress in these notes. (1 Rawle's Const. 37; 1 Kent's Com. Lect. 11 p. 211, 212.) The numbers considered. 1 Story's Const. § 706–708; 2 Curtis's Hist. of Const. passim. There was Hamilton's opinion in favor of tenure
*What was Hamilton's opinion?* during good behavior. Curtis's Hist. of the Const. 100, 105; Story's Const. § 709, note 2 in 3d Ed. The advantages of the present system and the classification fully discussed; Id. § 709–727.
*Effect of two votes?* Practically, the fact that each senator has one vote often divides the State upon questions of party interest.

*What has been the practice?* **29.** Where the election is by a joint convention of the two houses of the legislature, it is not necessary that there should be a concurrent majority of each house in favor of the candidate de-
*Cameron's case.* clared to be elected. Cameron's Case, United States Senate, 13th March, 1857. The election, however, must be substantially by
*28, 30* both houses, as distinct bodies. The mere fact that a majority of the joint body, or even of each body, is present, does not constitute the aggregate body a legislature, unless the two bodies, acting separately, have voted to meet, and have actually met accordingly.

Harlan's Case, United States Senate, 12th January, 1857; 10 Law Harlan's case?
Rep. 1–6.

In the case of John P. Stockton, of New Jersey, in 1866, it was Stockton's case? held that where the two bodies met in convention to elect a senator, and no one having, after numerous ballots, received a majority of the votes cast, and the convention then resolved to elect by plurality, and did so elect, it was not an election by the legislature, and Mr. Stockton was refused his seat.  Senate Journal, 4th Dec., 1865; 8th Jan., 30th Jan., and 26th March, 1866.

For the reasons which led to an equal representation in the sen-Why two ate, and for a longer term of service, see 2 Curtis's History of the senators? Constitution, p. 138–141, 165, 166, 186, 217.  This is one of the sections under which it has been urged that the right of the seceded States to representation in the senate is optional, absolute, 46. and unqualified.  While the precedent is that the reëstablishment of the representation depends upon the reëstablished 242. loyalty of the State, and the ability of the senators elected to 275, 279. take the test oath.

**30.** The mode of election has now been settled by the following act:—

CHAP. CCXLV.—*An Act to regulate the Times and Manner of hold-* July 25.1866, *ing Elections for Senators in Congress.* 14 St., 243.

*Be it enacted, &c.,* 1. That the legislature of each State which What legis-shall be chosen next preceding the expiration of the time for which latures of any senator was elected to represent such State in Congress, shall, States and when to on the second Tuesday after the meeting and organization thereof, elect sena-proceed to elect a senator in Congress, in the place of such senator tors? so going out of office, in the following manner: Each house shall What is the openly, by a viva voce vote of each member present, name one person mode of elec-for senator in Congress from said State, and the name of the person tion ? so voted for, who shall have a majority of the whole number of votes cast in each house shall be entered on the journal of each house by the clerk or secretary thereof; but if either house shall fail to give such majority to any person on said day, that fact shall be entered on the journal.  At 12 o'clock, meridian, of the day following that on which proceedings are required to take place, as aforesaid, the members of the two houses shall convene in joint assembly and the journal of each house shall then be read, and if the same person shall have received a majority of all the votes in each house, such person shall be declared duly elected senator to represent said State in the Congress of the United States; but if the same person shall not have received a majority of the votes in each house, or if either house shall have failed to take proceedings as required by this act, the joint assembly shall then proceed to choose by a viva voce vote of each member present, a person for the purpose aforesaid, and the person having a majority of all the votes of the said joint assembly, a majority of all the members elected to both houses being present and voting, shall be declared duly elected; and if no person shall receive such majority on the first day, the joint assembly shall meet at twelve o'clock, meridian, of each succeeding day during the session of the legislature, and take at least one vote until a senator shall be elected.

**What are the proceedings to elect a senator to fill a vacancy?** 2. Whenever, on the meeting of the legislature of any State, a vacancy shall exist in the representation of such State in the Senate of the United States, said legislature shall proceed, on the second Tuesday after the commencement and organization of its session, to elect a person to fill such vacancy, in the manner herein-before provided for the election of a senator for a full term; and if a vacancy shall happen during the session of the legislature, then on the second Tuesday after the legislature shall have been organized and shall have notice of such vacancy.

**How is the election certified?** 3. It shall be the duty of the governor of the State from which any senator shall have been chosen as aforesaid to certify his election, under the seal of the State, to the President of the Senate of the United States, which certificate shall be countersigned by the Secretary of State of the State.

**What is the classification?** [2.] Immediately after they shall be assembled, in consequence of the first election, they shall be divided, as equally as may be, into three classes. The seats of the senators of the first class shall be vacated at the expiration of the second year, of the second class at the expiration of the fourth year, and of the third class at the expiration of the sixth year, so that one-third may **If vacancies occur?** be chosen every second year; and if vacancies happen by resignation, or otherwise, during the recess of the legislature of any State, the executive thereof may make temporary appointments until the next meeting of the legislature, which shall then fill such vacancies.

**Is the senate permanent?** **31.** The senate is a permanent body; its existence is continued and perpetual. Cushing's Law of Legislative assemblies, 19.

But should a majority of the States persistently refuse to elect senators, the government would come to an end. Cohens v. Virginia, 6 Wh. 264; 5 Cond. 106.

**How vacated? Bledsoe's case.** **32.** The seat of a senator is vacated by a resignation addressed to the executive of a State, notwithstanding he may have received no notice that his resignation has been accepted. Bledsoe's Case, Cl. & Hall, 869.

**Can the executive fill a prospective vacancy? Lanman's case.** **33.** It is not competent for the executive of a State, during the recess of the legislature, to appoint a senator to fill a vacancy which will happen, but has not happened at the time of the appointment. Lanman's Case, Cl. & Hall, 871.

**How is the classification settled?** **34.** For a classification and list of senators, see Hickey's Constitution, 316–388. The classification is settled by lot when the senators first appear from a new State, in the mode adopted in the first classification, so as to prevent two vacancies occurring in the *For what purpose?* same State at the same time. (Journals of Senate, 15th May, 1789, 25, 26, edition of 1820.) 1 Story's Const. § 509. The classification gives some analogy to the principle of two years tenure in the house *How many senators?* of representatives, by the vacation of one-third of the terms every fourth of March. The whole number of States being now thirty-seven, the number of senators would be seventy-four; but ten States *46.* not being represented in the senate, there are only fifty-four senators *275, 279.*

[3.] No person shall be a senator who shall not have *What are the qualifications of senators?* attained to the age of thirty years, and been nine years a citizen of the United States, and who shall not, when elected, be an inhabitant of that State for which he shall be chosen.

**35.** The term "PERSON" here is subject to the same criticism as *What is meant by "person"?* to the qualifications of members of the house, and necessarily cannot be as comprehensive as "ALL OTHER PERSONS" in the 3d clause of the first section. See Farrar's Criticism, § 125–141. Words must *16, 24, 46.* receive their necessary signification and be construed according to *Is "senator" masculine?* the context, precedent and practice. "SENATOR" is sufficiently masculine, and is made certain by "*he.*" See Gallatin's Case, Cl. & *19.* Hall, 851; Shield's Case, who was rejected for want of nine years' *Gallatin's case? Shield's case?* naturalization, "at the commencement of the term for which he was elected." See Senate Journal, from 5th to 15th March, 1849. *93.* Shields was re-elected, and returned to the senate at its next *19.* session—was qualified, and took his seat.

[4.] The Vice-President of the United States shall *Who is president of the senate?* be President of the Senate, but shall have no vote, unless they be equally divided. *163 a.*

**36.** VI'CE [prep.], in place of the president. Webster's Dic. VI'CE. The reasons for this officer presiding discussed. Story's Const. § 732–741. The question of the inherent powers of the *What are the vice-president's powers?* vice-president is still open, it having been ruled in 1826, that he is without power, as presiding officer, except as it is given by the rules of the senate. Story's Const., § 739; 1 American Annual *88.* Register, 86, 87; 3 Id. 99; 4 Elliot's Debates, 311–315. By a rule of 1828, "every question of order shall be decided by the president without debate, subject to appeal to the senate." 3 Annual Reg. 99; Story's Const., § 740; 3 Jefferson's Manual, 15, 17.

**37.** The following have been the vice-presidents: John Adams, *Name the vice-presidents and their terms of office?* from 4 March 1789 to 3 March 1797; Thos Jefferson, from 4 March 1797 to 3 March 1801; Aaron Burr, from 4 March 1801 to 3 March 1805; George Clinton, from 4 March 1805 to 3 March 1813; Elbridge Gerry, from 4 March 1813 to 3 March 1817; Daniel D. Tompkins, from 4 March 1817 to 3 March 1825; John C. Calhoun, from 4 March 1825 to 3 March 1833; Martin Van Buren, from 4 March 1833 to 3 March 1837; Richard M. Johnson, from 4 March 1837 to 3 March 1841; John Tyler, from 4 March 1841 to 6 April 1841; George M. Dallas, from 4 March 1845 to 3 March 1849; Millard Fillmore, from 4 March 1849 to 10 July 1850; William R. King was elected in 1852 and was sworn as vice-president in 1853, in the island of Cuba, in accordance with act of 3d March, 1853. He died in Cuba, having never presided. John C. Breckinridge, from 4 March 1857 to 3 March 1861; Hannibal Hamlin, from 4 March 1861 to 3 March 1865; Andrew Johnson, from 4 March 1865 to 14 April 1865, when he was sworn as president in consequence of the assassination of Abraham Lincoln.

What officers do the senate choose? 172. 86.

[5.] The senate shall choose their other officers, and also a president *pro tempore*, in the absence of the vice-president, or when he shall exercise the office of President of the United States.

When does the presiding officer become president? 172. 168 *a*. 26.

**38.** This presiding-officer, under an act of Congress, becomes the President of the United States, in case of the death or disability of the president and vice-president. 1 St. § 9, p. 240; Brightly's Dig. 253. *Pro tempore* means for the time. But the law and practice is to elect a permanent presiding officer, who acts during the absence of the vice-president, and when the vice-president becomes President of the United States. The following is a list of these presiding officers, or presidents *pro tempore*:—

Name the presiding officers.

| Names of Presidents pro tempore of the Senate. | Attended. | Retired. |
| --- | --- | --- |
| John Langdon | 6 April 1789 | 21 April 1789 |
| John Langdon | 7 Aug. 1789 | 19 Aug. 1789 |
| Richard Henry Lee | 18 April 1792 | 8 May 1792 |
| John Langdon | 5 Nov. 1792 | 4 Dec. 1792 |
| John Langdon | 1 Mar. 1793 | 3 Mar. 1793 |
| John Langdon | 4 Mar. 1793 | 4 Mar. 1793 |
| Ralph Izard | 31 May 1794 | 9 June 1794 |
| Ralph Izard | 3 Nov. 1794 | 9 Nov. 1794 |
| Henry Tazewell | 20 Feb. 1795 | 3 Mar. 1795 |
| Henry Tazewell | 7 Dec. 1795 | 8 Dec. 1795 |
| Samuel Livermore | 6 May 1796 | 1 June 1796 |
| William Bingham | 16 Feb. 1797 | 3 Mar. 1797 |
| William Bradford | 6 July 1797 | 10 July 1797 |
| Jacob Read | 22 Nov. 1797 | 12 Dec. 1797 |
| Theodore Sedgwick | 27 June 1798 | 16 July 1798 |
| Theodore Sedgwick | 17 July 1798 | 17 July 1798 |
| John Lawrence | 6 Dec. 1798 | 26 Dec. 1798 |
| James Ross | 1 Mar. 1799 | 3 Mar. 1799 |
| Samuel Livermore | 2 Dec. 1799 | 29 Dec. 1799 |
| Uriah Tracy | 14 May 1800 | 14 May 1800 |
| John Eager Howard | 21 Nov. 1800 | 27 Nov. 1800 |
| James Hillhouse | 28 Feb. 1801 | 3 Mar. 1801 |

| Names of Presidents pro tempore of the Senate. | Attended. | Retired. |
|---|---|---|
| Abraham Baldwin | 7 Dec. 1801 | 14 Jan. 1802 |
| Abraham Baldwin | 17 April 1802 | 3 May 1802 |
| Stephen R. Bradley | 14 Dec 1802 | 18 Jan. 1803 |
| Stephen R. Bradley | 25 Feb. 1803 | 25 Feb. 1803 |
| Stephen R. Bradley | 2 Mar. 1803 | 3 Mar. 1803 |
| John Brown | 17 Oct. 1803 | 6 Dec. 1803 |
| John Brown | 23 Jan. 1804 | 9 Mar. 1804 |
| Jesse Franklin | 10 Mar. 1804 | 27 Mar. 1804 |
| Joseph Anderson | 15 Jan. 1805 | |
| Joseph Anderson | 28 Feb. 1805 | 2 Mar. 1805 |
| Joseph Anderson | 2 Mar. 1805 | 3 Mar. 1805 |
| Samuel Smith | 2 Dec. 1805 | 15 Dec. 1805 |
| Samuel Smith | 18 Mar. 1806 | 21 April 1806 |
| Samuel Smith | 2 Mar. 1807 | 3 Mar. 1807 |
| Samuel Smith | 16 April 1808 | 25 April 1808 |
| Stephen R. Bradley | 28 Dec. 1808 | |
| John Milledge | 30 Jan. 1809 | 3 Mar. 1809 |
| John Milledge | 4 Mar. 1809 | 7 Mar. 1809 |
| Andrew Gregg | 26 June 1809 | 28 June 1809 |
| Andrew Gregg | 27 Nov. 1809 | 18 Dec. 1809 |
| John Gaillard | 28 Feb. 1810 | |
| John Gaillard | 17 April 1810 | 1 May 1810 |
| John Gaillard | 3 Dec. 1810 | 11 Dec. 1810 |
| John Pope | 23 Feb. 1811 | 3 Mar. 1811 |
| William H. Crawford | 24 Mar. 1812 | 6 July 1812 |
| William H. Crawford | 2 Nov. 1812 | 3 Mar. 1813 |
| Joseph B. Varnum | 6 Dec. 1813 | 3 Feb. 1814 |
| John Gaillard | 18 April 1814 | 18 April 1814 |
| John Gaillard | 19 Sept. 1814 | 2 Mar. 1815 |
| John Gaillard | 4 Dec. 1815 | 30 April 1815 |
| John Gaillard | 2 Dec. 1816 | 3 Mar. 1817 |
| John Gaillard | 4 Mar. 1817 | 6 Mar. 1817 |
| John Gaillard | 1 Dec. 1817 | 18 Feb. 1818 |
| John Gaillard | 31 Mar. 1818 | 20 April 1818 |
| John Gaillard | 16 Nov. 1818 | 5 Jan. 1819 |
| James Barbour | 15 Feb. 1819 | 3 Mar. 1819 |
| James Barbour | 6 Dec. 1819 | 26 Dec. 1819 |
| John Gaillard | 25 Jan. 1820 | 15 May 1820 |
| John Gaillard | 13 Nov. 1820 | 3 Mar. 1821 |
| John Gaillard | 3 Dec. 1821 | 27 Dec. 1821 |
| John Gaillard | 1 Feb. 1822 | 8 May 1822 |
| John Gaillard | 2 Dec. 1822 | 2 Dec. 1822 |
| John Gaillard | 19 Feb. 1823 | 3 Mar. 1823 |
| John Gaillard | 1 Dec. 1823 | 20 Jan. 1824 |
| John Gaillard | 21 May 1824 | 27 May 1824 |
| John Gaillard | 6 Dec. 1824 | 3 Mar. 1825 |
| John Gaillard | 9 Mar. 1825 | 9 Mar. 1825 |
| Nathaniel Macon | 20 May 1826 | 20 Mar. 1825 |
| Nathaniel Macon | 2 Jan. 1827 | 13 Feb. 1827 |
| Nathaniel Macon | 2 Mar. 1827 | 3 Mar. 1827 |

| Names of Presidents pro tempore of the Senate. | Attended. | Retired. |
|---|---|---|
| Samuel Smith | 15 May 1828 | 26 May 1828 |
| Samuel Smith | 1 Dec. 1828 | 21 Dec. 1828 |
| Samuel Smith | 13 Mar. 1829 | 17 Mar. 1829 |
| Samuel Smith | 7 Dec. 1829 | 13 Dec. 1829 |
| Samuel Smith | 29 May 1830 | 31 May 1830 |
| Samuel Smith | 6 Dec. 1830 | 2 Jan. 1831 |
| Samuel Smith | 1 Mar. 1831 | 3 Mar. 1831 |
| Samuel Smith | 5 Dec. 1831 | 11 Dec. 1831 |
| Littleton W. Tazewell | 9 July 1832 | 16 July 1832 |
| Hugh Lawson White | 3 Dec. 1832 | 2 Mar. 1833 |
| Hugh Lawson White | 2 Dec. 1833 | 15 Dec. 1833 |
| George Poindexter | 28 June 1834 | 30 June 1834 |
| John Tyler | 3 Mar. 1835 | 3 Mar. 1835 |
| William R. King | 1 July 1836 | 4 July 1836 |
| William R. King | 28 Jan. 1837 | 3 Mar. 1837 |
| William R. King | 7 Mar. 1837 | 10 Mar. 1837 |
| William R. King | 13 Sept. 1837 | 12 Sept. 1837 |
| William R. King | 2 July 1838 | 16 Oct. 1837 |
| William R. King | 3 Dec. 1838 | 18 Dec. 1838 |
| William R. King | 25 Feb. 1839 | 3 Mar. 1839 |
| William R. King | 2 Dec. 1839 | 26 Dec. 1839 |
| William R King | 3 July 1840 | 21 July 1840 |
| William R. King | 7 Dec. 1840 | 15 Dec. 1840 |
| William R. King | 2 Mar. 1841 | 3 Mar. 1841 |
| William R. King | 4 Mar. 1841 | 4 Mar. 1841 |
| Samuel L. Southard | 11 Mar. 1841 | 15 Mar. 1841 |
| Samuel L. Southard | 31 May 1841 | 13 Sept. 1841 |
| Samuel L. Southard | 6 Dec. 1841 | 30 May 1842 |
| Willie P. Mangum | 31 May 1842 | 31 Aug. 1842 |
| Willie P. Mangum | 5 Dec. 1842 | 3 Mar. 1843 |
| Willie P. Mangum | 4 Dec. 1843 | 17 June 1844 |
| Willie P. Mangum | 2 Dec. 1844 | 3 Mar. 1845 |
| Willie P. Mangum | 4 Mar. 1845 | 4 Mar. 1845 |
| David R. Atchison | 8 Aug. 1846 | 10 Aug. 1846 |
| David R. Atchison | 11 Jan. 1847 | 14 Jan. 1847 |
| David R. Atchison | 3 Mar. 1847 | 3 Mar. 1847 |
| David R. Atchison | 2 Feb. 1848 | 8 Feb. 1848 |
| David R. Atchison | 1 June 1848 | 14 June 1848 |
| David R. Atchison | 26 June 1848 | 29 June 1848 |
| David R. Atchison | 29 July 1848 | 14 Aug. 1848 |
| David R. Atchison | 4 Dec. 1848 | 4 Dec. 1848 |
| David R. Atchison | 26 Dec. 1848 | 1 Jan. 1849 |
| David R. Atchison | 2 Mar. 1849 | 3 Mar. 1849 |
| David R. Atchison | 5 Mar. 1849 | 23 Mar. 1849 |
| William R. King | 6 May 1850 | 19 May 1850 |
| William R. King | 11 July 1850 | 30 Sept. 1850 |
| William R. King | 2 Dec. 1850 | 3 Mar. 1851 |
| William R. King | 1 Dec. 1851 | 31 Aug. 1852 |
| William R. King | 1 Dec. 1852 | 20 Dec. 1852 |
| David R. Atchison | 20 Dec. 1852 | 3 Mar. 1853 |

| Names of Presidents pro tempore of the Senate. | Attended. | Retired. |
|---|---|---|
| David R. Atchison | 5 Dec. 1853 | 7 Aug. 1854 |
| Jesse D. Bright | 4 Dec. 1854 | 3 Mar. 1855 |
| Jesse D. Bright | 3 Dec. 1855 | 8 Aug. 1856 |
| Jesse D. Bright | 21 Aug. 1856 | 30 Aug. 1856 |
| Jesse D. Bright | 2 Dec. 1856 | 5 Jan. 1857 |
| James M. Mason | 5 Jan. 1857 | 3 Mar. 1857 |
| Benjamin Fitzpatrick | 29 Mar. 1858 | 4 May 1858 |
| Benjamin Fitzpatrick | 24 Jan. 1859 | 10 Feb. 1859 |
| Solomon Foote | 18 July 1861 | 6 Aug. 1861 |
| Solomon Foote | 31 Mar. 1862 | 21 May 1862 |
| Solomon Foote | 20 June 1862 | 17 July 1862 |
| Solomon Foote | 18 Feb. 1863 | 4 Mar. 1863 |
| Daniel Clark | 25 April 1864 | 4 July 1864 |
| Daniel Clark | 9 Feb. 1865 | 19 Feb. 1865 |
| La Fayette S. Foster | 7 Mar. 1866 | 28 July 1866 |
| La Fayette S. Foster | 13 Dec. 1867 | 3 Mar. 1867 |
| Benjamin F. Wade | 4 Mar. 1867 | |

[6.] The senate shall have the sole power to try all impeachments. When sitting for that purpose, they shall be on oath or affirmation. When the President of the United States is tried, the Chief-Justice shall preside; and no person shall be convicted without the concurrence of two-thirds of the members present.

*How are impeachments tried?*

*Two thirds?*

**39.** For the doctrine of impeachment, see Peck's Trial, speeches 27, 191–194. for the prosecution and defence; Reports and Debates on the Impeachment of the President, December, 1867. A judgment of impeachment in the English House of Lords requires that at least twelve of the members should concur in it; and "a verdict by less than twelve would not be good." Com. Dig. Parliament. L. 17. The reasons why this power of impeachment was given to the senate are fully discussed in the Federalist, and in Story on the 36, 37. Const., and Rawle on the Const. Story's Const., § 743–775, and notes. The interest of the vice-president is supposed to disqualify him. Story's Const., § 777. For the action of the senate upon impeachment see the journal or record of the senate on trials of impeachment, from March 4, 1730, to March 3, 1851: 1. On the trial of William Blount, a senator of the United States, from December 17, 1798, to January 15, 1799; 2. On the trial of John Pickering, Judge of the New Hampshire District, from March 3, 1803, to March 12, 1803; 3. On the trial of Samuel Chase, one of the Associate Justices of the Supreme Court of the United States, from November 30, 1804, to March 1, 1805. The preceding cases will be found as an appendix to the third volume of the Legislative Journal of the Senate; 4. On the trial of James H. Peck, Judge of the Missouri District, from May 11, 1830, to May 25, 1830; and from December, 13, 1830, to January 31, 1831. The

*Where are the impeachment trials to be found?*

proceedings in this case will be found as an appendix to the Legislative Journal of the Senate of 1830, 1831, and also in volumes called Peck's Trial, Blount's Trial, Pickering's Trial, and Chase's Trial. For the mode of trial in cases of impeachment, see Story's Const., § 807–810; 2 Woodeson's Lect., 40, p. 603, 604; Jefferson's Manual, § 53.

*27, 191, 194.*

*What is the oath of the Senators?* The form of oath adopted by the Senate in Chase's case was as follows: " You solemnly swear or affirm, that in all things appertaining to the trial of the impeachment of ——, you will do impartial justice according to the Constitution and laws of the United States." (Chase's Trial, vol. 1, p. 12.) Report upon the impeachment of the President, 62.

*What is the question?* The question in Pickering's Case was : " Is John Pickering, district judge of the district of New Hampshire, guilty as charged in the —— article of the impeachment exhibited against him by the House of Representatives ?" Annals 2d Session 8th Cong. 364. In Chase's trial it was : " Mr.——, how say you; is the respondent, Samuel Chase, guilty or not guilty of a high crime or misdemeanor, as charged in the article of impeachment ?"    Ibid 2d Session 8th Congress, 564.)

*What is the judgment in impeachment?* [7.] Judgment in cases of impeachment shall not extend further than to removal from office, and disqualification to hold or enjoy any office of honor, trust, or profit, under the United States; but the party convicted shall nevertheless be liable and subject to indictment, trial, judgment, and punishment, according to law.

*What means judgment?* **40.** JUDGMENT here means the conclusion of law from the facts found upon the charges preferred by the House. In the trial of Judge Peck for having disbarred a lawyer, the defence was mainly rested upon the right of the court to punish for contempt, and the want of malice in the judge. Peck's Trial. Some have questioned whether if the defendant be found guilty, the judgment can be *less* than removal from office. Story's Const. 803. Shall not extend *further*, does not mean shall not *exceed* or *fall short*, but be exactly removal and *disqualification*, and nothing else. Farrar, p. 434., note 1.

*27, 39. 149. 191, 194.*

*Can the judgment be short of removal?*

In England the punishment extends to the whole punishment attached by law to the offense. (Comyn's Dig. Parliament, L. 41; 2 Woodeson, Lect. 40, p. 611–614). Story's Const., § 784. The sentence is limited to political punishment, and the party left to a trial for the criminal violation of the law by a jury. Story's Const. § 786.

*How far does the sentence extend?* DISQUALIFICATION.—The punishment touches neither his person nor property; but simply divests him of his political capacity. Mr Bayard, Blount's trial, 47–68, Phila., 1799. Id. 82. Story's Const., § 803.

Sec. 4. [1.] The times, places, and manner of hold- Who pre-
ing elections for senators and representatives, shall be times and
prescribed in each State by the legislature thereof; but elections?
the Congress may at any time by law make or alter　17
such regulations, except as to the places of choosing　18
senators.

**41.** When the legislature of a State has failed to "prescribe the What is the
times, places, and manner" of holding elections, as required by power of the
the Constitution, the governor may, in case of a vacancy, in his governor?
writ of election, give notice of the time and place of election; but
a reasonable time ought to be allowed for the promulgation of the
notice　Hoge's Case, Cl. & Hall, 135.

This power of Congress has only been exercised so far as to How far has
require the States to elect by districts, by the act of 1842, ch. 47. this power
(See Barnard's Protest, in December, 1843, and the debates of that of Congress
session,) and the election of Senators already referred to. These cised?
acts relate to the *manner* of elections, and the *places* so far as the　30
legislative halls are concerned in the election of senators. There
are those who contend that, under this power, the general powers, 274, 275,
and the thirteenth and fourteenth amendments, and the general What is
frame-work of the government, Congress may determine *who* shall meant by
vote at the elections for representatives; but whatever may be and manner?
said of other powers, the more settled opinion seems to be, that
the *times* relate to the days, the *places* to the precincts for voting, 274–279.
and the *manner* to the *viva voce* or ballot system, and the regula- 16–18.
tions for conducting the elections.

When Congress legislates on these points, the legislative "*regu-* What is the
*lations*," (which relate back to those three things) will cease. power of
Congress only has a superintending control. 1 Story's Const. § Congress
815–328. It cannot be said, with any correctness, that Congress subject?
can, in any way, alter the rights or qualifications of voters. 1
Story's Const., § 820. But it was argued differently by those who 17, 18.
opposed the ratification of the Constitution. Little was said in
the Conventions, The Federalist, Nos. 59, 60; 1 Elliot's Debates,
45–44, 67 68; 3 Id. 65. The Editor would say that the practice of
the States as to inappropriate times, the vacancies which exist
when sessions are called, and the experience in regard to secession
and rebellion render expedient that Congress should fix upon some
rule of uniformity.

As to the place of "choosing senators." This means that Con-　80
gress shall not say *where* the legislature shall sit. Story's Const.,
§ 823, note 2. The arguments of those who contend for the power 17, 18.
of Congress to determine *who* may vote, and who shall not be disfranchised, have been presented by Mr. Farrar, § 124–141. It is
now one of the irritating questions.—Ed.

[2.] The Congress shall assemble at least once in What are
every year: and such meeting shall be on the first of Congress?

Monday in December, unless they shall by law appoint a different day.

**When expire?** **42.** The constitutional term of Congress does not expire until twelve o'clock at noon on the 4th of March.   11 Stat. Appendix ii.

**Act of 22 Jan., 1867. 14 St. 378.** **When are the times of meetings?** **43.** "In addition to the present regular times of the meeting of Congress, there shall be a meeting of the Fortieth Congress of the United States, and of each succeeding Congress thereafter, at 12 o'clock meridian, on the fourth day of March, the day on which the term begins for which the Congress is elected, except that when the fourth of March occurs on Sunday, then the meeting shall take place at the same hour on the next succeeding day."

**When and for how long?** So that each Congress is now divided into three sessions: The first commences on the fourth day of March, and may continue its session until the first Monday in December; the second commences on the first Monday in December, and may continue until the next first Monday in December; the third commences on the first Monday in December, and must adjourn on the next fourth day of March, by the dissolution of the Congress.

**What are the powers of each House?** SEC. V.—[1.] Each house shall be the judge of the elections, returns, and qualifications of its own members; and a majority of each shall constitute a quorum to do business; but a smaller number may adjourn from day to day, and may be authorized to compel the attendance of absent members, in such manner, and under such penalties, as each house may provide.

**What are election returns and qualifications? 16-18, 29, 30, 41.** **44.** THE ELECTIONS in a general sense, means the right to determine who has been chosen by the "qualified electors" at the "times and places" and *returned,* according to "the regulations" prescribed by the laws of the States or by Congress wherein they shall have been superseded. Each case usually depends upon its own facts; and the object generally has been to ascertain who has received the highest number of lawful votes. The necessity and importance of this power discussed.   Story's Const. § 833.

**The returns?** **45.** THE RETURNS from the State authorities are *prima facie* evidence only of an election, and are not conclusive upon the house. Spaulding v. Mead, Cl. & Hall, 16, 18, 29, 30, 41, 157; Reed v. Cosden, Id. 353. And the refusal of the executive of a State to grant a certificate of election, does not prejudice the right of one who may be entitled to a seat.   Richard's Case, Id. 95.

**What of the qualifications? 19, 41, 35,** **46.** The "QUALIFICATIONS," in its narrower sense, would doubtless relate to the *age, citizenship,* and *inhabitancy* of the applicant as defined in the second clause of section 2, art. 1, and the third clause of section three of the same. But as the term "PERSON," if taken alone, in both might include a female, a lunatic or an idiot, a convicted felon, a person of notoriously bad character, or actually

at war with the United States, as during the rebellion, or one
coming from a State all of whose inhabitants are at war with
the United States, the term *"qualifications"* has, in practice, 275, 279.
received a more enlarged signification. Thus in the case of Mr.
Niles, in 1846, a committee was raised, in the senate, to inquire
into his mental capacity; the rebellion has caused a test oath,
which might reach persons in all the States, and does embrace          242.
majorities in some of them; a concurrent resolution was passed        70.
in 1866, in regard to the States lately in rebellion, which, it was
urged, limited this independent power of each house; the fourteenth amendment of the Constitution looks to a new *disqualifica-* 275-279.
*tion*, and all the reconstruction acts, it has been argued, intrench
upon this right.  At the time of this writing one committee is
investigating the subject of the *disqualifications* of certain members from Kentucky, and another the question as to whether
Maryland has a "republican form of government" within the           233.
meaning of the Constitution.

It may be pretty strongly inferred from messages and speeches
of President JOHNSON, and certainly it has been very clearly
expressed by some of the opposition statesmen in the senate and
house, that after the acts of reconstruction, that is, the formation
of amended constitutions and elections under the proclamations of
the President, the *"persons"* so chosen were entitled to their seats
without any superadded *"qualifications"* to those prescribed in this 277-279.
section, except the fact that they are "loyal men from loyal
States."

But the statesmen of the majority argue, that while these States
and these very members *elected* and *returned*, and the great bodies
of their constituents were claiming to be aliens to the United
States, and magistrates and people were engaged in war to resist
the authority of the government, they were not entitled to representation; and *a fortiori* they cannot send members with the
proper *"qualifications"* until the law-making power shall determine        233.
upon the terms of restoration; and that, certainly, the test oath is
a superadded *disqualification*, which the president's pardon cannot        242.
overcome.  On the other hand, it has been argued that, as that oath       177.
has been decided to be unconstitutional in some cases, it is so as to 142, 143.
members who are willing to swear to support the Constitution; that        242.
the president's pardon does remove all political disabilities; and
therefore, the test oath cannot apply to those who had been pardoned for their participation in the rebellion; and that the action
of the people, under the authority of the president, restores those
States and the citizens thereof, to all their rights, *in statu quo ante
bellum*.  These are the general arguments, for and against.  The
whole subject is a case not discussed in the formation of the Constitution; it is without precedent, because the frame-work of our
government differs from all others; therefore, the difficult problem 275-265.
must be worked out under its peculiar circumstances.

It is not within the plan of this work to give the opinions of the
Editor.  It may not be improper to remark, however, that there
seems to be more difference as to *who* shall accomplish the work of
restoration than *what* shall be done to accomplish it.  All seem to

agree that there *was* a time when the seceded States could not properly send members, even though such members possessed the constitutional *qualifications*; yet upon this the Constitution is silent. So the words *disloyalty* and *loyalty* are not in it. *Necessity* had to determine that those at war with the government could not vote on the question of supplies. But the time *when*, the power *which*, and the questions *how* and to *whom* political rights shall be restored or given, and indeed how far they are lost, are the matters of difference. Of course the actors in the drama, who believe that the ordinances of secession made the seceding States foreign and independent nations, and all the citizens who remained therein aliens,

**209.** and during the war alien enemies; that the "Confederate States" became a lawful belligerent power, which was only forced "to yield to superior numbers and means," have a kind of *estoppel in limine*, for which there is no other answer than that the friends of the United States held and have established the opposite theory.

The great misfortune in this and all political controversies is, that in discussions men neither weigh well nor define their words.

I can only pray that, in future editions, facts and precedents may enable the Editor to give the exact signification of terms.

What are the powers of each house?

[2.] Each house may determine the rules of its proceedings, punish its members for disorderly behavior, and, with the concurrence of two-thirds, expel a member.

Where are the rules to be found?

**47.** The "RULES" will be found in "Jefferson's Manual," and in the published manuals of each house. See Barclay's Digest; the standing rules printed by Francis Childs, in 1795; Jefferson's Manual; Dwarris on Statutes, 291; Hastel's Precedents; May's Treatise upon the Law, &c., of Parliament; Cushing's Rules of Proceeding, Debate, &c. All these works should be carefully studied by leading and efficient members of Parliamentary bodies. 1 Kent's Com. 238, and notes to 11th edition, where will be found an epitome of the rules.

What is the power as to contempts?

**48.** This does not exclude the power to punish for contempts others than members of the house. The Constitution says nothing of contempts. These were left to the operation of the common law principle, that all courts have a right to protect themselves from insult and contempt, without which right of self-protection, they could not discharge their high and important duties. Nugent's Case, 1 Am. L. J. 139; Anderson v. Dunn, 6 Wh. 204; 1 Story's Const. §§ 845-9; Bolton v. Martin, 1 Dall. 296; Sam. Houston's Case, 11 vol. of Benton's Condensed Debates, pp. 644, 658, where the whole case for striking Stanberry for words spoken in debate is given. This was a contempt not committed in the presence of the House, but upon the avenue, for words spoken and published. Houston was not a member of the House, and was punished by reprimand. Punishment for a breach of privilege should only be inflicted in cases of strong necessity. (Jarvis's Case, and Randolph & Whitney's Case); Houston's Case, 11 Benton's Debates 658.

Whatever may have a tendency to impair the freedom of debate, or
to detract from the independence of the representatives of the
people, is a breach of privilege.  Id. 669.   See the question discussed.  Jefferson's Manual; Tucker Blackstone App. note 200,
205; 1 Story on the Const. § 845-850, 3 ed.

**49.** It seems to be settled that a member may be expelled for For what
any misdemeanor which, though not punishable by any statute, is may a mem-
inconsistent with the trust and duty of a member.  Blount's Case, ber be ex-<br>pelled?
1 Story's Const. § 838;  Smith's Case, 1 Hall's L. J. 459;  Brooks'
Case, for assaulting Senator Sumner in the Senate Chamber, for 193, 194.
words spoken in debate.  It extends to all cases where the offense
is such, as in the judgment of the House, unfits him for parliamentary duties.  (1 Bl. Com. 163; Id. Christian's note, 167; Rex. v.
Wilkes, 2 Wilson's R. 251; Com. Dig. Parliament G. 5; 1 Hall's
Law Journ., 459, 466).  1 Story's Const. § 838.
    The Sergeant-at-arms has no authority to arrest by deputy.  F.
B. Sandborn's Case, 1 Kent's Com. 11 ed. 236, note 2.
    The power to punish for contempt is inherent in all legislative Whence are
assemblies.  1 Kent's Com. 236.  This has been denied in Eng- the powers<br>derived?
land.  (Kelly v. Carson, 4 Moore Privy Council; 63 Fenton v.
Hampton, 11 Id. 347).  Id.; Rex v. Flower, 8 T. 314; Yates v.
Lansing, 9 John. 417.  And see 1 Story's Const. 3d ed. § 845,
850, and his notes which exhaust the authorities.
    William Blount was expelled for an attempt to seduce an United 193, 194.
States interpreter from his duty, and to alienate the affections and
confidence of the Indians from the public officers residing among
them, &c.  (Journals of the Senate, 8th July, 1797; Serg. Const.
Ch. 28, p. 286), Story's Const. § 804.

**50.** On the 14th March, 1861, the Senate passed the following Who were
resolution: "Whereas the seats of Albert G. Brown and Jefferson expelled for
Davis of Miss., Stephen R. Mallory of Florida, Clement C. Clay, participa-<br>tion in the
jr. of Ala., Robt. Toombs of Ga., and Judah P. Benjamin of rebellion?
Louisiana, having become vacant: Therefore, *Resolved*, that the
Secretary be directed to omit their names respectively from the
roll."  Senate Journal, 14 March, 1861.  Jesse D. Bright of Indiana,
was also expelled for treasonable correspondence with Jefferson
Davis.  Senate Journal, 1 March, 1861.

[3.] Each house shall keep a journal of its proceed- What is the<br>rule as to
ings, and from time to time publish the same, except- Journals?
ing such parts as may, in their judgment, require
secrecy; and the yeas and nays of the members of Yeas and<br>nays?
either house, on any question, shall, at the desire of
one-fifth of those present, be entered on the journal.

**51.** The object is to ensure publicity.  Story's Const. § 840. What is the
These journals have been published in various editions and are object of the<br>Journal?
valuable sources of information.

Yeas and nays?

"YEAS AND NAYS" are simply a call for the record of each member's vote upon the questions stated by the Speaker.

State the power of adjournments.

[4.] Neither House, during the session of Congress, shall, without the consent of the other, adjourn for more than three days, nor to any other place than that in which the two houses shall be sitting.

What is the object of the power?

**52.** This places Congress independent of the President, except in cases of disagreement. Story's Const. § 813.

How of compensation?

SEC. VI.—[1.] The Senators and Representatives shall receive a compensation for their services, to be ascertained by law, and paid out of the treasury of the United States. They shall, in all cases, except treason,

Privileges?

felony, and breach of the peace, be privileged from arrest, during their attendance at the session of their respective houses, and in going to, and returning from the same; and for any speech or debate in either House, they shall not be questioned in any other place.

What is the compensation of members?

**53.** COMPENSATION.—The rate of compensation or pay has been several times increased to meet the exigencies of the diminished value of money. 1 Story's Const. § 858. It is now five thousand dollars per annum for the Senators and Representatives, and eight thousand dollars for the Speaker; and twenty cents a mile, by the nearest usually traveled route. 14 St. p. 323 § 17.

The members of the British Parliament receive no compensation. (1 Blackst. Com. 174, and Christian's note 34); Story's Const. § 853. The subject is one on which there was much division in the Convention. (Journal of the Convention, 67, 116–119, 142–151; 2 Elliot's Debates, 279, 280; 4 Elliot's Debates, 92–99. The reasons for and against discussed. Rawle on the Const. ch. 18, p. 179); Story's Const, § 851–858. See Confederation, ante Art. V., p. 11.

How fixed? And why? 53.

**54.** "TO BE ASCERTAINED BY LAW," removes the subject from the pride and parsimony, the local prejudices and local habits of any section of the Union. (3 Elliot's Debates, 279.) Story's Const. § 857.

What are their privileges? 43.

**55** THIS PRIVILEGE, which means freedom from arrest, has belonged to all legislative bodies on the Continent, and immemorially to the English Parliament. (1 Black. Com. 164, 165; Com. Dig. Parliament D. 17; Jefferson's Manual, § 3, *Privilege*; Benyon v. Evelyn, Sir O. Bridge. R. 334.) 1 Story on Const. §

859. It could not be surrendered without endangering the public liberties, as well as the private independence of the members. (1 Kent's Com. Lect. 11.   Bolton v. Martin, Dallas 296.   Coffin v. Coffin, 4 Mass., R. 1) Story's Const. § 869.   See *Ante* Art. V., p. 11.

It is not merely the privilege of the member or his constituents, but the privilege of the House also.   And every man must at his peril take notice who are the members of the house returned of record.   (4 Jefferson's Manual, 4), 1 Story's Const. § 860.

**56.** "TREASON, FELONY, OR BREACH OF THE PEACE."   This would seem to extend to all indictable offenses, as well those which are in fact attended with force and violence, as those which are only constructive breaches of the peace of the government, inasmuch as they violate its good order.  1 Bl. Com. 166; 1 Story's Const. § 865.   The words were borrowed from the common law, 14 Inst. 25; 1 Black. Com. 165; Com. Dig. Parliament D. Breaches of the peace include libels.   Rex v. Wilkes, 2 Wilson's R. 151.) Story's Const. § 865.

*(margin: From what offences? 192, 194.)*

**57.** ARREST.   They are privileged not only from arrest, both on judicial and mesne process, but also from the service of a summons or other civil process, while in attendance on their public duties. Geyer's Lesse v. Irwin, 4 Dall. 107; Nones v. Edsall, 1 Wall. Jr. 191; 1 Story's Const. § 860; Coxe v. McClenachan, 3 Dall. 478. Jefferson's Manual, § 3 and 4.

*(margin: From what arrest privileged?)*

The privilege is personal and does not extend to servants or property.   It is only for a reasonable time, *eundo, morando, et ad propria redeundo*.  (Holliday v. Pitt, 2 Str. R. 985; S. C. Cas. Temp. Hard. 28; 1 Black. Com. 165, Christian's note 21; Barnard v. Mordaunt, 1 Kenyon R. 125; 4 Jeff. Manual, § 3); Story's Const. § 861, 862, 864.

**58.** THE EFFECT of the arrest is, that it is a trespass *ab initio*, actionable and indictable, and punishable as a contempt of the house. (1 Black. Com. 164–166; Com. Dig. Parliament D. 17; Jefferson's Manual, § 3.)   Story's Const. § 863.   The member may also be discharged by motion to a court of justice, or upon a writ of *habeas corpus*.   (Jefferson's Manual, § 3; 2 Str. 990; 2 Wilson's R. 151; Cas. Temp. Hard. 28).   1 Story's Const. § 863.

*(margin: What is the effect of the arrest?)*

**59.** The privilege from arrest commences from the election and before the member takes his seat or is sworn.   (Jefferson's Manual, § 3; but see Comyn's Dig. Parliament D. 17.)   Story's Const. § 864.

*(margin: When does it commence?)*

**60.** One who goes to Washington duly commissioned to represent a State in Congress, is privileged from arrest, *eundo, morando et redeundo;* and though it be subsequently decided by Congress, that he is not entitled to a seat there, he is protected until he reaches home, if he return as soon as possible after such decision.   Dunton v. Halstead, 4 Penn. L. J. 237.

*(margin: In whose favor?)*

**61.** "AND FOR ANY SPEECH OR DEBATE IN EITHER HOUSE THEY SHALL NOT BE QUESTIONED IN ANY OTHER PLACE."

This secures the freedom of debate.   (2 Wilson's Law Sect. 156; 1 Black. Com. 164, 165.)   Story's Const. § 866.

*(margin: What is freedom of debate? 246, 247.)*

But this privilege is strictly confined to words spoken in the course of parliamentary proceedings, and does not cover things done beyond the place and limits of duty. (Jefferson's Manual, § 3) Story's Const. 866.

The privilege does not cover the publication of the speech by the member. (The King v. Creevy, 1 Maule and Selw. 273.   Coffin v. Coffin, 4 Mass. R. .1)   But see Houston's Case (Doddridge and Burgess Speeches in 1832).   Story on Const. § 866.

From what offices are senators and representatives excluded?
[2.] No senator or representative shall, during the time for which he was elected, be appointed to any civil office under the authority of the United States, which shall have been created, or the emoluments whereof shall have been increased, during such time; and no person holding any office under the United States, shall be a member of either house during his continuance in office.

How does the acceptance of one office vacate another?
**62.** The acceptance by a member of any office under the United States, after he has been elected to, and taken his seat in congress, operates as a forfeiture of his seat.   Van Ness's Case, Cl. & Hall, 122; Yell's Case in 1846-7.   Yell had been elected a volunteer colonel in Arkansas, and marched to Mexico.   He did not resign; but the governor ordered an election, and Newton was elected, and served out the term.   Continuing to execute the duties of an office
25.
under the United States, after one is elected to Congress, but before he takes his seat, is not a disqualification, such office being resigned prior to the taking of the seat.   Hammond v. Herrick, Cl. & Hall, 287; Earle's Case, Id. 314; Mumford's Case, Id. 316.

25.
A person holding two compatible offices or employments under the government is not precluded from receiving the salaries of both, &c.   (Converse v. The United States, 21 How. 463.)   9 Op. 508.

**63.** "DURING THE TIME FOR WHICH HE WAS ELECTED" does not reach the whole evil. (Rawle on the Const. ch. 19, p. 184; 1 Tucker's Black. App. 375.)   Story's Const. 867, 868.

What is the effect of holding incompatible offices?
A collector cannot, at the same time, hold the office of inspector of customs and claim compensation therefor.   Stewart v. The United States, 17 How. 116.

On the acceptance and qualification of a person to a second office, incompatible with the one he is then holding, the first office is *ipso facto* vacated. (The People v. Carrique, 2 Hill, 93.)   It operates
25.
as an implied resignation; an absolute determination of the original office. (Rex v. Trelawney, 3 Burr, 1616; Millward v. Thatcher, 2 T. R. 87; Wilcock on Municipal Corp. 240, 617; Ang. & Ames on Corp. 255.)   Paschal's Annotated Digest, note 200, p. 67; Biencourt v. Parker, 27 Tex. 262.

Where must originate revenue bills?
SEC. VII.—[1.] All bills for raising revenue shall

originate in the house of representatives; but the senate may propose or concur with amendments, as on other bills.

**64.** This is copied from a rule governing the English Parlia- What are ment. Story's Const. § 864. The reason is that the commons or bills? members of the house are the immediate representatives of the people. Id. Bills are the forms of enactments before they are acted upon by the house. Those for raising revenue are generally framed upon the estimate of the heads of departments.

**65.** REVENUE. That which returns or is returned; a rent, What is rev- (*reditus*); income; annual profit received from lands or other pro- enue? perty. (Cowell). Burrill's Law Dic. REVENUE.

Here it means what are technically called "money bills." Story's Const. § 874. In practice it is applied to bills to levy taxes in the strict sense of the word. (2 Elliot's Debates, 283, 284). Story's Const. § 880. And see 1 Tucker's Blacks. App. 261.

[2.] Every bill which shall have passed the house of What is the representatives and the senate, shall, before it become passing a law, be presented to the President of the United laws? States; if he approve, he shall sign it, but if not, he 165. shall return it, with his objections, to that house in which it shall have originated, who shall enter the What of the objections at large on their journal, and proceed to veto power? reconsider it. If, after such reconsideration, two-thirds of that house shall agree to pass the bill, it shall be sent, together with the objections, to the other house, How over- by which it shall likewise be reconsidered, and if ap- come? proved by two-thirds of that house, it shall become a law. But in all such cases the votes of both houses shall be determined by yeas and nays, and the names of the persons voting for and against the bill shall be entered on the journal of each house respectively. If any bill shall not be returned by the president within If the bill ten days (Sundays excepted) after it shall have been turned? presented to him, the same shall be a law, in like man- ner as if he had signed it, unless the Congress by their adjournment prevent its return, in which case it shall not be a law.

*When do bills take effect?*

**66.** Every bill takes effect as a law, from the time when it is approved by the president, and then its effect is prospective, and not retrospective. The doctrine that, in law, there is no fraction of a day, is a mere legal fiction, and has no application in such a case. In the matter of Richardson, 2 Story, 571 ; People v. Campbell, 1 Cal. 400. But this is denied to be law. In the matter of Welman, 20 Verm. 653 ; In the matter of Howes, 21 Id. 619. The practice of the presidents has been not to approve bills, not signed by the presiding officers before their actual adjournment.

*Can we go behind the record?*

We cannot go behind the written law. An act of Congress examined and compared by the proper officers, approved by the president and enrolled in the Department of State, cannot afterwards be impugned by evidence to alter and contradict it. 9 Op. 2, 3.

*What is the veto power?*

**67.** This returning of the bill commonly called the "VETO POWER," is simply the *negative power of the president*, which exists in the English Parliament. But the king's veto or negative is a final disposition of the bill. 1 Blacks. Com. 154. The privilege is a part of the king's prerogative never exercised since 1692 ; 1 Kent's Com. 226–229 ; De Lolme on Const. ch. 17, p. 390, 391.

*Define the word?*

"VETO ;" I (FORBID), the word by which the Roman tribunes expressed their negative against the passage of a law or other proceeding, which was also called interceding, (*intercedere*). (Adams' Roman Ant. 13, 145, 146.) Burrill's Law Dic. VETO. And see 1 Wilson's Law Lect. 448, 449 ; the Federalist, No. 51, 69, 73 ; Rawle's Const. Ch. 6, p. 61, 62 ; Burke's letter to the Sheriffs of Bristol in 1777, for the reasons why the exercise has been forborne.

*What are its objects?*

It is intended as a defence of the executive authority, and also as an additional security against rash, immature, and improper laws. Idem, and Story's Const. § 881–893.

The veto power was rarely exercised and never overcome during the first forty years of the government. (Story's Const. § 888.)

The most notable instances of its exercise to prevent legislation, which had really not been made issues in the popular contests for the presidency, were the vetos of President Jackson of the renewal

*74, 81.*

of the charter of the United States bank in 1832 ; and also of his veto of the Maysville Turnpike road. In both these messages the constitutional power of Congress was denied.

In the exciting contest of 1840, the recreation of a National bank was one of the favorite issues of the successful party. But Vice-President Tyler, having succeeded to the presidency, after the

*37.*

death of General Harrison, the exercise of the negative power created an obstacle which could not be overcome by a two-thirds vote.

*166.*

Some Internal improvement measures and the French Spoliation appropriations were also defeated by the negatives of President Polk. But the most notable instances of the exercise of the power have been during the administration of President Johnson.

First, in 1866, the defeat of what is called the " Freedmen's Bureau bill," may be classed among the measures incident to history, where the two-thirds majority could not be found to overcome the negative of the executive. But the passage of the " Civil Rights bill" and the several acts for the reconstruction of the rebel states (found in this volume), are the first instances wherein important measures have been passed by the requisite two-thirds majority. And as the president urged the unconstitutionality of the measures, particularly the last, the question of the duty of the executive to see the laws faithfully executed, which he still believes to be unconstitutional, or still to urge his objections after they had been overcome, according to prescribed forms, is for the first time before the judgment of the nation. The very fact that the measures are in regard to States, which the president contends are entitled to representation, may have no small influence upon his judgment. President's Message, Dec., 1861. *275-279.* *46.*

**68.** "Two Thirds."—On the 7th July, 1856, the senate of the United States decided, by a vote of thirty-four to seven, that two-thirds of a quorum only were requisite to pass a bill over the president's veto, and not two-thirds of the whole senate.   9 Law Rep. 196.   In the ratification of treaties, it is expressly provided that two-thirds of the senators present shall concur. And see Cushing's Law of Legislative Assemblies, § 2387; see Story's Const. § 891; 1 Kent's Com. 249, note b. *What is a Quorum?* *173.*

**69.** The president must receive the bill ten entire days before adjournment, or it will not become a law.   Hyde v. White, 24 Tex. 143, 145; Paschal's Annotated Dig. note 193, p. 62. *What of the ten days?*

[3.] Every order, resolution, or vote, to which the concurrence of the senate and house of representatives may be necessary (except on a question of adjournment), shall be presented to the President of the United States; and before the same shall take effect, shall be approved by him; or being disapproved by him, shall be repassed by two-thirds of the senate and house of representatives, according to the rules and limitations prescribed in the case of a bill. *What shall be presented to the president?* *52.* *244.* *Has he the veto?* *67.*

**70.** A joint resolution approved by the president, or duly passed without his approval, has all the effect of law.   But separate resolutions of either house of congress, except in matters appertaining to their own parliamentary rights, have no legal effect to constrain the action of the president, or of the heads of departments.   6 Opin. 680. *Have joint resolutions the effect of law?* *46.*

The "concurrent resolution" of 1866 in reference to the States in rebellion, not being admitted by either house, was not submitted to the president.

The reason for the exception as to adjournments is, that this is a power peculiarly fitted to be exercised by the two houses in order to secure their independence and prompt action.   Story's Const. § 892. *Why the exception as to adjournment?* *52.*

SEC. VIII.—The Congress shall have power—

With what
limitations
is the word
*power* to be
considered?
14.
41, 48.

133.

142, 144.
268, 269.
1, 148.

Are the fol-
lowing prop-
erly enumer-
ated powers?

Note p. 28,
30.

269.

**71.** POWER.—In this connection means authority to enact. It is to be taken in connection, 1, with the general declaration of the first section, that "all legislative POWER herein granted shall be vested in a Congress of the United States;" 2, with the last clause in this section, "to make all laws which shall be necessary and proper for carrying into execution the foregoing powers, and all other powers vested by this Constitution in the government of the United States, or in any department thereof;" 3, with the inhibitions in the 9th and 10th sections of this article; 4, with the IXth and Xth amendments; 5, with all the necessary powers growing out of other subjects contemplated by the Constitution.

Although the powers here following have been called by Mr. Hamilton, Mr. Jefferson, Mr. Madison, and almost by universal custom "*enumerated powers*," and are generally divided by Arabic numbers into eighteen clauses, yet it will be seen by reference to the authentic copy printed from the original, that, like the versification in the Bible, the *enumeration* has been the work of printers. Yet the practice of calling these special powers "*enumerated*" has too long obtained to ever be abandoned. Hamilton: Federalist, No. 83; Jefferson: Opinion on the Bank, 1781; Madison; Veto Message of 1817; Monroe: veto message of 1822; Farrar, § 283-288; Story's Const. § 981.

Were the fol-
lowing spe-
cial powers
actually
enumerated
in the origi-
nal draft of
the constitu-
tion?

The powers specifically granted to Congress are what are *called enumerated powers, and are numbered in the order in which they stand.* (Monroe, 4th May, 1822.) Story's Const. § 981. Certified copies of the Constitution have been printed by Hickey, Curtis, and Farrar, and now by the author, in which the *enumeration* of *articles* and *sections* appear; but there is none for the *clauses.* For convenience the enumeration of clauses is retained in [brackets]. The editor does not partake of the belief that the habit of calling the following powers *enumerated* has been a fruitful source of misconstruction; for without the figures every mind would number them for itself.

What are
the powers
and objects
of taxation?

**[2.]** To lay and collect taxes, duties, imposts, and excises; to pay the debts and provide for the common defense and general welfare of the United States; but all duties, imposts, and excises shall be uniform throughout the United States.

Define tax-
es?

22, 23.

**72.** "TAXES."—*Taxare.* In the civil law. To rate or value. Calv. Lex. To lay a tax or tribute. Spellman. In old English practice, to assess; to rate or estimate; to moderate or lay an assessment or rate. Burrill's Law Dic., TAX. A rate or sum of money assessed on the person or property of a citizen, by government, for the use of the nation or State. (Webster.) In a general sense—any contribution imposed by government upon individuals, for the use and service of the State: whether under the name of toll, tribute, tallage, gabel, impost, duty, custom, excise, subsidy, aid, supply, or other name. (Story, Const. § 472; 1 Kent's Com. 254-257. Burrill's Law Dic., TAXES; Tomlin's Law Dic. TAX.

In a stricter sense—a rate or sum imposed by government upon individuals (or polls), lands, houses, horses, cattle, possessions, and occupations; as distinguished from customs duties, imposts, and excises. (Id.; Webster.) This is the ordinary sense of the word. In New York, the term tax has been held not to include a street assessment. 1 Johns. 77, 80; Sharp v. Spear, 4 Hill, 76; People v. Brooklyn, 4 Comst. 419.) Literally, or according to its derivation—an imposition laid by government upon individuals, *according to* a certain *order* and proportion, (*tribulum certo ordine constitutum*). (Spelman, voc. TAXA) Id. Distinguished from eminent domain. People v. Brooklyn. 4 Comst. 422–425; s. c. 6 Barb. 214. "Taxes" means burdens, charges, or impositions, put or set upon persons or property for public uses; and this is the definition which the Code gives to tailage. 2 Inst. 522; Carth. 438; Matter of the Mayor, &c. 11 John. 80.

*What in a stricter sense?*

*What literally? 22. 144*

**73.** THE POWER TO LAY AND COLLECT taxes, duties, imposts, and excises, is co-extensive with the territory of the United States. Loughborough v. Blake, 4 Wh. 317.

*Over what extent of country? 22, 23.*

The power of taxation, as a general rule, is a concurrent power. The qualifications of the rule are the exclusion of the States from the taxation of the means and instruments employed in the exercise of the functions of the federal government. Van Allen v. The Assessors, 3 Wallace, 585.

*How far is the power concurrent?*

**74.** The States possess the power to tax the whole of the interest of the shareholder in the shares held by him in the national banks. Van Allen v. The Assessors, 3 Wallace, 588; approved, Bradley v. The People, 4 Wallace, 462. Chief-Justice Chase, in a dissentient opinion for himself and Justices Wayne and Swayne, reviewed McCulloch v. Maryland. 4 Wheat. 327, and Osborn v. the Bank of the United States, 9 Wheat. 73, Weston v. The city of Charleston, 2 Pet. 449, and questioned the power of Congress to authorize State taxation of national securities, either directly or indirectly. Van Allen v. The Assessors. 3 Wallace, 593.

*What power have the States to tax?*

A city cannot tax United States property within its limits. 9th Op. 291.

*What limitation as to the States?*

The jurisdiction of the States for the purposes of State taxation is supreme, and Congress can have no power or control in this regard. State Treasurer v. Wright, 28 Ill. 509; Gibbons v. Ogden, 9 Wh. 199.

The State has the right to collect taxes in gold or silver coin only; and Congress cannot control by its legal tender laws. State Treasurer v. Wright, 28 Ill. 509.

*82.*

The States cannot impose a tax upon the salaries of federal officers. (Dobbins v. The Commissioners of Erie County, 16 Pet. 435.) 9th Op. 477.

*97, 99, 155.*

**75.** DUTIES.—Almost equivalent to taxes and perhaps synonymous with the imposts. (Federalist Nos. 30, 36. Madison's letter to Cabell, 18th Sept. 1828; 3 Elliot's Debates, 289.) Story's Const. § 952; Hylton v. The United States, 3 Dall. 171, 177.

*What are duties? 72, 76.*

**76.** IMPOSTS.—A custom or tax levied on articles brought into a country. (United States v. Tappan, 11 Wheat. 419. A duty on

*Define imposts?*

imported goods and merchandise. Story's Const. 952. Id.    75.
Abridgment, § 472. Burrill's Law Dic. IMPOST. In a large sense,   144.
any tax, duty or imposition. Id.

**77.** EXCISE. An inland imposition upon commodities, charged What are
in most cases on the manufacturer. 2 Steph. Com. 579. A duty, excises?
or tax on certain articles produced or consumed at home.    144.
Wharton's Lex. EXCISE. 1 Bl. Com. 318. It includes also the
duties on licenses and auction sales. 2 Steph. Com. 581; 3 Id.
314. And see Story's Const. § 953. Andrews Rev. Laws, § 133;
Burrill's Law Dic. EXCISE. 2 Elliot's Debates, 209. Generally the
opposite of imposts. Story's Const. § 953.

Licenses under the act of June 30, 1864, "to provide internal What
revenue to support the government, &c." (13 Stat. 223), and the authority
amendatory acts, conveyed to the licensee no authority to carry on does a li-
the licensed business within a State. License Tax Cases, 5 Wal- fer?
lace, 462. The requirement of payment for such licenses is only a
mode of imposing taxes on the licensed business, and the prohibition under penalties, against carrying on the business without license
is only a mode of enforcing the payment of such taxes. The provisions of the act of Congress requiring such licenses, and
imposing penalties for not taking out and paying for them, are not
contrary to the Constitution or to public policy. Id.

The provisions in the act of July 13, 1866, "to reduce internal
taxation, &c." (14 Stat. 93), for the imposing of special taxes, in
lieu of requiring payment for licenses, removes whatever ambiguity
existed in the previous laws, and are in harmony with the Constitution and public policy. Id.

The recognition by the acts of Congress of the power and right    73.
of the States to tax, control, or regulate any business carried on What is the
within its limits is entirely consistent with an intention on the part power of the
of Congress to tax such business for national purposes. States?

A license from the Federal Government, under the internal revenue acts of Congress, is no bar to an indictment under a State law    267.
prohibiting the sale of intoxicating liquors. The *License Tax
Cases*, 5 Wallace, 462; Pervear v. Commonwealth; 5 Wallace, 475.

But very different considerations apply to the internal commerce What are
or domestic trade of the States. Over this commerce and trade the exclu-
Congress has no power of regulation nor any direct control. This sive rights of
power belongs exclusively to the States. No interference by Con- the States?
gress with the business of citizens transacted within a State is
warranted by the Constitution, except such as is strictly incidental
to the exercise of powers clearly granted to the legislature. Pervear v. Commonwealth, 470, 471.

The provisions in the act of July 13, 1866, "to reduce internal
taxation, &c." (14 Stat. 93), for the imposing of special taxes, in
lieu of requiring payment for licenses, removes whatever ambiguity
existed in the previous laws, and are in harmony with the constitution and public policy. Id.

The recognition by the acts of Congress of the power and right
of the States to tax, control, or regulate any business carried on
within its limits is entirely consistent with an intention on the part
of Congress to tax such business for National purposes.

A license from the Federal Government, under the internal revenue acts of Congress, is no bar to an indictment under a State law prohibiting the sale of intoxicating liquors. (The License Tax Cases, 5 Wallace, 462 affirmed.) Pervear v. The Commonwealth, 5 Wallace, 475.   267.

A law of a State taxing or prohibiting a business already taxed by Congress, as *ex. gr.*, the keeping and sale of intoxicating liquors,—Congress having declared that its imposition of a tax should not be taken to abridge the power of the State to tax or prohibit the licensed business—is not unconstitutional. Id. *Of prohibitory laws?*

**78.** "To Pay the Debts." The arrangement and phraseology (connected with what follows) shows that the latter part of the clause ("To provide for the common defence and general welfare,") was intended to enumerate the purposes for which the money thus raised was intended to be appropriated. (President Monroe's Message of 4th Dec. 1822.) Story's Const. § 978-981. *What means to pay the debts? 79, 80.* *74—77.*

This power to collect taxes, imposts, and excises, subjects to the call of Congress every branch of the public revenue, internal and external. (Monroe, Id.) Story's Const. § 981. And these powers give the right of appropriating to the purposes specified, according to the proper construction of the terms. Id.

*Statement of the public debt on the 1st day of January in each of the years from 1791 to 1842, inclusive, and at various dates in subsequent years to July 1, 1866.* *Examine the statement of the public debt?*

| On the 1st day of January.... | 1791 | $ 75,463,476 52 |
|---|---|---|
| | 1792 | 77,227,924 66 |
| | 1793 | 80,352,634 04 |
| | 1794 | 78,427,404 77 |
| | 1795 | 80,747,587 38 |
| | 1796 | 83,762,172 07 |
| | 1797 | 82,064,479 33 |
| | 1798 | 79,228,529 12 |
| | 1799 | 78,408,669 77 |
| | 1800 | 82,976,294 35 |
| | 1801 | 83,038,050 80 |
| | 1802 | 80,712,632 25 |
| | 1803 | 77,054,686 30 |
| | 1804 | 86,427,120 88 |
| | 1805 | 82,312,150 50 |
| | 1806 | 75,723,270 66 |
| | 1807 | 69,218,398 64 |
| | 1808 | 65,196,317 97 |
| | 1809 | 57,023,192 09 |
| | 1810 | 53,173,217 52 |
| | 1811 | 48,005,587 76 |
| | 1812 | 45,209,737 90 |
| | 1813 | 55,962,827 57 |
| | 1814 | 81,487,846 24 |
| | 1815 | 99,833,660 15 |
| | 1816 | 127,334,923 74 |
| | 1817 | 123,491,965 16 |

| | |
|---|---|
| On the 1st day of January....1818.......... | 103,466,633 83 |
| 1819.......... | 95,529,648 23 |
| 1820.......... | 91,015,566 15 |
| 1821.......... | 89,987,427 66 |
| 1822.......... | 93,546,676 98 |
| 1823.......... | 90,875,877 28 |
| 1824.......... | 90,269,777 77 |
| 1825.......... | 83,788,432 71 |
| 1826.......... | 81,054,059 99 |
| 1827.......... | 73,987,357 20 |
| 1828.......... | 67,475,043 87 |
| 1829.......... | 58,421,413 67 |
| 1830.......... | 48,565,406 50 |
| 1831.......... | 39,123,191 68 |
| 1832.......... | 24,322,235 18 |
| 1833 ........ | 7,001,032 88 |
| 1834.......... | 4,760,081 08 |
| 1835.......... | 351,289 05 |
| 1836.......... | 291,089 05 |
| 1837.......... | 1,878,223 55 |
| 1838.......... | 4,857,660 46 |
| 1839.......... | 11,983.737 53 |
| 1840.......... | 5,125,077 63 |
| On the first day of January,...1841.......... | 6,737,398 00 |
| 1842.......... | 15,028,486 37 |
| 1843.......... | 27,203,450 69 |
| On the first day of July ......1844.......... | 24,748,188 23 |
| 1845.......... | 17,093,794 80 |
| 1846.......... | 16,750,926 33 |
| 1847.......... | 38,956,623 38 |
| 1848.......... | 48,526.379 37 |
| 1849.......... | 64,704.693 71 |
| On the 1st day of December ..1850.......... | 64,228,238 37 |
| 1851.... ...... | 62,560,395 26 |
| On the 20th day of November.1852.......... | 65,131.692 13 |
| On the 30th day of December .1853.......... | 67,340,628 78 |
| On the first day of July ......1854.......... | 47,242,206 05 |
| 1855.......... | 39,969,731 05 |
| On the 17th day of November.1856.......... | 30,963,909 64 |
| On the 15th day of November.1857.......... | 29,060,386 90 |
| On the 1st day of July........1858.......... | 44,910,777 66 |
| 1859.......... | 58,754,699,33 |
| 1860.......... | 64,769,703 08 |
| 1861.......... | 90,867,828 68 |
| 1862.......... | 514.211,371 92 |
| On the 1st day of January....1863.......... | 1,098,793,181 37 |
| 1864.......... | 1,740,690,489 49 |
| 1865.......... | 2,682,593,026 53 |
| 1866.......... | 2,783,425,879 21 |

S. B. COLBY, *Register.*

TREASURY DEPARTMENT,
*Register's Office, November 22, 1866.*

Report of Secretary of Treasury on the Finances, p. 304.

The following is a statement of the public debt, June 30, 1866, exclusive of cash in the Treasury :—

| | | |
|---|---:|---:|
| Bonds, 10-40's, 5 per cent., due in 1904 | $171,219,100 00 | |
| Bonds, Pacific railroad, 6 per cent., due in 1895 and 1896 | 6,042,000 00 | |
| Bonds, 5-20's, 6 per cent., due in 1882, 1884, and 1885 | 722,205,500 00 | |
| Bonds, 6 per cent, due in 1881 | 265,317,700 00 | |
| Bonds, 6 per cent., due in 1880 | 18,415,000 00 | |
| Bonds, 5 per cent., due in 1784 | 20,000,000 00 | |
| Bonds, 5 per cent., due in 1871 | 7,022,000 00 | |
| | | $1,210,221,300 00 |
| Bonds, 6 per cent., due in 1868 | 8,908,341 80 | |
| Bonds, 6 per cent., due in 1867 | 9,415,250 20 | |
| Compound-interest notes, due in 1867 and 1868 | 159,012,140 00 | |
| 7-30 treasury notes, due in 1867 and 1868 | 806,251,550 00 | |
| | | 983,587,281 80 |
| Bonds, Texas indemnity, past due, not presented | 559,000 00 | |
| Bonds, treasury notes, &c., past due, not presented | 3,815,675 80 | |
| | | 4,377,65 80 |
| Temporary loan, ten days' notice | 120,176,196 65 | |
| Certificates of indebtedness, past due, not presented | 26,391,000 00 | |
| | | 146,567,096 65 |
| United States notes | 400.891,368 00 | |
| Fractional currency | 27,070,876 96 | |
| Gold certificates of deposit | 10,713,180 00 | |
| | | 438,675,424 96 |
| Total | | 2,783,425,879 21 |

The foregoing is a correct statement of the public debt, as appears from the books and Treasurer's returns in the Department, on the 1st of November, 1867.

## THE PUBLIC DEBT STATEMENT.

WASHINGTON, Nov. 6, 1867,
11:30 o'clock, P. M.

The following is the statement of the public debt of the United States on the 1st of November, 1867:—

DEBT BEARING COIN INTEREST.

| | |
|---|---:|
| Five per cent. bonds | $ 198,845,350 |
| Six per cent. bonds of 1857 and 1868 | 14,690 940 |
| Six per cent. bonds of 1881 | 283,676,600 |
| Six per cent. five-twenty bonds | 1,267,898,100 |
| Navy Pension fund | 13,000,001 |
| Total | $1,778,110,991 |

### DEBT BEARING CURRENCY INTEREST.

| | |
|---|---:|
| Six per cent. bonds. | $ 18,042,000 |
| Three-year compound-interest notes. | 62,558,940 |
| Three-year seven-thirty notes. | 334,607,700 |
| Three per cent. certificates. | 11,560,000 |
| Total. | $426,768,640 |

### MATURED DEBT NOT PRESENTED FOR PAYMENT.

| | |
|---|---:|
| Three-year seven-thirty notes, due August 15, 1867 | $ 3,371,100 |
| Compound-interest notes, matured June 10, July 15, August 15, and Oct. 15, 1867. | 9,316,100 |
| Bonds of Texas indemnity. | 262,000 |
| Treasury notes, acts July 17, 1861, and prior thereto | 163,661 |
| Bonds, April 15, 1842. | 54,061 |
| Treasury notes, March 3, 1863. | 868,240 |
| Temporary loan. | 4,168,375 |
| Certificates of indebtedness. | 34,000 |
| Total. | $18,237,538 |

### DEBT BEARING NO INTEREST.

| | |
|---|---:|
| United States Notes. | $ 357,164,844 |
| Fractional Currency. | 30,706,433 |
| Gold certificates of deposit. | 14,514,200 |
| Total. | $ 402,385,677 |
| Total debt. | $ 2,625,502,843 |

### AMOUNT IN THE TREASURY.

| | |
|---|---:|
| In coin. | $ 111,540,317 |
| In currency. | 22,458,080 |
| Total. | $ 133,998,398 |
| Amount of debt, less cash in the Treasury. | $ 2,491,504,450 |

HUGH McCULLOCH,
Secretary of the Treasury.

Report of the Secretary of the Treasury on the finances, p. 25. There has been some diminution of the public debt since the promulgation of this report.

Whatever may have been the theories and controversies about the powers of Congress to levy taxes for other purposes than to pay the debts of the United States, and as to whether indirect or direct taxes are most equal and just, it is certain that the enormous debt now existing, together with the necessarily increased expenses of supporting the government, will afford a fair opportunity of giving a trial to every mode of raising revenue. The **278.** DEBTS have been contracted. The great future question is, how shall the power to levy TAXES, &c., be *most* wisely exercised in order to pay them?

**79.** To PROVIDE FOR THE COMMON DEFENCE.—See this sentence contained in connection with the conclusion, that all duties, imposts, and excises shall be uniform throughout the United States. This provision operates exclusively on the power granted in the first part of the clause. (Monroe.) Story's Const., § 982.  *How is common defence construed? 10, 78.*

The object is to secure a just equality among the States in the exercise of that power by Congress. (Monroe.) Id., § 982.

The grant consists of two-fold power: to raise; and to appropriate the money. (Monroe.) Id., § 986.  *What two powers in the grant?*

The power in this clause is limited by the nature of the government only. Id., and § 991.

For a more limited doctrine, see President Jackson's veto message of the Maysville road bill, 27 May, 1830; 4 Elliot's Debates, 333–335; 4 Jefferson's Correspondence, 524; Jefferson's message, 2d Dec., 1806; Wait's State papers, 457, 458.  *72–77.*

The extent of the power has been very much debated, and perhaps the subject was exhausted in Congress, as reported in 4th Elliot's Debates, 236, 240, 265, 278, 280, 284, 291, 292, 332, 334, and in Hemphill's Report on Internal Improvements, 10th Feb., 1831; see also 1 Kent's Com., Lect. XII, 250, 251; Sergt's Const., ch. 28, 311–314; Rawle on the Const., ch. 9, p. 104; 2 United States Law Jour., April, 1826, p. 251, 264–280; Story's Const., ch. xiv.  *80.*

Every one will determine for himself the practice of the government from the appropriations for the Cumberland road in 1806, down to the Pacific railroads, and judge the value of precedents, according to his own theories. The speeches of Mr. Huger and Grimke in the South Carolina legislature, in 1830, may well be consulted by students. The term is necessarily connected with the next, " the general welfare."

The Confederate States Constitution contained this limitation:—

" To levy and collect taxes, duties, imposts, and excises, for revenue necessary to pay the debts, provide for the common defence, and carry on the government of the Confederate States; but no bounties shall be granted from the treasury, nor shall any duties or taxes on importations from foreign nations be laid to promote or foster any branch of industry; and all duties, imposts, and excises shall be uniform throughout the Confederate States." Paschal's Annotated Dig., 88.  *What was the Confederate States (rebel) Constitution?*

It will thus be seen that, as in the preamble of the Constitution of this peculiarly indoctrinated school, they took " TO PROVIDE FOR THE GENERAL WELFARE" *out of* their Constitution: while they left the " COMMON DEFENCE" *in*, although it was not one of the objects expressed in the preamble.  *5, 11.*

To leave no doubt of the intention to exclude the ideas which had divided the country upon the subject of internal improvements, the same Constitution contained this clause:—  *80–89.*

" 3. To regulate commerce with foreign nations, and among the several States, and with the Indian tribes; but neither this nor any other clause contained in the Constitution, shall ever be con-  *82–89.*

strued to delegate the power to Congress to appropriate money for any internal improvement, intended to facilitate commerce, except for the purpose of furnishing lights, beacons, and buoys, and other aids to navigation upon the coasts, and the improvement of harbors and the removing of obstructions in river navigation: in all which cases such duties shall be laid on the navigation facilitated thereby, as may be necessary, to pay the costs and expenses thereof." Paschal's Annotated Digest, p. 88.

The object of this was to prevent land internal improvements by the National government; and yet we find the same men as early as April 19th, 1862, appropriating a million and a half of dollars to aid in the construction of a railroad from New Iberia in Louisiana to Houston in Texas. Acts of Confederate States at large, 34. Like appropriations were made to complete the road from Danville to Raleigh. The amendment was in accordance with the extreme States rights or strict constructionists' views.

**Define the general welfare.**

**11, 79, 89.**

**79.**

**80.** "AND GENERAL WELFARE." Judge Story believed that the true import of the whole clause could be thus expressed: "The Congress shall have power to lay and collect taxes, duties, imposts, and excises, *in order* to pay the debts, and to provide for the common defence and general welfare of the United States." Story's Const. § 908. Thus limiting the power of the government to tax for providing for the common defence and general welfare. Id. and § 911–913.

**What is the power and the purpose?**

**22, 74.**

The laying taxes is the *power*, and the general welfare the *purpose* for which the power is to be exercised. Congress are not to lay taxes *ad libitum* for any purpose they please; but only to pay the debts or provide for the general welfare of the Union. In like manner they are not to do any thing they please, to provide for the general welfare; but only to lay taxes for that purpose. (Jefferson's Op. on the Bank of the United States 15 Feb. 1781; 4 Jefferson's Correspondence 524, 525.) Story's Const. § 926, 927, note 3; Elliot's Debates, 170, 183, 195, 328, 344; 3 Elliot's Debates, 262; 2 American Museum, 434; 2 Elliot's Debates, 81, 82, 311; 3 Elliot's Debates, 262, 290; 2 American Museum, 544.

The power does not interfere with the power of the states to tax for the support of their own governments. Congress is not empowered to tax for those purposes which are within the exclusive province of the States. Gibbons v. Ogden, 9 Wheat. 199; 1 Kent's Com. 251; Sergeant's Const. Ch. 28, p. 311–315. Rawle's Const. Ch. 9, p. 104; 2 United States L. I., April, 1826, 251–282.

**What are the rules for taxes?**

**22, 144, 145.**

**Define uniform?**

**81.** "ALL DUTIES TO BE UNIFORM." Congress has plenary power over every species of taxable property, except exports. But there are two rules prescribed for their government:—Uniformity, and apportionment. Duties, imposts and excises were to be laid by the first rule; and capitation and other direct taxes by the second. (Hylton v. The United States, 3 Dall. 171.) 1 Kent's Com. 255.

Taxes under this clause must be uniform; but need not be apportioned according to census. Idem. Yet "UNIFORM" must mean that the same duties shall be paid at all the ports in the "States and Territories," throughout the United States; and that

the same income taxes and excises should operate, alike including    91.
the District of Columbia. Loughborough v. Blake, 5 Wheat. 317.

The Indian tribes are not included in the excise law.    91, 92.

See " *uniform* " rule of naturalization.    93, 94.

[2.] To borrow money on the credit of the United To borrow.
States.

**82.** As first reported it read : " To borrow money [and emit    129.
bills] on the credit of the United States." To " emit bills," was    73.
stricken out, after debate, on the ground, that " *on the credit*," authorized the issuing of bills or notes by the government. Metropolitan Bank v. Van Dyke, 27 N. Y. R. 420 ; 3 Madison papers, 1343.

**83.** MONEY.—[*Moneta.*] Cash ; that is, gold and silver, or the What is
lawful circulating medium of the country, including bank notes, money?
when they are known and approved of and used in the market as 97, 98, 129.
cash. (Co. Litt. 207 a ; Lord Ellenborough, 13 East 20 ; Kent. in
Mann v. Mann, 1 Johns. Ch. R. 236.) Burrill's Law Dic. MONEY.
And money deposited in bank ; but not stocks. Hotham v. Sutton,
15 Ves. 319 ; Mann v. Mann, 1 Johns. Ch. p. 257.

For the necessity of this power, see the Federalist No. 41 ;
Story's Const. § 1065.

Treasury notes have been issued under the acts of 25th Feb. Treasury
1813, 26th December, 1814, 12th October, 1837, 31 January, 1842, notes on
31 August 1842, 22 July, 1846, 28 July, 1847, 23 December, 1857, authority
the 25th February, 1862, and the several subsequent acts. They issued?
are binding on the government. (Thorndyke v. The United States,
2 Mason, 1, 18.) Metropolitan Bank v. Van Dyck, 27 New York,
421. Some have drawn interest ; others not ; they all circulate as
money. And see the Pennsylvania Cases. 52 Penn. St. Rep.
15–100.

**84.** The United States bonds and indeed all the public securi-    73.
ties which have to be redeemed, and which circulate as currency
may properly be classified as *money* borrowed, or rather securities    22.
given for money borrowed on the credit of the United States. The
bonds issued and sold in market are technically so.

The states have no power to tax the loan of the United States. Can the
Weston v. City Council of Charleston, 2 Pet. 419–65 ; Bank of States tax
Commerce v. New York, 2 Black, 629. The Constitutional Court securities?
of South Carolina, in May, 1823, decided in favor of the power to
tax the loan. Judge Huger and two other judges, against four,
gave an opinion against the constitutionality of the law. 2 Pet.    22
452.

The sovereignty of a state extends to every thing which exists
by its own authority, or is introduced by its permission, but not to
those means which are employed by Congress to carry into execution powers conferred on that body by the people of the United
States. (Weston v. The City of Charleston, 2 Pet. 419.) Bank of
Commerce v. New York, 2 Black, 632.

This power is supreme within its scope and operation, and may
be exercised free and unobstructed by state legislation or authority.

(McCulloch v. The State of Maryland, 4 Wh. 116; Osborn v. The United States, 9 Wh. 732,) Bank of Commerce v. New York City, 2 Black. 632.

*Are treasury notes a constitutional legal tender?*

For the history of this section, see Metropolitan Bank v. Van Dyck, 27 N. Y. Rep. 419, *et seq* The power to issue notes is thus given, and the convention declined to prohibit the making them a legal tender in payment of either public or private debts. (Thorndyke v. United States, 2 Mas. 1, 18). Id. And after a full review

*82, 83.*

of the question of power, it was held that such notes may constitutionally be made a legal tender in payment of all debts between

*97-100.*

individuals. Metropolitan Bank v. Van Dyck, 27 N. Y. 451.

Congress has constitutional power to issue treasury notes of the United States, and make them lawful money, and a legal tender for the payment of debts. Shollenberger v. Brinton, 52 Penn. St. Rep. (2 P. F. Smith) 9,100; Brown v. Welch, 26 Ind. 116; Thayer v. Hedges, 23 Ind. 141; Bank of Indiana v. Reynolds, Law Reg. 1865. (But *Contra*, Judge Cadwalader. . Morrison v. Reading Railroad.) Shollenberger v. Brinton, 52 Penn. 49.

The Act of Congress of Feb. 25, 1862, authorizing the issue of such notes, is constitutional. Shollenberger v. Brinton, 52 Penn. St. Rep. (2 P. F. Smith) 9,100; Carpenter v. Northfield Bauk, 39 Vt. (4 Veasey) 49.

*Give the examples?*

The principal sum which redeems a ground-rent, is a "debt" within the meaning of the act. Shollenberger v. Brinton, 52, Penn, 9, 100.

A ground-rent payable in "*** dollars, lawful *silver money* of the United States of America," is redeemable by such notes. Id.

*155.*

So the half-yearly instalment of a ground-rent, payable in "*** dollars lawful silver money of the United States, each dollar weighing 16 dwt. 6 gr. *at least*." Mervin v. Sailor, 52 Penn. St. Rep. (2 P. F. Smith), 18, 45, 102.

So a ground-rent payable in "lawful money," or "lawful money of the United States." Davis v. Burton, 52 Penn. St. Rep. (2 P. F. Smith) 22; Kroener v. Calhoun, 52 Penn. St. Rep. (2 P. F. Smith) 24.

So a certificate of deposit of "*** gold, payable in like funds with interest." Sandford v. Hays, 52 Penn St. Rep. (2 P. F. Smith) 26; **Warner** v. Sauk Co. Bank, **20 Wis.** 494; Warnibold v. Schlicting, 16 Iowa, 243; Breitenbach v. Turner, 18 Wis. 140.

So a note for a sum of money marked in margin, "$14,145 specie," which by banker's rules, meant gold or silver coin. Graham v. Marshall, 52 Penn. St. Rep. (2 P. Smith) 28, 103

So a note for "*** dollars in gold," Laughlin v. Harvey, 52 Penn. St. Rep. (2. P. F. Smith) 30; Wood v. Bullens, 6 Allen (Mass.) 516, 518.

So, "or if paid in paper, the amount thereof necessary to purchase the gold, at the place of payment." (*Logansport* v. *Indiana.*) Brown v Welch, 26 Ind. 116.

The condition of a bond for payment of $3,000 "in good coins of United States, of a particular fineness, notwithstanding any laws which may now, or hereafter shall make any thing else a tender in payment of debt. *Held*, not payable in greenbacks. Dutton v. Pallant, 52 Penn. St. Rep. (2 P. F. Smith) 109.

"When treasury notes were made a legal tender in payment of debts, they were made the equivalent of coin as a means of payment, in all but the cases excepted by law." Brown v. Welch, 26 Ind. 117. *[margin: 97, 98. 99.]*

The outstanding debt of the United States for borrowed money usually called the loan, see note 78. *[margin: 78.]*

[3.] To regulate commerce with foreign nations, and among the several States, and with the Indian tribes. *[margin: What is the power as to commerce?]*

**85.** "To REGULATE." That is, to prescribe the rule by which commerce is to be governed. (Gibbons v. Ogden, 9 Wheat. 196.) Story's Const. § 1061. *[margin: How to regulate commerce? 191.]*

The power is exclusive, and leaves no residuum. (Gibbons v. Ogden, 9 Wheat. 209.) Story's Const. § 1072. See the Passenger Cases, 7 How. 283. *[margin: 79, 80.]*

But a State may pass police laws for the protection of its inhabitants against paupers. This is not a regulation of commerce. The city of New York v. Miller, 12 Pet. 102, 132; Story's Const. § 1072 a.

It is denied that the power "to REGULATE" is exclusively in Congress. (The License Cases, 5 How. 504.) Id. § 1072. And license laws. the primary object of which is to secure the health of the community. The License Cases, 5 How. 504; Story's Const. § 1072. *[margin: 89.]*

**86.** "COMMERCE" is traffic, but it is something more; it is intercourse. Gibbons v. Ogden, 9 Wheat. 191, 209.) United States v. Holliday, 3 Wallace, 417; Story's Const. § 1061, note 2. *[margin: What is commerce? 209.]*

Buying, selling. and exchanging is the essence of commerce. 3 Wall, 417. It also includes navigation, as well as traffic, in its ordinary signification; and embraces ships and vessels as the instruments of intercourse and trade, as well as the officers and seamen who navigate and control them. The power of Congress extends to all these subjects. People v. Brooks, 4 Denio, 469.

For the necessity of this power see the Federalist, Nos. 4, 7, 11. 22. 37; Gibbons v. Ogden, 9 Wheat. 225; Brown v. Maryland, 12 Wheat. 445, 446; Story's Const. §§ 1057. 1060.

To regulate the external commerce of the nation and the respective states. People v. Huntington, 4 N. Y. Leg. Obs. 187. The whole subject fully discussed. Id. But not to declare the status which any person shall sustain while in any State of the Union. The power can be exercised over persons as passengers, only while on the ocean, and until they come under State jurisdiction. It ceases when the voyage ends. and then the State laws control. Lemmon v. People, 26 Barb. 270; affirmed, 20 N. Y. 562. *[margin: 196. Can Congress declare the status of persons in the States? 18, 196.]*

**87.** "COMMERCE WITH FOREIGN NATIONS" means commerce between citizens of the United States and citizens or subjects of foreign governments, as individuals. United States v. Holliday, 3 Wallace, 417; Flannagan v. Philadelphia, 22 Penn. 219. The erection of wharves is subservient to commerce. Stevens v. Walker, 15 La. Ann. 577. *[margin: W th foreign nations. 231.]*

The giving of a license by a municipal corporation is not a regulation of commerce. Childers v. People, 11 Mich. 43.

The violation of a local law requiring such licenses, by the use of an unlicensed boat, though it be duly licensed for the coasting and foreign trade under the laws of the United States, is a punishable offense. Id.

A tax, the effect of which is to diminish personal intercourse, is a tax upon commerce. Linsing v. Washburn, 30 Cal. 534. The California tax-law upon Chinese is a violation of this section and unconstitutional. Id.

With foreign nations and among the several States? This power, like all others vested in Congress, is complete in itself, may be exercised to its utmost extent, and acknowledges no limitations other than are prescribed in the Constitution. Gibbons v. Ogden, 9 Wh. 196. Commerce with foreign nations, and among the several States, can mean nothing more than intercourse with those nations, and among those States, for the purposes of trade, be the object of trade what it may; and this intercourse must include all the means by which it can be carried on, whether by the free navigation of the waters of the several States, or by a passage over land through the States, where such passage becomes necessary to the commercial intercourse between the States. Corfield v. Coryell, 4 Wash. C. C. 388; Pennsylvania v. Wheeling & Belmont Bridge Co. 18 How. 421; Columbus Ins. Co. v. Peoria Bridge Co. 6 McLean, 70; Columbus Insurance Co. v. Curtenius, Id. 209; Jolly v. Terre Haute Drawbridge Co. Id. 237; United States v. Railroad Bridge Co. Id. 518. This clause confers the power to impose embargoes. Gibbons v. Ogden, 9 Wh. 191; United States v. The William, 2 Hall's L. J. 255, 272. And to punish crimes upon stranded vessels. United States v. Coombs, 12 Pet. 72. It does not, however, interfere with the right of the several States to enact inspection, quarantine, and health laws of every description, as well as laws for regulating their internal commerce. Gibbons v. Ogden, 9 Wh. 203; New York v. Miln, 11 Pet. 102; Conway v. Taylor, 1 Black. 633. Nor with their power to regulate pilots. Cooley v. Board of Wardens, 12 How. 299. Or to protect their fisheries. Smith v. Maryland, 18 How. 71; Dunham v. Lamphere, 3 Conn. 268.

State laws which violate? 79. **88.** A State law which requires the masters of vessels engaged in foreign commerce to pay a certain sum to a State officer, on account of every passenger brought from a foreign country into the State, or before landing any alien passenger in the State, conflicts with the Constitution and laws of the United States. Smith v Turner, 7 How. 263. (This decision was by a divided court, and is not conclusive authority. Smith v. Marston, 5 Tex. 432.) So does a state law, authorizing the seizure and imprisonment of free negroes brought into any port of the state, on board of any vessel, from any state or foreign port. Elkison v. Deliesseline, 2 Wh. Cr. Cas. 56; 1 Opin. 659. (But see 2 Opin. 426, *contra*.) And so does a state law which requires an importer to take a license, and pay fifty dollars before he should be permitted to sell a package of imported goods. Brown v. Maryland, 12 Wh. 419. Purvear v. Commonwealth, 5 Wall. 478. But a State law which imposes a tax on brokers dealing in foreign exchange, is not repugnant to this clause

of the Constitution. Nathan v. Louisiana, 8 How. 73. Nor is one
imposing a tax on legacies payable to aliens. Mager v. Grima, Id. 490.
Nor are the license laws of certain States, forbidding the sale of
spirituous liquors under less than certain large quantities. Thurlow
v. Massachusetts, 5 How. 504; The State v. Allmond, 4 Am. D. R.
533; California v. Coleman, 4 Cal. 467.

**89.** "AMONG THE SEVERAL STATES. This section quoted with
clause 18, and Art. VI., Sec. 2, and Art. X. of Amendments.
Gilman v. Philadelphia, 3 Wallace, 724.

Commerce includes navigation ; and comprehends the control for
that purpose, and to the extent necessary, of all navigable waters
of the United States which are accessible from a State other than
those within which they lie. For this purpose they are the public
property of the nation, and subject to all the requisite legislation of
Congress. (Gibbons v. Ogden, 9 Wheat. 191; Corfield v. Coryel, 4
Wash. C. C. R. 378.) Gilman v. Philadelphia, 3 Wallace, 724, 725.

The right includes the power to remove all obstructions, and
to provide for the punishment of offenders. The whole powers
which existed in the States before the adoption of the Federal
Constitution, and which have always existed in the Parliament in
England. Id.

It is for Congress to determine when its full powers shall be
brought into activity, and as to the regulations and sanctions which
shall be provided. (United States v. New Bedford Bridge, 1 Wood-
bury & Minot, 420. 421; United States v. Coombs, 12 Peters, 72;
New York v. Milne, 11 Peters, 102, 155.) Gilman v. Philadelphia, 3 Wallace, 725.

Wherever "commerce *among* the States" goes, the power of
the nation, as represented in this Court, goes with it to protect and
enforce its rights. (Gibbons v. Ogden, 9 Wheat. 191; Steamboat v.
Livingston, 3 Cowen. 713.) Gilman v. Philadelphia, 3 Wallace,
725.

The National Government possesses no powers but such as have
been delegated to it by the States, which retain all but such as they
have surrendered. The power to authorize the building of a
bridge is not to be found in the Federal Constitution. It has not
been taken from the States. Id. When the Revolution took place
the people of each State became themselves sovereign, and in that
character hold the absolute right to all their navigable waters and
the soil under them for their own common use, subject only to the
rights since surrendered by the Constitution to the general government (Martin v. Waddell, 16 Peters, 410.) Gilman v. Philadelphia,
3 Wallace, 726. *Ante* Preface, pp. viii., ix. The right of eminent
domain over the shores and the soil under the navigable waters, for
all municipal purposes, *belongs exclusively to the States within their
territorial jurisdiction*, and they only have the power to exercise
it. Id.

But this right can never be used to affect the exercise of any
national right of eminent domain or jurisdiction with which the
United States have been invested by the Constitution. (Pollard's
lessee v. Hogan, 3 Howard, 230.) Gilman v. Philadelphia, 3 Wallace, 726.

What is
commerce
among the
several
States?
133, 114, 274,
203.
86, 87.

What does
the right in-
clude?

203.

What is the
power of the
Supreme
Court to en-
force the
right?

What are the
powers of
the United
States?
71, 133, 269.

2, 6.

Eminent do-
main?

Can the
States use a
national
right?

**What subjects are under State control?** Inspection laws, quarantine laws, health laws of every description, as well as laws for regulating the internal commerce of a State, and those which respect turn-pike roads, ferries, &c., are component parts of the powers of a State. (Gibbons v. Ogden, 9 Wheat. 192) Gilman v. Philadelphia, 3 Wallace, 726. And also bridges. (People v. S. & R. R. R. Co., 15 Wend. 113.) Id.

**Pilot laws?** Pilot laws enacted in good faith are within the powers of the States. (Cooly v. The Board of Wardens, 12 Howard, 319.) Gilman v. Philadelphia, 3 Wallace, 727. Master v. Ward, 14 La. A. 289; Master v. Morgan, 14 Ib. 595.

**When is a law of Congress paramount?** But where Congress has acted the law is paramount. (Pennsylvania v. Virginia, 18 Howard, 430.) Gilman v. Philadelphia, 3 Wallace, 727, 729. Until Congress has exercised the power, the State may authorize obstructions which do not violate the Constitution. (Wilson v. Blackbird Creek Marsh Co. 2 Peters, 250.) Id. 727-729.

**When may the States exercise concurrent powers?** The States may exercise concurrent or independent power in all cases but three: 1. Where the power is lodged exclusively in the Federal Constitution. 2. Where it is given to the United States and prohibited to the States. 3. Where from the nature and subjects of the power, it must be necessarily exercised by the National Government exclusively. (Houston v. Moore, 12 Wheat. 419; Federalist No. 32.) Gilman v. Philadelphia, 3 Wallace, 730.

**What laws of a State are void?** A State law requiring an importer to take out a license before he shall sell a bale of goods is void. (Brown v. Maryland, 12 Wheat. 419.) Gilman v. Philadelphia, 3 Wallace, 730. Purvear v. Commonwealth, 5 Wall. 478. So the passenger laws from foreign countries. (Passenger's Cases, 7 Howard, 273.) Gilman v. Philadelphia, 3 Wall. 730. Not so of the State liquor-license laws. (License cases, 5 Howard, 504.) Gilman v. Philadelphia, 3 Wallace 730. Purvear v. Commonwealth, 5 Wall. 498. Congress may

**Bridges?** regulate all bridges over navigable waters, remove offending bridges, and punish those who shall thereafter erect them. Id. 731.

**Where does power of Congress not stop?** The power to regulate commerce does not stop at the jurisdiction or limits of the several States. (Gibbons v. Ogden, 9 Wheat. 190.) United States v. Holliday, 3 Wallace, 417.

**What were the powers as to slaves?** **90.** As to the power of Congress over the subject of commerce among the several States, see the Opinion of McLean, J., in Groves v. Slaughter, 15 Pet. 504; Taney, Ch. J., Id. 508; Baldwin, J., Id. 510. In Shelton v. Marshall, 16 Tex. 352, Wheeler, J., said:—As respects the power of the States over the subject of the Constitutional inhibitions in question (the introduction of slaves as merchandise), what we deem the sound and correct doctrine was stated by Chief-Justice Taney, in Groves v. Slaughter, 15 Pet. 508, viz.:—

"In my judgment, the power over this subject is exclusively with the several States: and each of them has a right to decide for itself, whether it will or will not allow persons of this description to be brought within its limits, from another State, either for sale or for any other purpose; and also to prescribe the manner and mode in which they may be introduced, and to determine their condition and treatment within their respective territories; and the action of the several States upon this subject cannot be controlled by Con-

gress, either by virtue of its power to regulate commerce, or by
virtue of any other power conferred by the Constitution of the
United States."

Congress may have power to prevent the obstruction of any Navigable
navigable stream which is a means of commerce between any two streams?
or more States. Works v. Junction Railroad, 5 McLean, 526;
Jolly v. Terre Haute Drawbridge Co. 6 Id. 237 ; Devoe v. Penrose
Ferry Bridge Co. 3 Am. L. J. 79. But a State law granting the ex-   203.
clusive privilege of navigating a part of an unnavigable stream,
which is wholly within the State, on condition of rendering such
part navigable, is not repugnant to the Constitution. Veazie v.
Moore, 14 How. 568. And see Wilson v. Blackbird Creek Marsh
Co. 2 Pet. 251.

**91.** If commerce or traffic or intercourse be carried on with an With the In-
Indian tribe, or with a member of such tribe, it is subject to be dian tribes?
regulated by Congress, although within the limits of a State. The Does the lo-
power is absolute, without reference to the locality of the tribe or cality of the
tribe cause a
the member of the tribe. United States v. Holliday, 3 Wallace, difference?
418. This power is not claimed as to any other commerce
originated and ended within the limits of a single State. Id.
So long as the tribal relations exist, the Indians who are connected with their tribes and under the jurisdiction of an agent, are
under the protection of the laws to regulate trade and intercourse
with the Indians. Id. The States cannot control the subject. Id.

Under the power to regulate commerce with the Indian tribes,
Congress has power to prohibit all intercourse with them, except
under a license. United States v. Cisna, 1 McLean, 254. So Congress has power to punish all crimes committed within the Indian
country, which was a part of the Louisiana territory, dedicated to
the Indians. The United States v. Rogers, 4 How. 567.

The United States has adopted the principle originally estab- What is the
lished by European nations, namely, that the aboriginal tribes of rule as to
ownership
Indians in North America are not regarded as the owners of the of soil?
territories which they respectively occupied. Their country was
divided and parceled out, as if it had been vacant and unoccupied
land. Id. If the propriety of exercising this power were now an
open question, it would be one for the law-making and political
department of the government, and not the judicial. Id.

The Indian tribes residing within the territorial limits of the   196.
United States, are subject to their authority ; and where the
country occupied by them is not within the limits of any one of the
States, Congress may by law, punish any offence committed there,
no matter whether the offender be a white man or an Indian. Id. ;
The United States v. Rogers, 4 How. 567.

The 25th section of the act of 30th June, 1834, extends the laws Intercourse
of the United States over the Indian country, with a proviso that law?
they shall not include punishment for "crimes committed by one
Indian against the person or property of another Indian." Id. This
exception does not embrace the case of a white man who, at mature
age, is adopted into an Indian tribe. He is not an "Indian" within
the meaning of the law. Id. 4 St. 729 ; 1 Brightly's Dig, 430, §
75 ; 4 Op. 72, United States v. Rogers, 4 How. 567.

The treaty with the Cherokees, concluded at New Echota, in 1835 allows the Indian council to make laws for their own people, or such persons as have connected themselves with them. But it also provides that such laws shall not be inconsistent with acts of Congress. The act of 1834, therefore, controls and explains the treaty. It results from these principles, that a plea, set up by a white man, alleging that he had been adopted by an Indian tribe, and was not subject to the jurisdiction of the circuit court of the United States, is not valid. Id.

What means commerce with the tribes? — Commerce *with* the Indian tribes, means commerce *with* the individuals composing those tribes. United States v. Holliday, 3 Wallace, 417.

The cotton grown in the Indian country and shipped to ports of the United States for sale, is not subject to the Internal revenue tax levied by the statutes of the 30th June, 1864, and the 13th July, 1866. The case of R. M. Jones. Attorney-General, H. Stanbery's opinion, of 24th July, 1867. The acts reviewed. Id.

All these provisions fortify the conclusion at which I have arrived, that cotton produced in the Choctaw nation does not come within their operation. A tax on cotton produced there or manufactured there, or sold there, cannot be levied, assessed or collected under the provisions of these acts. Nor is there any thing in these acts to forbid its removal or sale to any part of the United States. Being a production of the Indian country by express statutory enactment, it is not liable to any import or transit duty. There is no lien upon it for any tax at the place of production, nor is any permit for its removal necessary. "I am clearly satisfied that the omission in the various Internal revenue laws, to provide for the organization of collection districts over the Indian territory was not fortuitous or accidental, and that it was the settled purpose of Congress not to subject the persons or the productions of Indians existing under their regular tribal associations, to liability for any tax imposed by these acts.—If the provisions as to the specific article of cotton apply to Indian territory, I see no reason why all the other forms of tax provided for in these acts are not equally applicable to Indian territory. We must, consequently make them subject to taxation in reference to stamps, income, and descents in succession, as well as for other purposes. The intent of Congress not to include them in any sort of taxation, I think is clear enough from the language of the acts themselves. But all other considerations which apply to them, equally forbid this idea of Federal taxation. Their rights are defined by independent treaties. They are in a state of tutelage and protection under the United States. Laws in which they are not mentioned, are never understood to apply to them. Even when these Indians and their territory are situated within the bounds of a State of the Union, they are not subject to State taxation. In recent cases before the supreme court of the United States, at its December term, 1866, speaking of the condition of the Indian tribes under treaty with the United States, it used this language: 'The object of the treaty was to hedge the lands around with guards and restrictions, so as to preserve them for the permanent homes of the Indians. In order to accomplish this object they must be relieved from every species of levy, sale, and forfeiture—from a levy and sale for taxes, as well as the ordinary judicial levy and sale.' The Kansas Indians, 5 Wall. 760, 761. Again the Courts say, in reference to the tribal association of the Shawnees, that 'they are a people distinct from others, capable of making treaties, separated from the jurisdiction of Kansas, and to be governed exclusively by the government of the Union. If under the control of Congress, from necessity, there can be no divided authority.—If they have outlived many things they have not outlived the protection afforded by the Constitution, treaties, and laws of Congress.—It may be that they cannot exist much longer as a distinct people in the presence of the civilization of Kansas; but until they are clothed with the rights and bound to all the duties of citizens, they enjoy the privilege of total immunity from State taxation.' (Id. 755, 756). And again:—' As long as the United States recognizes their national character they are under the protection of the treaties and the laws of Congress, and their property is withdrawn from the operation of State laws.' (Id. 757.) Such is the well-established policy of the United States with regard to the total exemption of the Indian tribes from State taxation. The tenor of all the treaties shows that the idea of subjecting them to taxation by the General Government, was never entertained, and certainly hitherto it has never been attempted. I am, therefore, clearly of opinion that the particular cotton in question was not liable to taxation under our Internal revenue laws, either while in the Indian country or in transit through any collection district of the United States, or in the collection district where it may have been found or may have been sold. Until the Indians have sold their lands, and removed from them in pursuance of the treaty stipulations, they are to be regarded as still in their ancient possessions, and are in under their original rights, and entitled to the undisturbed enjoyment of them. (Fellows v. Blacksmith, 19 How. 366.) The New York Indians, 5 Wall, 770."

In the argument of the case of R. M. Jones before the Attorney-General, the Editor, who prosecuted the claim to have the tax, illegally collected, refunded, cited the following authorities: The State v. Ross, 7 Yerg. 74; United States v. Cisna, 1 McLean, 254; Cherokee Nation v. Georgia; Worcester v. Georgia; and Johnson v. McIntosh, cited elsewhere in this note. And the following cases to show that while Indians reside within the States as portions of tribes, they are not within State jurisdiction, as citizens subject to the burdens and benefits of State laws: Danforth v. Wear, 9 Wheat. 673; Lee v. Glover, 8 Cow. 189; Strong v. Waterman, 11 Paige, 807; Harmon v. Partier, 12 Sm. & Marsh. 425; Marsh v. Brooks, 8 How. 223; Fellows v. Lee, 3 Denio 628; Wall v. Williams, 8 Ala. 48 and 11 Ala. 826; Brashear v. Williamson, 10 Ala. 630; Parks v. Ross, 11 How. 427; Jones v. Laney, 2 Tex. 342. And as to the power of the United States over the Indian country, See United States v. Rogers, 4 Howard, 567.

What are the relations of the Indian tribes?

**92.** These various authorities settle the general propositions:
1. That the Indian tribes are dependent subordinate States,

whose political relations with the United States are defined by treaties.

2. That "commerce with the Indian tribes" is subject to the exclusive control of Congress, and it has only been regulated by treaties and intercourse laws.

81.

3. That Indians are not embraced by acts of Congress, unless they be named therein. Opinion of Judge Lewis, Commissioner of Internal Revenue, 1863.

And see 9 Op. 27. The Indians owe no allegiance to the United States. They may make war upon them without incurring the guilt of treason. Op. of Judge Lewis, Commissioner of Internal Revenue. "Though he holds his lands within the limits of the United States, he is not politically within its limits, nor has it jurisdiction over him." Judge Lewis. The stamp tax does not apply to the Indian reservations, when sold by the tribe; nor does any part of the laws in relation to Internal Revenue. Id. The court follows the executive as to the recognition of the tribal relations. Id. Cites The Cherokee Nation v. Georgia, 5 Peters, 1, and Worcester v. Georgia, 6 Peters, 515.

What as to naturalization? Bankruptcy?

**[4.] To establish a uniform rule of naturalization; and uniform laws on the subject of bankruptcies throughout the United States.**

What is naturalization?

17, 18, 205, 209.
What is expatriation?

274.

220, 221, 222.

Is the power exclusive?

Where alone is the power of naturalization?
120–123.

**93.** NATURALIZATION.—In its popular, etymological, and legal sense, signifies the act of adopting a foreigner and clothing him with all the privileges of a native citizen or subject. 9 Op. 359; Coke Litt. 199a; 1 Bl. Com. 374; 2 Kent's Com. 64–67. These laws are based upon the acknowledged principle of expatriation. Bates on Citizenship, 13. A naturalized citizen becomes a member of society, possessing all the rights of a native citizen, and standing on the footing of a native. The power is to prescribe a "uniform rule," and the exercise of this power exhausts it, so far as respects the individual. The Constitution then takes him up, &c. Osborn v. Bank of United States, 9 Wh. 827. *Expatriation* includes not only emigration out of one's native country, but *naturalization* in the country adopted as a future residence. 9 Op. 359; 8 Op. 125; Paschal's Annotated Digest, p. 920, note 1168, where the authorities are collected; Halleck's International Law 696; Rawle's Const. 95–101; Sergeant's Const. ch. 28, 30; 2 Kent's Com. 35, 42. The naturalized foreigner is protected against the conscript laws of his native sovereign. Ernest's Case, 9th Op. 357–363. The power to naturalize is exclusive in the Federal government. The Federalist, No. 32, 42; Chirac v. Chirac, 2 Wheat. 259, 269; Rawle's Const. 84–88; Houston v. Moore, 5 Wheat. 48, 49; Golden v. Prince, 3 Wash. C. C. R. 313, 332; 1 Kent's Com. 397.} Story's Const. § 1104; Thurlow v. Massachusetts, 5 How. 505; Smith v. Turner, 7 How. 556. The power must be exclusive or there could be no "UNIFORM RULE." (Federalist, No. 32;) Story's Const. 1104. While the Constitution gave to the citizens of each State the privileges and immunities of citizens in the several States, it, at the same time, took from the several States the power of naturalization, and confined that power exclusively to the Federal government. The right of naturalization was, therefore, with one accord, surrendered by the States, and confined to the Federal government. Golden v. Prince, 3 Wash. c. c. 314.  Naturalization is confined to **90.** persons born in foreign countries.  Scott v. Sandford, 19 How. 417–419.  The Constitution has conferred on Congress the right to **220, 17, 18.** establish uniform rules of naturalization, and this right is evidently exclusive. Id. 405.  Negroes cannot be naturalized. Id.  And **Negroes.** no law of a State, passed since the Constitution was adopted, can **274.** give any right of citizenship outside of its own territory. Id.  The **269.** naturalization law of 1790, only extended the privilege *"to aliens being free white persons."*  Id.  Citizenship at that time was perfectly understood to be confined to the white race. Id.  Congress might have authorized the naturalization of Indians, because they **Indians.** were aliens and foreigners. Id. 420.  For the latest collection of the naturalization laws and notes thereon, see Paschal's Anno- **91, 92, 220.** tated Digest, arts. 5392–5412; notes 1168–1172, and 148–150. A free white person born in this country, of foreign parents, is a citizen of the United States. (Lynch v. Clarke, 1 Sandford's Ch. R. 583.)  9 Op. 374.  This is a universal principle unless changed by statute, as in our own statute to prevent the alienage of children born abroad. 10 St. 604.  Bates on Citizenship, 13.

Allegiance on the one side, and protection on the other, con- **Who are cit-** stitute citizenship under the Constitution.  Smith v. Moody, 26 **izens?** Inda. 305.  Allegiance and protection constitute the sum of the **220-223.** duties and rights of a " natural born citizen of the United States." **What are the** Bates on Citizenship, 15.  Citizenship cannot depend on *color* or **duties of a** *caste.*  Id. 14–17.  Alienage is the only disability to citizenship **citizen?** recognized in the Constitution. Id.

**94.** UNIFORM SYSTEM OF BANKRUPTCY.—BANKRUPT [*banke-* **What is a** *rout*].  Literally from Law French *banke,* Lat. *bancus,* a bench, **bankrupt?** table, or counter, and *roupt* or *rout,* Latin *ruptus,* broken.  One **95.** whose bench or counter (place of business) is broken up.  In English law, a trader who secretes himself, or does certain other acts tending to defraud his creditors.  2 Bl. Com. 285, 471; Burrill's Law Dic. BANKRUPT; 4 Inst. Ch. 63; Story's Const. § 1112; Cooke's Bankrupt Laws, Intr. 1.  It is derived from the Roman law  Idem.  See Ogden v. Saunders, 12 Wheat. 264–270; Sturgis v. Crowninshield, 12 Wheat. 273, 275, 280, 306, 310, 314, 335, 369; and same case 4 Wheat. 122.  By the American law, bankrupts and bankruptcies are not confined to traders.  See Acts of April 4, 1800; December 19, 1803; Aug. 19, 1841; 2 March, 1867; James's Bankrupt Law, 1867, and notes; Taylor's Bankrupt Law; 2 Kent's Com. 390; 2 Story's Const. §§ 1111–1115; Stephens's Com. 180, 189.  The leading features of " a system established by law, as distinguished from ordinary law are, (1), the summary and immediate seizure of all the debtor's property (or the voluntary surrender of it); (2), the distribution of it among the creditors in general; and (3), the discharge of the debtor from future liability from debts then existing."  Archbold's Law and P. of Bankruptcy (11th ed.) b. 2, pp. 139, 235–237; 2 Burr. 829.  The American "SYSTEM" seems to have broken down the distinction between

"BANKRUPTCY" and insolvency.   Burrill's Law Dic., BANKRUPT.
Sturgis v. Crowninshield, 4 Wheat. 122, 194, 198, 203; 2 Kent's
Com. 321.

**What is bankruptcy? 94.**

**95.** BANKRUPTCY.—The act, state, or condition of a bankrupt.
A *status* or condition fixed by legislative provision. (2 Bell's Com.
214.)   A condition following upon the commission of certain acts
defined by law. (2 Stephens's Com. 191, 192; Williamson v.
Barrett, 13 How. 111. "A breaking up of the bank." Spencer v.
Billing, 3 Camp. 312.)   In a looser sense, the stopping and breaking up of business, because a man is insolvent, and utterly incapable of carrying it on. (Arnold v. Maynard, 2 Story's R. 354,
359. See Sturgis v. Crowninshield, 4 Wheat. 122, 195, 202). Burrill's Law Dic. BANKRUPTCY. The state of a man unable to pursue
his business, and meet his engagements, in consequence of the de-
rangement of his affairs.   Crabbe's Rep. 456, 465.   See Paschal's
Annotated Digest, BANKRUPTCY, note 278, p. 141.

**What right have the States to pass bankrupt laws?**

**How far do state bank rupt laws discharge debts?**

**96.** The States have authority to pass bankrupt laws, provided
they do not impair the obligation of contracts, and provided there be
no act of Congress in force to establish a uniform system of bankruptcy conflicting with such laws. Sturgis v. Crowninshield, 4 Wh.
132, 273, 275, 280, 306, 314, 335, 369; McMillan v. McNeil, Id. 209.
But an act of a State legislature which discharges a debtor from all
liability for debts contracted previous to his discharge, on his sur-
rendering his property for the benefit of his creditors, is invalid, so
far as it attempts to discharge, on the contracts with his creditors in other States than his residence.   Farmers & Mechanics' Bank
v. Smith, 6 Wh. 131. A mere insolvent law, however, is not within
the prohibition.   Ogden v. Saunders, 12 Wheat. 213, Mason v.
Haile, Id. 370; Boyle v. Zacharie, 6 Pet. 348, 635; Beers v. Houghton, 8 Id. 329; Suydam v. Broadnax, 14 Id. 67; Cook v. Moffat, 5
How. 295. The State bankrupt laws do not discharge debts contracted to citizens of other States, unless the contract be payable
within the state of the bankrupt. Beers v. Rhea, 5 Tex. 354. This
opinion reviews the various decisions of the supreme court of the
United States upon the subject, and concurs with their judgments,
though it is urged that the opinions have been inconsistent.
See Story's Conflict of Laws, § 338–423.   The reason of this
power is to prevent frauds where the parties or their property
may be removed into different States.   (The Federalist, No. 32.)
Story's Const. § 1105.

The Bankrupt Law of 1841 was held to be constitutional. Klein's
Case, 1 How. 277.  The power of Congress is not an exclusive grant;
it may, therefore, be exercised within constitutional limits by the
States. Sturgis v. Crowninshield, 4 Wheat. 122. See James's Bankrupt Law, p. 8. This book gives the Bankrupt Law of 1867, annotated.

**Money.**

[5.] To coin money, regulate the value thereof, and
of foreign coin; and fix the standard of weights and
measures.

**97.** To Coin.—To stamp and convert into money, as a piece of metal; to mint; in a more general sense, to form by stamping; as, to coin a medal. 2. To make or fabricate; to invent; to originate; as, to coin a word. Webster's Dic., Coin.

"To Coin Money," clearly means to mould into form a metallic substance of intrinsic value, and stamp on it its legal value. The thing so coined is itself " *money, ipse loquiter ;* but a treasury note is only a promise to pay money, and at the utmost, can only be, like a *bank bill,* or a bill of exchange, a representative of money. Griswold v. Hepburn, 2 Duvall's Ky. Rep. 29. The phrase means " to coin metal as the money of the United States " "They intend- ed that nothing else than metallic coin should be money, or be a legal tender, *immutum,* as *money.* Id. 33, 34. " Currency " is not money. Id. 33, 46, 47.

The articles of confederation read "To coin money and emit bills of credit." (*Ante,* Art. IX., p. 17.) The latter words were stricken out of a draft of the present Constitution. Id. The debate given in full. Id. 31,32; Madison papers, 1343–4–5–6; Daniel Webster; United States v. Marigold, 9 How, 567; Craig v. Missouri quoted. Id. 37, 38. And see the dissentient opinions, in the Pennsylvania legal tender cases. 52 Penn. State Reports, 1–100.

A contract may be satisfied by a payment of what is a legal tender at the time the contract is to be performed or the debt falls due, although in depreciated money. (Davies Reports, 48.) Shollenberger v. Brinton, 52 Penn. (2 P. F. Smith), 46. The constitutionality is maintained in the opinions of a majority of the judges, from pages 57 to 100.

This clause itself would carry along the right to regulate the value of money. (Madison's Letter to Cabell, 18th Sept., 1828.) Story's Const. § 1117.

**98.** Money.—Is the universal medium or common standard, by comparison with which the value of all merchandise may be ascer- tained; or it is a sign which represents the respective values of all commodities. (1 Black. Com. 276.) Story's Const. § 1118.

Our review of the legislation of Congress has shown us that Congress has uniformly declared the money so coined, and the value of which has thus been regulated, should be received as a legal tender in payment of debts equally, whether due to the government or to private individuals, &c. Metropolitan Bank v Van Dyck, 27 N. Y. 426.

The coin has no pledge of redemption; the intrinsic value is not a question; the treasury notes have a pledge for redemption; and they may become a substitute for coin. (Madison's Message.) Metropolitan Bank v. Van Dyck, 27 N. Y. R. 430, 431.

**99.** And Regulate the Value.—For a history of the acts regulating the value of money and prescribing legal tenders, see Metropolitan Bank v. Van Dyck, 27 N. Y. Rep. 424. This power is limited to the coining and stamping the standard of value upon what the government creates or shall adopt, and to punishing the offense of producing a false imitation of what may have been so created or adopted. Fox v. Ohio, 5 How. 433.

This power is exclusively in Congress. Rawle's Const. 102.

---

*Marginal notes:*

What is coin?

What to coin money? 82–84.

155.

72.

99, 100.

What is money? 83.

What is a legal tender? 82–84. 99, 100.

Has coin a pledge of redemption?

How regulate the value?

155

What are the
restrictions
as to legal
tender?

97.

84.

71.

**100.** There is no express grant of power to make gold and silver, or any thing else, a legal tender. Metropolitan Bank v. Van Dyck, 27 N. Y. Rep. 426. But the power has been uniformly exercised ever since the foundation of the government, unquestioned by any department of the Federal and State governments. This contemporaneous construction is to be received as evidence of the power. (Martin v. Hunter, 1 Wh. 421; Cohens v. Virginia, 6 Wh. 421; Briscoe v. The Bank of Kentucky, 11 Pet. 527; Moors v. The City of Reading, 21 Penn. 188; Norris v. Clymer, 2 Penn. 277; The People v. Green, 2 Wend. 274; The People v. Coutant, 11 Wend. 511.) Metropolitan Bank v. Van Dyck, 27 N. Y. Rep. 427–8. A discretionary power must exist somewhere in every government. Story's Const. § 425; Anderson v. Dunn, 6 Wh. 204, 220; Metropolitan Bank v. Van Dyck, 27 N. Y. Rep. 429.

Is intrinsic
value of con-
sequence?

97.

The intrinsic value of the metal on which money is coined is of no consequence. Id. 430.

Where a party deposited money with his banker upon general principles, it became a loan to the bank, which fact is not overruled by the word "gold," against the amount on the depositor's bank book. In such cases a tender of United States legal tender treasury notes is sufficient. The depositor cannot demand gold as his special deposit. Thompson v. Riggs, 5 Wallace.

What is a
standard?

**101.** "TO FIX THE STANDARD OF WEIGHTS AND MEASURES." TO FIX is to make permanent, to regulate. Webster's Dic. FIX. A STANDARD is that which is established by authority, as the rule to measure a quantity, as a gallon, a pound, or a weight. Webster. The States are not expressly inhibited from exercising this power; and in the absence of Congressional legislation, it has been tolerated. Rawle's Const. 102; Story's Const. § 1122.

What is a
ton?

101.

What is a
standard
pound of U.
S.?

**102.** "WEIGHTS AND MEASURES."—A "ton" is twenty hundred weight; each hundred weight being 112 pounds. Act of 30th Aug., 1842. 1 Brightly's Dig. 370, § 218.

The brass troy pound weight, procured by the Minister of the United States in London, in the year 1827, for the use of the mint, and now in the custody of the director thereof, shall be the standard troy pound of the mint of the United States, conformably to which the coin thereof shall be regulated.

How often is
standard
regulated?

It shall be the duty of the director of the mint to procure and safely keep a series of standard weights corresponding to the aforesaid troy pound, consisting of a one-pound weight, and the requisite subdivisions and multiples thereof, from the hundredth part of a grain to twenty-five pounds. And the troy weights ordinarily employed in the transactions of the mint, shall be regulated, according to the above standards, at least once in every year, under his inspection; and their accuracy tested annually in the presence of the assay commissioners, on the day of the annual assay. Act of 19th May, 1838, 4 St. 278; §§ 3, 4; 1 Brightly's Dig. p. 635, §§ 46, 47.

What is the
standard of
spirit
weight?

What proof spirit shall be held and taken to be that alcoholic liquor which contains one-half its volume of alcohol of a specific gravity of seven thousand nine hundred and thirty-nine ten thousandths (7,939) at sixty degrees Fahrenheit; and the Secretary of the Treasury is hereby authorized to adopt, procure, and prescribe for use such hydrometers, weighing and gauging instruments, meters, and other means for ascertaining the strength and quality of spirits subject to tax, &c., and to insure a uniform and correct system of inspection, weighing and gauging spirits subject to tax throughout the United States, &c.   Act of 2d March, 1867, 14 St. 481.

The following is the first general act of Congress which I find on the subject of weights and measures; and certainly it is of sufficient importance to occupy a place in a Manual of this kind:—

CHAP. CCCI.—*"An Act to authorize the use of the Metric System of Weights and Measures.* Act of 28th July, 1866, 14 St., 339,.

*Be it enacted, &c.,* That from and after the passage of this 340. act it shall be lawful throughout the United States of America to employ the weights and measures of the metric system; and no contract or dealing, or pleading in any court, shall be deemed invalid or liable to objection because the weights or measures expressed or referred to therein are weights or measures of the metric system. What is the standard of weights and measures?

2. The tables in the schedule hereto annexed shall be recognized in the construction of contracts, and in all legal proceedings, as establishing, in terms of the weights and measures now in use in the United States, the equivalents of the weights and measures expressed therein in terms of the metric system; and said tables may be lawfully used for computing, determining, and expressing in customary weights and measures the weights and measures of the metric system. The metric system. What schedule shall be recognized?

## MEASURES OF LENGTH.

What for measuring length?

| METRIC DENOMINATIONS AND VALUES. | EQUIVALENTS IN DENOMINATIONS IN USE. |
|---|---|
| Myriameter .............., 10,000 meters. | 6.2137 miles. |
| Kilometer................ 1,000 meters. | 0.62137 miles, or 3280 feet and ten inches. |
| Hectometer ............. 100 meters. | 328 feet and 1 inch. |
| Dekameter............... 10 meters. | 393.7 inches. |
| Meter ................... 1 meter. | 39.37 inches. |
| Decimeter .............. $\frac{1}{10}$ of a meter. | 3.937 inches. |
| Centimeter.............. $\frac{1}{100}$ of a meter | 0.2937 inches. |
| Millimeter.............. $\frac{1}{1000}$ of a meter. | 0.0394 inches. (0.03931) |

## MEASURES OF SURFACE.

Surface.

| METRIC DENOMINATIONS AND VALUES. | EQUIVALENTS IN DENOMINATIONS IN USE. |
|---|---|
| Hectare............. 10,000 square meters. | 2.471 acres. |
| Are............. ..... 100 square meters. | 119.6 square yards. |
| Centare.............. 1 square meter. | 1550 square inches. |

For measures of surface?

Capacity.                    MEASURES OF CAPACITY

For mea-
sures of
capacity.

| Names. | Number of liters. | Cubic measure. | Dry Measure. | Liquid or Wine Measure. |
|---|---|---|---|---|
| Kiloliter, or stere | 1,000 | 1 cubic meter........ | 1.308 cubic yards..... | 264.17 gallons. |
| Hectoliter ...... | 100 | $\frac{1}{10}$ of a cubic meter.... | 2 bushels & 3.35 pecks | 26.417 gallons. |
| Dekaliter....... | 10 | 10 cubic decimeters... | 9.08 quarts.......... | 2.6417 gallons. |
| Liter ....... .... | 1 | 1 cubic decimeter.... | 0.908 quarts........ | 1.0567 quarts. |
| Deciliter........ | $\frac{1}{10}$ | $\frac{1}{10}$ of a cubic decimeter | 0.1022 cubic inches... | 0.845 gills. |
| Centiliter....... | $\frac{1}{100}$ | 10 cubic centimeters.. | 0.6102 cubic inches.... | 0.388 fluid ozs. |
| Milliliter ....... | $\frac{1}{1000}$ | 1 cubic centimeter... | 0.061 cubic inches.... | 0.27 fluid dr's. |

Weights.                     WEIGHTS.

What stand-
ard of
weights ?

| Names. | No. of Grams. | Weight of what quantity of water at maximum density. | Avoirdupois weight. |
|---|---|---|---|
| Millier or Tonneau. | 1,000,000 | 1 cubic meter ......... | 2204.6 pounds. |
| Quintal ........... | 100,000 | 1 hectoliter............ | 220.46 pounds |
| Myriagram......... | 10,000 | 10 liters............... | 22.046 pounds. |
| Kilogram or kilo.... | 1,000 | 1 liter................ | 2.2046 pounds. |
| Hectogram ........ | 100 | 1 deciliter............ | 3.5274 ounces. |
| Dekagram.......... | 10 | 10 cubic centimeters ..... | 0.3527 ounces. |
| Gram ............. | 1 | 1 cubic centimeter ...... | 15.432 grains. |
| Decigram ......... | $\frac{1}{10}$ | $\frac{1}{10}$ of a cubic centimeter. | 1.5432 grains. |
| Centigram......... | $\frac{1}{100}$ | 10 cubic millimeters...... | 0.1543 grains. |
| Milligram......... | $\frac{1}{1000}$ | 1 cubic millimeter ...... | 0.0154 grains. |

What power
as to coun-
terfeiting ?

[6.] To provide for the punishment of counterfeiting the securities and current coin of the United States.

What is
counterfeit-
ing ?

**103.** COUNTERFEITING. [Law Latin, *Contrafactum.*] That which is made in imitation of something, but without lawful authority, or contrary to law, and with a view to pass the false for the true. (Wharton's Lex.)   Burrill's Law Dic., COUNTERFEITING.

The making in the semblance of true gold or silver coin any coin having in its composition a less proportion of the precious metal than is contained in the true coin, with intent to pass the same; or the altering of coin of lesser value, so as to make it resemble coin of the higher value.   Paschal's Annotated Digest,

Arts. 2113, 2114. See the Act to Punish, 1 Brightly's Dig., p. 215, Art. VII, §§ 73-79

Whether Congress has power to provide for the punishment of *passing* counterfeit coin, has been doubted. This power is certainly possessed by States. Metropolitan Bank v. Van Dyck, 27 N. Y. 420. But Congress may, without doubt, provide for punishing the offense of bringing into the United States, from a foreign place, false, forged, and counterfeit coins made in the similitude of coins of the United States; and also for the punishment of the offense of uttering and passing the same. United States v. Marigold, 9 How. 560; Metropolitan Bank v. Van Dyck, 27 N. Y. Rep. 450. In Fox v. Ohio, 5 How. 435, Mr. Justice McLean dissented; and insisted that Congress has the right (and has exercised it) to punish the uttering of counterfeit coin; and therefore the States have not the same power.

*Have the States power to punish counterfeiting?*

The right to punish the counterfeiting of the public coin is vested exclusively in Congress; and it cannot be concurrently exercised by the States; and such a State law is void. Mattison v. The State of Missouri, 3 Mo., 421.

In Fox v. The State of Ohio, this court have taken care to point out that the same Act might, as to its character, tendencies, and consequences, constitute an offense against both the State and the Federal governments, and might draw to its commission the penalties denounced by either, as appropriate to its character in reference to each. (Fox v. Ohio, 5 How. 433.) United States v. Marigold, 9 How. 560; Story's Const. § 1123, note 4.

And see United States v. King, 5 McLean, 203; United States v. Burns, Ibid. 23; United States v. Brown, 4 Ibid, 142; United States v. Morrow, 4 W. C. C. R. 733; United States v. Gardner, 10 Pet. 618; Commonwealth v. Hutchinson, 2 Pars. 354; United States v. Hutchinson, 7 Penn. Law J. 365.

## [7.] To establish post-offices and post-roads.

**104.** "ESTABLISH" is the ruling term; post-offices and post-roads are the subjects on which it acts. The power is thereby given to fix on towns, court houses, and other places throughout our Union, at which there should be post-offices, the routes by which mails should be carried from one post-office to another, to fix the rate of postage, and to protect the post-offices and mails from robbery. (President Monroe's Message, 4th May, 1822, pp. 24-27.) Story's Const. § 1129, of third edition.

*What is the just import of these words, and the extent of the grant?*

The word "ESTABLISH," in other parts of the Constitution, is used in a general sense. Thus, "to *establish* justice;" "and *establish* this Constitution;" "to *establish* a uniform rule of naturalization and system of bankruptcies;" "such inferior courts as Congress may ordain and *establish*;" "the *establishment* of this Constitution;" "an *establishment* of religion."

*8, 13, 93-95, 195, 243, 245. Define establish.*

The clear import of the word is, to create, form, and fix in a settled manner. Story's Const. § 1131.

*101.*

The controversy has been between the power to *make* the roads and the power to fix on and declare them mail routes, after the extending settlements have opened, established, adopted, or *built* roads and paths. See the subject fully discussed in Story's Const. chap. XVIII. § 1124–1150; and Notes to **Third Edition**; and 1 Kent's Com. Lect. XII. 267–268.

The Confederate Constitution added this sentence: "But the expenses of the Post-Office Department, after the first of March, in the year of our Lord eighteen hundred and sixty-three, shall be paid out of its own revenues." Paschal's Annotated Digest, 88.

The first year's history of the insurgent government demonstrated the impracticability of the restriction.

What are post-offices ? **105.** POST-OFFICES.—As understood, under the Confederation, and since carried out by statutes, and in practice, post-offices may be defined to be the General Post-Office at Washington, presided over by one of the President's advisers, called the Postmaster-General. This office was first held by Dr. Franklin, in 1775. (Story's Const. § 1126, note 1.) It is now an immense palace (with over a hundred rooms), erected and owned by the government, wherein the whole of the postal service of the United States is superintended and the business directed, and where all contracts for mail service are let, and the accounts therefor are settled. The Postmaster-General is assisted by three Assistant Postmaster-Generals, an Auditor, and several hundred clerks. Every postmaster in the United States is a deputy to the Postmaster-General. There are numerous route agents and detectives ; and every line of post-roads is well known and carefully watched. Every place in the United States, whether in office, house, tent, booth, boat, vessel, car, wagon, or box, where the mails are opened and the mail matter delivered, is called a "POST OFFICE," and the sworn and bonded deputy who opens and delivers

19, 35, 169. the written and printed matter received, is called a "POSTMASTER ;" although many of them might be called "POSTMISTRESSES," as ladies are frequently appointed of late years.

Describe the postal service. The first post-office ever established in America seems to have been under an act of Parliament in 1710. (Dr. Lieber's Encyc. Amer., POSTS.) In England the first regular mode adopted was in 1642. (Malkin's Introductory Letter.) In 1790 there were 75 post-offices in the United States; 1,875 miles of post-roads; the amount of postage was $37,935. In 1828 there were 7,530 post-offices ; 115,176 miles of post-roads, and the amount of postage was $1,659,915. (The American Almanac Repository, Boston, 1830, p. 217; American Almanac for 1832, p. 134; Dr. Lieber's Encyc. Americana, Article POSTS.) Story's Const. § 1125 (3d ed., note 1.) In 1866 there were 23,828 post-offices; 180,921 miles of post-roads ; amount of postage, $14,386,986.21.

For the rates of foreign postage, and monthly valuable statistics, see "United States Mail and Post-Office Assistant," New York.

The rates for letters are three cents for every half ounce, in the United States. All mail matter is charged by weight.

What improvement as to carrying suggested? It is questionable whether the government could peaceably return to the unequal charges of our fathers. It can be hoped, that some public man may yet develop the idea, that a system of carrying the mails by weight would be practicable ; more just to the carriers ; more economical to the government ; and immensely bene-

ficial to the people, as thereby the carrying need not to be profess-
edly limited to *paper;* but (like our immense express companies,
which first forced upon the government the weight system of
tariffs,) every thing might be carried and charged for by the ounce,
with a direct responsibility upon the government for safe delivery.

To the "regulations" of rates may be added the volume of
laws and regulations sent out every year, which establish "post-
offices and post-roads," and regulate the service and punish infrac-
tions of the law.

**106.** "Post Roads."—Every railroad, turnpike, wagon-road, *What are*
path, river, creek, ocean, sea, gulf, lake, and pond, over which *post-roads?*
mails are transported, may be denominated post-roads.

Every person and corporation engaged in carrying and deliver- *Who are*
ing the mails, is called a mail carrier or contractor; and they all *mail car-*
act under official responsibility. It may at once be deduced that *riers?*
the books, maps, reports and information to be gathered from the
General Post-Office Department is the most valuable to the student
of geography in the United States.

Among the "REGULATIONS" are the rates for carrying mail- *What are the*
matter, which, in 1846, were changed from the senseless method *rates of*
of charging the "single letter" at 25 cents and the "double let- *charges and*
ter" in proportion, regardless of weight or value, to the common *the charges?*
sense tariff of weights. The present laws regulating post-offices
and post-roads, the rates of postage, the franking privilege, and the
whole mail service, will be found in books issued by the Postmaster-General, and in Brightly's Dig. pp. 363 to 383; see also 2 Brightly's Dig. 750 to 800.

It is under this power that Congress has adopted the mail regula- *What are*
tions of the Union, and punishes all depredations on the mail. *the powers*
Sturtevants v. City of Alton, 3 McLean, 393. The power to estab- *of Congress?*
lish post-roads is restricted to such as are regularly laid out under
the laws of the several States. Cleveland, Painesville and Ashtabula
R. R. Co. v. Franklin Canal Co., Pittsburg L. J., 24th December,
1853; Pennsylvania v. Wheeling and Belmont Bridge Co., 18 How.
421; Dickey v. Turnpike Road Co., 7 Dana, 113; 1 Kent's Com. 281,
282.

But under this power Congress may make, repair, keep open, and *73-80.*
improve post-roads. Dickey v. Turnpike Road Co. 7 Dana, 113.
For conflicting views, see 1 Kent's Com. 11th ed. p. 268, note c.

Nothing which tends to facilitate the intercourse between the
States, can be deemed unworthy of the public care. Federalist,
No. 42.

**[8.]** To promote the progress of science and the *What is the*
*power as to*
useful arts, by securing, for limited times, to authors *authors and*
*inventors?*
and inventors the exclusive right to their respective
writings and discoveries.

**107.** To PROMOTE [*Promoveo, pro* and *moveo,* to move] is here *To promote*
used to advance, foster, and encourage, by all the liberal legislation
which can aid. Worcester's Dic. PROMOTE.

6

**Progress.**   THE PROGRESS [*Progressus, Projredior, advancement*], that is the growth, advancement of, and constant progression. Worc. Dic. PROGRESS.

**Define science.**   SCIENCE. [SCIENTIA, from *Scio, Scire* to know.] Knowledge. It is used here in the sense of Abstract, *Mental,* Mathematical, Natural, and Physical Science. (See the whole definitions and synonyms,) Webster's Dic. SCIENCE.

As practically illustrated by our legislation, the word has no limitation in the whole range of literature and knowledge, since all authors have a right to obtain copy-rights for their books, maps, pictures, and every thing printed and first published as such in the United States.    Clayton v. Stone, 2 Paine, 383 ; Jollie v. Jaques, 1 Blatch. 618 ; Binns v. Woodruff, 4 W. C. C. 48 ; Wheaton v. Peters, 8 Wheat. 591.

**Arts.**   " AND USEFUL ARTS."—ART [*Ars, Artis*]. The power of doing something not taught by nature.    Worcester's Dic. ART.

This word is also intimately connected with science.

**Distinguish between science and art.**   The distinction between Science and Art is, that *Science* is a body of principles and deductions, to explain the nature of some matter.    An Art is a body of precepts, with practical skill for the completion of some work.    *Science* teaches us to know ; an *Art* to do.    In *Art* truth is means to an end ; in Science it is the only end.    Hence the practical arts are not to be classed among the sciences.    (Whewell.)    Worc. Dic. SCIENCE. Science never is engaged, as art is, in productive application. (Kearslake) Worcester.

**Define se-cure.**   BY SECURING.—[*Securus, se* and *cura*, or without care.] Here used, by protecting in the exclusive use of ; to make certain ; to put beyond hazard ; to assure ; to insure ; to guaranty.    Worcester's Dic. SECURE.

**Why a limit-ed time?**   " FOR A LIMITED TIME."—Not perpetually ; but for a reasonable time.    The Acts of Congress have generally fixed the limit of fourteen years, which was the period in England when the Consti-tution was adopted.    2 Bl. Com. 406, 407, Christian's notes, 5, 85 ; Millar v. Taylor, 4 Burroughs, 2303 ; Rawle's Const. ch. 9, pp. 105, 106 ; 2 Kent's Com. Lect. 36, pp. 299–306.    The case in Burroughs, 2303, exhausts the whole ancient learning on the subject of copy-rights.    It is a grant by the government to the author of a new and useful invention, of the exclusive right for a term of years, the practising that invention.    Curtis on Patents, p. LX.

"USEFUL," *utility*, has been long exploded as an unnecessary and superfluous condition.    Millar v. Taylor, 4 Bur., 2303 ; Hall's New York edition, 182.    Puffendorf, Lib. 4 c. 5, p. 378, note 1.

**Who is an author?**   " TO AUTHORS."    [*Auctor.*]    He to whom any thing owes its origin ; originator ; creator ; maker ; first cause.    One who com-pletes a work of science or literature ; the first writer of any thing distinct from a translator or compiler.    Worc. Dic. AUTHOR.

**How are copy-rights secured?**   In the United States, an author has no exclusive property in a published work, except under some act of Congress.    Whea-ton v. Peters, 8 Pet. 591 ; Jefferys v. Boosey, 30 Eng. L. & Eq. 1 ; Dudley v. Mayhew, 3 Comstock, 12.    It had been decided in Great

Britain before the revolution, to be a common law right. Story's Const. § 1152. Overruled. Dudley v. Mayhew, 3 N. Y. (3 Col st.) 12.

The power is confined to authors and inventors; and cannot be extended to the introducers of new works or inventions. Story's Const § 1153. See Federalist, No. 43; 1 Tuck. Black. Com. App. 265, 266; Hamilton's Report on Manufactures, § 8, pp. 235, 236; Livingston v. Van Ingen, 9 John. 507; Journal of Convention, 260, 261, 327–329.

**108.** AND INVENTORS." [*Invenio; in*, and *venio*, to come.]     Who are inventors?
To *invent* is to devise something new, not before made, or to modify and combine things before made or known, so as to form a new whole. Wore. Dic. INVENT. One who invents; a contriver. This right was saved out of the statute of monopolies in the reign of King James the First, and has ever since been allowed for a limited period, not exceeding fourteen years. 2 Black. Com. 406, 407; Christian's notes, 5, 8; 2 Kent's Com. Lect. 36, pp. 306–315.

Patents are entitled to a liberal construction, since they are For what are not granted as restrictions upon the rights of the community, but patents granted? "to promote the progress of science and the useful arts." Blanchard v. Sprague, 3 Sumner, 535; Grant v. Raymond, 6 Pet. 218; Hogg v. Emmerson 6 How. 486; Brooks v. Fisk, 15 Id. 223. The power of Congress to legislate upon the subject of patents is plenary, by the terms of the Constitution; and as there are no restraints on its exercise, there can be no limitation of its right to modify them at its pleasure, so that they do not take away the rights of property in existing patents. McClurg v. Kingsland, 1 Id. 206. Evans v. Eaton, 3 Wheat. 545; s. c. 7 Wheat. 356; Evans v. Hettish, 7 Wheat. 453; Blanchard v. Sprague, 3 Sumner, 541. Therefore, Congress has the power to grant the extension of a patent which has been renewed under the act of 1836. Bloomer v. Stolley. 5 McLean, 158. Its power to reserve rights and privileges to assignees, on extending the term of a patent, is incidental to the general power conferred by the Constitution. Blanchard's Gun-Stock Turning Factory v. Warner, 1 Blatch. 258.

Perhaps there is nothing which has tended more to the rapid development of American genius, character, and improvement, than the laws securing to authors and inventors their rights. The Patent Office is, perhaps, the most commodious house in America. There are collected the applications, specifications, drawings, and models of the inventors, whose works have dispensed with the hand-labor of more millions than the world now contains. From this office issues annually a report of the current inventions. No lover of the development of his country should visit Washington without giving himself a week to examine the wonderful mysteries of the Patent Office.

For a most able treatise upon the law of patents, the reader is referred to the very able work of Curtis on Patents, 1867; to the "PATENT LAWS," issued by the Patent Office; 1 Brightly's Dig. COPY RIGHT, p. 193; Patents, 721, and accurate notes: 2 Brightly, 353.

[9.] To constitute tribunals inferior to the Supreme Court.

**109.** To CONSTITUTE here means to create and organize, defining the jurisdiction.

TRIBUNAL [Lat. TRIBUNAL.] Bench of a judge; hence courts of justice, subject to the superior jurisdiction of the Supreme Court. Webster's Dic., TRIBUNAL.

Do State decisions about real property control? See American Insurance Company v. Canter, 1 Pet. 546. This power affords no pretext for abrogating any established law of property, or for removing any obligation of her citizens to submit to the rule of the local sovereign. Suydam v. Williamson, 24 How. 433. Where any principle of real property has been settled in a State court, the same rule will be applied by this court. (Jackson v. Chew. 12 Wh. 162; Beauregard v. New Orleans, 18 How. 497); Suydam v. Williamson, 24 How. 432, 434. Even to the over-ruling of our decisions, which have not been followed by the State courts. (Arguello v. The United States, 18 How. 539; League v. Egery, 24 Id. 265-6; Foote v. Egery, Id. 268); Suydam v. Williamson, Id. 434. In the last cases, we followed the interpretation of the Supreme Court of Texas, rather than our own, upon the 4th article of the National Colonization Law of Mexico. Suydam v. Williamson, 24 How. 434. In a case of conflict of jurisdiction between the court of a State and that of the United States, that which first attaches should hold. Taylor v. Carryl, 20 How. 583.

What tribunals have been established under this power? The tribunals which have been established under this power are the Circuit Courts and the District Courts of the United States, between which have been divided the controversies between litigants. See Brightly's Digest, pp. 124 to 129, 228 to 234.

And to these may properly be added the court of claims, which has a special limited jurisdiction in certain suits against the United States, and the commissions and tribunals created at different times for the trial of certain land claims arising under the treaties with France, Spain, and Mexico.

Define the special power on crimes. [10.] To define and punish piracies and felonies committed on the high seas, and offenses against the law of nations.

What is to define? **110.** To DEFINE is to give the limits or precise meaning of a word or thing in being; to make, is to call into being. Congress has power to *define*, not to make, the laws of nations; but Congress has the power to make rules for the government of the army and navy. James Speed, Attorney-General, upon the right to try by Military Commission, the conspirators to murder President Lincoln, July, 1865, p. 4.

129.

111.

How has Congress defined? **111.** To PUNISH, in this sentence, is to inflict the penalty of the law, which, in cases of piracy, is, by the law of nations, death. Had Congress simply declared that piracy should be punished with death, the offense would have been sufficiently *defined*. Congress may as well *define* by using a word of known and determinate meaning, as by an express enumeration of all the particulars in-

110.

cluded in that term. But it was intended not merely to define
piracy as known to the law of nations, but to enumerate what
crime in the national code should be deemed piracy. And so the
power has been practically expounded by Congress. (United States
v. Smith, 5 Wheat. 153–163.)    Story's Const. § 1159; 1 Stat. 113,
3 Stat. 600.

**112.** "PIRACY" is robbery or forcible depredation on the *high* What is pi-
*seas*, without lawful authority, and done, *animo furandi*, in the racy?
spirit and intention of universal hostility.  1 Kent's Com. 183;
Story's Const. § 1160.  The acts which, if committed upon land,
would have amounted to felony there.  7 East. Pl. of the Crown, 796.
It is the same offense at sea with robbery on land.  1 Kent's Com.
183; Wharton's Am. Crim. Law, §§ 2816–2855. The crime of piracy
is defined by the law of nations with reasonable certainty.  United
States v. Smith, 5 Wh. 153.  And see Story's Const. § 1158, 1159;
The Federalist, No. 4; Rawle on the Const., ch. 9, p. 107;  2 A pirate?
Elliott's Debates, 389, 390.  A PIRATE is a rover and robber upon
the sea, an enemy to the human race.  Cowel; Webster; 3 Inst.
113; Burrill's Law Dic., PIRATE; 4 Bl. Com. 71–73.    Piracy is
defined by Congress in the Acts 13 April, 1790, 1 Stat. 113; and 15
May, 1820, 3 Stat. 600.  Brightly's Dig. 207, 208.

**113.** FELONY comprises every species of crime which occa- What is fel-
sioned, at common law, the forfeiture of lands and (or) goods. ony?
All offenses which are capital, and some which are not capital.
(Co. Litt. 391; 2 Black. Com. 93–98;) Story's Const. 192–194, 1161. 192, 193.
Felony is a loose term, and needs to be defined.  (Federalist,
No. 42; Elliott's Debates, 389, 390); Story's Const. § 1160;
Burrill's Law Dic., FELONY. where there are many learned cita-
tions of original authors.  Woodeson's Lec. 306.
   Felony on the high seas seems not to be of a technical common What is fel-
law, but of civil law definition.  (United States v. Smith, 5 Wheat. ony on the
153, 159; 3 Inst. 112; Co. Litt. 391, a); Story's Const. 1162. high seas?
   The Acts of 26 March. 1804, 2 Stat. 290; 3 March, 1825, 4 St.
115; 3 March, 1835, 4 St. 775; 8 Aug. 1846, 9 St. 73, all define
and punish felony.  1 Brightly's Dig. 208–211.

**114.** "HIGH SEAS" [*Altum mare.*] Not only the waters of the What are the
ocean, which are out of sight of land, but the waters on the sea-coast, high seas?
below low-water mark, whether within the territorial boundaries
of a nation or of a domestic State.  (United States v. Pirates, 5
Wheat. 184, 200, 204, 206; United States v. Wilberger, 5 Wheat, 76,
94). Story's Const. § 203, 1164. And see, 4 Black. Com. 110; Con-
stable's Case, 5 Co. Rep. 106; 3 Inst., 13; 2 East's P. C. 802, 803;
Hale in Harg. Law tracts, ch. 4, p. 10; 1 Hale's P. C., 423, 424.
   As to the States of the Union, "High Seas" may here be taken
to mean that part of the ocean which washes the sea-coast, and is
within the body of any county, according to the common law; and
as to foreign nations, any waters on their seacoast below low-water
mark. (Rawle's Const. ch. 9, p. 147; 3 Id. 439, 441; Sergt's. Const.
ch. 28, [ch. 30]; 1 Kent's Com. Lect. 17, p. 342; United States v.
Grush, 5 Mason's R. 290); Story's Const. § 1164; 1 Kent's Com.

397; Waring v. Clark, 5 How. 453, 462; Pyrodus v. Howard, 7 Pet. 342, 324; Howard v. Ingersoll, 13 How. 421, 424; Schooner Harriet, 1 Story's R. 259 Jones v. Root, 6 Mass. 435; The case of Waring v. Clarke, 5 How. 451-504, exhausts the whole learning on the subject. 13 How. 421-424; Angel on Tide-waters, ch. 3, p. 53; Id. ch. 1, pp. 15-34.

**What are offenses against the law of nations?**

**192-124.**

**217-223.**

**Are all offenses crimes?**

**252-255.**

**255.**

**115.** "OFFENSES AGAINST THE LAW OF NATIONS."—Many of the *offenses* against the law of nations, for which a man may, by the laws of war, lose his life, his liberty, or his property, are not *crimes*. It is an offense against the laws of nations and of war to break a lawful blockade, to hold communication or intercourse with the enemy, to act as spy (is an offense against the laws of war, and the punishment for which, in all ages, has been death); to violate a flag of truce, to unite with banditti, jayhawkers, guerillas, or any other unauthorized marauders. And yet these are not crimes. Some of the offenses against the laws of war are crimes, and some not. Because they are crimes, they do not cease to be offenses against those laws; nor because they are not crimes or misdemeanors do they fail to be offenses against the laws of war. Murder is a crime, and the murderer, as such, must be proceeded against in the form and manner prescribed in the Constitution; in committing the murder an offense may also have been committed against the laws of war. For that offense he must answer to the laws of war, and the tribunals legalized by that law.

There is, then, an apparent but no real conflict in the constitutional provisions. *Offenses* against the laws of war must be dealt with and punished under the Constitution as the laws of war, they being a part of the law of nations, direct; *crimes* must be dealt with and punished as the Constitution, and laws made in pursuance thereof, may direct. (Speed on the Conspirators, July, 1865.)

**Define the law of nations.**

**Can Congress change the laws of nations?**

**117, 118.**

**116.** "LAW OF NATIONS."—A code of public instruction, which defines the rights and prescribes the duties of nations in their intercourse with each other. 1 Kent's Com. 1, 2; Halleck's International Law, § 1, and numerous citations.

Mr. Randolph, then Attorney-General, said: "The law of nations, although not specifically adopted by the Constitution, is essentially a part of the law of the land. Its obligation commences and runs with the existence of a nation, subject to modification on some points of indifference." (See opinion Attorney-General, vol. 1, page 27.) Hence Congress may define those laws, but cannot abrogate them; or, as Mr. Randolph says, may "modify on some points of indifference." (Speed on the Conspirators), July, 1865.

That the laws of nations constitute a part of the laws of the land is established from the face of the Constitution, upon principle and by authority. Id.

But the laws of war constitute much the greater part of the law of nations. Like the other laws of nations, they exist and are of binding force upon the departments and citizens of the government, though not defined by any law of Congress. Id.

Congress can declare war. When war is declared, it must be,
under the Constitution, carried on according to the known laws
and usages of war amongst civilized nations. Id.

[11.] To declare war, grant letters of marque and
reprisal, and make rules concerning captures on land
and water.

**117.** "To Declare War."—See Confederation, Art. IX. p. 14.

"To declare," may be as well by a formal recognition, as by a
declaration in advance. Thus in our war with Great Britain in
1812: "That war be, and is hereby declared to exist, between the
United Kingdom of Great Britain and Ireland and the dependencies
thereof, and the United States of America and their territories."
Act of 1812, ch. 102; 2 St. 755; Story's Const. § 1174; Talbot v.
Seaman, 1 Cranch, 28; Bas v. Tingey, 4 Dall. 37.

And in the war with Mexico, in 1846, after the commencement
of hostilities: "Whereas war exists, with Mexico, by the act of
Mexico." 9 St. 9.

So in the qualified war with France, in 1798, which was regulated
by sundry acts confining the war within certain limits. Rawle's
Const. ch. 9, p. 109.

During the rebellion, the existence of the civil war was recognized
in a number of acts of Congress, but there was no formal recognition of the war.

To declare war in Great Britain is the exclusive prerogative of
the Crown; and in other countries, it is usually, if not universally,
confided to the executive department. (1 Tucker's Black. App.
271; 4 Black. Com. 257, 258.) Story's Const. § 1170. See Federalist, No. 41. See Halleck's International Law, ch. 20–24, pp. 289–
992.

War is "that state in which a nation prosecutes its right by
force." The Prize Cases, 2 Black, 666. (A state of forcible conten-
tion; of armed hostility between nations. Grotius de jure bell. lib.
1. c. 1.) Civil war exists when the regular course of justice is
interrupted by revolt, rebellion, or insurrection, so that courts of
justice cannot be kept open. The Prize Cases, 2 Black, 667.
Congress alone has the power to declare a national or foreign war;
but not against a State, or any number of States, under the Constitution. But the President may resist the insurrection without a
declaration of war. The Prize Cases, 2 Black's Rep. 668, 669.

A civil war is waged because the laws cannot be peaceably
enforced by the ordinary tribunals of the country through civil process and by civil officers. Speed on the power to execute the
assassins of the President, p. 5.

**118.** As a consequence of the power of declaring war, and
making treaties, the government possesses the power of acquiring
territory, either by conquest or by treaty. American Ins. Co. v.
Canter, 1 Pet. 542; Scott v. Sandford, 19 How. 393. In this case,
the power to acquire territory is not rested upon any particular
power in the Constitution, but is unqualifiedly asserted to exist. Id.

229-232.

What is the effect of war upon the citizens?

250, 251.

446-7. It would seem to be rested upon the power to admit new States. Id. All contracts made by the citizens of one country with the citizens or subjects of another, which countries are at war with each other, are void. Griswold v. Edrington, 16 Johns. 444. In this case, Chancellor Kent exhausts the whole learning upon the subject down to 1819. He says: "The law has put the sting of disability into every kind of voluntary communication and contract with an enemy which is made without the special permission of the government." (16 Johns. 483); Jackson v. Johnson, 11 Johns. 418; 1 Kent's Com. 66; The Ann Dodson, 2 Wh. 27; The Mary & Susan, 1 Wh. 57; 2 Cond. 599; The Julia, 8 Cr. 181-203; 3 Cond. 152. When one nation is at war with another nation, all the subjects or citizens of the one are deemed in hostility to the subjects or citizens of the other; they are personally at war with each other, and have no capacity to contract. White et al. v. Burnley, 20 How. 249; Ogden v. Lund, 11 Tex. 690. The court is bound judicially to know when war existed. Id.; The Prize Cases, 2 Black, 666. The inhabitants are not permitted to pass from the one country to the other. Ogden v. Lund, 11 Tex. 690. The military upon the frontier, from the necessity of the case, must be charged with the duty of preventing such intercourse. Id. To prevent the running of a ferry between Texas and Mexico, while the United States and Mexico were at war, was lawful, and affords no ground of action against the officer. Id. 692. See Constitution of the Confederate States, same section. Paschal's Annotated Dig., note 217. These general rules of law are applicable alike to civil and international wars: that all people, of each State or district, in insurrection against the United States, must be regarded as enemies, until, by the action of the legislature and the executive, or otherwise, that relation is permanently changed. (The Prize Cases, 2 Black, 687.) Mrs. Alexander's Cotton, 2 Wall. 419; The Venice, 2 Wall. 274; The Prize Cases, 2 Black, 666.

What was the effect of the late rebellion?

This power necessarily extends to all legislation necessary to the prosecution of war with vigor and success, except such as interferes with the command of the forces and the conduct of the campaign. Ex parte Milligan, 4 Wallace, 139.

When two governments, foreign to each other, are at war, or when a civil war becomes territorial, all of the people of the respective belligerents become, by the law of nations, the enemies of each other. Speed.

Does this justify marauders?

15, 116.

But this only authorizes hostility by those who are empowered by the express or implied command of the State, &c.

*Hence it is that, in land wars, irregular bands of marauders are liable to be treated as lawless banditti, not entitled to the protection of the mitigated usages of war as practiced by civilized nations.* (Wheaton's Elements of International Law, page 406, 3d edition; Speed on the Assassins, p. 9.)

112.

"A pirate, an outlaw, or a common enemy to all mankind may be put to death at any time. It is justified by the *law of nature and nations*." (Patrick Henry; 3 Elliott's Debates on Federal Constitution, p. 140; Speed.)

How were the assassins tried?

The assassins were tried by military commission and convicted, and a part of the conspirators executed, and a part of them sentenced to imprisonment for life. See the volumes containing the trial of the conspirators; and see the trial of Surratt.

Until Congress passes laws upon the subject of war and reprisals no private citizen can enforce such rights; and the judiciary is incapable of giving them any legitimate operation. (Brown v. United States, 8 Cr. 1.) Story's Const. § 1177. And although Mrs. Alexander had taken the oath of amnesty, while she remained in rebel territory she had no standing in court. Mrs. Alexander's Cotton. 2 Wall. 421. The cotton captured on the land by the naval forces, in a rebellious State, was not the subject of prize. See 9 Op. 524, 525; (Speed, 4–10). The Queen of England recognized the Confederates as neutrals, on the 13th May, 1861. Id. 669. The President must determine when insurrection exists. The Prize Cases, 670. His proclamation of blockade, of 19th April, 1861, is conclusive upon the courts; and neutrals were bound by it. Id. Under this very peculiar Constitution, although the citizens owe a supreme allegiance to the Federal Government, they owe also a qualified allegiance to the State in which they are domiciled. Their persons and property are subject to its laws, and they are liable to be treated as enemies. Id. 673. When the legislative authority has declared war, the executive authority, to whom its execution is confided, is bound to carry it into effect; he has a discretion vested in him, as to the manner and extent; but he cannot lawfully transcend the rules of warfare established among civilized nations. Brown v. United States, 8 Cr. 153. The Supreme Court of the State of Pennsylvania has decided that the United States conscription is unconstitutional. Judge Woodward gave the decision. The following is an abstract:— He starts with the idea that the conscription levies upon, takes, and destroys the militia of the States, and in spite of the States. He shows that in 1706 and 1707 a conscription was attempted in the British Parliament, but laid aside as unconstitutional; and he reasons that our fathers, in making the Federal Constitution, never intended to give a central government power over life and liberty not found even in the British constitution. Standing armies are the jealousies of Britons. Our fathers never intended to raise them by force, independent of the States. General Washington, in suppressing the whisky rebellion of Pennsylvania, paid the most scrupulous attention to the rights, and interests, and laws of Pennsylvania. Citizens cannot be made deserters of before they have been soldiers, as the conscription act declares.

"There are other features of the conscript law that deserve criticism; but not to extend my opinion further, I rest my objection to its constitutionality upon these grounds:—

"1st. That the power of Congress to raise and support armies does not include the power to draft the militia of the States. 2d. That the power of Congress to call forth the militia cannot be exercised in the forms of this enactment. 3d. That a citizen of Pennsylvania cannot be subjected to the rules and articles of war until he is in actual military service. 4th. That he is not placed in such actual service when his name has been drawn from a wheel, and ten days'

*[Marginal notes:]* Define the relations during the late rebellion.

To whom is allegiance due? 17, 220.

What are the president's powers?

What as to conscription?

124.

130.

notice thereof has been served upon him." Kneedler v. Lane, 9 Wright, 331; 48 Penn. 331.

**130–133.** The conscript laws of the Confederacy, which declared every man from seventeen to fifty years of age a soldier, were held, by a majority of the Supreme Court of Texas (under this same power) to be constitutional, Mr. Justice Bell dissenting. Paschal's Annotated Digest, notes 217–219; *Ex parte* Coupland; 26 Tex. 394.

**What of marque and reprisal?** **119.** "GRANT LETTERS OF MARQUE AND REPRISAL." This power would be incident to the power to declare war. (See Mr. Madison's Letter to Mr. Cabell, 18th Sept., 1828.) Story's Const. § 1175.

**Define marque.** **120.** MARQUE is, in public law, the frontier boundary of a country. And "to grant" is permission to pass the frontier of a country in order to make reprisals. (See March's Letters of Marque; 1 Bl. Com. 258.) Burrill's Law Dic., MARQUE. Generally used as synonymous with "*reprisal.*" 1 Black, Com. 258. See Halleck's International Law, 391–393; Wheaton's International Law, part 4, chap. 2, sec. 10.

**121.** "REPRISAL." [*Reprisalia.*] A retaking; taking back; recaption. The repossessing one's self of a thing unjustly taken by another. 3 Bl. Com. 4. A taking of one thing in satisfaction for another (*captio rei unius in alterius satisfactionem*)—frequently used in the plural *reprisalia.* Spelman; *Loccende Jur. Mar.* lib. 3, C. 5; 1 Kent's Com's 61.

**What is the meaning of reprisal?** A taking in return; a taking by way of retaliation. Burrill's Law Dic. REPRISAL. In this case, letters of "*marque and reprisal*" (words used as synonymous, the latter [reprisal] signifying a taking in return, the former ["*letters* of marque"], the passing the frontiers in order to such taking) contain an authority (grant) to seize the bodies or goods of the subjects of the offending State wherever they may be found, until satisfaction is made for the injury. (1 Black. Com. 258, 259; Bynkershoek on War, ch. 24, p 182, by Duponceau; *Valin,* Traité des Prises, pp. 223, 321; 1 Tuck Black. Com., App. 271; 4 Elliot's Debates, 251.) Story's Const. § 1176. Halleck, 391, 393.

**What is the power as to armies?** [12.] To raise and support armies; but no appropriation of money to that use shall be for a longer term than two years.

**122.** This power did not exist under the Articles of Confederation. For discussions of the limitation and necessities of this power, see 4 Elliot's Debates, 220, 221; 1 American Museum, 270, 273, 283; 5 Marshall's Life of Washington, App., note 1, Id. ch. 3, p. 125, 126; ch. 5, p. 212–220; ch. 6, p. 238–248; 2 Elliot's Debates, 9 3, 285, 286, 307. 308, 309. 319, 320, 430, 438; Federalist, Nos. 23, 24–29, 41; Story's Const. § 1168–1198, 3d ed. and notes.

**Define to raise and support.** **123.** "TO RAISE AND SUPPORT," in practice, means to educate, commission, enlist, draft, conscript, feed, clothe, transport and pay officers and men.  See Brightly's Digest, 55-90 and notes; 2 Id. 9-50.  During peace as well as war.  Story's Const. § 1186-1198.

**124.** "ARMIES."—Collections or bodies of men, armed for war, Define and organized in companies, battalions, regiments, brigades and armies. divisions, under their proper officers.  Webster's Dic. Army.  All the military in the service of the United States are called the ARMY of the United States.  The power to raise large bodies of men and divide them into "ARMIES" has only been exercised three times since the formation of the government, viz.:  In the war with Great 117, 118. Britain, 1812, with Mexico, 1846. and during the late rebellion.

The Army of the United States consists of five regiments of What is the artillery, ten regiments of cavalry, forty-five regiments infantry, present the Professors and Corps of Cadets of the United States Military army? Academy, and the officers and men of the different departments and corps, under the control of the War Department.  The ranks of the commissioned officers of this army are :  General (Ulysses S. Grant);  Lieutenant-General (William T. Sherman);  Major-General (five);  Brigadier-General (ten);  Colonel;  Lieutenant-Colonel; Major ;  Captain ;  Lieutenant, first and second.  14 Stat. 332 ;  and see the Reports of Sec. of War, 1866 and 1867; and the Army Register.  At the close of the rebellion, the army consisted of over a million of men. rank and file, which had been raised by enlistment, drafts, and bounties.  The power is unlimited, being an indispensable incident to the power to declare war.  See Story's Const. 123. § 1178-1192, and the references; 2 Elliot's Debates, 285, 286. 307, 308, 430;  Federalist, Nos. 23, 24, 25, 28.  See 1 Brightly's Dig. 55-90; 2 Id. 9-50.

**125.** Congress has a constitutional power to enlist minors, in What is the the navy or army, without the consent of their parents.  United power of States v. Bainbridge, 1 Mass. 71; Case of Emanuel Roberts, 2 enlistment? Hall's L. J. 192; United States v. Stewart, Crabbe, 205 ; Commonwealth v. Murray, 4 Binn. 487; Commonwealth v. Barker, 5 Id., 423; Commonwealth v. Morris, Phil. R 381: *Ex parte* Brown, 5 118. Cr. C. C. 554.  Public policy requires that a minor shall be at liberty to enter into a contract to serve the State, whenever such contract is not positively forbidden by the State itself.  Commonwealth v. Gamble, 11 S. & R. 94; The King v. Rutherford Grays, 1 Barn and Cress, 345.  The act of 21st June, 1862, § 2, 12 Stat. 140, 141. 620, repealed the act of 28th September, 1850, which required the consent of parents or guardians for the enlistment of minors, since which repeal minors, between the ages of eighteen and twenty-one, may be enlisted without the consent of the parent or guardian. Follis's Case, 10 Leg. 276.  But see United States v. Wright, 2 Leg. Int. 21, and Commonwealth v. Carter, Id.; Henderson's Case, Id. 187, where it is held that the act of 1802 is still in force, and that such enlistment is void.  In Shirk's Case, however, a discharge under similar circumstances was refused  20 Leg. Int. 260.  The oath of enlistment, though conclusive upon the recruiting officer, is not so upon the courts.  Webb's Case, 10 Pittsburg, L. J. 106. *Contra,* United States v. Taylor, 29 Leg. Int. 284; Jordan's **case,**

11 Am. L. R. 749.  A prisoner of war, paroled by the enemy, is not entitled to his discharge, although a minor, until exchanged. Henderson's Case, 20 Leg. Int. 181 ; 2 Brightly's Dig. p. 24, note.

Each individual in a republic, as in a monarchy, can be required to perform military duty without his consent, if the demand is made by a proper exercise of the national will.  *Ex parte* Coupland, 26 Tex., 394.  This follows from the unrestricted power to declare war.  Id.  (Cites Hurd on *Habeas Corpus*, 8; United States v. Bainbridge ; Mass. 71; Federalist, 187.)  "Militia" is not synonymous with " arms-bearing men ;" and it was held that when the citizens were conscripted into the "Confederate States" service (under the same clauses), they had no right to choose their officers. Id. 396, 397.  When a citizen goes into the army raised by Congress, either voluntarily, or in obedience to the law requiring him to do so, he does this as a citizen, and not a militia-man. Id. 397.  Paschal's Annotated Digest, 217–220, p. 88–91.

For the time being, the right of the State government over him ceases.  The opinion endeavors to reconcile this view with the doctrines of States Rights, and held the Confederate conscript law to be constitutional *during* the necessity. Id. 397–405.  Mr. Justice Bell reviewed the 41st, 29th, 45th and 4th numbers of the Federalist, and denied the constitutionality of the law. Id. 405–430.

This power has led to the establishment of the War Department, presided over by a Secretary and Assistant Secretary of War, to which are attached the following departments, the heads of which have the rank of Brigadier-General, viz.: Adjutant-General, Quartermaster, Subsistence, Pay, Medical, Ordnance, and Bureau of Military Justice ; there are four Inspectors-General, with the rank of Colonel, and also an Engineer and Signal Corps. The Chief of Engineers has the rank of Brigadier-General, and the chief signal officer ranks as Colonel of cavalry.

**126.** BUT NO APPROPRIATION TO THAT USES HALL BE FOR A LONGER TERM THAN TWO YEARS.  Congress may vote the supplies for but one year or a shorter period, but, imperatively, no appropriation shall be for a longer period than two years. (Federalist, Nos. 26, 41 ; 2 Elliot's Debates, 93, 308, 309.) Story's Const. § 1188, 1189, 1190.

The English Parliament is not thus restricted. 1 Black. Com. 414, 415; Tucker's Appendix, 271, 272, 379 ; Federalist, No. 41; Story's Const. § 1190.

[13.] To provide and maintain a navy.

**127.** "TO PROVIDE AND MAINTAIN," in this clause, is about equivalent "*to raise and support,*" in the preceding clause.  The present splendid navy of the United States, with its immortal history, is the best refutation of the arguments which were urged against this necessary branch of the service.  See Articles of Confederation, Art. IX. ante p. 14.  See Federalist, Nos. 11, 24, 29, 41 ; 2 Elliot's Debates, 319–324 ; Virginia Resolutions and Report, 7th and 11th Jan., 1800, pp. 57–59 ; 5 Marshall's Life of Washington, 523–531, Story's Const. § 1193–1198.

**128.** "NAVY;" [*Navigation—from Navis*, a ship.]—"To build Define navy. and equip a navy." Articles of Confederation, ante Art. IX. p. 14. The present words are more broad and appropriate. Story's Const. § 1194. It practically means not only to build and equip, but to organize, provide, and maintain a naval department, 127. naval school, coast survey, naval armament, merchant marine; and it is the strongest arm of our harbor defenses, as well as a powerful engine of attack and offensive warfare. 1 Brightly's Digest, 657–680; 2 Id., 315–387.

It is the natural result of the sovereignty over the navy of the United States, that it should be exclusive. Whatever crimes, therefore, are committed on board of public ships of war of the 110, 116. United States, whether they are in port or at sea, are exclusively cognizable and punishable by the government of the United States. The public ships of sovereigns, wherever they may be, are deemed to be extra-territorial, and enjoy the immunities from the local jurisdictions belonging to their sovereign. (See United States v. Bevans, 3 Wheat. 336, 390. The Schooner Exchange, 7 Cr. 116.) Story's Const. § 1168.

This grant of power has been developed in the organization of a Navy Department, over which presides a Secretary of the Navy (at present GIDEON J. WELLES), an Assistant Secretary of the Navy, and other appropriate officers of the bureau.

The ranks of the Naval officers are: Admiral, Vice-Admiral, Commodore, Captain, Commander, Lieut.-Commander, Lieutenant, Master, Ensign, Midshipman. 2 Brightly's Digest, 315, 316, 318; 14 Stat., 515, 516.

[14.] To make rules for the government and regula- How to tion of the land and naval forces. govern the forces?

**129.** "To MAKE RULES," in this connection, means to pre- Define to scribe the rules of conduct; that is, to enact the necessary laws make rules? "for the government and regulation of the land and naval forces." 133, 233, 240. This Congress has done by the enactment of the rules and articles of war, which are always in the hands of military and naval offi- 120–127. cers, and have become exceedingly familiar to our volunteer civilians during the late war.

For these "Rules" see 1 Brightly's Dig. pp. 73–83, ch. XVI. Arts. I–CL; 2 Brightly, 24–27; 2 St. 359; 12 St. 316, 330, 339, 354, 589, 595, 598, 735, 754; 13 St. 145, 356, 489.

[15.] To provide for calling forth the militia to exe- What power cute the laws of the Union, suppress insurrections, militia? and repel invasions.

**130.** MILITIA.—The national soldiery of a country, as distin- Define mili guished from a standing military force, consisting of the able-bodied tia? male inhabitants of a prescribed age, who are enrolled, officered, mustered, and trained according to law, but are called into active service 234, 235. only on emergent occasions, such as to suppress insurrections and repel invasions, for the public defense. (Act of Congress, 8 May,

1792; 1 Kent's Com. 262, 266.) Burrill's Law Dic., MILITIA; 1 Brightly's Dig., 619, 624, and notes; 2 Id., 299; 525–597.

**189.** The act of 1795, which confers power on the President to call forth the militia in certain exigencies, is constitutional; and the President is the exclusive and final judge whether the exigency has arisen. Martin v. Mott, 12 Wh. 19; Vanderheyden v. Young. 11 Johns. 150. The power to repel invasion includes the power to provide against the attempt or danger of invasion. Martin v. Mott, **234, 235.** 12 Wh. 19; 6 Cond. 417. Those called out according to law are subject to court-martial. (Houston v. Moore, 3 Wh. 433.) Martin v. Mott, 6 Cond. 421; Moore v. Houston, 3 Serg. and R. 167; 1 Kent's Com. 267; Bates on *Habeas Corpus*, 5th July, 1861. The President cannot exercise this power. Bates, 18th April, 1861.

**What are the president's powers?** It belongs exclusively to the President to judge when he has the authority to call forth the militia, and his decision is conclusive upon all others. Martin v. Mott, 12 Wheat. 19; 1 Kent's Com. 279; and see the same, 244–250; Story's Const. § 1210–1215; Bates on *Habeas Corpus*, 5th July, 1861.

**235.** And also upon the Courts of the United States. Luther v. Borden, 7 How. 1.

The power is to be exercised upon sudden emergencies, upon great occasions of State, and under circumstances which may be vital to the existence of the Union. Luther v. Borden, How. 18, 19, 31, 32; Story's Const. § 1211.

The President may make his requisitions directly upon the executives of the States, or by orders directed to any subordinate officers of the militia. Houston v. Moore, 5 Wheat. 15–16; see 1 Kent's Com. 277–279.

**When do the militia become national?** The militia is the militia of the States, respectively, and not of the United States. When called into the service of the General Government, they become national militia after they are mustered at the place of rendezvous designated by national authority, and not until then. (Houston v. Moore, 5 Wheat; Martin v. Mott, 12 Wheat. 19.)

**Define laws of the Union.** **131.** LAWS OF THE UNION.—This Constitution, and the laws of the United States which shall be made in pursuance thereof, and all treaties made, or which shall be made, under the authority of **233–240.** the United States, shall be the supreme law of the land. Art. 6, cl. 2. The laws of the Union are of course this supreme law; and the execution of this power is coextensive with the whole subject of constitutional legislation. But the exigency can only arise when there is an actual or threatened resistance to the laws of the United States. See Bates on *Habeas Corpus*, 5th July, 1861.

**Define insurrection.** **132.** INSURRECTIONS.—It has often been contended that insurrection here only means that "domestic violence" mentioned in **234, 235.** the fourth section of the fourth article, and hence that the power can only be exercised when the legislature or executive of a State demands it.

But insurrection seems to have been treated as resistance to law by a force too strong for the ordinary *posse comitatus.* (2 Elliot's Debates, 292–309; Federalist, No. 29.) Story's Const.

§ 1201.  It doubtless has reference to the violences of a domestic faction, or sedition, as contradistinguished from invasion by a foreign enemy.  Id.  And the insurrection may as well be against United States as State authority.

In the Southern States, the word "insurrection" was almost exclusively confined to "risings" by the slave population.

Insurrection is synonymous with sedition, rebellion, revolt.  Webster's Dic., REBELLION.

**133.** "INVASIONS" is here doubtless coupled with the guaranty of the United States "to protect every State against invasion." (Art. IV. sec 4.)  But the "invasion" would be none the less so if invited by State authorities, or if no call should be made by the legislature or governor of an invaded State.  The act of 1795 seemed to restrict the idea to invasions by a foreign enemy, as in the wars of 1812 and 1846.  1 St. 424; 1 Brightly's Dig. 440 and notes.

235.

Define invasion? 234, 235.

[16.] To provide for organizing, arming, and disciplining the militia, and for governing such part of them as may be employed in the service of the United States; reserving to the States, respectively, the appointment of the officers and the authority of training the militia according to the discipline prescribed by Congress.

What is the power as to organizing the militia?

**134.** This "ORGANIZING, ARMING, AND DISCIPLINING THE MILITIA," would include the whole legislation upon the subject.  But practically the power has not been fully exercised in time of peace.  It has indeed generally been left to the States, except as to the tactics and the distribution of arms, by quotas among the States.  See Act of 8th May, 1792, ch. 33, 1 St. 271; Act of 12th May, 1820, ch. 97; Act of 1821, ch. 68, 3 St. 577; Story's Const. § 1203; 1 Brightly's Dig. 619–624.  2 Id. 299 and notes.  MILITIA here means the body of arms-bearing citizens, as contradistinguished from the regular army.  Webster's Dic. MILITIA.  See Coupland, ex parte, 26 Tex. 411, 412.  For the discussions upon this subject, see 2 Elliot's Debates, 301–318; Luther Martin, 4 Elliot's Debates, 34, 35.  If Congress neglect to exercise this power, the States have a concurrent right to do so.  Houston v. Moore, 3 Sergt. and Rawle, 369.  See Houston v. Moore, 5 Wheat. 1–56.  And see Luther v. Borden, 7 How. 1 : Story's Const. § 1207.

What does organizing &c., include?

Define militia?

The militia of the several States are not subject to martial law unless they are in the actual service of the United States.  Mills v. Martin, 19 Johns. 7.  And this does not commence until their arrival at the place of rendezvous.  Houston v. Moore, 5 Wh. 20.  So far as Congress has provided for organizing the militia, the legislative powers of the States are excluded.  Id. 51; Houston v. Moore, 3 S. & R. 169.  But a State legislature may lawfully provide for the trial, by courts-martial, of drafted militia who shall re-

Is conscription constitutional? 113, 124.

fuse or neglect to march to the place of rendezvous, agreeably to the orders of the Governor, founded on the requisition of the President of the United States. Id. The act of the Congress of the United States, of the 3d March, 1863, 12 Stat. at Large, § 172, declared, that all citizens of the United States, &c., "are hereby declared to constitute the national forces, and shall be liable to perform military duty in the service of the United States, when called out by the President for that purpose." In New York, it has been determined, that this act is unconstitutional, on the ground that it attempted to create a *national militia*, a power not granted to the Federal Government, which is only empowered to raise an army and navy; whilst the militia is but a *State* force, though liable to be called into the service of the United States, by the President, in case of emergency. The People v. Stephens, before McCunn, J., at Chambers, 14th July, 1863. In Pennsylvania, however, Cadwallader, J., decided that the act was constitutional. Antrim's Case, 20 Leg. Int. 200; 2 Brightly's Dig. 40, note *a*; Kneedler v. Lane, 9 Wright, 238. See *ex parte* Coupland, 26 Tex. 394, where it was held that a conscript law, which declared all men between the ages of 17 and 50 years, was constitutional.

**What is the power over the militia?** **135.** When called out, they are subject to the rules and articles of war, save only that, when tried by court-martial, the court shall be composed of militia officers. (1 Brightly's Dig. p. 622, sec. 4; p. 82, sec. 270.) Atty. General Bates, 18th April, 1861.

The obvious theory of the Constitution and law is, that whilst Congress shall prescribe, by general rules, an uniform militia system for the States, securing the enrollment of all the able-bodied white male citizens, and maintaining the system of discipline and field exercise observed in the regular army (1 Brightly, 621), yet that the details, militia organization, and management shall be left to the State governments, requiring that only an annual report of the condition of the service shall be left to the President. Idem.

This power was first exercised to suppress the insurrection in Pennsylvania, in 1794. (5 Marshall's Life of Washington, ch. 8, pp. 576–592; 2 Pitk. His. ch. 23, pp. 421–592; the next, during the war of 1812, with Great Britain; and the last was the memorable occasion, to suppress the rebellion, on the 13th of April, 1861, and during its continuance. See the Act of 1795, 1 St. 424; Houston v. Moore, 3 Sergt. & R. 169; and S. C. 5 Wheat. 60; Martin v. Mott, 12 Wheat. 19; Duffield v. Smith, 3 Sergt. & R. 590; Vanderheyden v. Young, 11 Johns. 150.

**Where has congress exclusive power of legislation?** [17.] To exercise exclusive legislation in all cases whatsoever over such district (not exceeding ten miles square), as may, by cession of particular States and the acceptance of Congress, become the seat of the Government of the United States, and to exercise like authority over all places purchased by the consent of the legislature of the State in which the same shall be,

for the erection of forts, magazines, arsenals, dock-
yards, and other needful buildings. And,

**136.** " Exclusive Legislation over the District."—This By what
provision was executed by the cession of the District of Columbia states was
by Maryland and Virginia; and the legislation by Congress over ceded ?
the inhabitants and public property there ever since. See 1 Brightly's Dig. p. 233–252. Congress retroceded to Virginia, Alexandria
and the surroundings, so that the District is, in fact, only about
seven miles square. For the reasons for this exclusive government,
see the Federalist, No. 43 ; 2 Elliot's Debates, 92, 321, 322, 326 ;
Rawle's Const. ch. 9, p. 112, 113. See 2 Brightly's Dig. 233–252.

The site was selected by President WASHINGTON, after whom
the capital was named. The inhabitants are citizens of the United
States ; and might constitutionally have a local legislature. See
the Federalist, No. 43 ; United States v. Bevans, 3 Wheat. 336, 388.

In its exercise, Congress acts as the legislature of the Union.
Cohens v. Virginia, 6 Wheat. 424. The elective franchise allows
no distinction on account of race or color. 14 Stat. 375.

**137.** This includes the power of taxation. Loughborough v. Define the
Blake, 5 Wh. 317. The charter of the City of Washington did not powers ?
authorize the corporation to force the sale of lottery tickets in 136, 137.
States whose laws prohibited such sales. Cohens v. Virginia, 6
Wh. 264.

The right of exclusive legislation carries with it the right of
exclusive jurisdiction. United States v. Coryell, 2 Mas. 60 91 ;
6 Opin. 577. Even to recapture by military force. 9 Op. 521. This
second clause binds all the United States. (Cohens v. Virginia,
6 Wheat. 224.) Story's Const. § 1229.

Congress has the right to punish murder in a fort, or other Define the
place within its exclusive jurisdiction; but no general right to pun- jurisdiction
ish murder committed within any of the States. Idem. The power over forts?
to legislate in these places, ceded by a State, carries with it, as an
incident, the right to make that power effectual. Cohens v. Virginia, 6 Wheat. 428. Congress does not act as a local legislature,
but exercises this particular power, like all other powers, in its
h h character as the legislature of the Union. Id.; Story's
Const. § 1234. But the purchase of lands by the United States for
public purposes, within the territorial limits of a State, does not of
itself oust the jurisdiction or sovereignty of such State, over the
lands so purchased. United States v. Coryell, 2 Mas. 60. The
Constitution prescribes the only mode by which they can acquire
land as a sovereign power; and, therefore, they hold only as an
individual when they obtain it in any other manner. Commonwealth v. Young, Brightly, 302 ; People v. Godfrey, 17 Johns. 225 ;
United States v. Traver, 2 Wh. Cr. Cas. 490 ; People v. Lent, Id.
548. It seems, however, that the States have not the right to
tax lands purchased by the United States for public purposes,
although the consent of the legislature may not have been given
to the purchase. United States v. Weise, 2 Wall. Jr. 72. And see
7 Opin. 628. And see Commonwealth v. Cleay, 8 Mass. 72;

Rawle's Const. ch. 27, p. 238; Sergeant's Const. ch. 28 [ch. 30];
1 Kent's Com. Lect. 19, pp. 402-404; Story's Const. § 1222-1224.

After a cession by a State, it cannot take cognizance of any acts
done in the ceded places after the cession.  And the inhabitants
of those places cease to be inhabitants of the State, and can no
longer exercise any civil or political rights under the laws of the
State.  But if there has been no cession, the State jurisdiction still
remains.  (The People v. Godfrey, 17 Johns. 225; Commonwealth
v. Young, 1 Hall's Journal of Jurisprudence, p. 47; 1 Kent's Com.
Lect. 19, p. 403, 404; ch. 28 [ch. 30]; Rawle's (Const. ch. 27, p. 238-
240;) Story's Const. § 1127.

**What are the general powers of Congress?**
**71.**

[18.] To make all laws which shall be necessary and
proper for carrying into execution the foregoing
powers, and all other powers vested by this Constitution in the Government of the United States, or in any
department or office thereof.

**Define necessary?**
**269, 258, 259.**

**138.** This does not mean absolutely necessary, nor does it
imply the use of only the most direct and simple means calculated
to produce the end.   Commonwealth v. Lewis, 6 Binn. 270-1;
McCulloch v. Maryland, 4 Wh. 413; Metropolitan Bank v. Van
Dyck, 27 N. Y. Rep. 438-9.   And, therefore, Congress had power
to charter the Bank of the United States, as a necessary and useful
instrument of the fiscal operations of the government.  Id. 316,
422.   So, also, Congress has power, under this general authority, to
provide for the punishment of any offenses which interfere with,
obstruct, or prevent commerce and navigation with foreign States
and among the several States, although such offenses may be done
on land.   United States v. Coombs, 12 Pet. 78.  *Necessary* and
*proper* are to be considered synonymous terms.  Metropolitan Bank
v. Van Dyck, 27 N. Y. Rep. 439.   There is no warrant for saying
that the powers shall be construed *strictly.*  A reasonable import
of terms should be given.  (Martin v. Hunter, 1 Wh. 304, 326-7.)
Metropolitan Bank v. Van Dyck, 27 N. Y. Rep. 413, 415.  See
Federalist, 33, 44.

**Is this a power or a limitation?**
**93, 94.**

This section is among the powers of Congress, not the limitations; it enlarges and adds to, but does not diminish or lessen the
powers.  (McCulloch v. Maryland, 4 Wh. 413.)   Metropolitan Bank
v. Van Dyck, 27 N. Y. Rep. 443.   Under this power, Congress
may exempt the national securities from taxation.  (The People v.
The Tax Commissioners, 2 Black, 620.)  Metropolitan Bank v. Van
Dyck, 27 N. Y. Rep. 444.  Where the power is given to Congress,
it must judge of the means necessary to effect the end.  The end
must be legitimate.  Metropolitan Bank v. Van Dyck, 27 N. Y.
Rep. 445, 450; The United States v. Marigold, 9 How. 560.  Under
clause 4. and the power to coin money, Congress has the power to

**62, 63,**
**97-99.**

make the notes of the Government a legal tender.  Metropolitan
Bank v. Van Dyck, 27 N. Y. Rep. 454.

This power was greatly assailed.  See Federalist, 42, 43, 44; 1
Elliot's Debates, 293, 294, 300; 2 Id. 196, 342; Tuck. Black.

Com. Appendix, 286, 287; Hamilton on Banks, 1 Hamilton's Works, 121; McCulloch v. Maryland, 4 Wheat. 406, 407, 419; Calhoun's Essay on the Constitution; Story's Const. Ch. XXIV. § 1236–1258.

"Power" is the ability or faculty of doing a thing; and employing the means necessary to its execution; the right to make laws; Story's Const. § 1237, 1241. *Define power? 71, 93.*

Powers given by the Constitution, imply the ordinary means of execution. (McCulloch v. Maryland, 4 Wheat. 409; 4 Elliot's Debates, 217–221.) Story's Const. 1237.

"Expressly delegated," was in the Articles of Confederation. (*Ante* p. 9, Art. II). Story's Const. § 1238. *269.*

The plain import of the clause is, that Congress shall have all the incidental and instrumental powers necessary and proper to carry into execution all the express powers. It neither enlarges any power specifically granted, nor is it a grant of any new power to Congress. Story's Const. § 1243. Some have gone further than this. Governor Randolph, 2 Elliot's Debates, 342; Mr. Gerry in 1791, 4 Elliot's Debates, 225, 227. *Ex parte* Coupland, 26 Tex. 415, 416. *What is the import of the clause?*

The power must be *expressed*, or be an incident. Virginia Report and Resolutions, Jan. 1800, p. 33, 34; 1 Tuck. Black. Com. App. 287, 288; President Munroe's Exposition and Message, 4th May, 1822, p. 47.

The degree of necessity cannot control. 1 Hamilton's works, 118, 120.

"Necessary" often means no more than *needful, requisite, incidental, useful* or *conducive to.* Story's Const. § 1248. *Define necessary?*

The word "necessary" has no fixed character peculiar to itself, as in "*absolutely necessary* for executing its inspection laws," as contrasted with this *necessary and proper,* proves." Story's Const. § 1248–1250. See McCulloch v. Maryland, 4 Wheat, 413–418. *146–149, 162–164.*

"Proper" has a sense, admonitory and directory. It requires that the means should be *bona fide* appropriate to the end. McCulloch v. Maryland, 4 Wheat. 419, 420; Story's Const. § 1253. *Define proper?*

Among the necessarily incidental powers may be classed the right to acquire and govern territory; the right to contract and sue; to punish offenders on board ships; to protect collectors of revenue, men in the postal service, and army contractors. (Dugan v. The United States, 3 Wheat. 173, 179, 180; United States v. Tingey, 5 Peters, 115; United States v. Bevans, 3 Wheat. 388; The Exchange, 7 Cranch, 116; S. C., 2 Peters, 439; Osborn v. Bank of United States, 9 Wheat. 365, 366); Story's Const. § 1256–1258, and note 2. *What may be classed among the incidental powers? 232–4.*

The law must be necessary and proper. As to necessary, it must be borne in mind that no power can execute itself. * * The means are auxiliary powers * * ; that is implied powers. * * * * * * * * * *269.*

But the law must also be proper as well as necessary. * * That is, even implied powers are subject to important conditions, when used as means to carry powers or rights into execution. * They must be carried into execution so as not to injure others; and as connected with and subordinate to this, that where the implied powers or means used come in contact with the implied powers or means used by another, in the execution of the powers or rights vested in it, the less important should yield to the more important, the convenient to the useful, and both to health and safety; because it is proper they should do so. (Calhoun's Discourse on the Const.)

124.     *Ex parte* Coupland, 26th Tex. 416, 417. The learned Judge also quotes to the same effect from McCulloch v. Maryland.

The question is not, whether or not the power to raise armies is granted; but whether to raise them by *conscription* is implied. (Mr. Munroe's plan in 1814 contrasted.)  Id.

What is the inhibition as to the African slave trade?

Sec. IX.—[1.] The migration or importation of such persons as any of the States now existing shall think proper to admit, shall not be prohibited by the congress prior to the year one thousand eight hundred and eight; but a tax or duty may be imposed on such importation, not exceeding ten dollars for each person.

Define migration?

98.

24.

65–92.

**139.** MIGRATION OR IMPORTATION OF PERSONS.—"Migration" here, doubtless, means *immigration;* but as connected with "importation," it is used nearly synonymously with that term; and both have reference to the "PERSONS" who formed the basis of the African slave-trade. This trade was abolished on the 2d of March, 1807. 2 St. 428; 1 Brightly's Dig. 837. Those who wish to consult the statutes on this subject, and the luminous decisions upon a question now mostly obsolete in the United States, are referred to Brightly's Dig., chapter "SLAVE-TRADE," vol. 1, p. 835, and notes thereon; Scott v. Sandford, 19 How. 397; 1 Kent's Com. Lect. 9, pp. 192–203; Cobb on Slavery; Story's Const. § 1331, 1334; 2 Pitk. History, ch. 20, pp. 261, 262; 2 Elliot's Debates, 335, 336; 3 Id. 97, 98, 250, 251; Federalist, 42.

This section has no application to the State governments. Butler v. Hopper, 1 Wash. c.c. 499.

Define person?
24, 35, 46.

The word "PERSON" may fairly be said to refer to an imported African, and bears some analogy to the same word in Art. I., sec. 2, clause 3.

65–92.

Migration seems appropriately to apply to voluntary arrivals, as importation does to involuntary arrivals; and so far as an exception from a power proves its existence, this proves that the power to regulate commerce applies equally to the regulation of vessels employed in transporting men, who pass from place to place voluntarily, as to those who pass involuntarily. (Gibbons v. Ogden, 9 Wheat. 206–230.) Story's Const. 1387.

When may the privilege of *Habeas Corpus* be suspended?

[2.] The privilege of the writ of *habeas corpus* shall not be suspended, unless when in cases of rebellion or invasion the public safety may require it.

**140.** The PRIVILEGE of the writ must here mean the right to Define priv-
the writ.   See Burrill's Law Dic., PRIVILEGE. ilege?

The power to issue the writ is not the privilege; to ask for it, is   141.
Attorney-General Bates on *Habeas Corpus*, 5th July, 1861.

This privilege the President may suspend in time of such a   189.
rebellion.   Id.   Only in the cases contemplated by the act of Congress relative to rebellion.   Id.

It results that the President is not obliged to answer a writ of Can the
*habeas corpus*.   Id.   He is not answerable to the judiciary as Presi- President
dent.   Id.   The courts cannot revise his political actions.   Id.   suspend it?
204.

**141.** HABEAS CORPUS—No doubt it means here to have the Define
body; or the writ then known as the *habeas corpus, ad faciendum,* Habeas
*subjiciendum, et recipiendum,* to do, submit to, and receive whatso- Corpus?
ever the judge or court awarding the writ shall adjudge in that   140.
behalf.   3 Bl. Com. 131; 2 Kent's Com. 22; Steph. Com. 135; Burrill's Law Dic., HABEAS CORPUS; Story's Const. § 1339.   These
authors give the several writs.

As a co-ordinate power of the government, the President could
not be made amenable to this writ, for military arrests made during the rebellion.   Id.

For the meaning of the term *Habeas Corpus* resort must be had Where must
to the common law; but the power to award the writ, by any of we look for
the courts of the United States, must be given by written law. tion?
(Bollman, Swartwout's Case, 4 Cr. 93); Bates on *Habeas Corpus*;
Story's Const. § 1339.   And the writ means the writ *ad subjicien-*
*dum.*   (Luther v. Borden, 7 Howard, 1; Fleming v. Page, 9 How.
615; Cross v. Harrison, 10 How. 189; Santissima Trinidad, 7
Wheat. 305; Martin v. Mott, 12 Wheat. 29. Id.

It matters little whether it be called the peace or war
power.   Id.

It is a writ of right, which every person is entitled to, *ex merito*
*justitiæ.*   (4 Inst. 290.)   2 Kent's Com. Lect. XXIV. p. 26.   This
lecture fully discusses the subject.   And see Yates v. Lansing, 5
Johns. 282, and 6.   Id. 387; Story's Const.

The writ was never suspended except by the act of 12th March, When was it
1863, 12 St. 755; 2 Brightly's Dig. 196; Story's Const. § 1342; first sus-
2 Jeff. Cor. 274, 291, 344. pended?

It would seem, as the power is given to Congress to suspend the
writ in cases of rebellion or invasion, that the right to judge,   140.
whether the exigency had arisen, must exclusively belong to that
body.   (Martin v. Mott, 12 Wh. 19.)   Story's Const. 1342.   This
is denied in the opinion of Attorney-General Bates to President
Lincoln.

The federal courts have power to issue the writ of *habeas corpus* When may
only when necessary in aid of their jurisdiction, in a case pending. the Federal
*Ex parte* Everts, 7 Am. L. R. 79; overruling United States v. the writ?
Williamson, 4 Id. 11.   The case of a father claiming the custody of
an infant child, is not one in which a *habeas corpus* can issue, by a
court of the United States, as ancillary to the exercise of its jurisdiction.   Id.   Nor can a circuit court issue such a writ, although
the father be a citizen of another State, as the matter in dispute is
incapable of a pecuniary estimation.   Id.   A *habeas corpus* issued

by a State court has no authority within the limits of the sovereignty of the United States.  If served on a marshal having a **What is the power of the State Courts?** prisoner in custody, under authority of the United States, he should, by a proper return, make known the authority by which he holds him; but, at the same time. it is his duty not to obey the State process, but to execute that of the United States. Ableman v. Booth, 21 How. 506.  The federal courts have power to apply the writ of *habeas corpus* to all cases which it would reach at common law; provided it be not issued to any person in jail, unless confined under and by color of the authority of the United States. *Ex parte* Des Rochers, 1 McAllister, 68.  A State court, on a writ of *habeas corpus* issued at the relation of one committed on process from a federal court, cannot go behind the commitment and inquire into the grounds of it.  Williamson v. Lewis, 18 Leg. Int. 172.

**What department of the government only can suspend the writ?** The privilege of the writ of *habeas corpus* can only be suspended by act of Congress.  *Ex parte* Merryman, 24 Law Rep. 78; 9 Am. L. R. 524; Jones v. Seward, 3 Gr. 431. But see McQuillan's Case, 9 Pittsburgh Leg. I. 27; 27 Law Rep. 129; and Bates on *Habeas Corpus*.  The federal judges have exclusive jurisdiction on *habeas corpus*, whenever the applicant is illegally restrained of his liberty, under or by color of the authority of the United States, whether by virtue of a formal commitment or otherwise.

**What is the power of the State Courts over persons held in military service?** *Ex parte* McDonald, 9 Am. L. R. 662.  Much diversity of opinion appears to exist, as to the power of the State courts to discharge, on *habeas corpus*, a person illegally held in the military service of the United States.  Some judges hold that the State courts have jurisdiction to discharge one enlisted contrary to the acts of Congress.  Wilson's case, 18 Leg. Int. 316; Dobb's Case, 9 Am. L. R. 565; Commonwealth v. Carter, 20 Leg. Int. 21; Henderson's Case, Id. 181; Webb's Case, 10 Pittsburgh Leg. I. 106; *contra*, Phelan's Case, 9 Abbott, 286. And in Carney's Case, Chief-Justice Lowrie discharged a person from military arrest, who, after having been exempted from the conscription by the board of enrolment, was arrested on the pretext that they had reconsidered their decision. 14th August, 1863, MS.  On the contrary, it has been held that the State courts have no jurisdiction to inquire into the validity of the draft on *habeas corpus*. Spangler's Case, 11 Am. L. R. 596; Jordan's Case, Id. 749.  And that they have no power to discharge from the custody of the provost marshal one held for desertion, though enlisted contrary to law. Shirk's Case, 3 Gr. 460. This, however, was said by Leonard, J., in the Supreme Court of New York, to be founded on a misconception of the case of Ableman v. Booth; and Barrett, having been illegally enlisted, was discharged, notwithstanding a charge of desertion. Barrett's Case, 12 Pittsburgh Leg. I. 90.  See also Follis's Case, 19 Leg. Int. 276; United States v. Wright, 20 Id. 21; McCall's Case, Id. 108; Commonwealth v. Rogers, 10 Pittsburgh Leg. I. 178; Stevens's Case, 24 Law Rep. 205; *Ex parte* McDonald, 9 Am. L. R. 662; United States v. Taylor, 20 Leg. Int. 284; *In re* Hicks and Archibald, 11 Pittsburgh Leg. I. 25; Com. v. Wright, 3 Gr. 437.

In Vallandigham's Case, Judge Leavitt refused an application for a writ of *habeas corpus*, on the ground that the imprisonment was under military authority, and that, although a civilian, he was held for trial before a military commission, for disloyal practices; the country being engaged in war, and the military necessities requiring that the power to arrest parties under such circumstances should be exercised by the President, as commander-in-chief. Vallandigham's Trial, 259. Where a prisoner is held on original federal (not judicial) process, the State courts have concurrent jurisdiction with those of the United States, to inquire into the legality of the detention on *habeas co·pus*. Bressler's Case, 3 Gr. 447; citing 10 Johns. 328; 7 Cow. 471; 5 Hill, 16; 2 South, 555; 12 N. H. 194; 11 Mass. 63; 24 Pick. 267; 7 Cush. 285; 7 Barr. 336. The State judges have no power, on *habeas corpus*, to inquire into cases of commitment or detainer, under the authority of the federal government. Hopson's Case, 12 Am. L. R. 189. A return to a *habeas corpus*, by a provost marshal, that the prisoner is held as a deserter from the army, under the authority of the United States, is sufficient, without the production of the body; the State courts having no jurisdiction to inquire into the truth of the fact alleged in the return. Id. The proceedings on a writ of *habeas corpus* in the federal courts, are governed by the common law of England as it stood at the adoption of the Constitution, subject to such alterations as Congress may prescribe. *Ex parte* Kaine, 3 Blatch. 1. See *Ex parte* Aernam, Id. 160.

*[margin note: And when held by the military power?]*

By the act of 3d March, 1863, § 1, 12 Stat. 755 (2 Brightly, 196), it is declared:—" During the present rebellion, the President of the United States, whenever, in his judgment, the public safety may require it, is authorized to suspend the writ of *habeas corpus* in any case throughout the United States, or any part thereof."

*[margin note: Give the date and the language of the act to suspend the writ?]*

Upon a return to a writ of *habeas corpus*, that the relator was held by virtue of an order issued by the Secretary of War, by direction of the President, for endeavoring to prevent, and discouraging enlistments in the army, and that the privilege of the writ of *habeas corpus* had been suspended by the President, the writ was dismissed without inquiry into the validity of the arrest, or the legality of the cause of complaint. Kulp v. Ricketts, 3 Gr. 420. And see Vallandigham's Trial, 259.

On the 15th September, 1863, the President, by proclamation, suspended the privilege of the writ of *habeas corpus*, during the rebellion, throughout the United States, in all "cases when, by the authority of the President of the United States, the military, naval, and civil officers of the United States, or any of them, hold persons under their command or in their custody, either as prisoners of war, spies, or aiders or abettors of the enemy, or officers, soldiers, or seamen, enrolled, drafted, or mustered or enlisted in or belonging to the land or naval forces of the United States, or as deserters therefrom, or otherwise amenable to military law, or the rules and articles of war, or the rules or regulations prescribed for the military or naval service by authority of the President of the United States, or for resisting a draft, or for any other offense against the military or naval service." In Commonwealth *ex rel.* Cozzens v. Frink, on *habeas corpus*, **before** Judge Thompson of the Supreme Court of

*[margin note: And the President's proclamation?]*

Pennsylvania, it was decided, that the courts will take judicial notice that the rebellion no longer continues, and with it ends the power of the President to suspend the *habeas corpus*, and to order the arrest of a citizen, without warrant, if any he ever possessed, by virtue of this act. In that case, a provost-marshal made return to a writ of *habeas corpus*, that the relator was detained by him as a prisoner, under the authority of the President of the United States; this return, however, was adjudged insufficient, and the prisoner was discharged from military arrest. Philadelphia "Ledger," 6th July, 1865. 13 Am. L. R. 700.

Mrs. Surratt's case? In Mrs. Surratt's Case, Judge Wylie, of the Supreme Court of the District of Columbia, issued a writ of *habeas corpus* to inquire into the legality of her conviction by a military commission ; but was compelled to acknowledge himself powerless to enforce obedience to the writ, and the prisoner was executed in pursuance of the sentence. 7th July, 1865.

See 2 Brightly's Dig. title *Habeas Corpus*, 140, 141. Mr. Brightly also refers to the pamphlet of Horace Binney, against the constitutionality of the act.

But see Attorney-General Bates on *Habeas Corpus*, 5th July, 1861.

What is the jurisdiction of the Supreme Court of the United States? 199-201. The circuit court may certify a proceeding for a *habeas corpus*, upon a division of opinion, as in other "causes" or "suits." (Bollman's Case, 4 Cranch, 75; case of Tobias Watkins, 3 Pet. 193; The United States v. Daniel, 6 Wheat. 562; Weston v. The City Council of Charleston, 2 Pet. 419; Cohens v. Virginia, 6 Wheat. 264; Holmes v. Jennison, 14 Pet. 540.) *Ex parte* Milligan, 4 Wallace, 110-113, 117.

If a party is unlawfully imprisoned, the writ of *habeas corpus* is his appropriate legal remedy. It is his *suit* in a court to recover his liberty. (Holmes v. Jennison, 4 Pet. 540.) *Ex parte* Milligan, 4 Wallace, 113, 132.

The act of Congress "relating to *habeas corpus* and regulating proceedings in certain cases," was approved March 3d, 1863. (12 St. 755.) *Ex parte* Milligan, 4 Wallace, 114. This act was constitutional. Id. 133.

The President suspended the writ by proclamation, dated 15th September, 1863. Id.

Does the suspension authorize arrests? The suspension of the writ does not authorize the arrest of any person, but simply denies to one arrested the privilege of this writ in order to obtain his liberty. *Ex parte* Milligan, 4 Wallace, 115. The act recited. Id. The Chief-Justice and Justices Wayne, Swayne and Miller dissented from this. Id. 137.

The suspension of the privilege of the writ of *habeas corpus* does not suspend the writ itself. It issues as a matter of course, and on the return made to it, the court decides whether the party applying is denied the right of proceeding any further with it. Id. 131.

When will it live in contempt cases? The supreme court will not grant the writ to bring up a party imprisoned for contempt, except on a certificate of division of opinion, because such a commitment is a criminal proceeding. *Ex parte* Kearney, 7 Wheat. 38; Anderson v. Dunn, 6 Wheat. 204; Sergeant's Constitutional Law, 66, 67; James Buchanan, Peck's Trial, 435.

The laws of Pennsylvania in relation to the writ of *Habeas* When for persons enlisted in the navy?
*Corpus* reviewed.    Opinion of Attorney-General, Henry Stanbery
in Gormley's case, 6th Oct., 1867.    And also the several acts of
Congress of 1789, 1833, 1842, and 1863, upon the subject of *Habeas
Corpus*.    None of these acts declare the jurisdiction of the courts
of the United States to be exclusive of the State courts.    Id.

From an examination of the acts of 1789, 1806, 1809, 1820,
1837, 1845, and July 1, 1864, it appears that minors between
the ages of thirteen and eighteen may be enlisted in the
navy with the consent of their parents or guardians, to serve
until the age of twenty-one years; and that minors above eighteen
years may be enlisted without such consent.    Id.

The weight of authority is in favor of the power of the State
courts to hear the application of enlisted persons or persons held by
United States authority, and to discharge or remand them.    Id.
The production of the body is the life of the writ.    Id.

But judicial convictions and sentences by the United States
courts are exceptions to the rule.

Neither the regularity nor validity of the proceedings can be
called in question by any other court, State or Federal, by *habeas
corpus*.    (Ableman v. Booth, 21 How. 506, 526.)    Stanbery's opinion in Gormley's Case.

" We do not question the authority of a State court or judge, who Define the demarcation between the powers of United States and State Courts?
is authorized by the laws of the State to issue the writ of *habeas
corpus*, to issue it in any case where the party is imprisoned within
its territorial limits, provided it does not appear when the application is made, that the person imprisoned is in custody under
authority of the United States.    The court or judge has a right to
inquire into this mode of proceeding for what cause and by what
authority the prisoner is confined within the territorial limits of the
State sovereignty.    And it is the duty of the marshal or other person having the custody of the prisoner, to make known to the
judge or court, by a proper return, the authority by which he
holds him in custody.    This right to inquire, by means of *habeas
corpus*, and the duty of the officer to make a return, grows necessarily out of the complex character of our government, and the
existence of two distinct and separate sovereignties within the
same territorial space, each of them restricted in its power, and
each, within its own sphere of action, prescribed by the Constitution of the United States, independent of the other.    But after the
return is made, and the State judge or court judicially apprised
that the party is in custody under the authority of the United
States, they can proceed no further.    They then know that the
prisoner is within the dominion and under the jurisdiction of
another government, and that neither the writ of *habeas corpus* or
any other process issued under State authority can pass over the
line of division between the two sovereignties.    He is then within
the dominion and exclusive jurisdiction of the United States.    If
he has committed an offense against their laws, they alone can
punish him.    If he is wrongfully imprisoned, their tribunals can
release him and afford him redress.    And although, as we have said,
it is the duty of the marshal, or other person holding him, to make
known by a proper return the authority under which he detains

him, it is at the same time imperatively his duty to obey the process of the United States, to hold the person in custody under it, and to refuse obedience to the marshal or process of any other government.  And, consequently, it is his duty not to take the prisoner, or suffer him to be taken, before a State judge, or court, upon a *habeas corpus* under State authority.  No State judge or court, after they are judicially informed that the party is imprisoned under the authority of the United States, has any authority to interfere with him or to require him to be brought before them. And if the authority of a State, under form of judicial process or otherwise, should attempt to control the marshal or other authorized officer or agent of the United States in any respect, in the custody of his prisoner, it would be his duty to resist it and call to his aid any force that might be necessary to maintain the authority of the law against illegal interference.  No judicial process, whatever form it may assume, can have any authority outside of the limits of the jurisdiction of the court or judge by whom it is issued ; and an attempt to enforce it beyond these boundaries is nothing less than lawless violation.  (United States v. Booth, 21 How. 526? ") Stanbery in Gormley's Case ; 1 Kent's Com. 32, 11th Edition, note 1.

This general language is to be confined to process issued by the United States courts, not to any other kind of imprisonment. (Hurd on *Habeas Corpus*, 284.)   Stanbery.

It was the duty of Commodore Selfridge to produce the body of the marine.  Id.   The decision of the Secretary of the Navy was revoked, and the Commodore ordered to obey the writ of the Court of Quarter Sessions of Pennsylvania.  New York Herald of 7th Oct., 1867.

Attainder and *ex post facto?* [3.] No bill of attainder or *ex post facto* law shall be passed.

Define Bill of Attainder ? **142.** A BILL OF ATTAINDER is a legislative act which inflicts punishment without a legal trial.  And it includes bills of pains and penalties.  (Story's Const. § 1344.)  Cummings v. The State of Missouri, 4 Wallace, 323.  They may be directed against individuals or a whole class.  Id.   And inflict punishment absolutely or conditionally.  Id.  Gaines v. Buford, 1 Dana, 510.

Give example of such? 19. The Constitution of Missouri, which required an expurgatory oath of all priests, teachers, &c., was in effect, a bill of attainder. Cummings v. State of Missouri, 4 Wall. 323, 325.

The test oath required of Attorneys (note 242) of the courts of the United States, partakes of the nature of a bill of pains and penalties, and it is subject to the constitutional inhibition against the passage of bills of attainder, under which general designation they are included.  *Ex parte* Garland, 4 Wallace, 377 ; H. Stanbery's Opinion of 24th May, 1867, p. 14.

In Cummings v. The State, (4 Wallace, 326), we considered the meaning of a bill of attainder and of an *ex post facto* law in the clause of the Constitution forbidding their passage by the States, and it is unnecessary to repeat here what we there said.  A like prohibition is contained in the Constitution against enactments of this kind by Congress. *Ex parte* Garland, 4 Wallace, 378.

Attorneys and counsellors are not officers of the United States. Are attorneys offi-
Id. They are officers of the court, and hold during good behavior, neys offi-
and can only be deprived of their offices for misconduct ascertained cers?
and declared by the judgment of the court, after opportunity to be
heard has been afforded. (*Ex parte* Heyfron, 7 Howard, Mississippi,
127; Fletcher v. Dangerfield, 20 California, 430.) Id.

Their appointments and removal are judicial acts, and they can
only be deprived of the right for moral and professional delinquency.
(In the matter of the application of Henry W. Cooper, 22 New
York (8 Smith), 81; *Ex parte* Secombe, 19 How. 9.) *Ex parte*
Garland, 4 Wallace, 379. The removal cannot be effected by an
act of Congress requiring new qualifications. (Cummings v. Missouri. 4 Wallace, 329.) *Ex parte* Garland, 4 Wallace, 380. Such
laws are forbidden both to Congress and the States. Id. 386.

In the opinion by Mr. Justice Miller, expressing the dissent of What was
Chief-Justice Chase, Justices Davis, Swayne, and himself, he the dissent?
defines " ATTAINDER," in the language of Sir Thomas Tomlins, as
"the stain or corruption of blood of a criminal capitally condemned ; the immediate and inseparable consequence of the common law, on the pronouncing the sentence of death." *Ex parte*
Garland, 4 Wallace, 387.

Bills or acts of attainder were laws which declared certain persons
attainted, and their blood corrupted, so that it had lost all heritable
quality. *Ex parte* Garland, 4 Wall. 387.

The power to pass attainders is forbidden in this section to Con- Is the power
gress, in section nine to the States, and in section three of article forbidden to
III., it is declared that no attainder of treason shall work corrup- States?
tion of blood or forfeiture, except during the life of the person    150.
attainted. *Ex parte* Garland, 4 Wallace, 387, 388.

Attainders were convictions and sentences pronounced by the Define at-
legislative department, instead of the judicial; the sentence pro- tainders at
nounced and the punishment inflicted were determined by no common
previous law or fixed rule; the investigation into the guilt of the law?
accused, if any were made, was not necessarily or generally conducted in his presence, or that of the counsel, and no recognized
rule of evidence governed the inquiry. (Story's Const. § 1344.)
*Ex parte* Garland, 4 Wallace, 389. (A bill of attainder may affect
the life of an individual, or may confiscate his property, or both.
Fletcher v. Peck, 6 Cr. 138; 1 Kent's Com. Lect. 19. p. 382.)

The act of Congress and the Constitution of Missouri, requiring    18.
expurgatory oaths, do not come within the definitions, and are    143.
not bills of attainder. *Ex parte* Garland, 4 Wallace, 388.

They designate no criminal, either by name or description, declare no guilt, pronounce no sentence and inflict no punishment,
and can, in no sense, be bills of attainder. Justice Miller in *ex
parte* Garland, 4 Wallace, 390. See 2 Woodeson's Lectures, 622–
624.

**143.** *Ex post facto* laws are such as create or aggravate crime, Define *ex
or increase the punishment, or change the rules of evidence for the post facto?
purpose of conviction. Calder v. Bull, 3 Dall. 390; Cummings v.

Missouri, 4 Wallace, 326; Shepherd v. People, 25 N. Y. 406. The phrase only applies to penal and criminal laws, which inflict for-
**158.** feitures or punishment, and not to civil proceedings which affect private rights retrospectively. Watson v. Mercer, 8 Pet. 110; Carpenter v. Pennsylvania, 17 How. 463; Fletcher v. Peck, 6 Cr. 138; Society for the Propagation of the Gospel v. Wheeler, 2 Gall. 138; United States v. Hall, 2 Wash. C. C. 366; Commonwealth v. Lewis, 6 Binn. 271; Locke v. New Orleans, 4 Wallace, 173. There is nothing in the Constitution which forbids Congress to pass laws violating the obligation of contracts, though such a power is denied to the States. Evans v. Eaton, Pet. C. C. 323; Mayer v. Knight, 27 Tex. 719; Paschal's Annotated Digest, note 220, p. 91, and note 157, p. 42.

An *ex post facto* law renders an act punishable in a manner it was not punishable when committed. (Fletcher v. Peck, 6 Cranch, 138.)
Give an Cummings v. Missouri, 4 Wallace, 326. An act repealing a law on
example? which a grant rests and annulling the title, is, in effect, an *ex post*
**18.** *facto* law. Idem. The Constitution of Missouri, which disqualified
**122.** all persons who had aided in the rebellion or sympathized with the rebels, unless they took an expurgatory oath, was in effect an *ex post facto* law. Cummings v. Missouri, 4 Wallace, 327.

Some of the things enumerated in the oath were not offenses when committed; and therefore are within the definition of an *ex post facto* law. "They impose a punishment for an act not punishable at the time it was committed." Id. So the clauses which imposed a further penalty was *ex post facto*, because "they impose additional punishment to that prescribed when the act was committed." (Fletcher v. Peck, 6 Cranch, 138.) Cummings v. Missouri, 4 Wallace, 328. (For the Missouri oath, see Constitution of Missouri, Article II., 1 New York Convention Manual, p. 348.)

This provision to secure the liberty of the citizen, cannot be evaded by the form in which the power of the State is exerted. Id.
To what In the cases of Cummings and Garland, Mr. Justice Miller de-
class of cases livered the dissentient opinion for Chief-Justice Chase, Justices
does *ex post* Davis, Swayne, and himself. He held that all the cases agree, that
*facto* only the term *ex post facto* is to be applied to criminal and penal cases
apply? alone, and not to civil proceedings. (Watson v. Mercer, 8 Pet. 88;
**159.** Calder v. Bull, 3 Dall. 386; Fletcher v. Peck, 6 Cr. 87; Ogden v. Saunders, 12 Wheat. 266; Satterlee v. Matthewson, 2 Pet. 380.) *Ex parte* Garland, 4 Wallace, 390, 391.
**238.** They make acts done before the passage of the law, and which were innocent when done, criminal, and punish such actions; or change the punishment and inflict greater punishment than the law annexes to the crime when committed; or they alter the rules of evidence and receive less or different testimony than the law required at the time of the commission of the offense. (Calder v. Bull, 3 Dall. 386.) *Ex parte* Garland, 4 Wall. 391; Cummings v. Missouri, 4 Wall. 325, 326; Shepherd v. People, 25 N. Y. (11 Smith) 406.
**158.** The true distinction, is between *ex post facto* laws and retrospective laws. (Calder v. Bull.) *Ex parte* Garland, 4 Wallace, 391.

The minority held that the test oath to attorneys in the act of

Congress, and the expurgatory oath in the Constitution of Missouri are not within the definition of an *ex post facto* law.  Id.

And for further learning on the subject, see Carpenter v. Pennsylvania, 17 How. 456; Baugher v. Nelson, 9 Gill. 299; The Federalist, Nos. 44, 49; Journal of Convention, Supp. 431; 2 Am. Museum, 556; 2 Elliot's Debates, 343–354; Ogden v. Saunders, 12 Wheat. 266, 303, 329, 330, 335; 1 Kent's Com. Lect. 19, pp. 381, 382.

[4.] No capitation, or other direct tax, shall be laid, unless in proportion to the *census* or enumeration hereinbefore directed to be taken.

*What is the inhibition as to direct taxes?*

**144.** "CAPITATION," [Lat. caput, the head] or, as they are more commonly called, poll-taxes, that is taxes upon the polls, heads, or persons, of the contributors, are direct taxes.  (See Smith's Wealth of Nations, B. 5, ch. 2, art. 4; The Federalist, No. 36; 2 Elliot's Debates, 209.) Story's Const. § 954; Hylton v. United States 3 Dall. 171; Loughborough v. Blake, 5 Wh. 320–1.  This section, compared with the 8th and 9th, and the 2d section of the 1st art.  Hylton v. United States, 1 Cond. 84.  A tax on carriages, expenses, or income is not a direct tax.  Id.

*Define capitation?*

*22, 51, 85.*

Taxes on lands, houses, &c., are direct taxes.  (1 Tucker's Black. Com. App. 232, 233; Hylton v. United States, 3 Dall, 171; The Federalist, No. 21; Loughborough v. Blake, 5 Wheat. 317–325.) Story's Const. § 954.  The poll-tax was to be considered direct on account of the slaves.  Id.

In a general sense, all contributions imposed by the government upon individuals for the service of the State, are called taxes, by whatever name they may be known, whether by the name of tribute, tithe, tailage, impost, duty, gabel, custom, subsidy, aid, supply, excise, or other name.  They are divided into direct and indirect taxes.  Under the former are included taxes on land, or other real property; under the latter, taxes on articles of consumption.  (Federalist, Nos. 21, 36; Smith's Wealth of Nations; B. 5, ch. 2, Pt. 2, Arts. 1 and 2 and App.; Loughborough v. Blake, 5 Wheat. 317–319.) Story's Const. § 950.

*What are all contributions imposed by government called?*

*72, 77.*

If South Carolina considers the revenue laws unconstitutional, and has a right to prevent their execution in the port of Charleston, there would be a clear constitutional objection to their collection in every port, and no revenue could be collected anywhere; for all imposts must be equal.  President Jackson's Proclamation, 10th December, 1832: Story's Const. § 1053a, note 1.  It will also be found in Benton's Thirty Years in the Senate.  No document has ever more strongly stated the principles upon which the government suppressed the rebellion.

*What was the view of nullification?*

For an exhaustive treatise on "TAXES," see Story's Const. 3 ed. book 3, ch. IV.

Direct taxes must be by the rule of apportionment.  The License Cases, 5 Wall. 471.

*22, 51.*

**Define census?**

**145.** "CENSUS."—Lat. in the Roman law. A numbering or enrollment of the people, with a valuation of their fortunes (*personarum et bonorum descriptio*). (Brissonius.) The right of being enrolled in the census books. (Butler's Corpus Jur. 27.) [Law Lat.] In old European law, a tax or tribute (*tributum*); a toll (*Esprit des lois*, liv. 30, c. 14). Burrill's Law Dic., CENSUS.

**21, 22.**

In this clause it doubtless has reference to Article 1, clause 3, which declares that "Representatives and direct taxes shall be apportioned among the several States which may be included in the Union according to their respective *numbers*," the basis of which, as has been seen, was to number every soul, but to exclude two-fifths of the slaves from the ratio of representation. But since the destruction of slavery, all the "*numbers*" found by the future

**24.**
**275, 285.**

censuses must be counted, unless the new basis proposed by the fourteenth amendment shall have been adopted. This has naturally been one of the great points of controversy upon the reconstruction question. It is a legitimate fruit of the revolution.

**How many census reports?**

To the philosophical statesman there has been nothing in the execution of the Constitution so valuable as the Census Reports and the Compendiums thereof, running through eight decades. The information and the classification have improved every year, until the present able head of the bureau has almost reduced the tables to perfection. Nothing is hazarded in saying that, had these reports been carefully studied, the Union never would have encountered its severe struggle.

**What are the inhibitions as to commerce?**

[5.] No tax or duty shall be laid on articles exported from any State. [6.] No preference shall be given by any regulation of commerce or revenue to the ports of

**144.**
**61.**

one State over those of another; nor shall vessels bound to, or from, one State, be obliged to enter, clear, or pay duties in another.

**Can there be any duty on exports?**

**146.** "No TAX OR DUTY."—The power is thus wholly taken away to interfere with the subject of exports. Story's Const. § 1014; Sergeant's Const. ch. 28, p. 346; Rawle's Const. ch. 10, p. 115, 116; United States v. Brig William. 2 Hall's Law Jour. 255, 259, 260. The subject was well considered in the Convention. Journals of Convention, 222, 275, 301, 318, 377; 2 Curtis's Hist. Const. 290, 304.

The clause was stricken out of the Constitution of the Confederate States. This clause read: "No preference shall be given by any regulation of commerce to the ports of one State over those of another."

And very heavy export duties were levied upon cotton, first by military orders, and afterward by statute. Paschal's Annotated Digest, p. 90, § 7.

The omission in regard to vessels was to correspond with their amendment in regard to commerce.

**147.** "No PREFERENCE."—[Lat. *prefero*, the act of preferring.]

—This means, that "all duties, imports and excises, shall be uniform <sup></sup>What means preference? throughout the United States." See Story's Const. § 1016–1031, 81. 3d edition and notes; Journals of the Convention, 227, 303, 304; Federalist, No. 44.

An "IMPOST," or duty on imports, is a custom or tax levied on articles brought into a country. "IMPORTS," are the articles themselves which are brought into the country. "A DUTY ON IMPORTS" is not merely a duty on the act of importation, but it is a duty on the thing imported. (Brown v. Maryland, 12 Wheat. 449.) Story's Const. § 1013–1031, 1072a–1072i, note 3.

*Define impost? Import? 75–77.*

The power of the State inspection laws is retained, subject to the revision and control of Congress. (Gibbons v. Ogden, 9 Wheat. 203–206, 210, 235, 236, 311; Brown v. Maryland, 12 Wheat. 419, 438, 439, 440.) Story's Const. § 1016, 1017; Curtis's Hist. Const. 189, 281, 282, 285, 290–297.

*Where is the power of inspection?*

Inspection laws form a portion of the immense mass of legislation, which embraces every thing in the territory of a State not surrendered to the general government. Inspection laws, quarantine laws, and health laws, as well as laws for regulating the internal commerce of a State, and others, which respect roads, fences, &c., are component parts of State legislation, resulting from the residuary powers of State sovereignty. No direct power over these is given to Congress, and, consequently, they remain subject to State legislation, though they may be controlled by Congress when they interfere with their acknowledged powers. (See the authorities above cited; Federalist, Nos. 7, 22; Gibbons v. Ogden, 9 Wheat. 199–201.)

*77–81.*

*269.*

**148.** "VESSELS BOUND."—This clause has reference to the coasting trade, and the intercommunication by lakes, bays, rivers, and creeks—a trade, the tonnage of which exceeds all our foreign tonnage by over a thousand *per cent.* The vastness of this commerce and its total exemption from taxation, show the immense value of the Union.

*Define vessels bound?*

A State law requiring the payment of pilotage fees, does not infringe this clause. Cooley v. Board of Wardens, 12 How. 314–15; Pennsylvania v. Wheeling & Belmont Bridge Co. 18 Id. 421.

[7.] No money shall be drawn from the treasury, but in consequence of appropriations made by law; and a regular statement and account of the receipts and expenditures of all public money, shall be published from time to time.

*What are the restrictions over the treasury?*

**149.** "NO MONEY," &c.—The definition of money here, is sufficiently comprehensive to embrace every kind of currency received and expended by the government.

*What means money here? 82–84, 98, 99.*

The Confederate States Constitution contained this further restriction: "Congress shall appropriate no money from the Treasury, except by a vote of two-thirds of both houses, taken by yeas and nays, unless it be asked and estimated for by some one of the heads of departments, and submitted to Congress by the President;

*How did the Confederate States Constitution vary?*

•

or for the purpose of paying its own expenses and contingencies; or for the payment of claims against the Confederate States, the justice of which shall have been judicially declared by a tribunal for the investigation of claims against the government, which it is hereby made the duty of Congress to establish." Paschal's Annotated Digest, pp. 90, 91. As it was contemplated that the cabinet officers should have seats upon the floor, with the privilege of discussion; and as "the President may approve any appropriation, and disapprove any other appropriation in the same bill," this was certainly a great increase of executive power. A bill not estimated for had to receive a two-thirds vote, then encounter opposition by the head of department on the floor; and finally pass by a two-thirds vote over the President's veto. Paschal's Annotated Digest, pp. 87, 88, Art. I., § 6, 7, Clauses, 2, 2.

A court of claims was created by the act of 24th Feb., 1855; but the final power to allow or disallow the judgment of the court, still remains. 9 St. 612; 1 Brightly's Digest, 198.

**What is the creditor's remedy?** Whether the public moneys at the disposal of the postmaster-general, are technically in the treasury or not, the spirit of this provision applies to them, and ought to be faithfully observed in their expenditure. 3 Opin. 13. No other remedy exists for a creditor to the government. than an application to Congress for payment; he cannot have a lien on the public property in his possession or custody. United States v. Barney, 3 Hall's L. J. 130; 2 Wh. Cr. Cas. 513.

The reports of the receipts and expenditures are made to Congress annually, by the Secretary of the Treasury; and they form an important part of the executive documents of the nation.

**What are the inhibitions as to nobility and presents?** [8.] No title of nobility shall be granted by the United States; and no person holding any office of profit or trust under them, shall, without the consent of the Congress, accept of any present, emolument, office, or title of any kind whatever, from any king, prince, or foreign state.

**Define nobility?** **150.** "No Title of Nobility."—[Lat. *Nobilitas.*]—Being noble, whether by antiquity of family, or letters patent by the sovereign. Worcester's Dic., Nobility.—Here, the collective body of titled and privileged persons in a State; the aristocratic and patrician class; the peerage; as the English *nobility*, the French, German, Russian nobility. Webster's Dic., Nobility; 1 Black. Com. 156–157.

Perfect equality is the basis of all our institutions. Story's Const. § 1351. A privileged order would certainly destroy our republican form of government. (See sec. X). The same restriction is upon the States. Id.

**Define office?** **151.** "No Person holding any Office."—Office. [Lat. *Officium*, or *opificium*; from *opus*, work, and *facio*, to do.] Here a public charge or employment. Worcester's Dic., Office.—Thus a marshal of the United States, cannot at the same time, hold the office of commercial agent of France.   6 Op. 409.

As to the object, see the Federalist (No. 84; 1 Tuck. Black) Com. App. 295–296; Rawle on the Const. ch. 10, p. 120 ; Story's Const. § 1352. An amendment was proposed in 1803, extending the prohibition to all private citizens.   But it has never yet been ratified.   Story's Const. § 1352.

SEC. X. [1.]   No State shall enter into any treaty, alliance, or confederation; grant letters of marque and reprisal; coin money; emit bills of credit; make any thing but gold and silver coin a tender in payment of debts; pass any bill of attainder, *ex post facto* law, or law impairing the obligation of contracts, or grant any title of nobility.

*What are the unqualified inhibitions upon the State?*

**152.** REMARK.—It will be observed that to Congress is either given or denied all the powers herein inhibited to the States except " to make any thing but gold and silver coin a legal tender," "emit bills of credit," or "pass any law impairing the obligation of contracts." Thus to the President, by and with the advice of the Senate, is given the right to enter into treaties, alliances, or confederations. To Congress is given the right to coin money and grant letters of marque and reprisal; and from Congress is denied the power to create a title of nobility or pass *ex post facto* laws. About the power of Congress to emit bills of credit, make tenders in payment of debts, or to pass laws impairing the obligation of contracts, the Constitution is silent. Neither of these powers is reserved to the States under the tenth amendment; for they are expressly prohibited. Those who deny them to Congress do so upon the ground, that because they are denied to the States and not granted to Congress, they do not exist in either government. But on the other hand, it is answered, that the right to borrow money on the credit of the United States carries the right to emit bills of credit and to make them lawful tenders; and, as *ex post facto* laws relate to crimes, the power to pass bankrupt laws carries along the power to impair the obligation of contracts by the Federal Government. The whole ground is narrow; and hence we have to be controlled by the precedents of the past and what is necessary and proper. None deny the concurrent power of Congress to make gold and silver coin a tender in payment of debts. But the argument is that it can make nothing else a lawful tender.

*Which of these powers are given or denied to the United States?*
*178.*
*97, 98.*
*99, 173.*
*150.*
*158.*
*269.*
*78, 82.*
*143, 156.*
*94–96.*

**153.** To ENTER INTO ANY TREATY, &c., TO "COIN MONEY."— These powers being national cannot exist in the States. Federalist, No. 44; Rawle's Const. ch. 10, p. 136. They belonged to the Confederation, *ante*, p. 11, Art. 6. The same remark is true as to letters of marque and reprisal and coining money. Story's Const. § 1354–1357.

*Why are national powers denied?*
*178, 195.*

**154.** EMIT BILLS OF CREDIT.—To constitute a bill of credit within the Constitution, it must be issued by a State, involve the

*Define a bill of credit?*

7*

**83.**
faith of the State, and be designed to circulate as money, on the credit of the State, in the ordinary uses of business. Briscoe v. Bank of Kentucky, 11 Pet. 257, 311; Woodruff v. Trapnall, 10 How. 204. As to what are such bills of credit, see Craig v. Missouri, 4 Pet. 410, 434–448; same case, 8 Pet. 40; Woodruff v. Trapnall, 10 How. 205; McFarland v. The Bank of Arkansas, 4 Ark. 410; Darrington v. State Bank of Alabama, 13 How. 12; Curran v. Arkansas, 15 How. 317–18. The loan certificates of Missouri were bills of credit, and formed no valid consideration for a contract. Mankster v. The State, 1 Mo. 321; Lopez v. The State, 1 Mo. 451; Craig v. Missouri, 4 Pet. 410, 435. And see State of Indiana v. Warm, 6 Hill, 33; Delafield v. State of Illinois, 26 Wend., 192; Sturges v. Crowinshield, 4 Wheat. 204–205; Madison's Letter to C. J. Ingersol, 2d Feb. 1811. Story's Const. § 1358–1373.

Bills of credit in the colonies were understood to apply to all paper money, whether funds were provided for their repayment or not. (See 2 Hutch. Hist. 208, 381.) Story's Const. § 1368. This author and the cases cited exhaust the whole learning upon the subject.

"Emit bills of credit," was omitted in the Constitution of the Confederate States. The result was that many of the States issued large amounts of bills intended to circulate as money. Paschal's Annotated Digest, p. 91, Arts. 806–811.

**Where does the power as to legal tenders reside?**

**269.**

**53, 97, 98.**
**155.** "MAKE ANY THING BUT GOLD AND SILVER COIN A TENDER IN PAYMENT OF DEBTS."—The things in this article, not also prohibited to Congress, are allowed to be exercised by it, if the power come within the purview of either of the express or implied powers granted. Metropolitan Bank v. Van Dyck, 27 N. Y. Rep. 418, 423, 442.

"The interpretation which I give to this clause is, that the United States possess power to make any thing besides gold and silver a legal tender. * * They have a right to make bank paper a legal tender. Much more then, have they the power of causing it to be received by themselves in payment of taxes." (4 Elliot's Debates, 367, 368; Mr. Alston of South Carolina.) Metropolitan Bank v Van Dyck, 27 N. Y. R. 418; The Pennsylvania Cases, 52 Penn. St. R. (2 Smith) 1–100.

**What may be a legal tender?**
There is no express delegation of power to Congress to legislate on the subject of legal tenders, neither is there any prohibition in the Constitution, upon Congress forbidding such legislation, or declaring what shall or shall not make a legal tender; the omission was not accidental. Metropolitan Bank v. Van Dyck, 27 N. Y. 422.

It was the opinion of Mr. Madison, that Congress would have the power to declare bills or notes issued on the credit of the United States, a legal tender, unless prohibited by the Constitution. Metropolitan Bank v. Van Dyck, 27 N. Y. 419, 420, 422, 423, 426.

**83.**
The first legal tender act was in favor of foreign coin. (Act 1st July, 1793.) Metropolitan Bank v. Van Dyck, 27 N Y. 424, where are cited all the acts on the subject.

A contract dated 16th December, 1851, payable "in gold or silver coin, lawful money of the United States," may be paid in United States legal tender notes, as lawful money of the United States. Rodes v. Bronson, 34 N. Y. R. 649. When the contract matured, it was payable in the only lawful money of the country. The power §3, 97–99. of Congress to declare treasury notes legal tenders for debts contracted previously to its passage, as well as those contracted subsequently, has been affirmed by this court. (Metropolitan Bank v. Van Dyck, 34 N. Y. R. 654.)   Rodes v. Bronson, 34 N. Y. 654.

A law of Congress to change the currency in which a contract Does a law may be discharged, does not impair the obligation of the contract. of Congress (Faw v. Marsteller, 2 Cr. 20; Dowmans v. Dowmans, 1 Wash. the currency Virg. 26; Pong v. Lindsay, Dyer, 82; Barrington v. Potter, Dyer, impair the 81 B. fol. 67; United States v. Robertson, 6 Pet. 644; Conkey v. contracts? Hart, 4 Kern. 22; Mason v. Haile, 12 Wh. 370.)  Metropolitan Bank v. Van Dyck, 27 N. Y. Rep. 455–8.

The above authorities also settle, that if a contract be made payable in a particular currency, and that currency ceases to exist before it is due, it must be discharged in the lawful currency at the date of maturity. See, particularly, Faw v. Marsteller, 2 Cr. 20, and Metropolitan Bank v. Van Dyck, 27 N. Y. Rep.

A law will not be held to be unconstitutional, unless it is clearly When will a and plainly so. (Morris v. The People, 3 Den. 381; *Ex parte* law be held McCollom, 1 Cow. 564; Fletcher v. Peck, 6 Cr. 87; Ogden v. San- to be uncon- ders, 12 Wh. 29; Adams v. Howe, 14 Mass. 345.)  Metropolitan stitutional? Bank v. Van Dyck, 27 N. Y. Rep. 460.

**156.** "PASS ANY BILL OF ATTAINDER OR EX POST FACTO LAW." Define *ex* —These terms relate to criminal law only; but as the words "*ex* *post facto* *post facto* law, or law impairing the obligation of contracts," are law? only separated by a comma, many of the judges treat the words in 142–143. this connection as synonymous; and thus seem to make *ex post facto* apply to contracts.

The critical reader is referred to the phrase in Burrill's law dictionary, for the civil law origin of the term, wherein will be found its exact application. *Quæ ab initio inutilis fuit institutio, ex post facto non convalescere non potest.*  Translated: An institution or act which was of no effect at the beginning (when made or done), cannot acquire force or validity from after matter. *Nunquam crescit ex post facto præteriti delicti æstimatio.* The estimate of the character of a past offense is never enhanced by after matter. See 1 Kent's Com. 409. Here follows an instance where it is used in reference to contracts.

*Ex post facto,* literally construed, operating upon a previous fact, yet the restricted sense stated, is the one in which it has always been held. It was the sense in which it was understood at the time the Constitution was adopted, both in this country and in England. (1 Blackstone's Com. 46; Calder v. Bull, 3 Dallas, 390.)  Locke v. New Orleans, 4 Wallace, 173, 174.

**157.** THE OBLIGATION OF THE CONTRACT.—The laws which What laws exist at the time and place of the making of the contract, enter enter into into and form a part of it; and they embrace alike those which the obliga- affect its validity, construction, discharge and enforcement. contract?

**155-159.** (Green v. Biddle, 8 Wheat. 92; Bronson v. Kinzie. 1 How. 319; McCracken v. Hayward, 2 How. 612; People v. Bond, 10 California, 570; Ogden v. Sanders, 12 Wheat. 231.) Von Hoffman v. City of Quincy, 4 Wallace, 550. (This principle has been denied. Farnsworth v. Vance, 2 Coldwell (Tenn.) Rep. 111.)

**160-161.** As, if the acts so change the remedies as materially to impair the rights and interests of the owner, they are just as much a violation of the compact as if they overturned his rights and interests. (Green v. Biddle, 8 Wheat. 92.) Von Hoffman v. City of Quincy, 4 Wallace, 551. Or the Illinois two-thirds twelve months stay law. (1 Howard, 297.) Id. Or the State bankrupt insolvent laws, as to anterior contracts. Sturges v. Crowinshield, 4 Wheat. 122.) Id. But not as to subsequent contracts. Ogden v. Sanders, 1 Wheat. 213.) Id.

**How are the validity and remedy connected?**

**155.** The ideas of validity and remedy are inseparable, and both are parts of the obligation, which is guarantied by the Constitution against invasion. The obligation of the contract "is the law which binds the parties to perform their agreement." (Sturges v. Crowninshield, 12 Wheat. 257.) Von Hoffman v. City of Quincy, 4 Wallace, 552; Story v. Furnam, 25 N. Y. (11 Smith), 223. Where the State incorporated a bank, with no other stockholder than the State, which issued bills, for which all the bank assets were legally bound (and which provided that the issues were receivable for all public dues), laws which withdrew the funds from the bank, and appropriated them to various other purposes than paying the notes of the bank, impaired the obligation of the contract, and were unconstitutional. (Bronson v. Kinzie, 1 How. 311; McCracken v. Hayward, 2 How. 608.) Curran v. The State of Arkansas, 15 How. 310. The guaranty that the bills were receivable for all public dues, was a contract with the bill-holders; and to repeal the guaranty, impaired the contract as to bills then in circulation. Woodruff v. Trapnall, 10 How. 205; affirmed.

**What of the repeal of bank charters?**

**157.** Hawthorn v. Caleff, 2 Wall. 23. A law repealing a bank charter, does not impair the obligation of a contract, because the property *bona fide* held, is still a fund for the creditors. (Muma v. The Potomac Co. 8 Pet. 281.) Curran v. Arkansas, 15 How. 310, 331; This seems not to be so, as to creditors, where the corporators are liable personally for the issues. Corning v. McCulloch, 1 Comst. 47, 49; Conaut v. Van Schaick. 24 Barb. 87; Bronson v. Kinzie, 1 How. 311; Hawthorne v. Caleff, Id. 311. The legislature may repeal the guaranty that the bills shall be received for all public dues; but the repeal only operates upon future issues, the guaranty remaining as to those outstanding. Woodruff v. Trapnall, 10 How. 206.

**What is the doctrine of bridges?** A bridge charter, which declared that no other bridge should be built within the designated limits, is a contract, within the meaning of the Constitution. Bridge Proprietors v. Hoboken Co. 1 Wall. 146-7. But a railroad bridge is not a bridge, within the meaning of a statute of New Jersey of 1790. Bridge Proprietors v. Hoboken Co. 1 Wall. 147. A railroad bridge does not necessarily impair the right of an ordinary toll-bridge. (Mohawk Bridge Co. v. Utica & S. R. R. Co. 6 Paige, 564; Thompson v.

New York & Harlem R. R. Co. 3 Sandf. 625; McRae v. Wilmington Raleigh R. R. Co. 17 Conn. 56; Enfield Toll-bridge v. The Hartford & New Haven R. R. Co. 17 Conn. 56;) Bridge Proprietors v. Hoboken, 1 Wall. 150–1. As to what a ferry privilege is, see Conway v. Taylor, 1 Black. 603; Hartford Bridge Co. v. Union Ferry Co. 29 Conn. 210. It may be granted by Kentucky without the concurrent assent of Ohio. Id. (Cites Trustees of Newport v. Taylor, 6 J. J. Marsh, 134.)

A contract is an agreement to do or not to do a particular thing. (Sturges v. Crowinshield, 4 Wheat. 197; Green v. Biddle, 8 Wheat. 92; Ogden v. Saunders, 12 Wheat. 256, 297, 302, 316, 335; Gordon v. Prince, 3 Wash. C. C. Rep. 319.) Story's Const. § 1376. *Define a contract? 160.*

This provision has never been understood to embrace other contracts than those which respect property, or some object of value, and confer rights which may be asserted in a court of justice. Dartmouth College v. Woodward, 4 Wh. 629. A private charter is such a contract. Id. 518. So also an act incorporating a banking institution. Providence Bank v. Billings, 4 Pet. 514; Gordon v. Appeal Tax Court, 3 How. 133; Planter's Bank v. Sharp, 6 Id. 301; Curran v. Arkansas, 15 Id. 304. And a grant of land by the legislature of a State. Fletcher v. Peck, 6 Cr. 87; Terrett v. Taylor, 9 Id. 43. And so is a compact between two States. Green v. Biddle, 8 Wh. 1; Allen v. McKean, 1 Sumn. 276. And see 2 Pars. on Cont. 509. An appointment to a salaried office, however, is not a contract, within the meaning of the Constitution. Butler v. Pennsylvania, 10 How. 402; Commonwealth v. Mann, 5 W. & S. 418; Commonwealth v. Bacon, 6 S. & R. 322; Barker v. Pittsburgh, 4 Barr, 49; Jones v. Shaw, 15 Tex. 577. All contracts are subject to the right of eminent domain existing in the several States; and the exercise of this power does not conflict with the Constitution. West River Bridge Co. v. Dix, 6 How. 507; Rundle v. Delaware & Raritan Canal Co., 14 Id. 80; The State v. De Lesdernier, 7 Tex. 99. *To what contracts only does the inhibition apply?*

It is a compact between two or more persons. (Fletcher v. Peck, 6 Cranch, 136; s. c. 2 Pet. Cond. 321.) Story's Const. § 1376. *160.*

A law of a State, issuing transferable swamp land-scrip, and exempting the land from taxation, for ten years or until reclaimed, constituted a contract, between the State and the holders of the land-scrip, issued under the act. McGee v. Mathis, 4 Wallace, 155.

An act of incorporation is a contract between the State and the stockholders. All courts, at this day, are estopped from questioning the doctrine. (Dartmouth College v. Woodward, 4 Wheat. 418.) The Binghampton Bridge, 3 Wallace, 72. *Is an act of incorporation a contract?*

Such contracts are construed liberally by the government. The Binghampton Bridge, 3 Wallace, 74. Nothing is to be taken by intendment against the State. The Binghampton Bridge, 3 Wallace, 75; The Charles River Bridge, 11 Peters, 544; Jefferson Br. Bank v. Skelley, 1 Black. 446. But the State may grant franchises by reference to another statute on the same subject-matter.

Id. After the grant of such franchises, the restraint is upon the legislature itself. Id.

The Supreme Court of the United States will determine for itself, irrespective of the State decisions, what is the contract of a State, Jefferson Branch Bank v. Skelley, 1 Black (U. S.), 442, 443.

**What contracts are included?**

**155.**

It includes executory as well as executed contracts. (Fletcher v. Peck, 6 Cranch, 137; s. c. 2 Pet. Cond. R. 321, 322.) Story's Const. § 1376. Whoever may be the parties to them. (Fletcher v. Peck, 6 Cranch, 87.) Von Hoffman v. City of Quincy, 4 Wallace, 549.

Because the State is not a single sovereign, but a part of the Union, whose Constitution is supreme and imposes limits upon the legislatures of the several States. (New Jersey v. Wilson, 7 Cranch. 164; Terret v. Taylor, 9 Cranch, 43.) Von Hoffman v. City of Quincy, 4 Wallace, 550.

Also express and implied contracts The grantor is estopped by both. (Fletcher v. Peck, 6 Cr. R. 137; s. c. 2 Cond. R. 321, 322; Dartmouth College v. Woodward, 4 Wheat. R. 657, 658, 688, 689.) 1 Story's Const. § 1377.

And assessments upon the stockholders of banks which have gone into liquidation. Commonwealth v. Cochituate Bank, 3 Allen, Mass. 42.

**What of retrospective laws?**

**571.**

**158. MERELY RETROSPECTIVE.**—Because a law is merely retrospective, does not bring it within the prohibition. Locke v. New Orleans, 4 Wallace, 173.

The Constitution does not prohibit the States from passing retrospective laws generally, but only *ex post facto* laws. Watson v. Mercer, 8 Pet. 110. Retrospective laws, divesting vested rights, are impolitic and unjust; but they are not *ex post facto* laws within the meaning of the Constitution, nor repugnant to its provisions (Albee v. May, 2 Payne, 74), unless they impair the obligation of a contract. Baltimore & Susquehanna R. R. Co. v. Nesbit, 10 How. 401. Should a statute declare, contrary to the general principles of law, that contracts founded upon an illegal or immoral consideration, whether in existence at the time of passing the statute, or which might hereafter be entered into, should nevertheless be valid and binding upon the parties, all would admit the retrospective character of the enactment; but it would not be repugnant to the Constitution of the United States. Satterlee v. Mathewson, 2 Pet. 412; Curran v. Arkansas, 15 How. 10; Aspinwall v. The Commissioners, &c., 22 How. 365; Dartmouth College v. Woodward, 4 Wh. 628. For the same inhibitions in the Constitution of Texas, see Paschal's Annotated Dig. 168, 170.

**155-155.**

The prohibition has no reference to the degree of impairment. The largest and least are alike forbidden. Sturges v. Crowinshield, 12 Wheat. 257; Green v. Biddle, 8 Wheat. 84; Von Hoffman v. City of Quincy, 4 Wall. 552; Planter's Bank v. Sharp, 6 How. 327; Farnsworth v. Reaves, 2 Coldwell, 111. Its value must not be diminished by legislation. (Planter's Bank v. Sharp, 6 How. 327.) Von Hoffman v. City of Quincy, 4 Wallace, 553.

That is directly, and not incidentally, and only by consequence. Von Hoffman v. City of Quincy, 4 Wall. 553.

The States may abolish imprisonment for debt. Beers v. Houghton, 9 Peters, 359; Mason v. Haile, 12 Peters, 373; Sturgis v. Crowninshield, 4 Peters, 200.) Von Hoffman v. City of Quincy, 4 Wallace, 553.

**159.** EXEMPTIONS.—And the States may exempt from forced sale the necessary implements of agriculture, the tools of a mechanic, and articles of necessity in household furniture—the things which in civilized communities belong to the remedy. Von Hoffman v. City of Quincy, 4 Wall. 553. The exact limit between right and remedy must be determined in every case upon its own circumstances. Id. If the right be impaired the law is void. (Bronson v. Kinzie, 1 Howard, 311; McCracken v. Hayward, 2 How. 608.) Von Hoffman v. City of Quincy, 4 Wallace, 554. The question between the remedy and the other parts of the contract cannot be considered *res integra*. (1 Kent's Com. 456; Sedg. on Stat. and Const. Law, 652; Mason v. Haile, 12 Wheat. 379.) Id. *(How do exemption laws impair contracts? 157-160)*

A State may disable itself by contract from exercising its taxing power in particular cases. (New Jersey v. Wilson, 7 Cranch, 166; Dodge v. Woolsey, 18 How. 331; Piqua Branch v. Knoop, 16 How. 331.) Von Hoffman v. City of Quincy, 4 Wallace, 554.

The legal obligation of a contract consists in the remedy given by law to enforce its performance, or to make compensation for the failure of performance. Johnson v. Higgens, 3 Metcf. (Ky.), 566. A law which forbade the rendering of judgments for a given time was constitutional. Id. So, where a State has authorized a municipal corporation to contract and tax, to meet its engagements, the power cannot be withdrawn until the contract is satisfied. (People v. Bell, 10 California, 570; Dominic v. Sayre, 3 Sand. 555.) Von Hoffman v. City of Quincy, 554. It is a trust which neither the State nor corporation can annul. Id. *(In what does the legal obligation consist? 157)*

**160.** STAY LAWS.—Statutes relating to levies on executions may be applicable to levies made before their enactment, as they affect the remedy and not the right. Grosvenor v. Chesley, 48 Maine, 369; Coriell v. Ham, 4 Greene (Iowa), 455; Swift v. Fletcher, 6 Minn. 550. *(How do stay laws impair contracts? 159)*

But redemption laws, as to judgments upon anterior contracts, are unconstitutional. Scobey v. Gibson, 17 Ind. 572; Iglehart v. Wolfin, 20 Ind. 32.

And the laws for the release and discharge of securities. Swift v. Fletcher, 6 Minn. 550.

So of laws allowing the debtor to remove without subjecting his property to sale, so far as concerns judgment liens accruing prior to their passage. Tillotson v. Millard, 7 Minn. 513.

The legislature cannot extend the time for redeeming lands sold at tax sales. Robinson v. House, 13 Wis. 341. Nor apply appraisement laws to anterior contracts. Rosier v. Hale, 10 Iowa (2 With.), 470.

The Supreme Court of the United States will determine for itself, irrespective of the decision of the State courts, what is a contract *(How will the S. C. construe?)*

By what will the S. C. of U. S. be governed in defining a contract? 155, 109.

within the meaning of the Constitution. Jefferson Branch Bank v. Skelley, 1 Black, 443. A law authorizing a redemption of property sold by forced sale, impairs the obligation of a contract, and is unconstitutional as to mortgages and contracts of anterior date to the redemption law. Bronson v. Kinzie, 1 How. 311; McCracken v. Hayward, 2 How. 612–615; Gantly v. Ewing, 3 How. 716–7; Howard v. Bugbee, 24 How. 464–5; Bunn v. Gorgus, 41 Penn. St. R. 441; Weaver v. Mailot, 15 La. 395; Billmeyer v. Evans, 40 Penn. St. R. 324. The legislature of a State has a right to bind the State by contract, so as to exempt persons, corporations, and things from taxation. The Richmond R. R. Co. v. The Louisa R. R. Co. 13 How. 71; Gordon v. The Appeal Tax Court, 3 How. 33; New Jersey v. Wilson, 7 Cr. 164; Jefferson Branch Bank v. Skelley, 1 Black, 447–8. But the intention to exempt must be clear. Id.; Gilman v. The City of Sheboygan, 2 Black, 513. And the *privilegia favorabilia* will be narrowly construed. Rector, &c. v. The County of Philadelphia, 24 How. 302.

Do laws which affect the remedy only impair?

**161.** LAWS WHICH AFFECT THE REMEDY ONLY.—Where there is no direct constitutional prohibition, a State may pass retrospective laws, such as in their operation may affect suits pending, and give to a party a remedy which he did not previously possess, or modify an existing remedy, or remove an impediment in the way of legal proceedings. (Hepburn v. Curts, 7 Watts, 300; Shenly v. Commonwealth, 36 Penn. State, 57; Foster v. Essex Bank, 16 Mass. 245; Rich v. Flanders, 39 N. H. 325.) Freeborn v. Smith, 2 Wall. 175. The legislature may pass private acts authorizing sales by administrators, in a different manner from the general statutes regulating the subject. (Mason v. Wait, 4 Scam. 134.) Florentine v. Barton, 2 Wall. 216–7. Judicial sales of lands to pay the debts of a decedent's estate, are in the nature of a proceeding *in rem*, and the purchaser need only look to the order of sale. The State court is presumed to have correctly settled every judicial question, including the constitutionality of the act of assembly. (Grignon v. Astor, 3 How. 319.) Florentine v. Barton, 2 Wall. 216. The inhibition against impairing the obligation of contracts is upon the States not the United States. (Evans v. Eaton, 1 Pet. C. C. Rep. 322; In the matter of Klein, 1 How. 277; Kunzler v. Kohaus, 5 Hill, 325.) Metropolitan Bank v. Van Dyck, 27 N. Y. 453.

The cases which draw the distinction between *ex post facto* laws; the laws impairing the obligation of contracts; retrospective laws, and laws which only affect the remedy, will be found fully collected in Paschal's Annotated Digest, notes 61, 157, 168, 410, 1107–1109. And for a very learned and exhaustive treatise upon the whole subject, see Story's Const. Book III. ch. XXXIV., § 1374–1400.

What of usurious contracts?

The States may pass laws validating contracts which were usurious and void when made. Welsh v. Wadsworth, 30 Conn. 149. But not to operate unreasonably and unjustly upon antecedent rights. Id. And may change the interest laws relieving from penalties. Wood v. Kennedy, 19 Ind. 68. And the laws of costs as to pending suits. Taylor v. Keeler, 30 Conn. 324. But not the compensation of rights already vested. State v. Auditor,

Costs?

3? Miss. 287. And providing for the validity of marriages. Goshen v. Richman, 4 Allen (Mass.), 458. And changing the presumptions in favor of tax sales. Hickor v. Tallman, 38 Barb. N. Y. 608. And curing irregularities in conveyances, as to the parties and subsequent purchasers; but not to disturb vested rights. Thompson v. Morgan, 6 Minn. 292.  *Evidence? Convey-ances?*

[2.] No State shall, without the consent of the Congress, lay any imposts or duties on imports or exports, except what may be absolutely necessary for executing its inspection laws; and the net produce of all duties and imposts, laid by any State on imports or exports, shall be for the use of the treasury of the United States; and all such laws shall be subject to the revision and control of the Congress. [3.] No State shall, without the consent of Congress, lay any duty of tonnage, keep troops or ships-of-war in time of peace, enter into any agreement or compact with another State, or with a foreign power, or engage in war, unless actually invaded, or in such imminent danger as will not admit of delay.  *What are the inhibitions upon the States without the consent of Congress?*

**162.** For the definitions of "imposts" and "duties" see 75-77. notes 75 to 77. For a history of this clause, see journals of the Convention, 222, 227, 275, 301, 303, 318, 377 and 378.

"AN IMPOST OR DUTY ON IMPORTS," is a custom or tax levied on articles brought into the country. Brown v. Maryland, 12 Wheat. 446, 447. Imports are things imported—the articles themselves which are brought into the country. It is not merely a duty on the act of importation, but it is a duty on the thing imported. It is not confined to a duty levied while the article is entering the country, but extends to a duty levied after it has entered the country. (Brown v. Maryland, 12 Wheat. 419, 446, 447.) Story's Const. § 1019; see Gibbons v. Ogden. 9 Wheat. 199–201. The power to impose duties on imports is exclusive in Congress. Pervear v. The Commonwealth, 5 Wall. 479. A charge on vessels by the State for the benefit of the master and warders of the port is unconstitutional. The Southern Steamship Company v. The Master, &c. 6 Wall.  *What is a duty on imports? 138. 274. 86–89.*

It was really intended to make the vast inter-state commerce as nearly free as possible. The ordinance of the city of Houston requiring wharfage duties of steamboats, does not infringe this provision of the Constitution. Sterrett v. Houston, 14 Tex. 166.

"EXCEPT WHAT MAY BE ABSOLUTELY NECESSARY."—This is the strongest qualification of "necessary" See McCulloch v. Maryland, 4 Wheat. 316; Kent's Com. 398–401; Story's Const. § 1033.  *Necessary?*

**Inspection?**    "INSPECTION."—The tax or duty of inspection, is frequently, if not always, paid while the article is in the bosom of the country. Brown v. Maryland, 12 Wheat. 420.

The exception was made because the **tax** would otherwise have been within the prohibition. Id.  See the subject discussed. Id. The State has no right to tax the goods imported, in the hands of the importer. Id.  This language means the same thing as the inhibition on the United States against laying a tax on articles exported from any State. Id. Story's Const. § 1030.  Upon the same principles, or their analogies, it was held that the State of Maryland had not the constitutional right to tax the branch of the United States bank located in Maryland.  McCulloch v. Maryland, 1 Wheat. 316; Kent's Com. 398, 401; Story's Const. § 1033–1053. The sale of liquors within a State is subject exclusively to State control.  (License cases, 5 Wall. 462.)  Pervear v. The Commonwealth, 5 Wall. 479.

**What is tonnage?**    **163.** "LAY ANY DUTY OF TONNAGE, &c."—This form of expression occurs nowhere else in the Constitution.  TONNAGE [*tonnagium*] is a custom or impost upon wines or other merchandise exported or imported, according to a certain rate per ton. (Spelman; Cowell.)  Burrill's Law Dic.: A duty or impost upon ships estimated per ton.  Webster's Dic., TONNAGE.

**Define troops?**    **164.** "KEEP TROOPS OR SHIPS-OF-WAR IN TIME OF PEACE."—This means organized troops, or armies, and a navy; because these are national powers.  See Articles of Confederation, *ante*, p. 12,
**122, 123.**    Art. VI.; Story's Const. § 1401–1409.  In certain emergencies, States may raise troops to repel invasions or suppress insurrections. Story's Const. § 1404.  Luther v. Borden, 7 How. 1.

**Define agreement or compact?**    "AGREEMENT OR COMPACT," properly applies to such as regarded what might be deemed mere private rights of sovereignty, such as boundaries, land, and other internal regulations for the mutual
**152.**    comfort and convenience of States bordering on each other.  Story's
**178.**    Const. § 1403.  These words are used in their broadest sense; they were intended to cut off all negotiation and intercourse between the
**223–225.**    State authorities and foreign nations.  Holmes v. Jennison, 14 Pet. 572, 574.  And, therefore, no State can, without the consent of Congress, enter into any agreement or compact, to deliver up fugitives from justice from a foreign State, who may be found within its limits.  Id.; 3 Opin. 661.  This prohibition is political in its character, and has no reference to a mere matter of contract, or to the grant of a franchise which in nowise conflicts with the powers delegated to the general government by the States.  Union Branch R. R. Co. v. East Tennessee & Georgia R. R. Co. 14 Ga. 327.  A compact entered into between two States, with the assent of Congress, is binding on those States and the citizens of each.  Fleeger v. Pool, 1 McLean, 185.  See Story's Const. § 1403; 1 Tucker's Black. Com. App. 301.

## ARTICLE II.

**Where is the executive power?**    SEC. I.—[1.] The executive power shall be vested in a President of the United States of America.  He shall hold his office during the term of four years, and

together with the Vice-President, chosen for the same *The term of office?*
term, be elected as follows.

**165.** THE EXECUTIVE POWER.—The object of this department is *What is the object?*
to insure the execution of the laws. 1 Kent's Com. 285. With
energy in the executive and safety to the people. Story's Const.
§ 1417. The ingredients for energy, are unity, duration, adequate
provisions for its support; and, for safety, a due dependence on
the people, and a due responsibility to the people. (Federalist, No.
70; 1 Kent's Com. Lect. 13, pp. 253, 254.) Story's Const. § 1418.

The powers of the President are not executive only. The veto *Define the executive power?*
power and the appointing power are not strictly executive powers;
no more so than when exercised by Congress or the States. Bates
on *Habeas Corpus*, 5th July, 1861. He is a civil magistrate, to *67, 199.*
whom all military officers are subordinate. Id. In calling out the
militia to see the laws faithfully executed, he acts as a civil
magistrate upon the same principle that a court calls out the
*posse.* Id. In times of great danger, when the very existence of
the nation is assailed, the President may order military arrests. Id.

We must not forget that this power of appointment to office is *179.*
essentially an executive function. It belongs essentially to the *174.*
executive department rather than to the legislative or judicial. If
no provision on the subject had been made by the Constitution, it
would have been held appurtenant to the President as the head of
the executive department specially charged with the execution of
the laws. Stanbery on the executive power. See Confederation,
*ante* Article VI. p. 14; 2 Elliot's Debates, 358; Federalist, Nos.
67, 70, 1 Kent's Com. 271–303; Journal of Convention, 68, 89,
96, 136, 211, 222, 324, 332, 333; 2 Pitk.'s Hist. 252; 2 Curtis'
Hist. of Const. ch. III., pp. 56–60; Story's Const. ch. XXXVI.,
§ 1440–1448, and voluminous notes of the 3d edition.

A proposition was made in the Convention for an executive
with a plurality of persons. Journal of Convention, 124. Mr.
Calhoun advocated a dual executive at a later day. See Calhoun's Essay on the Const.; Story's Const. § 1426–1429.

**166.** The following is the list of Presidents who have been *Who have been the presidents?*
chosen under this Constitution:—

| NAME. | NATIVITY. | RESIDENCE. | SERVICE. | |
|---|---|---|---|---|
| George Washington. | Virginia. | Virginia. | 4 March, 1789, | 4 March, 1793. |
| George Washington. | " | " | " " 1793, | " " 1797. |
| John Adams. | Massachusetts. | Massachusetts. | " " 1797, | " " 1801. |
| Thomas Jefferson. | Virginia. | Virginia. | " " 1801, | " " 1805. |
| Thomas Jefferson. | " | " | " " 1805, | " " 1809. |
| James Madison. | " | " | " " 1809, | " " 1813. |
| James Madison. | " | " | " " 1813, | " " 1817. |
| James Monroe. | " | " | " " 1817, | " " 1821. |
| James Monroe. | " | " | " " 1821, | " " 1825. |
| John Quincy Adams. | Massachusetts. | Massachusetts. | " " 1825, | " " 1829. |
| Andrew Jackson. | South Carolina. | Tennessee. | " " 1829, | " " 1833. |
| Andrew Jackson. | " | " | " " 1833, | " " 1837. |
| Martin Van Buren. | New York. | New York. | " " 1837, | " " 1841. |
| William H. Harrison. | Virginia. | Ohio. | " " 1841, | 4 April, 1841. |
| John Tyler. | " | Virginia. | 6 April, 1841, | 4 March, 1845. |
| James K. Polk. | North Carolina. | Tennessee. | 4 March, 1845, | " " 1849. |
| Zachary Taylor. | Virginia. | Louisiana. | " " 1849, | 9 July, 1850. |
| Millard Fillmore. | New York. | New York. | 10 July, 1850, | 4 March, 1853. |
| Franklin Pierce. | New Hampshire. | New Hampshire. | 4 March, 1853, | " " 1857. |
| James Buchanan. | Pennsylvania. | Pennsylvania. | " " 1857, | " " 1861. |
| Abraham Lincoln. | Kentucky. | Illinois. | " " 1861, | " " 1865. |
| Abraham Lincoln. | " | " | " " 1865, | 14 April, 1865. |
| Andrew Johnson. | North Carolina. | Tennessee. | 15 April, 1865, | |

*When and how long?*

How are
electors
appointed?

[2.] Each State shall appoint, in such manner as the legislature thereof may direct, a number of electors equal to the whole number of senators and representatives to which the State may be entitled in the Congress; but no senator or representative, or person holding an office of trust or profit under the United States, shall be appointed an elector.

Disqualifi-
cations?

Define
electors?

**167.** "ELECTORS," as here used, mean the persons chosen to cast the votes in the first instance for President and Vice-President. All the legislatures have, long since, directed that they shall be "*appointed*," that is, chosen by the people, except South Carolina, which appointed by the legislature. See Story's Const. § 1472; 3 Elliot's Debates, 100, 101.

16-17.

Thus the "electors" for members of Congress, indirectly choose the "electors" for President, Vice-President, and Senators.

But the House of Representatives in one contingency, and the Senate in another, may choose the President. Therefore, however chosen, it results that the President is, indirectly, chosen by the same electors who choose the popular branch of the State legislature.

How many
electors?
23.

Necessary
to a choice?

As there are now thirty-seven States, the senators represent 74 electoral votes; add to these 243 representatives, and the electoral vote of 1868 will be 317; necessary to a choice 159. That is if no new State be added by the second session of the fortieth Congress; and if all the non-reconstructed States be allowed to vote. The number of electoral votes to which Virginia, North and South Carolina, Georgia, Florida, Alabama, Mississippi, Louisiana, Arkansas and Texas, would be entitled, under the apportionment are 70.

46.
175-185.

The question as to whether these States shall vote, and *who* shall choose the electors, is now one of the exciting issues of the day. See Story's Const. § 1454–1488.

The attempted independence of the electors has failed. Story's Const. § 1463; Rawle's Const. ch. 5, p. 58.

## [ARTICLE XII.—AMENDMENT.]

How is the
President
elected?

167.

[**1**]. The electors shall meet in their respective States, and vote by ballot for President and Vice-President, one of whom, at least, shall not be an inhabitant of the same State with themselves; they shall name in their ballots the person voted for as President, and in distinct ballots the person voted for as Vice-President;

How are the
votes certi-
fied?

and they shall make distinct lists of all persons voted for as President, and of all persons voted for as Vice-President, and the number of votes for each, which

list they shall sign and certify, and transmit sealed to
the seat of the government of the United States,
directed to the President of the Senate; the President of the Senate shall, in the presence of the Senate
and House of Representatives, open all the certificates, And
and the votes shall then be counted; the person hav-  counted?
ing the greatest number of votes for President shall
be the President, if such number be a majority of the
whole number of electors appointed; and if no person
have such majority, then from the persons having the If no
highest numbers, not exceeding three, on the list of  election?
those voted for as President, the House of Representatives shall choose immediately by ballot the President.
But in choosing the President, the votes shall be taken How do the
by States, the representation from each State having  States vote?
one vote; a quorum for this purpose shall consist of a
member or members from two-thirds of the States, and
a majority of all the States shall be necessary to a
choice.   And if the House of Representatives shall If the
not choose a President, whenever the right of choice refuse to
shall devolve upon them, before the fourth day of  choose?
March next following, then the Vice-President shall  172.
act as President, as in the case of the death or other
constitutional disability of the President.

**168.** The original read as follows:—
"[3.] The electors shall meet in their respective States, and vote What was
by ballot for two persons, of whom one at least shall not be an in-  the repealed
habitant of the same State with themselves. And they shall  section?
make a list of all the persons voted for, and of the number of
votes for each; which list they shall sign and certify, and transmit sealed to the seat of the government of the United States,
directed to the President of the Senate.  The President of the
Senate shall, in the presence of the Senate and House of Representatives, open all the certificates, and the votes shall then be
counted.  The person having the greatest number of votes shall be
the President, if such number be a majority of the whole number
of electors appointed; and if there be more than one who have
such majority, and have an equal number of votes, then the House
of Representatives shall immediately choose by ballot one of them
for President; and if no person have a majority, then from the five
highest on the list the said House shall in like manner choose the

President. But in choosing the President, the votes shall be
taken by States, the representation from each State having one
vote; a quorum for this purpose shall consist of a member or
members from two-thirds of the States, and a majority of all the
States shall be necessary to a choice. In every case, after the
choice of the President, the person having the greatest number of
votes of the electors shall be the Vice-President. But if there
should remain two or more who have equal votes, the Senate
shall choose from them by ballot the Vice-President."

When
do the
electors
meet and
vote?

The electors shall meet on the first Wednesday in December, by
act 1st March, 1792. 1 Stat. 239. Before the first Wednesday
in January, by the same act. On the second Wednesday in February, by the same act. In the election of 1864, the votes of
Louisiana, Arkansas, and Tennessee for President were given, but
not counted. Virginia, North Carolina, South Carolina, Georgia,
Florida, Alabama, Mississippi, and Texas, did not vote in this
election. On a motion to discharge a defendant arrested upon a
*capias ad respondendum*, by a marshal appointed by the President
*de facto*, of the United States, the court will not decide the question
whether he has been duly elected to that office. Peyton v. Brent,
3 Cr. C. C. 424.

If ever the tranquillity of this nation is to be disturbed and its
liberties endangered by a struggle for power it will be upon the
subject of the choice of a President. 1 Kent's Com. 274.

If there be four candidates and two of them have an equal number of votes, the Constitution makes no provision. Story's Const.
§ 1471.

If the
electors do
not choose
a Vice-
President?

12th Amend.

[**2.**] The person having the greatest number of
votes as Vice-President shall be the Vice-President, if
such number be a majority of the whole number of
electors appointed; and if no person have a majority,
then from the two highest numbers on the list the
Senate shall choose the Vice-President : a quorum for
the purpose shall consist of two-thirds of the whole
number of Senators, and a majority of the whole number shall be necessary to a choice.

**168***a.*   There has, thus far, been no necessity for the Senate to
exercise this power. For a list of Vice-Presidents see note 17.

What are
the qualifi-
cations of
Vice-Presi-
dent?
12th Amend.

[**3.**] But no person constitutionally ineligible to the
office of President shall be eligible to that of Vice-
President of the United States.

**168***b.*   For commentaries on this amendment see 1 Kent's
Com. 260, 262; Rawle on the Const. ch. 5, pp. 54, 55; Story's
Const. § 1468–1473.

[3.] The Congress may determine the time of choosing the electors, and the day on which they shall give their votes; which day shall be the same throughout the United States. <sub></sub>

*What is the power of Congress as to the time of election?*

**168c.** On the Tuesday next after the first Monday in November; by act 23d January, 1845. 5 Stat. 721.

*When to be held?*

On the first Wednesday in December; by act 1st March, 1792. 1 Stat. 239. All the States now choose the electors by the people. See Story's Const. § 1475, 1476.

[4.] No person except a natural born citizen, or a citizen of the United States at the time of the adoption of this Constitution, shall be eligible to the office of President; neither shall any person be eligible to that office who shall not have attained to the age of thirty-five years, and been fourteen years a resident within the United States.

*What are the qualifications for President?*

*18, 19, 35.*

*220-222.*

**169.** "A NATURAL BORN CITIZEN."—Not made by law or otherwise, but *born*. And this class is the large majority; in fact the mass of our citizens; all others are exceptions specially provided for by law. As they become citizens, *by birth*, so they remain citizens during their natural lives, unless, by their own voluntary act, they expatriate themselves and become citizens or subjects of another nation. For we have no law (as the French have) to *decitizenize* a citizen who has become such either by the natural process of birth or the legal process of adoption. Attorney-General Bates on Citizenship, 29th November, 1862, p. 8.

*Who are eligible?*

*274.*

The Constitution does not make the citizens (it is, in fact, made by them). It only intends and recognizes such of them as are natural, home-born, and provides for the naturalization of such of them as are alien, foreign-born, making the latter, as far as nature will allow, like the former. Id. We have no middle class or denizens. (1 Sharswood's Bl. Com. 374.) Id. 9. But Attorney-General Legaré thought there might be. (4 Opin. 147.) Id. The example of a Roman citizen and St. Paul's case and claim thereto cited. Id. Paul's is a leading case of the "*Jus Romanum;*" it is analagous to our own; it establishes the great *protective rights* of the citizen, but, like our own national Constitution, it is silent about his *powers*. Id. 12.

*Does the Constitution make the citizens?*

*93.*

*279.*

"NATURAL BORN CITIZEN" recognizes and reaffirms the universal principle common to all nations, and as old as political society, that the people born in a country do constitute the nation, and, as individuals, are *natural* members of the body politic. Bates on Citizenship, p. 12.

*Define natural born?*

*220.*

Every person born in the country is, at the moment of birth, *prima facie* a citizen. Id.

*Nativity* furnishes the rule, both of duty and of right, as between the individual and the government. (2 Kent's Com. Part 4, Lect.

*What does nativity imply?*

25; 1 Bl. Com. ch. 10, p. 365; 7 Coke's Rep. and (Calvin's Case, 11 State Trials, 70) Doe v. Jones, 4 Term. 300; Shanks v. Dupont, 3 Pet. 246; Horace Binney, 2 Am. Law Reporter, 193.) Bates on Citizenship, p. 12.

**170.** "OR A CITIZEN OF THE UNITED STATES AT THE TIME OF THE ADOPTION OF THIS CONSTITUTION."—The declaration of independence of 1776, invested all those persons with the privilege of citizenship who resided in the country at the time, and who adhered to the interests of the colonies. (Ingliss v. The Sailors' Snug Harbor, 3 Pet. 99, 121.) United States v. Ritchie, 17 How. 540; Paschal's Annotated Digest, note 350, p. 209.

There can be few of the class of the foreign born, such as Alexander Hamilton, who are now surviving, who are eligible to the presidency. Considering the ages of all such, no person of foreign birth can now ever be President of the United States under this Constitution. (See Story's Const. § 1479; Journals of Convention, 267, 325, 361.) Still, in this case, as in the qualifications of senators and representatives in Congress, the question is not so clear as to who are "natural born citizens of the United States." Are the *ante-nati* of the Republic of Texas, for example, "natural born citizens of the United States?" They were born upon what is *now* soil of the United States; but they were not "citizens at the moment of their births." About the *post nati* there can be no doubt; but, according to the principles of Calvin's case, which was so learnedly and quaintly discussed, none of the *ante-nati* of our *acquired* territories have now the full *status* of citizenship; and certainly they are no other than adopted or naturalized citizens, in contradistinction to "natural born citizens." See Calvin's Case, 11 State Trials, 70 *et seq.*

And here, again, the language of this clause has to be construed in connection with other clauses and the general understanding of *mankind.* For there is nothing in this clause to indicate *sex* unless it be the word "PRESIDENT." Our advocates for equal "*Woman's Rights*" might consider this a very narrow definition; and they might even urge that the pronoun "he," in other clauses, does not protect woman from the severest criminal statutes; nor would it deprive woman of the guaranties accorded to "him" and "himself," standing for the antecedent of "person" in the Vth and VIth amendments.

The claims of males to be alone entitled to be "*Senators*" and "*Representatives*," is believed to rest alone upon the *masculinity* of the word, the single "*he,*" and the common sense and understanding of men. These remarks are not made in any speculative or hypercritical spirit, but to impress upon the reader the necessity of applying the same common-sense tests to this Constitution as to all other instruments. That is, not to construe it alone by the very technicalities of the words in a single member of a sentence; but to apply to it the same rules of interpretation which we apply to all other instruments, laws, and statutes. That is to construe it by its language, nature, reason, and spirit, objects and intention, and the interpretations of contemporaneous history, having an eye to

*Side notes:*

Who besides natural born are eligible? 220.

274

85, 19.

220.

46.

252–263.

How is the Constitution to be interpreted?

the old law, the mischief and the remedy. See Story's Const.
chapters three, four, and five, and voluminous references.

**171.** "WHO SHALL NOT HAVE ATTAINED THE AGE OF THIRTY What does
YEARS."—This is a limitation upon the people themselves. If all the age fix?
of the nation speak with one united voice, they cannot constitutionally make any man President who happens to be under thirty-
five. Bates on Citizenship, p. 18.

"FOURTEEN YEARS' RESIDENCE."—By "residence" is to be understood, not an absolute inhabitancy within the United States during
the whole period; but such an inhabitancy as includes a permanent domicile in the United States. Story's Const. § 1479.

[5.] In case of the removal of the President from If there be a
office, or of his death, resignation, or inability to dis- the Presi-
charge the powers and duties of the said office, the then be-
same shall devolve on the Vice-President, and the President?
Congress may by law provide for the case of removal,     36.
death, resignation, or inability, both of the President
and Vice-President, declaring what officer shall then
act as President, and such officer shall act accordingly
until the disability be removed, or a President shall be
elected.

**172.** The following is the act of Congress for filling vacancies: Act of
"Sec. 8. In case of removal, death, resignation, or inability both March 1,
of the President and Vice-President of the United States, the 239.
President of the Senate *pro tempore*, and in case there shall be no 38, 26.
President of the Senate, then the Speaker of the House of Repre- If in the
sentatives, for the time being, shall act as President of the Vice-Presi-
United States until the disability be removed or a President shall dency?
be elected.

"9. Whenever the offices of the President and Vice-President When shall
shall both become vacant, the Secretary of State shall forthwith there be a
cause a notification thereof to be made to the executive of every election?
State, and shall also cause the same to be published in at least one
of the newspapers printed in each State, specifying that electors
of the President of the United States shall be appointed or chosen
in the several States within thirty-four days preceding the first
Wednesday in December then next ensuing: *Provided*, there shall
be the space of two months between the date of such notification
and the said first Wednesday in December; and if the term for
which the President and Vice-President last in office were elected,
shall not expire on the third day of March next ensuing, then the
Secretary of State shall specify in the notification that the electors
shall be appointed or chosen within thirty-four days preceding the
first Wednesday in December in the year next ensuing; within
which time the electors shall accordingly be appointed or chosen,
and the electors shall meet and give their votes on the said first

Wednesday in December, and the proceedings and duties of the said electors and others shall be pursuant to the directions prescribed in this act." Act of 1 March, 1792, § 8, 9. 1 Stat. 239. Brightly's Dig. 253, 254. The Constitution does not provide for a vacancy in case of non-election. Therefore, the constitutionality of some parts of this act has been doubted. Story's Const. § 1480–1484; Rawle's Const. ch. 5, p. 57; 1 Tucker's Black. App. 320; 2 Elliot's Debates, 359, 360.

*Suppose there is no election?*

WILLIAM HENRY HARRISON having died on the 4th day of April, 1841, JOHN TYLER took the oath of office as President, on the 6th day of April, 1841; ZACHARY TAYLOR died on the 9th day of July, 1850, and the next day MILLARD FILLMORE took the presidential oath; ABRAHAM LINCOLN was assassinated by John Wilkes Booth, on the 14th day of April, 1865, and, on the 15th, ANDREW JOHNSON was inaugurated President.

*What Vice-Presidents have become Presidents?*

*What of the President's compensation?*

[6.] The President shall, at stated times, receive for his services a compensation, which shall neither be increased nor diminished during the period for which he shall have been elected, and he shall not receive within that period any other emolument from the United States or any of them.

*What is the amount?*

**173.** The President's salary was fixed at twenty-five thousand dollars per annum, by the act of 18th Feb., 1793. 1 St. 318, Brightly's Digest 818.

The government provides and furnishes a mansion for his use. For the wisdom of this independence in regard to salary, see 1 Kent's Com. 263; Federalist, No. 73; Story's Const. § 1486.

[7.] Before he enter on the execution of his office, he shall take the following oath or affirmation:—

*What is the President's oath?*

242.

"I do solemnly swear (or affirm), that I will faithfully execute the office of President of the United States, and will, to the best of my ability, preserve, protect, and defend the Constitution of the United States."

**174.** The President is the only officer required to take this oath. Metropolitan Bank v. Van Dyck, 27 N. Y. Rep. 408.

This oath embraces all the laws, Constitution, treaties, and statutes. And it constitutes the President, above all other officers, the guardian, protector, and defender of the Constitution. Bates on *Habeas Corpus*, 5th July, 1861. See Stanbery on vacancies. The acts of 1795 and 1807, came in aid of these duties. Id.

*What does to faithfully execute embrace?*

"FAITHFULLY TO EXECUTE THE OFFICE OF PRESIDENT."—This embraces the general office of the executive, and also the official powers not in their nature executive, such as the veto power; the

treaty-making power; the appointing power, and the pardoning      165.
power. Bates on *Habeas Corpus*, 5th July, 1861.

SEC. II.—[1.] The President shall be commander-in- What
chief of the army and navy of the United States, and President's
of the militia of the several States, when called into 124-178.
the actual service of the United States; he may      130.
require the opinion, in writing, of the principal officer
in each of the executive departments, upon any subject relating to the duties of their respective offices,      177.
and he shall have power to grant reprieves and par- 40, 191.
dons for offenses against the United States, except in
cases of impeachment.      194.

**175.** "COMMANDER-IN-CHIEF."—This was to give the exercise Why com-
of power by a single hand. See 1 Kent's Com. Lect. 13, p. 283; 3 mander?
Elliot's Debates, 103; Story's Const. § 1491, 1492; Rawle's Const.
ch. 20, p. 193. The power may be delegated. Id.  5 Marshall's
Life of Washington, ch. 8, pp. 583, 584, 588.

The President is not obliged to take, personally, the command of Must he
the militia, when called into the service of the general government, command in
but he may place them under the command of officers of the army person?
of the United States, to whom, in his absence, he may delegate the
powers vested in him by the Constitution. Any officer of the army
may, therefore, be required, by orders emanating from the President, to perform the appropriate duties of his station in the militia,
when in the service of the United States, whenever the public
interest shall so require. But this power must be exercised in
strict accordance with the right of appointment of militia officers,
which is expressly reserved to the States. 2 Opin. 711-12. See
2 Story's Const. § 1490-2. As commander-in-chief, the President
has the right to decide what officer shall perform any particular      165.
duty, and, as supreme executive magistrate, he has the power of
appointment. Congress could not take away this power. 9 Op.
468, 518. But this power is to be used only in the manner prescribed by the legislative department. 9 Op. 518.

The President has unquestioned power to establish rules for the What rules
government of the army, and the Secretary of War is his regular may the
organ to administer the military establishment of the nation, and establish?
rules and orders promulgated through him must be received as
the acts of the executive, and, as such, are binding on all within 129, 134.
the sphere of his authority. (United States v. Eliason, 16 Pet.
291.) But this power is limited, and does not extend to the repeal
or contradiction of existing statutes, nor to the making of provisions of a legislative nature. (6 Opin. 10.) Bates, 18th April,
1861.

But the powers of the President over the militia, only commence when those of the governors cease; that is, when the

militia are called into the actual service of the United States. Id.
The President cannot establish a bureau of militia. Id.

**What of opinions in writing?**

**176.** "OPINIONS IN WRITING."—This practice commenced with the administration of President Washington. The depository of such opinions has generally been in the State department. The attorney-general frequently gives opinions to the President, as the law officer of the government, which are published in the current series.

**What are the Departments, and who are the cabinet?**

The "DEPARTMENTS" are now called the State, the Treasury, the War, the Navy, the Post-office, the Attorney-General's, and the Interior departments. The heads of these are known as the President's advisers or cabinet officers. Their respective duties are defined by statutes, which will be found collected under appropriate heads in Mr. Brightly's Digest.

The opinions are more frequently given in secret cabinet councils. But Mr. Jefferson thought the separate opinions in writing more consistent with the Constitution. (4 Jeff.'s Corresp. 143, 144.) Story's Const. § 1493, note 3. Upon the reconstruction laws, President Johnson took the opinions in council; and he seems to have authorized their publication.

**Define reprieves?**

**177.** "REPRIEVES."—The withdrawing of a sentence of death for an interval of time, whereby the execution is suspended. 4 Bl. Com. 394; Burrill's Law Dic., REPRIEVE; *Ex parte* Wells, 18 How. 307, 315; Story's Const. 3d Ed. p. 305, § 1505. The power is not to pardon, but to *grant* reprieves and pardons. *Ex parte* Wells, 18 How. 316.

**Define pardon?**

"AND PARDONS."—In common parlance, forgiveness, release, remission. *Ex parte*, Wells, 18 How. 307. In law every pardon has its particular denomination. They are general, special or particular, conditional or absolute, statutory, not necessary in some cases, and in some grantable of course. Id.

Here it is meant, that the power is to be used according to law; that is, as it had been used in England, and these States when they were colonies. Id. That is, according to the principles of the English common law, at the time of the adoption of this Constitution. (United States v. Wilson, 7 Pet. 162.) *Ex parte* Wells, 18 How. 309. Hence, when the words "to grant pardons" were used in the Constitution, they conveyed to the mind the authority as exercised by the English crown, or by its representatives in the colonies. Id.; Cathcart v. Robinson, 5 Pet. 264, 280; Flavel's Case, 8 Watts and Sergeant, 197.

A pardon is said by Lord Coke to be a work of mercy, "whereby the king, either before attainder, sentence, or conviction, or after, forgiveth any crime, offense, punishment, execution, right, title, debt, or duty, temporal or ecclesiastical." (3 Inst. 233.) *Ex parte* Wells, 18 How. 311, 312. The whole subject discussed. Id.

**When may the President pardon?**

He may pardon as well before trial and conviction as afterward. 6 Opin. 20. (See the proclamations of amnesty in relation to the rebellion.) And after the expiration of the imprisonment which forms a part of the sentence. Stetler's Case, Phila. R. 302. He may grant a conditional pardon; *Ex parte* Wells, 18 How. 307; 1

Opin. 341; provided the condition be compatible with the genius
of our Constitution and laws. Id. 482. Where the condition is
such that the government has no power to carry it into effect, the
pardon will be in effect unconditional. 5 Id. 368. See Flavell's
Case, 8 W. & S. 197; United States v. Wilson, 7 Pet. 161; People In what
v. Potter, 1 Parker C. R. 47. The pardoning power includes that cases?
of remitting fines, penalties, and forfeitures, under the revenue
laws; 2 Pet. 329; the laws prohibiting the slave-trade; 4 Id. 573;
fines imposed on defaulting jurors, 3 Id. 317; 4 Id. 458; for a
contempt of court; 3 Id. 622; and in criminal cases; Id. 418;
even treason, amnesty proclamations, and warrants. And the
same power is possessed over a judgment, after security for its
payment shall have been given, as before. Id. But the President
has no power to remit the forfeiture of a bail-bond. 4 Id. 144.
Nor, it seems, can he, by a pardon, defeat a legal interest or right
which has become vested in a private citizen; as, for example, the
vested right of an officer making a seizure. United States v.
Lancaster, 4 Wash. C. C. 64; 4 Opin. 376; 6 Id. 615; and see 5
Id. 532, 579. The grant of the pardoning power neither requires
nor authorizes the President to re-examine the case upon new facts;
nor to grant a pardon upon the assumption of the new facts alleged.
1 Opin. 359. A pardon is a private though official act; it must be Must the
delivered to and accepted by the criminal, and cannot be noticed by pardon be
the court, unless brought before it judicially by plea, motion, or accepted?
otherwise. United States v. Wilson, 7 Pet. 150. The President
alone can pardon offenses committed in a territory in violation of       231.
acts of Congress 7 Opin. 761. He has power to order a *nolle*      232.
*prosequi* in any stage of a criminal proceeding, in the name of the
United States. 5 Id. 729. He pardoned the rebels upon their
taking the oath of amnesty, with certain exceptions, by general
proclamation. The warrants issued to those within special exceptions were all conditional.

The power to pardon is unlimited, with the exceptions stated. What is the
It extends to every offense known to the law, and may be exercised extent of the
at any time after its commission, either before legal proceedings power?
are taken, or during their pendency, or after conviction and judgment. This power of the President is not subject to legislative
control.

Congress can neither limit the effect of his pardon, nor exclude Can Con-
from its exercise any class of offenders. The benign prerogative of gress limit
mercy cannot be fettered by any legislative restrictions. *Ex parte* the pardon?
Garland, 4 Wall. 380.

A pardon reaches both the punishment prescribed for the offense What does
and the guilt of the offender; and when the pardon is full, it re- the pardon
leases the punishment and blots out the existence of the guilt; so reach?
that in the eye of the law the offender is as innocent as if he had
never committed the offense. If granted before conviction, it pre-
vents any of the disabilities consequent upon conviction from
attaching; if granted after conviction, it removes the penalties and
disabilities, and restores him to all his civil rights; it makes him,
as it were, a new man, and gives him a new credit and capacity.
*Ex parte* Garland, 4 Wallace, 380, 381. This court is obliged to
conform to these principles. Judge Duval, in the case of the United

States v. Devine, Texas, June Term, 1867. There is only one limitation to its operation; it does not restore offices forfeited, or property or interests vested in others in consequence of the conviction and judgment. (4 Blackstone's Com. 402 ; 6 Bacon's Abridgment, tit. Pardon ; Hawkins, book 2, ch. 37, § 44 and 54.) *Ex parte* Garland, 4 Wallace, 381.

What is the effect of the pardon of the rebels? 142, 143, 242, 254.

The pardon produced by the petitioner is a full pardon "for all offenses, from participation, direct or implied, in the rebellion." This relieves him from all penalties and disabilities attached to the offense of treason, committed by his participation in the rebellion. So far as that offense is concerned, he is thus placed beyond the reach of punishment of any kind. (*Ex parte* Garland, 4 Wallace, 381.) The United States v. Devine, before Judge Duval, in the United States Circuit Court for the Western District of Texas, June Term, 1867. The expurgatory oath required by attorneys cannot affect an attorney, who had been previously such of the court, after pardon. Congress cannot inflict punishment beyond the reach of executive clemency. *Ex parte* Garland, 4 Wallace, 381.

242. 274.

The remission of a penalty after it has been paid has no effect. Edwin M. Stanton, Attorney-General, 3d Jan. 1861.

See 1 Kent's Com. 11 Ed. Part II. Lect. 13, p. 283–285 and notes; Story's Const. § 1494, 1504 ; Federalist, No. 74 ; 2 Wilson's Law Lect. 198–200 ; 2 Elliot's Debates, 366 ; Rawle's Const. ch. 17, p. 178.

What is the power of the President as to treaties and appointments? 179.

[2.] He shall have power, by and with the advice and consent of the Senate, to make treaties, provided two-thirds of the Senators present concur ; and he shall nominate, and by and with the advice and consent of the Senate, shall appoint ambassadors, other public ministers and consuls, judges of the Supreme Court, and all other officers of the United States, whose appointments are not herein otherwise provided for, and which shall be established by law. But the Congress may by law vest the appointment of such inferior officers, as they think proper, in the President alone, in the courts of law, or in the heads of departments.

183.

**178.** "HE SHALL HAVE POWER, BY AND WITH THE ADVICE AND CONSENT OF THE SENATE, TO MAKE TREATIES, PROVIDED TWO-THIRDS OF THE SENATORS PRESENT CONCUR."

How is the advice usually given?

This "advice and consent" is usually given after the treaty, or appointment is made and signed by the President. The work is then sent to the Senate, to ask the "CONCURRENCE of two-thirds." But it is in the option of the President to ask the advice and con-

sent of the Senate in advance, and it was so asked by President
Polk upon the ratification of the Treaty with Great Britain, in
1846, relative to Oregon.  See 5 Marshall's Life of Washington,
ch. 2, p. 223; Executive Journal, 11th Aug. 1790, pp. 60, 61;
Rawle's Const. ch. 7, pp. 63, 64; Story's Const. § 1523; see Senate
Journal and Debates of July. 1846, upon the Oregon Treaty.

"MAKE TREATIES."—[*Fœdus.*]  An agreement between two or
more independent States.  Brande.  An agreement, league, or contract between two or more nations or sovereigns, formally signed
by commissioners properly authorized, and solemnly ratified by the
several sovereigns, or the supreme power of each State.  Webster's
Dic., TREATY; Burrill's Dic., TREATY.  See Halleck's International
Law, ch. 34, pp. 189, 841.

A treaty is, in its nature, a contract between two nations; not a
legislative act.  It does not generally effect, of itself, the object to
be accomplished, especially so far as its operation infra-territorial,
but is carried into execution by the sovereign power of the respective parties to the instrument.  Foster & Elam v. Neilson, 2 Peters,
314.

In the United States a different principle is established.  Our
Constitution declares a treaty to be the law of the land.  It is, consequently, to be regarded in courts of justice as equivalent to an
act of the legislature, wherever it operates of itself without the aid
of any legislative provision.  But when the terms of the stipulation import a contract, when either of the parties engages to perform a particular act, the treaty addresses itself to the political,
not the judicial department; and the legislature must execute the
contract before it can become a rule for the court.  Id.

The power extends to every kind of treaty.  Story's Const. § 1508.
But the power cannot be exercised to override other parts of the
Constitution, and to destroy the fundamental principles of the gov-
ernment.  Id.; Woodeson's Elem. of Jurisprudence, 31; 4 Jeff's
Corresp. 2, 3, 498; Rawle's Con t. 63–75. See the power discussed.
Story's Const. § 1508, 1523; Ware v. Hylton, 3 Dall. 272–276.

**179.** "HE SHALL NOMINATE."—The word as here used means
to recommend, in writing to the Senate, the name of an appointee
for confirmation.  It is in this form the "advice of the Senate" is
asked.  This is the sole act of the President, and is voluntary.
Marbury v. Madison, 1 Cr. 137; 1 Peter's Cond. 270; Story's
Const. § 1548.

But the practice, when the Senate is not in session (and I think
sometimes when it is), is, that the President fills vacancies, and
the appointee qualifies and enters upon the duties of his office.  In
such cases, the NOMINATION is not confined to the PROVISIONAL
appointee; but the President *may* and often *does* appoint another.
See Stanbery on appointments to office. 14–19.

"AND BY AND WITH THE ADVICE AND CONSENT OF THE SENATE
SHALL APPOINT."—It will be observed that, as in the *nomination,*
the duty is imperative—"*shall nominate,*" "*shall appoint.*"

This power to fill vacancies is in the President, with the assent
of the Senate, whilst that body is in session, and in the President
alone when the Senate is not in session.  There is no reason upon

Margin notes: What is a treaty? | 199. | 199. 240. | Define nominate? 184. | Appoint?

which the power to fill a vacancy can be limited by the state of things when it first occurred. On the contrary, the only inquiry is as to the state of things when it is filled.

**What is the effect of an appointment during the recess?**
**189.**
All admit that whenever there is a vacancy existing during the session, whether it first occurred in the recess or after the session began, the power to fill it requires the concurrent action of the President and Senate. It seems a necessary corollary to this, that where the vacancy exists in the recess, whether it first occurred in the recess or in the preceding session, the power to fill is in the President alone. If, during the recess, the power is not in the President, it is nowhere, and there is a time when for a season the President is required to see that the laws are executed, and yet denied every means provided for their execution. Stanbery.

**What is the effect of the confirmation?**
Nevertheless, it comes back to the point that the President can only "appoint," with the concurrence of the Senate; and all the appointments whether during the recess, or the session of the Senate are provisional only, and subject to the concurrence, in common parlance, "ratification," of that body.

**What powers can the President confer?**
Hence his power at all times to vacate offices and to fill vacancies. He can, by his own act, do every thing but give full title to his appointees, and invest them with the right to hold during the official term. That he cannot do without the consent of the Senate; but such is his power over officers, that, after the Senate has consented to his nomination, or in common parlance, has confirmed it, the nominee is not yet fully appointed, or even entitled to the office, for it still remains with the President to give him a commission or to refuse it, as he may deem best; and without the commission there is no appointment. This was held by the Supreme Court in Marbury v. Madison, 1 Cr. 137, 155, 156; and when to that decision we add the doctrine recognized by the same court in *Ex parte* Hennen, (13 Pet. 213), we see how fully the appointment and removal of officers is held to be a necessary incident of executive power. Stanbery, 18, 19.

The nomination and appointment are voluntary acts, and distinct from the commissioning. Marbury v. Madison, 1 Cr. 155–6. Even after confirmation, the President may, in his discretion, withhold a commission; and, until a commission has been signed, the appointment is not fully consummated. (4 Opin. 218). Stanbery.

**What is the effect of the commission?**
**184.**
When the Senate has concurred and the "commission" is signed by the President, even before delivery, the appointment is complete, and the officer has vested legal rights which cannot be resumed. Marbury v. Madison, 1 Cr. 156; United States v. Le Baron, 19 How. 74; Story's Const. § 1548–1554. Mr. Jefferson refused to act upon this decision, and claimed the power to withhold the commission. 4 Jeff. Corr. 75, 317, 372; Rawle on the Const. 166; Story's Const. § 1553, note 1.

To "appoint," and to "commission," are not one and the same thing. Marbury v. Madison, 1 Cr. 155. The commission is not necessarily the appointment, although conclusive evidence of the fact. Id.; United States v. Le Baron, 19 How. 74.

When the appointee refuses to accept, the successor is nominated in his place, and not in the place of the person who had been pre-

viously in the office and had created a vacancy. (Marbury v.
Madison, 1 Cr. 137–156.) Story's Const. § 1554.  See also John-
son v. United States, 5 Mason, 425, 438, 439; United States v.
Kirkpatrick, 4 Wheat. 733, 734; Bowerbank v. Morris, Wallace
Cir. R. 425, 438, 439; Thompson's Case, 3 P. Will. 194; Boucher
v. Wiseman, Cro. Eliz. 440; Burch v. Maypowder, 1 Vt. 400.

**180.** "AMBASSADORS, OTHER PUBLIC MINISTERS, AND CONSULS." What is an
—"AMBASSADORS," comprehend the highest grade only of public Ambassa-dor?
ministers.  Story's Const. § 1525.  See Grotius, Vattel, Martens,
Wicquefort, Halleck (ch. 9, pp. 200–239) and Wheaton, Title, 202.
AMBASSADORS.  For a better definition, see note 202.

Ambassadors could not include consuls, hence the enlargement
of the enumeration.  Story's Const. § 1525; Federalist, No. 42.
See ante, p. 14, Art. IX.

**181.** "PUBLIC MINISTERS AND CONSULS."—CONSULS.—For the 188.
derivation of the word consul (consulere, consulatus, comes, comi- Define con-
tatus), see Co. Litt. lib. 3, note 20; Burrill's Law Dic, CONSUL. suls?
The name of a chief magistrate among the Romans, and of Earls,
from consulendo, among the Britons.  Bract. fol. 5, b.  ; 1 Bl. Com.
227.  For the origin, history, and duty of consuls, see Halleck's
International Law, ch. 15, 239–269, and the many learned authorities there cited.

In commercial and international law, a public agent, appointed
by a government to reside in a foreign country (and usually in
seaports), to watch over its own commercial rights and privileges,
and the commercial interests of its citizens or subjects.  1 Kent's
Com. 41.

**182.** "JUDGES OF THE SUPREME COURT, AND ALL OTHER What offi-
OFFICERS OF THE UNITED STATES, WHOSE APPOINTMENTS ARE cers can
NOT HEREIN OTHERWISE PROVIDED FOR, AND WHICH SHALL BE dent
ESTABLISHED BY LAW." appoint?
Judges of the Supreme Court are defined in the Constitution. 179.
(Art. III. sec. 1.)

The effect of this and other clauses of the Constitution, on the
subject of the appointments to office, is to declare that all offices
under the federal government, except in cases where the Constitution itself may otherwise provide, shall be established by law.
United States v. Maurice, 2 Brock. 96.

Every thing concerning the administration of justice, or the
general interests of society may be supposed to be within the
meaning of the Constitution, especially if fees and emoluments are
annexed to the office.  But there are matters of temporary and
local concern, which, although comprehended in the term officers,
have not been thought to be embraced by the Constitution.
(Lehman v. Sutherland, 3 Serg. Rawle, 149.)  Attorney-General Stanbery's Opinion on the Reconstruction Laws, 24th May,
1867, p. 12.

**183.** "BUT THE CONGRESS MAY VEST BY LAW THE APPOINT- Where else
MENT, ETC., OF INFERIOR OFFICERS IN THE PRESIDENT ALONE, IN appointing
THE COURTS OF LAW, OR IN THE HEADS OF DEPARTMENTS."—Here power be
vested?

8*

**179-182.**

**Officers commissioned?**

the duty of commissioning is distinct from the appointment. The legislature might require commissions. Marbury v. Madison, 1 Cr. 157; Story's Const. § 1548.

Clerks of courts are such officers; and, in such cases, the power of removal is incident to the power of appointment. *Ex parte* Hennen, 13 Pet. 230, 259. And may be exercised by the court which appointed. Id.

The President cannot appoint a commissioner of bail, affidavits, &c. That power belongs to the circuit courts. Bates, 24th June, 1861.

**Tenure of office?**

**Can the President remove as well as appoint?**

**179, 180.**

**184.** THE POWER OF REMOVAL. The power of the President to appoint to office, necessarily includes the power to remove all officers appointed and commissioned by him, where the Constitution has not otherwise provided. Therefore he may remove a territorial judge, in his discretion. 5 Opin. 288 ; 3 Id. 673 ; 4 Id. 603, 608-9; 4 Elliot's Debates, 350; *Ex parte* Hennen, 13 Pet. 259. And he may cause a military officer to be stricken from the rolls, without a trial by court-martial, notwithstanding a decision in his favor by a court of inquiry. 4 Opin. 1.; 2 Story's Const. § 1538 ; Stanbery, 17-19. But see act of 13th July, 1866, in this note; Story's Const. § 1519-1554.

**To what is the Senate's action confined.**

**193, 194.**

The Senate cannot originate an appointment; its constitutional action is confined to a simple affirmation or rejection of the President's nominations; and such nominations fail whenever it disagrees to them. 3 Opin. 188; Stanbery, 18.

This clause gives him power to appoint diplomatic agents of any rank, at any place, and at any time, in his discretion, subject to the approbation of the Senate ; and this power cannot be limited by act of Congress. 7 Opin. 186.

**185.**

**Art. III., Sec. 1.**

**184.**

Nothing is said about the power of removal by the executive of any officers whomsoever. As, however, the tenure of office of no officers except those in the judicial department, is, by the Constitution, provided to be during good behavior, it follows, by irresistible inference, that all others must hold their offices during pleasure, unless Congress shall have given some other duration to their office. (1 Lloyd's Debates, 511, 512.) Story's Const. § 1537; Keenan v. Perry, 24 Tex. 258. In the absence of a constitutional or statutory provision, the power of removal would seem to be incident to the power of appointment. (*Ex parte* Hennen, 13 Pet. 259.) Keenan v. Perry, 24 Tex. 258.

As far as Congress constitutionally possesses the power to regulate and delegate the appointment of "inferior officers," so far they may prescribe the term of office, the manner in which, and the persons by whom, the removal, as well as the appointment to office, shall be made. (Marbury v. Madison, 1 Cranch, 137, 155.) Story's Const. § 1537. See Monroe's Message of 12th April, 1822, 1 Executive Journal, 286; Sergt's Const. ch. 29 [31]; 5 Marshall's Life of Washington, ch. 3, p. 196-200 ; 1 Lloyd's Debates, 351-366. and 450-600; Id. 1-12.

The removal takes place in virtue of the new appointment, by mere operation of law. *Ex parte* Hennen, 13 Pet. 300; Federalist, No. 77.

"The consent of the Senate would be necessary to displace as well as to appoint." (Federalist, No. 77.) Story's Const. § 1540.

While Mr. Madison claimed the power to remove, he said, "the wanton removal of meritorious officers would subject him (the President) to impeachment." (1 Lloyd's Debates, 503; and see Id. 351, 366, 450, 480–600; 4 Elliot's Debates, 141–207.  *191-194.*

The first limitation on the President's power of removal is as follows: "And no officer in the military or naval service shall, in time of peace, be dismissed from service except upon, and in pursuance of, the sentence of a court-martial to that effect, or in commutation thereof." Act of 13th July, 1866, 14 St. p. 92, § 5.  *How are the military removed?*

In the differences between the President and Congress, the question was again discussed by the thirty-ninth Congress; and although not very elaborately argued, the positions taken for and against the power were urged, and will be found in the Congressional Globe of that session, and in the President's veto of the following law :—

### An Act regulating the Tenure of certain Civil Offices.

"SEC. 1. Every person holding any civil office to which he has been appointed by and with the advice and consent of the Senate, and every person who shall hereafter be appointed to any such office, and shall become duly qualified to act therein, is, and shall be entitled to hold such office until a successor shall have been in like manner appointed and duly qualified, except as herein otherwise provided: *Provided*, That the Secretaries of State, of the Treasury, of War, of the Navy, and of the Interior, the Postmaster-General, and the Attorney-General, shall hold their offices respectively for and during the term of the President, by whom they may have been appointed, and for one month thereafter, subject to removal by and with the advice and consent of the Senate.  *Act of March 2, 1867, 14 St. 430.*  *What is tenure of civil officers?*  *With what exceptions?*

"2. When any officer appointed as aforesaid, excepting judges of the United States Courts, shall, during a recess of the Senate, be shown, by evidence satisfactory to the President, to be guilty of misconduct in office, or crime, or for any reason shall become incapable or legally disqualified to perform its duties, in such case, and in no other, the President may suspend such officer and designate some suitable person to perform temporarily the duties of such office until the next meeting of the Senate, and until the case shall be acted upon by the Senate, and such person so designated shall take the oaths and give the bonds required by law to be taken and given by the person duly appointed to fill such office; and in such case it shall be the duty of the President, within twenty days after the first day of such next meeting of the Senate, to report to the Senate such suspension, with the evidence and reasons for his action in the case, and the name of the person so designated to perform the duties of such office. And if the Senate shall concur in such suspension, and advise and consent to the removal of such officer, they shall so certify to the President, who may thereupon remove such officer, and, by and with the advice and consent of the Senate, appoint another person to such office. But if the Senate shall refuse to concur in such suspension, such officer so suspended shall forthwith resume the functions of  *When may the President suspend and temporarily appoint?*  *To whom to report?*  *If the Senate refuse to concur?*

his office, and the powers of the person so performing its duties in his stead shall cease, and the official salary and emoluments of such officer shall, during such suspension, belong to the person so performing the duties thereof, and not to the officer so suspended: *Provided, however,* That the President, in case he shall become satisfied that such suspension was made on insufficient grounds, shall be authorized, at any time before reporting such suspension to the Senate as above provided, to revoke such suspension and reinstate such officer in the performance of the duties of his office.

*May the President revoke the removal?*

"3. The President shall have power to fill all vacancies which may happen during the recess of the Senate, by reason of death or resignation, by granting commissions which shall expire at the end of their next session thereafter. And if no appointment, by and with the advice and consent of the Senate, shall be made to such office so vacant or temporarily filled as aforesaid during such next session of the Senate, such office shall remain in abeyance, without any salary, fees, or emoluments attached thereto, until the same shall be filled by appointment thereto, by and with the advice and consent of the Senate; and during such time all the powers and duties belonging to such office shall be exercised by such other officer as may by law exercise such powers and duties in case of a vacancy in such office.

*If the Senate refuse to concur in vacancies?*

"4. Nothing in this act contained shall be construed to extend the term of any office the duration of which is limited by law.

*What limit on term?*

"5. If any person shall, contrary to the provisions of this act, accept any appointment to, or employment in, any office, or shall hold or exercise, or attempt to hold or exercise, any such office or employment, he shall be deemed, and is hereby declared to be, guilty of a high misdemeanor, and, upon trial and conviction thereof, he shall be punished therefor by a fine not exceeding ten thousand dollars, or by imprisonment not exceeding five years, or both said punishments, in the discretion of the court.

*What penalty for accepting or exercising office contrary to this act?*

"6. Every removal, appointment, or employment, made, had, or exercised, contrary to the provisions of this act, and the making, signing, sealing, countersigning, or issuing of any commission or letter of authority for or in respect to any such appointment or employment, shall be deemed, and are hereby declared to be, high misdemeanors, and, upon trial and conviction thereof, every person guilty thereof shall be punished by a fine not exceeding ten thousand dollars, or by imprisonment not exceeding five years, or both said punishments, in the discretion of the court: *Provided,* That the President shall have power to make out and deliver, after the adjournment of the Senate, commissions for all officers whose appointment shall have been advised and consented to by the Senate.

*And for removal, &c., contrary to the act?*

"7. It shall be the duty of the secretary of the Senate, at the close of each session thereof, to deliver to the Secretary of the Treasury, and to each of his assistants, and to each of the auditors, and to each of the comptrollers in the treasury, and to the treasurer, and to the register of the treasury, a full and complete list, duly certified, of all the persons who shall have been nominated to and rejected by the Senate during such session, and a like list of

*When may the President commission?*

*How are rejections to be certified?*

all the offices to which nominations shall have been made and not confirmed and filled at such session.

"8. Whenever the President shall, without the advice and consent of the Senate, designate, authorize, or employ any person to perform the duties of any office, he shall forthwith notify the Secretary of the Treasury thereof; and it shall be the duty of the Secretary of the Treasury thereupon to communicate such notice to all the proper accounting and disbursing officers of his department.

"9. No money shall be paid or received from the treasury, or paid or received from or retained out of any public moneys or funds of the United States, whether in the treasury or not, to or by or for the benefit of any person appointed to or authorized to act in or holding or exercising the duties or functions of any office contrary to the provisions of this act; nor shall any claim, account, voucher, order, certificate, warrant, or other instrument. providing for or relating to such payment, receipt, or retention, be presented, passed, allowed, approved, certified, or paid by any officer of the United States, or by any person exercising the functions or performing the duties of any office or place of trust under the United States, for or in respect to such office, or the exercising or performing the functions or duties thereof; and every person who shall violate any of the provisions of this section shall be deemed guilty of a high misdemeanor, and, upon trial or conviction thereof, shall be punished therefor by a fine not exceeding ten thousand dollars, or by imprisonment not exceeding ten years, or both said punishments, in the discretion of the court." Passed over the President's veto, 2 March. 1867.

See the Debates in 1789, on the question Whether the heads of departments were "inferior officers?" 1 Lloyd's Debates, 480–600; 2 Id. 1–12. The result of the debate seems to have been that they were not. (Rawle's Const. ch. 14, pp. 163, 164; Sergeant on the Const. ch. 29 [ch. 31]; see President Monroe's Message of 12th April, 1822.) Story's Const. § 1536–1539. The President was overruled by the Senate, which contended that, as Congress possessed the power to make rules and regulations for the land and naval forces, they had a right to make any which would promote the public service; that Congress fixes the promotions, and every promotion is a new appointment, which requires ratification. (Sergeant's Const. ch. 29) [ch. 31.]

The power to *nominate* does not naturally or necessarily include the power to remove; and if the power to appoint does include it, then the latter belongs conjointly to the executive and Senate. Story's Const. § 1538. It results, and is not separable from the appointment itself. (*Ex parte* Hennen, 13 Pet. 213.) Story's Const. § 1538; Federalist, No. 77.

The power to remove by the President was affirmed during the administration of President Washington by the casting vote of the Vice-President. Senate Journal, July 18, 1789, p. 42. The question was much agitated again during the administration of President Jackson. Finally the power has been denied, in the shape of the tenure of office bill. during the administration of

*Side notes:*

What is the duty of the Secretary in such case?

What restrictions as to pay?

What penalty for violation?

Are the Cabinet inferior officers?

179.

President Johnson, because of the peculiar attitudes of a President and a Congress elected at the same time, and upon the same platform of principles. Without pretending to assert positively the constitutionality of the law, the editor ventures to predict, that no political party will ever entirely remove the restrictions, and leave the tenure of office wholly and exclusively at the will of the President. The real evil results from the too great patronage in the hands of the executive, and the corrupting influences, for a long time so openly employed, by the distribution of federal patronage to control State elections. The evil could only be reached and Presidential elections rendered peaceful and safe by an organic change, which would place the choice of federal magistrates where the constitutions of the States have generally placed them—in the hands of the people. If time has demonstrated that the elective democratic principle may be left to the wisdom of choice, why could not the rule apply to many grades of federal officers?

*23f*

*What is the power to fill vacancies?*
*184, § 3.*

[3.] The President shall have power to fill up all vacancies that may happen during the recess of the Senate, by granting commissions which shall expire at the end of their next session.

*If the vacancies occur during the session.*
*184.*

**185.** "ALL VACANCIES THAT MAY HAPPEN DURING THE RECESS OF THE SENATE."—Mr. Wirt, in 1823, Mr. Taney, in 1832, and Mr. Legaré, in 1841, concur in opinion that vacancies first occurring *during* the session of the Senate may be filled by the President *in* the recess. Mr. Mason, in a short opinion given in 1845, held that vacancies *known to exist* during the session could not be filled *in* the recess; but in a more elaborate opinion, written in 1846, he

*25.*
*32.*

expresses general concurrence with his three predecessors. All these concurring opinions give a construction to the meaning of the words; and they agree that these words are not to be confined to vacancies which first occur *during* the recess, but may apply to vacancies which first occur *during* the session and continue in the recess. Attorney-General Stanbery on the President's power in the matter of appointments to office, 30th Aug. 1866, p. 4.

*How may the vacancy occur?*
*179.*

1. The vacancy may not have become known during the recess; 2. It may have occurred by the failure of the Senate to act upon a nomination; 3. Or, upon a nomination and confirmation, where the party so nominated and confirmed refuses in the recess to accept the office; 4. Or by the rejection of the nominee of the President in the last hour of the session; 5. Or by the failure of the President to make a nomination during the session

*143.*

or after a rejection of his nominee. Id.

*What means "that may happen"?*

The subject-matter is a *vacancy*. It implies duration—a condition or state of things which may exist. I incline to think, upon the mere words, that we might construe them precisely as if the phrase were, "If it happen that there is a vacancy in the recess," or, "If a vacancy happen to exist in the recess." Id. 5, 6.

But if the office first occur during the recess; or if it be created during the session and the President fail to appoint, he cannot appoint during the recess. The word "HAPPEN" has relation to some casualty, not provided for by law. (The appointment of the Ministers to Ghent, in 1813; Senate Journal of 20th April, 1822; 2 Executive Journal, pp. 415, 500; 3 Executive Journal, 297.) Story's Const. § 1559.

He may fill, during a recess of the Senate, a vacancy that occurred by expiration of commission during a previous session. 1 Opin. 631. So he may fill a vacancy which has occurred by the expiration of a former temporary appointment, the Senate having neglected to act on a nomination to fill the office. 3 Id. 673; 4 Id. 523; 2 Id. 525; 4 Id. 36:.

**186.** "WHICH SHALL EXPIRE AT THE END OF THE SESSION."— Length of commission? The commission of an officer appointed during a recess, who is afterward nominated and rejected, is not thereby determined: it continues in force until the end of the next session, unless sooner determined by the President. 2 Opin. 336; 4 Id. 30.

It was upon this state of facts that Mr. Taney gave his opinion What means "which shall expire at the end of the session"? in 1832, and held on this point that "the vacancy did take place in the recess," and that "the former appointment continued during the session, and there was no vacancy until after they adjourned." Stanbery on filling vacancies, 6. 184.

If the President appoint and commission, both expire at the end of the next session. If he nominate the same person, and the Senate concur, it is a new appointment; and the bond given "to fill up the vacancy," does not apply to acts done under the new appointment and commission (United States v. Kirkpatrick, 9 Wheat. 720, 733, 734, 735.) Story's Const. § 1538.

SEC. III.—He shall, from time to time, give to the Congress information of the state of the Union, and recommend to their consideration such measures as he shall judge necessary and expedient. He may, on extraordinary occasions, convene both houses, or either of them; and in case of disagreement between them, with respect to the time of adjournment, he may adjourn them to such time as he shall think proper. He shall receive ambassadors and other public ministers. He shall take care that the laws be faithfully executed, and shall commission all the officers of the United States. *What are the duties enjoined upon the President? Further powers?*

**187.** "GIVE INFORMATION OF THE STATE OF THE UNION, AND RECOMMEND," &c.—The opening messages of Presidents Washington and John Adams were delivered in person and answered. 1 Benton's Cond. Debates; Story's Const. 3d ed. § 1561, note 1. See *How are the opinions given?*

1 Tuck. Bl. Com. 343–345; Federalist, No. 78; Rawle's Const. ch. 16, p. 171.

The practice was changed by President Jefferson; and ever since all messages have been delivered in writing. This "information of the state of the Union," embraces the reports of all the departments, and altogether they constitute what are called the executive documents of the government, which are valuable repositories for statesmen and students. Calls are often made by Congress on the President and the heads of departments, for information on special matters.

**Have extra sessions been called?**

**188.** "MAY CALL CONGRESS TOGETHER AND ADJOURN," &c.— This power of convening Congress in extra session, has been frequently exercised, both in regard to Congress and the Senate. Never could the necessity of the power be more forcibly demonstrated than upon the occasion of its exercise by President Lincoln, in April, 1863. See Federalist, No. 78; Rawle's Const., ch. 16, p. 171.

It is not remembered that the occasion ever has arisen for the President to exercise the power to adjourn Congress.

**What does "ambassadors and other public ministers" embrace? 180, 181, 202.**

The power to receive AMBASSADORS AND OTHER PUBLIC MINISTERS carries along the power to receive consuls, and they never act without *exequaturs.* Rawle's Const. ch. 24, pp. 224, 225. Story's Const. § 1564–1572. See Federalist, No. 42; 1 Kent's Com. Lect. 2, pp. 40–44. Halleck's International Law, p. 242, § 4; Fynn, British Consuls abroad, pp. 34–55; 2 Phillimore on International Law, § 246, 258.

In case of a revolution, or dismemberment of a nation, the judiciary cannot take notice of any new government or sovereignty, until it has been duly recognized by some other department of the government, to whom the power is constitutionally confided. (United States v. Palmer, 3 Wheat. 610, 634, 643; Hays v. Gelston, 3 Wheat. 246, 323, 324; Rose v. Himley, 4 Cr 441; the Divina Pastora, 4 Wheat. 52, and note 65; the Nuestra Señora de la Caridad, 4 Wheat. 497.) Story's Const. § 1566.

**What is the duty of the President to see the laws executed? 204.**

**189.** "HE SHALL TAKE CARE THAT THE LAWS BE FAITHFULLY EXECUTED."—That is, to execute the laws to the extent of the defensive means placed in his hands. 9 Op. 524.

The Supreme Court of the United States cannot enjoin the President from seeing the laws faithfully executed. Mississippi v. Johnson, 4 Wallace, 498. Where an executive officer is clothed with discretion, the act to be done is executive, and beyond judicial control. (Marbury v. Madison, 1 Cranch, 137; Kendall, Postmaster-General v. Stockton and Stokes, 12 Pet. 527.) Id.; The State v. The Southern P. R. R. 24 Tex. 117; Paschal's Annotated Digest, note 191.

**174, 175.**

It is of the very essence of executive power, that it should always and everywhere be capable of, and be in, full exercise. There shall be no cessation—no interval of time when there may be an incapacity of action. Stanbery on filling vacancies, 8, 9.

Under this power the governor (the President) ought to order suits in all cases where the laws are infracted and the rights of the government invaded. The State v. Delesdenier, 7 Tex. 95.

**190.** "SHALL COMMISSION ALL OFFICERS."—This seems to be 185, 185. more properly connected with the appointing of officers; but it is not one and the same thing.  Marbury v. Madison, 1 Cr. 156–7; Story's Const. § 1548.

As incident to this power, he has authority to appoint commis- *What are* sioners and agents to make investigations required by acts or reso- *the Presi-* lutions of Congress; but cannot pay them, except from an appro- *dent's powers?* priation for that purpose. 4 Opin. 248. It is not, in general, judicious for him, in the exercise of this power, to interfere in the functions of subordinate officers, further than to remove them for any neglect or abuse of their official trust. 3 Id. 287. But where combinations exist among the citizens of one of the States, to obstruct or defeat the execution of acts of Congress, and the question of the constitutionality of such laws is made in suits against a marshal of the United States, the President is justified in assuming his defense on behalf of the United States. 6 Id. 220, 500.

The various acts of President Lincoln, in calling out the militia, organizing an army, and proclaiming a blockade of the Southern ports, in April, 1861, for the suppression of the rebellion, were approved, ratified, and confirmed by a joint resolution of Congress, in August, 1861. The President was the judge of his powers, and the court is bound by his acts. The Prize Cases, 2 Black, 666.

SEC. IV.—The President, Vice-President, and all *Impeach-* civil officers of the United States, shall be removed *Who may be* from office on impeachment for, and conviction of, *impeached?* treason, bribery, or other high crimes and misdemeanors.

**191.** "CIVIL OFFICERS."—The remedy is strictly confined to *27, 39, 40.* civil officers, in contradistinction to military.  Story's Const. § 690, 691.

A senator or representative in Congress is not such civil officer. *Who are* Blount's Trial, 22, 102; Wh. St. Tr. 260,°316; 1 Story's Const. *civil* § 793, 802. See 2d vol. Senate Journal (1797), 383–393. Nor is a *officers?* territorial judge, not being a constitutional, but a legislative office only. 3 Opin. 409. But United States circuit and district judges are subject to impeachment. Peck's Trial, 20, and Chase's Trial.

No previous statute is necessary to authorize an impeachment *Where must* for any official misconduct. What are, and what are not high *we look for* crimes and misdemeanors, is to be ascertained by a recurrence to *definitions?* the rules of the common law. 1 Story's Const. § 799. Peck's Trial, 499. For the rules of proceedings prescribed in cases of impeachment, see Peck's Trial, 56–9.

Blount was expelled as a senator for a "high misdemeanor;" but the Senate refused to consider him a "civil officer," liable to "impeachment." See 2 Senate Journal, pp. 383–397. The "high misdemeanor," was not in the violation of any particular statute. *What is an*

"An impeachment before the Lords by the Commons in Great *impeach-* Britain, in Parliament, is a prosecution of the *already known and* *the common* *established law,* and has been frequently put in practice, being a *law?*

27, 39, 177.  presentment to the most high and supreme court of criminal jurisdiction by the most solemn grand inquest of the whole kingdom."
(4 Blackstone, 259); and when this most high and supreme court
of criminal jurisdiction is assembled for the trial of a person impeached for a violation of the "already known and established
law," it must proceed according to the known and established law,
for although "the trial must vary in external ceremony, it differs
not in essentials from criminal prosecutions before inferior courts.
The same rules of evidence, the same legal notions of crimes and
punishments prevail." (Woodeson, vol. 2, 611.)  Minority report
on the Impeachment of the President, 62.  See 2 Chase's Trial, 137;
Rawle's Const. 204.

What must   **192.** "TREASON AND BRIBERY."—TREASON against the United
the treason  States shall consist only in levying war against them or in adher-
be against?  ing to their enemies, giving them aid and comfort.  Art. 3, sec. 3.
215.  The treason must be against the United States.  (Rawle's Const.
ch. 22, p. 215.)  Story's Const. § 802.

BRIBERY is the offense of taking any undue reward by a judge,
juror, or other person concerned in the administration of justice, or
by a public officer, to influence his behavior in his office, (4 Black.
Com. 139, and Chitty's note; 3 Inst. 145; 4 Burr, 2494; 1 Russel
on Crimes, 151.)  Burrill's Law Dic., BRIBERY.

For what   For this definition resort must necessarily be had to the com-
must it be  mon law.  Story's Const. § 796; Peck's Trial.
defined?
No other *crimes* than bribery and treason can regularly be
inquired into as ground of impeachment.  Rawle's Const. ch. 22,
p. 215.  But neither this point, nor whether any other than a public
officer can be impeached, has been authoritatively settled.  Story's
Const. § 802, 803.

Define high   **193.** "HIGH CRIMES."—Crime or misdemeaner is an act com-
crimes?  mitted, or omitted, in violation of a public law, either forbidding or
27, 39, 194,  commanding it.  4 Bl. Com. 5.  This general definition compre-
212, 223.  hends both crimes and misdemeanors.  Id.  Crime, in a narrower
sense, is distinguished from a misdemeanor, as being an offense of
a deeper and more atrocious dye, and usually amounting to a
felony.  4 Bl. Com. 5; Burrill's Law Dic., CRIME; Minority report
on the Impeachment of the President, 61.  A breach or violation
of some public right or duty to a whole community, considered as
a community, in its social aggregate capacity; as distinguished
from civil injury.  4 Bl. 5.

The violation of a right, when considered in reference to the evil
tendency of such violation, as regards the community at large.
4 Stephen's Com. 55; 1 Id. 127, 128.  In this sense it includes misdemeanors.  Burrill's Law Dic., CRIME.

Define mis-   **194.** "MISDEMEANOR" is a less heinous species of crime; an
demeanor?  indictable offense not amounting to felony.  4 Bl. Com. by Chitty, 5,
27, 39, 192,  note; Burrill's Law Dic., MISDEMEANOR.  Properly speaking, crime
193.  and misdemeanor are synonymous.  Id.; 4 Steph. Com. 57.

In general, a *misdemeanor* is used in contradistinction to *felony*,
and comprehends all indictable offenses which do not amount to
felony; as perjury, battery, libels, conspiracies, attempts and so-

licitations to commit felonies, &c. 4 Bl. Com. notes 5, 6; Paschal's Annotated Digest, 1658-1660.

The case of Judge Humphries, at the commencement of the rebellion, was upon charges of disloyal acts and utterances, some of which clearly did not set forth offenses indictable by statute of the United States, and yet upon all those charges, with one exception only, he was convicted and removed. Report upon the Impeachment of the President, 52, 53. The minority say that they amounted to treason, because he advised secession by Tennessee, after the ordinance by South Carolina and the levying war by that State. Id. 68.

It has been insisted that none but an offense against a statute of the United States is impeachable. (1 Chase's Trial, 9-18, 47, 48; 4 Elliot's Debates, 262; Rawle's Const. ch. 29, p. 273.) Story's Const. § 796; Minority Report on the Impeachment of the President, 61. *Must the offense be against a statute? 192.*

Where any offense is punishable by an act of Congress, it ought to be impeachable. Story's Const. § 796.

So political offenses, impeachable at common law, may be so classified. Id. § 764, 763, 797, 798, 799; Jefferson's Manual, § 53, title, IMPEACHMENT; Blount's Trial, 29-31, 75-80; Farrar, § 494-496; Curtis' Com. p. 360.

No one of the cases yet tried rests upon statutable misdemeanors. Story's Const. § 799; Report upon the Impeachment of the President, pp. 51-53.

For the English parliamentary cases, see 2 Woodeson's Law Lect. 40, p. 602; Comyn's Dig. *Parliament*, 28-40; Story's Const. § 800.

Mr. Madison said: "He (the President) will be impeachable by this House, before the Senate, for such an act of maladministration: the wanton removal of meritorious officers would subject him to impeachment and removal from his high trust." (Lloyd's Debates, 503, 351, 450; 4 Elliot's Debates, 141.) Farrar's Const. § 495, 496. *What were Madison's views? 184-186.*

Whether offenses not connected with office are impeachable is still unsettled. Story's Const. § 803-805.

While this work was running through the press, a majority of the judiciary committee (on the 25th November, 1867) made a report to the House of Representatives (in response to a resolution of the House), wherein they impeached ANDREW JOHNSON, President of the United States, of "High crimes and misdemeanors." The report was signed by five members; the minority, including the chairman, dissented. The report is long, and the evidence is voluminous. *State the history of the President's impeachment?*

The committee did not charge the violation of any criminal statute. The charges are sundry usurpations of congressional power; willful efforts to defeat the work of reconstruction in the rebel States, and the encouragement of those who were engaged in the rebellion. All the charges hinge upon this one point. But, in the specifications, there are sundry charges of the violation of statute law: particularly in using money appropriated for other purposes to support the President's own reconstruction measures; in levying taxes; using United States property; restoring abandoned and captured property; ordering the dispersal of the Louisiana Convention; and conspiracies with and pardons of prominent rebels, and appointing them to office. See Report, 1–47, 55–59.

State the legal argument of the minority? 143.
It is urged by the minority of the committee, that an impeachment will only lie for offenses which are indictable; that the house is to impeach for offenses, not to create them; that nothing is penal except crimes (13 Encyc. Brit. 275); that Blackstone's definition of municipal law (1 Bl. Com. 44) is to be observed; that no *ex post facto* law shall be passed; that the definitions of crime (the same stated in this note) are to control; that, in the trial, the Senate, like the House of Lords, is a high criminal court, governed by the same rules of law and evidence as other criminal
212.
courts; that the fact that the party can be convicted in another court proves this (2 Chase's Trial, 137); that they must be "*crimes*," such as are entitled to jury-trial (Art. III. Sec. 2); that Blount's trial was for crimes (but against what criminal law is not shown); that while Pickering's offense may not have been criminal, the plea of insanity was ignored, and the case is a disreputable precedent; that Chase must have been acquitted because mere misconduct as a judge was not a crime or misdemeanor. In Blount's case,
49.
several of the charges were proved. They were; "With intending to carry into effect a hostile expedition in favor of the English against the Spanish possessions of Louisiana and Florida; with attempts to engage the Creek and Cherokee Indians in the same expedition; with having alienated the affections of the said Indians from Ben. Hawkins, an agent of the United States among the Indians, the better to answer his said purposes; with having seduced James Cary, an interpreter of the United States among the Indians, for the purpose of assisting in his criminal intentions; and with having attempted to diminish the confidence of the Cherokee Indians in relation to the boundary line, which had been run in consequence of the treaty which had been held between the United States and the said Indians." (1 Annals of 5 Cong. 499, 919.) That the plea to the jurisdiction was sustained, on the ground that Blount was not a civil officer. (Id. 2318, 2319.) That while Peck was only arraigned for misconduct, or official misbehavior, he did not
197.
*demur* to the charge, but affirmed the justice of his action; that if the point, that a judge may be tried for want of "good behavior," may be admitted, it cannot apply to the President, whose tenure is for four years; that the charges against Humphries were
217.
of treason, because they were words and acts *after* the levying of war by South Carolina; that a fair review of the English cases shows that Parliament rested all cases upon some indictable offense, though it is admitted that definitions have been strained; fifty-five cases given by Hatsell are named (p. 71); where the effort to explain fails, the precedents are boldly attacked; the current of precedents is cited to show that the federal courts can only entertain jurisdiction of crimes, defined and made penal by Congress (United States v. Hudson, 7 Cr. 32; United States v. Coolidge, 1 Wheat. 415; *Ex parte* Bollman and Swartwout, 4 Cr. 95; United States v. Lancaster, 2 McLean, 33, and various others, 77, 78): that the same principle should apply to the high court of impeachment; that "other high crimes and misdemeanors," means such as may be declared by the law-making power of the United

States, (Rawle's Const. 265); and the rest of the report is principally devoted to the facts. Report upon Impeachment of the President, 64–78. The whole argument is, that the impeachment must be for treason within the constitutional definition; for bribery within the then common-law definition; or if for other high crimes and misdemeanors, then they must be such as are created by some penal enactment of Congress; and not such as existed at, and were impeachable by, the common law. The majority of the committee assume that high crimes and misdemeanors may consist in oppressive, unjust, corrupt, and unauthorized official misconduct, although not indictable. It is not within the plan of this work to give the conclusions of the author, derived from the same class of reading. This hour of the country's history is not fortunate for a calm investigation. If we admit the conclusions of the minority report, the difficulty is only removed; for still the question would remain—which of the statute offenses would be the subject of impeachment? Shall they be piracy, homicide, larceny, forgery, counterfeiting, robbery, defalcations, or any one of the hundred felonies and misdemeanors spread over the statutes? And shall they be confined to offenses committed within the criminal jurisdiction of the United States? Such only are indictable. Or may an impeachment be for an infamous crime against the laws of a foreign country?

The question being now afloat upon the sea of public opinion, he can only hope that future writers may have more satisfactory guides. The house by a large majority sustained the minority report and refused to impeach, but still it can hardly be regarded as settling the principle, that nothing is impeachable except what is indictable as an offense against the United States.

## ARTICLE III.

SEC. 1.—The judicial power of the United States, shall be vested in one Supreme Court, and in such inferior courts as the Congress may, from time to time, ordain and establish. The judges, both of the supreme and inferior courts, shall hold their offices during good behavior; and shall, at stated times, receive for their services, a compensation, which shall not be diminished during their continuance in office.

*Define the judicial power?*

*Tenure of office? 194.*

*Compensation?*

**195.** "THE JUDICIAL POWER OF THE UNITED STATES."—*Judicialis, judex*, a judge, or *judicium*, a judgment. Burrill's Law Dic., JUDICIAL. It is the power to hear and determine controversies between litigants, upon proper cases of law and fact presented for adjudication.

*Define judicial power?*

*8, 210, 213.*

The object was to establish a judiciary for the United States, a necessary department, which did not exist under the Confederation. (Federalist, Nos. 22, 28. 80, 81; 2 Wilson's Law Lect. ch. 3, p. 201; 3 Elliot's Debates, 142, 143; Osborn v. United States

*What was the object?*

Bank, 9 Wheat. 818, 819; 1 Kent's Com. Lect. 14, pp. 290–297.) Story's Const. § 1574; Montesquieu's Spirit of Laws, b. 11, ch. 6; Rawle's Const. ch. 21, p. 199. Chisholm v. Georgia, Dall. 419, 474. For the great necessity and duties of a national judiciary, also see Cohens v. Virginia, 6 Wheat. 384–390; Id. 402–404, 415; Marbury v. Madison, 1 Cr. 137; Curtis' Commentaries, § 2. With jurisdiction to the full extent of the Constitution, laws, and treaties of the United States. Osborn v. United States Bank, 9 Wheat. 819; Martin v. Hunter, 1 Wheat. 328.

How is the power contradistinguished from the law?

233.

JUDICIAL POWER, as contradistinguished from the power of the laws, has no existence. Courts are the mere instruments of the law and can will nothing. Their discretion is a mere legal discretion. Judicial power is never exercised for the purpose of giving effect to the will of the judge; but always of the legislature or will of the law. Osborn v. Bank of United States, 9 Wheat. 818, 819, 866; 1 Kent's Com. Lect. 14, p. 277; 3 Story's Const. § 1574, note 3 of 3d edition. But must regard the Constitution as paramount. Marbury v. Madison, 1 Cr. 178; 1 Kent's Com. Lect. 20, pp. 448, 460; Cohens v. Virginia, 6 Wheat. 414.

On what does the jurisdiction depend? 210, 211.

The jurisdiction of the courts of the United States depends exclusively on the Constitution and laws of the United States. Livingston v. Jefferson, 1 Brock. 203; American Insurance Co. v. Canter, 1 Pet. 511; 1 Curtis' Com. § 4: United States v. Drenner, Hemp. 320; United States v. Alberti, Id. 444. The federal courts have the right to determine their own jurisdiction. (The United States v. Peters, 5 Cr. 115; The United States v. Booth, 21 How. 506.) Freeman v. Howe, 24 How. 459–461.

Define "shall be vested?" 211.

"SHALL BE VESTED" is mandatory upon the legislature. Its obligatory force is so imperative, that Congress could not, without a violation of its duty, have refused to carry it into operation. Martin v. Hunter, 1 Wheat. 304, 328–337; 1 Kent's Com. Lect. 14, pp. 290–293. Congress can only VEST the power in courts created by itself. Id.; Story's Const. § 1501–1503. The words afford an absolute grant of judicial power. Id.; Story's Const. § 1594.

State the divisions of power? 141, 165. 199.

275. 109.

All legislative power *shall be vested* in a Congress; all executive power in a President; all judicial power *shall be* (not may be) *vested* in *one* Supreme Court and in such inferior courts, &c. These powers are thus absolutely vested, and it is the duty of Congress to vest the *whole judicial* power. (Martin v. Hunter, 1 Wheat. 304, 337.) Story's Const. § 1590, 1591; 1 Kent's Com. Lect. 11, p. 221. And yet it cannot be denied that the *duty* of Congress to *vest* the whole judicial power, by proper legislation, is one thing; and the *power* to enforce that duty through any other department of the government. or to exercise it until distributed by legislation, is another.—[EDITOR.

What is the Supreme Court? 210, 211.

"IN ONE SUPREME COURT."—SUPREME, here means the highest national tribunal, with both original and appellate jurisdiction. But this can only have original jurisdiction in two classes of cases; those affecting ambassadors, &c.; and where a State is a party. (Martin v. Hunter, 1 Wheat. 304, 337.) Story's Const. § 1593. Congress cannot vest any portion of the power in State courts, only in courts established by itself.

**196.** "Such Inferior Courts"—Congress, having the power State the to establish inferior courts, must, as a necessary consequence, have power over the right to define their respective jurisdictions. Sheldon v. Sill, 8 inferior courts? How. 448-9; Osborn v. United States Bank, 9 Wh. 738; Turner 194, 195. v. Bank of North America, 4 Dallas. 10; McIntyre v. Wood, 7 Cr. 505; Kendall v. United States, 12 Pet. 616; Cary v. Curtis, 3 How. 245.

Therefore, "Inferior Courts" have to be ordained and Why established in order that the whole "judicial power" may be inferior courts? exercised. (Martin v. Hunter, 3 Cr. 316.) Story's Const. § 1593.

Congress has the exclusive power of legislating over the terri- 231, 232. tories, and consequently the Supreme Court has appellate jurisdiction over the courts established therein. (Benner v. Porter, 9 How. 235, 236.) Freeborn v. Smith, 2 Wall. 173. And see American Insurance Co. v. Canter, 1 Pet. 511; Hunt v. Palao, 4 How. 589; Benner v. Porter, 9 How. 214, as to the character of territorial courts.

The commissioners of the Circuit Courts of the United States are What are officers exercising functions of justices of the peace under the commissioners? laws of the commonwealth. Sim's Case, 7 Cush. 731. Congress 224, 225. might appoint justices, without commissioning them as judges, 197, 198. during good behavior, or giving them fixed salaries. Id. 194.

**197.** "The Judges both of the Supreme and Inferior Define good Courts shall hold their offices during good behavior."— behavior? The meaning of this is for life or until impeachment, unless, 191-194. indeed, there be power to abolish circuits and districts, and thus 40. to dispense with supernumerary or objectionable incumbents.

For a full note of the State Constitutions, as to tenure, see 1 Kent's Com. 11th edition, p. 295, note (a.)

The territorial judges are not of this class, as they only hold four years. (American Insurance Co. v. Canter, 1 Pet. 546.) Benner v. Porter, 9 How. 244.

Judges for a term of years.—Courts in which the judges hold What are their offices for a specific number of years, are not constitutional constitu- courts, in which the judicial powers conferred by the Constitution tional courts? can be deposited. American Ins. Co. v. Canter, 1 Pet. 511, 546. The Supreme Court of the United States was last organized Give the as follows:—Allotment, &c., of the Judges of the Supreme Court of allotment? the United States, as made April 8, 1867, under the Acts of Congress of July 23, 1866, and March 2, 1867.

| NAME OF THE JUDGE, AND STATE WHENCE COMING. | NUMBER AND TERRITORY OF THE CIRCUIT. | DATE AND AUTHOR OF THE JUDGE'S COMMISSION. |
|---|---|---|
| CHIEF-JUSTICE. Hon. S. P. CHASE, Ohio. | FOURTH. MARYLAND, WEST VIRGINIA, VIRGINIA, NORTH CAROLINA, AND SOUTH CAROLINA. | 1864. December 6th. PRESIDENT LINCOLN. |

| NAME OF THE JUDGE, AND STATE WHENCE COMING. | NUMBER AND TERRITORY OF THE CIRCUIT. | DATE AND AUTHOR OF THE JUDGE'S COMMISSION. |
|---|---|---|
| ASSOCIATES. Hon. JAMES M. WAYNE, Georgia. | FIFTH. GEORGIA, FLORIDA, ALABAMA, MISSISSIPPI, LOUISIANA, AND TEXAS. | 1835. January 9th. PRESIDENT JACKSON. |
| Hon. SAML. NELSON, New York. | SECOND. NEW YORK, VERMONT, AND CONNECTICUT. | 1845. February 14th. PRESIDENT TYLER. |
| Hon. R. C. GRIER, Pennsylvania. | THIRD. PENNSYLVANIA, NEW JERSEY, AND DELAWARE. | 1846. August 4th. PRESIDENT POLK. |
| Hon. N. CLIFFORD, Maine. | FIRST. MAINE, NEW HAMPSHIRE, MASSACHUSETTS, AND RHODE ISLAND. | 1858. January 12th. PREST. BUCHANAN. |
| Hon. NOAH H. SWAYNE, Ohio. | SIXTH. OHIO, MICHIGAN, KENTUCKY, AND TENNESSEE. | 1862. January 24th. PRESIDENT LINCOLN. |
| Hon. S. F. MILLER, Iowa. | EIGHTH. MINNESOTA, IOWA, MISSOURI, KANSAS, AND ARKANSAS. | 1862. July 16th. PRESIDENT LINCOLN. |
| Hon. DAV. DAVIS, Illinois. | SEVENTH. INDIANA, ILLINOIS, AND WISCONSIN. | 1862. December 8th. PRESIDENT LINCOLN. |
| Hon. S. J. FIELD, California. | NINTH. CALIFORNIA, OREGON, AND NEVADA. | 1863. March 10th. PRESIDENT LINCOLN. |

HENRY STANBERY, of Kentucky, Attorney-General; DANIEL WESLEY MIDDLETON, of the District of Columbia, Clerk; R. C. PARSONS, of Ohio, Marshal.

The following have been Chief-Justices of the Supreme Court of the United States:—

| | Name. | Term of Service. | Born. | Died. |
|---|---|---|---|---|
| Give a list of the Judges? | John Jay, N. Y. | 1789–1795 | 1745 | 1829 |
| | John Rutledge, S. C. | 1795–1795 | .... | 1800 |
| | Oliver Ellsworth, Conn. | 1796–1801 | 1752 | 1807 |
| | John Marshall, Va. | 1801–1835 | 1755 | 1835 |
| | Roger B. Taney, Md. | 1836–1864 | 1777 | 1864 |
| | Salmon P. Chase, O. | 1864–.... | 1809 | .... |

The following have been Associate Justices:—

| Name. | Term of Service. | Born. | Died. |
|---|---|---|---|
| John Rutledge, S. C. | 1789–1791 | .... | 1800 |
| William Cushing, Mass. | 1789–1810 | 1733 | 1810 |
| James Wilson, Penn. | 1789–1798 | 1742 | 1798 |
| John Blair, Va | 1789–1796 | 1732 | 1800 |
| Robert H. Harrison, Md. | 1789–1789 | 1745 | 1790 |
| James Iredell, N. C. | 1790–1799 | 1750 | 1799 |
| Thomas Johnson, Md. | 1791–1793 | 1732 | 1819 |
| William Paterson, N. J. | 1793–1806 | 1743 | 1806 |
| Samuel Chase, Md | 1796–1811 | 1741 | 1811 |
| Bushrod Washington, Va. | 1798–1829 | 1759 | 1829 |
| Alfred Moore, N. C. | 1799–1804 | 1755 | 1810 |
| William Johnson, S. C. | 1804–1834 | .... | 1834 |
| Brockholst Livingston, N. Y. | 1806–1823 | 1757 | 1823 |
| Thomas Todd, Ky | 1807–1826 | .... | 1826 |
| Joseph Story, Mass. | 1811–1845 | 1779 | 1845 |
| Gabriel Duvall, Md | 1811–1835 | 1751 | 1844 |
| Smith Thompson, N. Y. | 1823–1845 | 1767 | 1845 |
| Robert Trimble, Ky. | 1826–1829 | .... | 1829 |
| John McLean, Ohio. | 1829–1861 | 1785 | 1861 |
| Henry Baldwin, Penn. | 1830–1846 | 1779 | 1846 |
| James M. Wayne, Ga. | 1835–1867 | 1786 | 1867 |
| Philip P. Barbour, Va. | 1836–1841 | .... | 1841 |
| John Catron, Tenn. | 1837–1865 | 1786 | 1865 |
| John McKinley, Ala | 1837–1852 | .... | 1852 |
| Peter V. Daniel, Va. | 1841–1860 | 1785 | 1860 |
| Samuel Nelson, N. Y. | 1845– | 1792 | .... |
| Levi Woodbury, N. H. | 1845–1851 | 1790 | 1851 |
| Robert C. Grier, Penn. | 1846– | 1794 | .... |
| Benjamin R. Curtis, Mass. | 1851–1857 | 1809 | .... |
| James A. Campbell, Ala. | 1853–1856 | 1802 | .... |
| Nathan Clifford, Me. | 1858– | 1803 | .... |
| Noah H. Swayne, Ohio. | 1862– | 1805 | .... |
| Samuel F. Miller, Iowa. | 1862– | 1816 | .... |
| David Davis, Illinois. | 1862– | 1815 | .... |
| Stephen J. Field, California. | 1863– | 1817 | .... |

Efforts were made at the Supreme Court clerk's office, and at the State Department, to obtain more accurate information as to the respective dates of service, but without success.

**198.** The "COMPENSATION" of Judges is at present as follows: Chief-Justice, six thousand five hundred dollars; Associate Justices, six thousand dollars each.   10 Stat. 655; Brightly's Dig. 819.   The District Judges' salaries vary from three thousand five hundred dollars to five thousand five hundred dollars. *State the present compensation?*

This compensation prohibits the imposition of a tax upon a judge's salary. Commonwealth v. Mann, 5 W. & S. 415.   Congress may give the Circuit Court original jurisdiction in any case to which the appellate jurisdiction extends.   (Osborn v. The Bank of the United States, 9 Wh 821.)   Jones v. Seward, 41 Barb. 272-3. *Can it be taxed?*

9

And see United States v. Bevans, 3 Wheat. 336. When
the Act of Congress directs the transfer of the case, wo
have nothing to do with the validity of the law as a defense to the
action. (Story's Const. ch. 38, § 903, 906, *et seq.*; Martin v.
Hunter, 1 Wh. 304; Cohens v. Virginia, 6 Wh. 364; Osborn
v. The Bank of the United States, 9 Wh. 738.) Jones v. Seward,
41 Barb. 273. As to what cases will be transferred from the State
to the federal court, see 1 Brightly's Dig. Laws U. S. p. 128,
§ 19, notes *d, e, g,* and *h;* Smith v. Rines, 2 Sumn. 338; Wilson
v. Blodget, 4 McLean, 363; Hubbard v. The Northern R. R. Co. 25
Vt. 715, 719; Welch v. Tenent, 4 Cal. 203; Ladd v. Tudor, 3
W. & M. 325. No suit can be removed in which a State is a
party. New Jersey v. Babcock, 4 Wash. C. C. 344. After the
proper steps for removal, any subsequent proceedings in the State
courts are illegal. Gordon v. Longest, 16 Pet. 97; 1 Kent's
Com. 295.

Sec. II.—[1.] The judicial power shall extend to all
cases, in law and equity, arising under this Constitution, the laws of the United States, and treaties made,
or which shall be made under their authority; to all
cases affecting ambassadors, other public ministers,
and consuls; to all cases of admiralty and maritime
jurisdiction; to controversies to which the United
States shall be a party; to controversies between two
or more States; between a State and citizens of
another State; between citizens of different States;
between citizens of the same State, claiming lands
under grants of different States, and between a State,
or the citizens thereof, and foreign States, citizens
or subjects.

**199.** Judicial Power, as contradistinguished from legislative
power and executive power, is the power to hear and determine
all the cases of law and fact, which arise between the government
and parties, or between parties, under this Constitution, the law
of nations, and the laws and treaties of the United States, which
shall be legally brought within the cognizance and jurisdiction of
any of the courts or judicial tribunals established under the Constitution. It was intended to be a separate department of the
government, possessing all the "judicial power" of the national

government except upon the single jurisdiction of impeachment.
Not a power to control the other departments of the government
in their official actions, but to act independently of them under the
Constitution and laws.

But the judicial power does not extend to all *questions* which
arise under the Constitution, laws, and treaties, because many of

these are political, and have to be solved by other departments of
the government.  Thus:—

"TREATIES."—Where the title to property depended on the **Has the**
question, whether the land was within a cession by treaty to the **judiciary**
United States, after our government, legislative and executive, **struction of**
had claimed jurisdiction over it, the courts must consider that **all treaties,**
question as a political one, the decision of which having been made **or what is**
in this manner, they must conform to it. (Foster v. Neilson, 2 Pet. **the rule?**
309; United States v. Arredondo, 6 Pet. 711, 712; Garcia v. **178, 24.**
Lee, 12 Pet. 520, 521; Williamson v. Suffolk Ins. Co., 13 Pet. 441,
920.) Luther v. Borden, 7 How. 56.

So the protection of the Indians in their possessions seems to be **As to the**
a political question. (Cherokee Nation v. Georgia, 5 Pet. 20.) Id. **Indians?**
So as to State boundaries, unless agreed to be settled, as a judicial **91-92.**
question. (Rhode Island v. Massachusetts, 12 Pet. 736, 738; **State boun-**
Garcia v. Lee. Id. 520.) Id. And they have agreed upon this **daries?**
court to settle such questions. Rhode Island v. Massachusetts, 12 **195.**
Pet. 737. And so of foreign treaties, as to confiscations. (Barclay **274.**
v. Russel, 3 Ves. 424, 434.) Id. And generally as to political
treaties. (Carnatic v. The East India Company, 2 Ves. jr. 56.)
Luther v Borden, 7 How. 56. So as to which must be regarded
as the rightful government abroad between two contending parties, **As to revo-**
is never settled by the judiciary, but is left to the general govern- **lutions?**
ment. (The Cherokee Nation v. Georgia, 5 Pet. 50; Williams v.
Suffolk Ins. Co. 13 Pet. 419; Rose v. Himley, 4 Cr. 241; United
States v. Palmer, 3 Wheat. 634; Gilston v. Hoyt, Id. 246; The
Divina Pastora, 4 Wheat. 64.) Luther v. Borden, 7 How. 56, 57.

The same rule has been applied in a contest as to which is the **233, 235.**
true Constitution, between two, or which possesses the true legislative power in one of our own States. (Scott v. Jones, 5 How.
374.) Luther v. Borden, 7 How. 57.

Congress is the legislative department of the government; the **110.**
President is the executive department. Neither can be restrained **195.**
in its action by the judicial department; though the acts of both,
when performed, are, in proper cases, subject to its cognizance.
Mississippi v. Johnson, 4 Wall. 500.

A CASE arises, within the meaning of the Constitution, **Define a**
whenever any question respecting the Constitution, laws, or treaties **case?**
of the United States, has assumed such a form, that the judicial **140, 141.**
power is capable of acting on it. Osborn v. United States Bank, 9 **198, 210.**
Wh. 819; Jones v. Seward, 41 Barb. 272; Curtis' Com. § 7; Ex **263, 264.**
parte Milligan, 4 Wallace, 112, 114. LAW, in this article, and **201.**
COMMON LAW, in the seventh amendment, mean the same thing;
that is, not merely *suits* which the common law recognized among
its old and settled proceedings, but suits in which legal rights were
to be ascertained and determined in contradistinction to those
where equitable rights are administered. (Parsons v. Bedford, 3
Pet. 447.) Fenn v. Holmes. 21 How. 486 (cites Strother v. Lucas,
6 Pet. 768; Parish v. Ellis, 16 Pet. 453-4; and Bennett v. Butter-
worth, 11 How. 669). And see Sheirburne v. De Cordova, 24
How. 423. Or, where the proceeding is in the admiralty. Parsons
v. Bedford, 3 Pet. 447; Robinson v. Campbell, 3 Wh. 212. The

action of ejectment, or trespass to try title, cannot be supported on
the common-law side of the United States Court, upon the inchoate
titles recognized by the State statutes.  Fenn v. Holmes, 21 How.
481 ; Hooper v. Scheimer, 23 Id. 249; Sheirburne v. De Cordova,
24 Id. 423.

This class of cases is without reference to who are the parties.
Curtis' Com. § 3–17.  See Van Ness v. Packard, 2 Pet. 137, 144;
Wheaton v. Peters, 8 Pet. 591 ; Terrett v. Taylor, 9 Cr. 43 ; Town
of Pawlet v. Clarke, Id. 292.

When considered?   But a "CASE" can only be considered when the subject is submitted to it by a party who asserts his rights in the form prescribed
by law.  (Osborn v. Bank of the United States, 9 Wh. 819.)  Curtis'
Com. § 7.    And see Robinson v. Campbell, 2 Wh. 212, 221, 223;
Parsons v. Bedford, 3 Pet. 433, 416, 447.  That is, there must be a
judicial proceeding.  Curtis' Com. § 10, 11; Osborn v. Bank of
United States, 9 Wheat. 738, 819, 821.

The record must show that the Constitution or some law or
treaty was drawn in question.  (Lawter v. Walker, 12 How. 149;
Mills v. Brown, 16 Pet. 525.)  Railroad Co. v. Rock, 4 Wall. 180.

And under the 25th section of the judiciary act, the decision must
be against the validity of the act, treaty, or Constitution; not in
favor of it.  Ryan v. Thomas, 604.

Define a case in equity? 199.   **200.** BY "CASES IN EQUITY," are to be understood suits in
which relief is sought according to the principles and practice of the
equity jurisdiction as established in English jurisprudence.  Robinson v. Campbell, 3 Wh. 222–3; United States v. Howland, 4 Id.
108; Lanman v. Clark, 2 McLean, 570–1 , Lanman v. Clark, 4 Id.
18; Gordon v. Hobart, 2 Sumn. 401; Pratt v. Northam, 5 Mas.
95; Cropper v. Coburn, 2 Curtis' C. C. 465.  And see 1 Curtis'
What is the true test of equity jurisdiction?   Com. § 7–9, 19a–30.  The true test of equity jurisdiction is,
whether there is a plain, adequate, and complete remedy at law in
the same courts.  United States v. Howland, 4 Wheat. 108;
Boyce's Executors v. Grundy, 3 Pet. 210, 215 , Gould v. Gould, 3
Story R. 516, 536; Gaines v. Chew, 2 How. 619, 645; Williams v.
Benedict, 8 How. 107 ; Curtis' Com. § 23–38.  Not according to
the practice of the State courts, but the distinctions in England.
Robinson v. Campbell, 3 Wheat. 222, 223.

When does a case arise?   **201.** A CASE is said to "ARISE" under the Constitution or laws
of the United States, whenever its correct decision depends on the
construction of either.  Cohens v. Virginia, 6 Wh. 379.  A bill in
equity to enforce a specific performance of a contract to convey a
103.   patent, is not a "case arising under the laws of the United States"
as to patents, so as alone to give jurisdiction to its Courts.  Nes-
mith v. Calvert, 1 W. & M. 34.  A case in admiralty, is not a case
arising under the Constitution, but the jurisdiction is as old as
admiralty itself.  The Amer. Ins. Co. v. Canter, 1 Pet. 545.  This
255–259.   article is reconcilable with the 5th amendment, and the several judiciary acts on the subject of trial by jury.  Parsons v. Bedford, 3
Pet. 444; Story's Const. § 1645; Chisholm v. Georgia, 2 Dall. 419,
What is a case?   433, 437 ; S. C., 635, 640, 642.

A "CASE" is a controversy between parties which has taken a

shape for judicial decision.  Marshall's speech, 5 Wheat. App. 16, **199.**
17; Osborn v. Bank of United States, 9 Wheat. 819.  A CASE is a suit
in law or equity, instituted according to a regular course of judicial 121-p. 124.
proceedings; and when it involves any question arising under the
Constitution, treaties, or laws of the United States, it is within the
judicial power confided to the Union.  (See 1 Tuck. Black. Com.
418–420; Madison's Virginia resolutions and report, January, 1800,
p. 28; Marbury v. Madison, 1 Cr. 137, 173, 174; Owing v. Norwood, 5 Cr. 344; 2 Elliot's Debates, 418, 419; Martin v. Hunter,
1 Wheat. 304; Cohens v. Virginia, 6 Wheat. 264, 378–392.)
Story's Const. § 1647–1656.  It consists of the right of the one
party as well as the other.  Cohens v. Virginia, 6 Wheat. 379.

**202.**  "IN ALL CASES AFFECTING AMBASSADORS, OTHER PUBLIC How are
MINISTERS AND CONSULS."—These classes are usually distinguished foreign
in diplomacy:—1. AMBASSADORS, who are the highest order, who are representa-
considered as personally representing their sovereigns; 2. ENVOYS fied? tives classi-
EXTRAORDINARY AND MINISTERS PLENIPOTENTIARY; 3. MINISTERS 180, 181, 210.
RESIDENT, AND MINISTERS CHARGÉ D'AFFAIRES.  Mere chargés
d'affaires are deemed of still lower rank.  Dr. Lieber's Encyc. Am.
Art. MINISTERS, FOREIGN: Vattel, B. 4 chap. 6, § 71–74.  And
see Schooner Exchange v. McFadden, 7 Cr. 116, 138; Story's
Const. § 1658, 3d ed. 494. note 1.  Whatever their rank and grade
public ministers of every class are the immediate representatives
of their sovereigns.  Id.

The federal courts have jurisdiction of all suits "affecting" Is it neces-
public ministers, although they may not be parties to the record. sary they
Osborn v. United States Bank, 9 Wh. 854–5.  See United States v. should be
Ortega, 11 Wh. 467; United States v. Ravara, 2 Dall; 297, S. C., 4 the record?
Wash. C. C. 531.  The recognition of the executive of the United
States is conclusive as to the public character of the party. Dupont
v. Pichon, 4 Dall. 321; United States v. Ortega, 4 Wash. C. C.
531; Curtis' Com. § 31–35; Story's Const. § 1660–1662, notes to
3d ed.

**203.**  "ADMIRALTY AND MARITIME JURISDICTION."—The cases What is
are:—1. Captures made *jure belli* upon certain waters, and all admiralty
questions of prize and other incidents arising therefrom; 2. and mari-
Crimes and offenses against the laws of the United States com- diction? time juris-
mitted upon the same waters; 3. Civil acts, torts, and injuries 110–116.
committed upon the same waters not under claim or color of exercising the rights of war, as assaults and personal injuries; col-
lisions of ships, illegal seizures, or depredations upon property;
illegal dispossession of ships, seizures for breaches of revenue
laws, and salvage services.  Curtis' Com. § 37; and see same,
§ 38–52; Marshall's Speech, 5 Wheat. App. 16; Martin v. Hunter, 1 Wheat. 335; Story's Const. § 1666, 1669, 3d ed., note 1;
Abbott on Shipping, P. 2, chap. 4, pp. 132–138, and notes to
American editions; 1 Kent's Com. Lect. XVII., pp. 342–352, and
notes.  But the torts must be upon the navigable waters, and not
partly on land.  (Thomas v. Lane, 2 Sumner, 9; The Huntress,
Davies, 85; United States v. McGill, 1 Wash. C. C. 463; s. c., 4
Dall. 346; Plumer v. Webb, 4 Mas. 383, 384.)  The Plymouth, 3
Wall. 333, 334.

<table>
<tr><td>

**How far does the jurisdiction extend?**

</td><td>

The Admiralty clause embraces what was known and understood in the United States, as the admiralty and maritime jurisdiction, at the time when the Constitution was adopted. Genesee Chief v. Fitzhugh, 12 How. 443; New Jersey Steam Navigation Co. v. Merchants' Bank, 6 Id. 244; Waring v. Clark, 8 Id. 411; Tunno v. The Betsina, 5 Am. L. R., 408; The Huntress, Davies, 83. And also extends the power so as to cover every expansion of jurisdiction. Waring v. Clarke, 5 How. 458.

</td></tr>
</table>

**Why was maritime used?**

The word "maritime" was added to guard against any narrow interpretation of the preceding word "admiralty." Story's Const. § 1666. In Hine v. Trevor, 4 Wall. 561–569, Mr. Justice Miller reviewed the steamboat Thomas Jefferson, 10 Wh. 428; The steamboat Orleans, 11 Pet. 175; Warring v. Clark, 8 How. 441; The Genesee Chief, 12 How. 457 (which overruled the first two); Fritz v. Bull, 12 How; The Moses Taylor, 4 Wall. 411; The statute of 1845, 5 St. 726; of 1789, 1 St. 77, and deduced the following rules :—

**What was the extent and division of admiralty jurisdiction?**

1. The admiralty jurisdiction is not limited to tide water, but covers the entire navigable waters of the United States; 2. The original jurisdiction in admiralty, exercised by the district courts, by virtue of the act of 1789, is exclusive, not only of the federal courts, but of the State courts also; 3. The jurisdiction of admiralty causes arising on the interior waters of the United States, other than the lakes and their connecting waters, is conferred by the Act of September 24th, 1789; 4. The admiralty jurisdiction exercised by the same courts, on the lakes, and the waters connecting those lakes, is governed by the Act of 3d February, 1845; 5. The Acts of the State legislatures, which virtually give admiralty remedies on the navigable rivers, are unconstitutional and void. 4 Wall. 569.

Since the case of the Genesee Chief (12 How. 457), navigable waters may be substituted for tide-waters. The Plymouth, 3 Wall. 34.

**Enumerate some of the cases?**

The jurisdiction of the admiralty courts in this country, at the time of the Revolution, and for a century before, was more extensive than the high court of admiralty in England. Paschal's Annotated Digest, note 89; The Genesee Chief, 12 How. 455. This jurisdiction extends to the navigable lakes and rivers of the United States, without regard to the ebb and flow of the tides of the ocean. Genesee Chief v. Fitzhugh, 12 How. 443. It embraces all maritime contracts, wheresoever the same may be made or executed, and whatever may be the form of the stipulations; and also all torts and injuries committed upon waters within its jurisdiction. De Lovio v. Boit, 2 Gall. 398; Gloucester Ins. Co. v. Younger, 2 Curt. C. C. 322; Philadelphia & Havre de Grace Towboat Co. v. Philadelphia, Wilmington & Baltimore Railroad Co. 5 Am. L. R. 230. All crimes and offenses against the laws of the United States. Corfield v. Coryell, 4 Wash. C. C. 371; United States v. Bevans, 3 Wh. 336. And all cases of seizures for breaches of the revenue laws, and those made in the exercise of the rights of war. The Vengeance, 3 Dall. 297; The Sally, 2 Cr. 406; The New Jersey Steam Navigation Co. v. Merchants' Bank, 6 How. 344. Another class of cases, in which jurisdiction has always been exercised by the admiralty courts in this country, but which is denied in England, are suits by ship-carpenters and material-men, for repairs and necessaries made and furnished to ships, whether foreign, or in the port of a State to which they do not belong, or in the home port, if the municipal laws give a lien for the work and materials. Gardner v. The New Jersey, 1 Pet. Adm. 227; Stevens v. The Sandwich, Id. 233, n.; Zane v. The Brig President, 4 Wash. C. C. 453; The Ship Robert Fulton, 1 Paine, 620; Davis v. A New Brig, Gilp. 473; The General Smith, 4 Wh. 438; Wick v. The Samuel Strong, 6 McLean, 590; Curtis' Com. § 36–52.

The jurisdiction extends to the seizure of cotton upon rivers in the States in rebellion. Mrs. Alexander's Cotton, 2 Wall. 419. But cotton seized upon land could not be the subject of lawful prize, although it was subject to capture, notwithstanding it was private property. Id. *117, 118.*

**204.** "CONTROVERSIES TO WHICH THE UNITED STATES SHALL BE A PARTY."—1. The jurisdiction is not conferred upon any particular court; Congress must therefore designate the tribunal; 2. Cognizance is not given of all controversies, but only of some; 3. "Controversies" seem to embrace only civil suits. Cohens v. Virginia, 6 Wheat. 264, 411, 412; Story's Const. § 1674–1681; Curtis' Com. § 56, 57. *Where is the jurisdiction when the United States is a party?*

The United States can only be sued in cases where it has consented to be sued by act of Congress. Curtis' Com. § 57; Story's Const. § 1677, 1678. As in suits for the confirmation of land grants and in the Court of Claims. Curtis' Com. § 100–102. *When can the United States be sued?*

A suit against the President to prevent the enforcement of the reconstruction laws, was held to be a suit against the executive of the United States, and dismissed for want of jurisdiction. Mississippi v. Johnson, 4 Wall. 498. Georgia v. Stanton, 6 Wall. 000.

**205.** "TO CONTROVERSIES BETWEEN TWO OR MORE STATES." —This means States of the Union.

This clause about suits between States, includes a suit brought by one State against another, to determine a question of disputed boundary. Rhode Island v. Massachusetts, 12 Pet. 657; Alabama v. Georgia, 23 How. 510. And only applies to those States that are members of the Union, and to public bodies owing obedience and conformity to its Constitution and laws. Scott v. Jones, 5 How. 377. And a State is within the operation of this clause only when it is a party to the record, as a plaintiff or defendant, in its political capacity. Osborn v. United States Bank, 9 Wheat. 738; 1 Curtis' Com. § 59, 63. The Cherokee nation is not a State, within the meaning of the Constitution, either foreign or domestic—nor had it the right to sue Georgia before the Supreme Court of the United States. The Cherokee Nation v. Georgia, 5 Pet. 1, 16–20. *What may be included by a State against a State? s. 9, 223– 228.*

As early as 1792, this court exercised original jurisdiction, without any further legislation than the act of 1789. (Brailsford v. Georgia, 2 Dall. 402, 415; Oswald v. Georgia, Dall.; Chisholm v. Georgia, 2 Dall. 419, 478; New Jersey v. New York, 5 Pet.

Upon whom should the process be served? 284; Grayson v. Virginia, 3 Dall. 320.) These cases settle that the process should be served upon the chief executive and attorney-general of the State. Kentucky v. Ohio, 24 How. 96–7. Where the governor sues or is sued, in his official capacity, it is a suit by or against the State. Id. 97, 99; Governor of Georgia v. Madrazo, 1 Pet. 110. A mandamus is an ordinary process to which a State is entitled, where it is applicable. (Kendall v. The United States, 12 Pet. 615; Kendall v. Stokes, 3 How. 100.) Kentucky v. Ohio, 24 How. 97–8.

For the necessity of this jurisdiction, see Federalist, No. 80; Kent's Com. Lect. 14; Chisholm v. Georgia, 2 Dall. 437–445; Sergeant's Const. Introduction, 11–16; New York v. Connecticut, 4 Dall. 3; Fowler v. Lindsay, 3 Dall. 411; 3 Elliot's Debates, 281; 2 Elliot's Debates, 418; Penn v. Lord Baltimore, 1 Vesey, 444; Story's Const. § 80, 489, 1679–1681; 1 Chalm. Annals, 480–490.

The jurisdiction is a necessity to prevent a resort to the sword. Story's Const. § 1681. See Ableman v. Booth, 21 How. 506; Curtis' Com. 60–70.

A State obtained an injunction to prevent the construction of a bridge which would impede the navigation of the Ohio River. Pennsylvania v. Wheeling & Belmont Bridge Co. 13 How. 518.

271, 272. The 11th article of the amendments has forbidden suits by individual citizens against the States.

If the judicial power does not extend to *all* controversies between States, it excludes none. Rhode Island v. Massachusetts, 12 Pet. 657; Curtis' Com. § 60.

Its mere interest in a corporation will not oust the jurisdiction, U. S. Bank v. Planters' Bank, 9 Wheat. 904, 966; Curtis' Com. § 66. See also Bank of the Commonwealth of Kentucky v. Wistar, 2 Pet. 318.

It seems the court will look into the interest of the State, where it claims to be a party. Pennsylvania v. Wheeling Bridge Co. 13 How. 518, 539; Curtis' Com. § 70.

205, 203, 211, 271, 272. **205a.** "BETWEEN A STATE AND THE CITIZENS OF ANOTHER STATE."—Before the eleventh amendment (1793), it was held, that this authorized suits to be brought *against*, as well as *by* States, where the plaintiff was a citizen of another State. Chisholm v. Georgia, 2 Dall. 419–478; Cohens v. Virginia, 6 Wheat. 406; Curtis' Com. § 60.

Can a citizen sue a State? 271, 272. But this power of a citizen to sue a State is removed by the eleventh amendment. For the history and object of the amendment, see Cohens v. Virginia, 6 Wheat. 406 *et seq.*; Curtis' Com. § 62. But where a State recovers a judgment against a citizen a writ of error will still lie. Id.; Cohens v. Virginia, 6 Wheat. 409.

When is a State within the rule? 271. A State is within the operation of this original clause of the Constitution, only when it is a party to the record, as plaintiff or defendant, in its political capacity. Osborn v. Bank of United States, 9 Wheat. 738; Curtis' Com. § 63–65. New York v. Connecticut, 4 Dall. 3; Story's Const. § 1680, 1681.

Where a State is a party to the record, the question of jurisdiction is decided by inspection. Id.

The State is only a party when it is on the record as such.

(Fowler v. Lindsay, 3 Dall. 411, 415; S. C. 1 Pet. Com. 190, 191; New York v. Connecticut, 4 Dall. 1–6; United States v. Peters, 5 Cr. 115, 139; 1 Kent's Com. Lect. 15, p. 302.) Story's Const. § 1685.

**206.** "CONTROVERSIES BETWEEN CITIZENS OF DIFFERENT STATES." —"CONTROVERSIES" is synonymous with civil suits. Curtis' Com. § 73. It may be deduced: 1. That they are all citizens of the United States, who are domiciliated in a State; (Scott v. Sandford, 19 How. 393.) 2. And they are suits where one party is a citizen of one State, and the other a citizen of another. Curtis' Com. § 73. The *situation* of the parties, rather than their *characters* determines the jurisdiction. Id. At the commencement of the suit. Connoly v. Taylor, 2 Peters, 556, 564.

This clause does not embrace cases where one of the parties is a citizen of a territory, or of the District of Columbia. Hartshorn v. Wright, Peters C. C. 64; Scott v. Jones, 5 How. 377; Hepburn v. Elszey, 2 Cr. 445; Corporation of New Orleans v. Winter, 1 Wh. 91; Gassies v. Ballou, 6 Pet. 761; 1 Kent's Com. Lect. 17, p. 360; Story's Const. § 1693, 1694; Curtis' Com. § 77. Citizenship, when spoken of in the Constitution, in reference to the jurisdiction of the federal courts, means nothing more than residence. Lessee of Cooper v. Galbraith, 3 Wash. C. C. 546; Gassies v. Ballou, 6 Pet. 761; Shelton v. Tiffin, 6 How. 163; Lessee of Butler v. Farnsworth, 4 Wash. C. C. 101. But a free negro of the African race, whose ancestors were brought to this country and sold as slaves, is not a citizen within the meaning of the Constitution, nor entitled to sue in that character in the federal courts. Scott v. Sandford, 19 How. 393–4. But see the Civil Rights Bill, note 6, p. 55; 14 St. p. 27, § 1; Paschal's Annotated Digest, Art. 5382. A corporation created by, and transacting business in a State, is to be deemed an inhabitant of the State, capable of being treated as a citizen, for all purposes of suing and being sued. Louisville R. R. Co. v. Letson, 2 How. 497; Marshall v. Baltimore & Ohio R. R. Co. 16 Id. 314; Wheeden v. Camden & Amboy R. R. Co. 4 Am. L. R. 296. The judiciary act confines the jurisdiction, on the ground of citizenship, to cases where the suit is between a citizen of a State and a citizen of another State; and, although the Constitution gives a broader extent to the judicial power, the actual jurisdiction of the circuit courts is governed by the act of Congress. Moffat v. Soley, 2 Paine, 103; Hubbard v. Northern R. R. Co. 25 Vt. 715. So, too, in the same act, there is an exception, that where suit is brought in favor of an assignee, there shall be no jurisdiction, unless suit could have been brought in the courts of the United States, had no assignment been made. This is a restriction on the jurisdiction conferred by the Constitution; and yet this provision has been sustained by the Supreme Court since its organization. Assignee of Brainard v. Williams, 4 McLean, 122; Sheldon v. Sill, 8 How. 441. The Constitution has defined the limits of the judicial power, but has not prescribed how much of it shall be exercised by the circuit courts. Turner v. Bank of North America, 4 Dall. 10; McIntyre v. Wood, 7 Cr. 506; Kendall v. United States, 12 Pet. 616; Cary v. Curtis 3 How. 245.

*Margin notes:* Controversies? 199–201. Who are citizens of a State? 17, 19, 25, 93, 169, 220–222. What determines the jurisdiction? What does citizenship mean? 6, 18, 93, 170, 220. 274. 274. 222.

9*

It is well understood by those experienced in the jurisprudence of the United States, that Congress has conferred upon the federal courts but a portion of the jurisdiction contemplated by the Constitution. Clarke v. City of Janesville, 4 Am. L. R. 593. The plaintiffs should distinctly aver that they are citizens of different States; and in the absence of such averment, the judgment will be reversed for want of jurisdiction. (Bingham v. Cabott, 3 Dall. 382; Jackson v. Ashton, 8 Pet. 148; Capron v. Van Noorden, 2 Cr. 126; Montalet v. Murray, 4 Cr. 46.) Scott v. Sandford, 19 How. 420. Curtis' Com. § 79, note 4. But if the citizenship be denied, it should be by plea in abatement, or it should otherwise appear in the record. Id. See 1 Brightly's Dig. p. 126, sec. 17, and notes thereon. The Constitution of the Confederate States omitted this jurisdiction. Paschal's Annotated Dig. p. 92. In other respects it corresponded to this section and the eleventh amendment. Id.

How must the citizenship be averred?

The citizenship must be expressly averred, or the facts which constitute it must be set forth. (Turner v. Bank of North America, 4 Dall. 8; Montalet v. Murray, 4 Cr. 46; Bailey v. Dozier, 6 How. 23.) Curtis' Com. § 78.

See the Judiciary Act of September 24, 1789, 1 St. 78; 1 Brightly's Digest, p. 126 and notes.

What is the extent of the jurisdiction?

The Judiciary Act of 1789 limited jurisdiction of national courts so far as they are determined by citizenship, "to suits between a citizen of the State in which the suit is brought and a citizen of another State," and except in relation to revenue cases this limitation remains unchanged. Ins. Co. v. Ritchie, 5 Wall. 542. In consequence of nullification the jurisdiction was extended to "all cases in law or equity arising under the revenue laws of the United States for which other provisions have not already been made." (4 Stat. 632.) Id. And by this act many suits brought in the State courts were removed into the circuit courts (Elliott v. Swartwout, 10 Pet. 137; Bend v. Hoyt, 13 Pet. 267); Ins. Co. v. Ritchie, 5 Wall. 542. The fiftieth section of the Internal Revenue Act of 1854 extended the act of 1833 to all cases arising under the laws for the collection of internal duties. (12 Stat. 241.) Id. But the act of 1866 repealed the fiftieth section aforesaid, without any saving of such causes as were then pending, and said that "the act of 1833 shall not be so construed as to apply to cases arising under act of 1864," &c. This ousted jurisdiction in the causes then pending. Id. When the jurisdiction of a cause depends upon a statute, the repeal of which takes away the jurisdiction, or it is prohibited by a subsequent statute, it can no longer be exercised. (Rex v. Justices of London, 3 Burrow, 1456; Norris v. Crocker, 13 How. 229.) Ins. Co. v. Ritchie, 5 Wall. 544. But where the case would be removable under the new provision, and it is the opinion of the circuit judge that it ought to be retained, the jurisdiction is not lost. City of Philadelphia v. Collector, 4 Wall. 720–30.

As respects the proof of the residence or domiciliation to constitute citizenship, see Shelton v. Tiffin, 6 How. 163, 185

Can a corporation be a citizen?

A corporation, whose members are citizens of a different State from the other party, is a citizen of a different State. Hope Ins.

Co. v. Boardman, 5 Cr. 57; Bank of United States v. Devaux, 5 Cr. 61; United States v. Planters' Bank, 9 Wheat. 410; Story's Const. § 1695; Curtis' Com. § 76, 78. The doctrine is to be extended to its creation and place of business. The Commercial & Railroad Bank of Vicksburg v. Slocomb, 14 Pet. 60.

**207.** "BETWEEN CITIZENS OF THE SAME STATE CLAIMING LANDS UNDER GRANTS OF DIFFERENT STATES."—A grant of land is a title emanating from the sovereignty of the soil.

Cases of grants made by different States are within the jurisdiction, notwithstanding one of the States, at the time of the first grant, was part of the other. Town of Pawlet v. Clark, 9 Cr. 292. It is the grant which passes the legal title; and if the controversy is founded upon the conflicting grants of different States, the federal courts have jurisdiction, whatever may have been the prior equitable title of the parties. Colson v. Lewis, 2 Wh. 377. Notwithstanding one State may have originally covered the territory of both. The question is, have the grants been made by different States? Id.; Curtis' Com. § 80.

**208.** "CONTROVERSIES BETWEEN A STATE OR THE CITIZENS THEREOF, AND FOREIGN STATES, CITIZENS, OR SUBJECTS."—This was intended to give cognizance to the federal judiciary where foreign States, or individual foreigners, are parties. See Chappedelaine v. De Chenaux, 4 Cr. 306, 308; Brown v. Strode, 5 Cr. 303.

An Indian tribe, or nation, within the United States, is not a "foreign State," within the meaning of this clause. Cherokee Nation v. Georgia, 5 Pet. 1. See this case for a definition of the relations of the Cherokees, as a dependent subordinate State. The very term "nation," so generally applied to them, means "a people distinct from others." Worcester v. Georgia, 6 Pet. 619.

**209.** "FOREIGN CITIZENS OR SUBJECTS."—If the party to the record be an alien, he is within this clause, whether he sue in his own right, or as trustee, if he has a substantive interest as a trustee. Chappedelaine v. De Chenaux, 4 Cr. 306. And if the nominal plaintiff, although a citizen, sue for the use of an alien, who is the real party in interest, the case is within the jurisdiction. Browne v. Strode, 5 Id. 303. A foreign corporation is an alien for this purpose. Society for the Propagation of the Gospel v. Town of New Haven, 8 Wh. 464. Possibly enlarged to creation and residence. Commercial & Railroad Bank of Vicksburg v. Slocomb, 14 Pet. 60; Curtis' Com. § 81.

The opposite party must be a citizen, and this must appear from the record. Jackson v. Twentyman, 2 Pet. 136.

A mere declaration of intention to become a citizen, under the naturalization laws, is not sufficient to prevent an alien from being regarded as a foreign subject, within the meaning of this clause. Baird v. Byre, 3 Wall. Jr.

An alien is a stranger born; a person born in another or foreign country, as distinguished from a native or natural born citizen or subject. In English law, born out of the legiance or allegiance of the king. Co. Litt. § 128, 129a; 7 Co. 31; 1 Bl. Com. 366, 373; 2 Steph. Com. 426–429. In American law,

*Marginal notes:*

207, 220, 221

What is a grant?

When are grants by different States?

205, 205a, 211.
What was the object of this provision?

Is an Indian tribe a foreign State?

91.

What aliens can sue?

Suppose a nominal plaintiff sue for an alien?

206, 220, 221.

Is there jurisdiction where both parties are aliens?

6, 19, 93, 220.
Who are aliens?

274.  one born out of the jurisdiction of the United States; 2 Kent's Com. 50; Burrill's Law Dic., ALIEN.

What are the rights of aliens to recover real estate?  At common law an alien cannot maintain a real action or one for the recovery of real estate. (Co. Litt. 129; Shepherd's Touchstone, 204; Roscoe on Real Actions, 197; Littleton, § 198.)  White v. Sabariego, 23 Tex. 246.

And see Jones v. McMasters, 20 How. 8, 20, 21; Paschal's Annotated Digest, notes 147–150, 237–240; 1168–1170a, and the numerous cases upon the rights of aliens there cited. Lanfear v. Hunly, 4 Wall. 209; McDonough v. Millandon, 3 How. 707; Semple v. Hagar, 4 Wall. 433, 434; 1 Daniel, ch. 53; Bayes v. Hogg, 1 Hayw. 485; Orser v. Hoag, 3 Hill, 79.

What are the aliens' rights to take and hold?  But an alien may take lands and may hold them against every person except the king, and against the king until inquisition of office. And if the alien be naturalized, before seizure by the government, the alien's title vests absolutely, and by relation relates back to the date of the purchase.  Fairfax v. Hunter. 7 Cr. 603; Cox v. McIlvaine, 2 Cond. 86; Chirac v. Chirac, 2 Wheat. 259; Hughes v. Edwards, 9 Wheat. 489; Carneal v. Banks, 10 Wheat. 181; Jackson v. Clarke, 3 Wheat. 1; Craig v. Leslie, 3 Wheat. 563, 589; Craig v. Radford, 3 Wheat. 594; Orr v. Hodgson, 4 Wheat. 453; Fox v. Southack, 12 Mass. 148; Jackson v. Adams, 7 Wend. 376; Jackson ex dem. Culverhouse v. Beach, 1 John's Cases. 399; S. C. 4 Johns. 75; Bradwell v. Weeks, 1 Johns. 206; Moore v. White, 6 Johns. Chan. 360; Cross v. De Valla, 1 Wall. 13; Osterman v. Baldwin, U. S. S. C., Dec. 7, 1867; 6 Wall. 000. The annexation of Texas removed the alienage from citizens of the United States. Osterman v. Baldwin, 6 Wall. 000; Cryer v. Andrews, 11 Tex. 170–183; Paschal's Annotated Digest, notes, 148, 237, 238; McKinney v. Sabariego, 18 How. 239.

The disability of the alien to maintain the real action is personal, and, at common law, relates, not to the date of acquiring the property, but of bringing the suit. 1 Chitty's Pl. 470, 471; 7 Bacon's Abridgment, Tit. USES AND TRUSTS, E. 2, p. 89; 1 Id. ALIEN, D, 137; Coke Litt. 129; Id. (B. 3) p. 6; Comyn's Dig., ALIEN (C.), p. 301; Kemp v. Kennedy, 1 Pet. C. C. R. 40; affirmed 5 Cr. 173; 2 Cond. 223.

What is the jurisdiction of the Supreme Court?  [2] In all cases affecting ambassadors, other public ministers and consuls, and those in which a State shall be party, the Supreme Court shall have original jurisdiction. In all the other cases before mentioned,

Appellate?  the Supreme Court shall have appellate jurisdiction, both as to law and fact, with such exceptions and under such regulations as the Congress shall make.

**210.** The Supreme Court has no original jurisdiction except in the two classes of cases mentioned in the first clause. Story's Const. § 1702. And to that extent it would seem to be exclusive. United States v. Ravara, 2 Dall. 297; Marbury v. Madison, 1 Cr. 137.

"CASES" here is applied as a generic term to all the objects designated by "case" and "controversy" in the preceding clause. Curtis' Com. § 83. See "case" and "controversy" defined. Id.; *ante*, n. 199; Martin v. Hunter, 1 Wheat. 304, 333; Curtis' Com. § 124–130. If the words "to all cases" give exclusive jurisdiction in cases affecting foreign MINISTERS, they may also give exclusive jurisdiction, if such be the will of Congress, in cases arising under the Constitution, laws, and treaties of the United States. (Cohens v. Virginia, 6 Wheat. 392–399.) Story's Const. § 1713. *[How is the term cases applied? 199–201.] [181, 182, 202.]*

But it does not mean that the court has jurisdiction of every "CASE" or *question* which may arise under the Constitution, laws, or treaties. These often necessarily devolve upon Congress or the executive, according as the law shall direct. (Luther v. Borden, 7 How. 1.) Curtis' Com. § 84–85a. The word is therefore limited to such "cases" as arise between parties, or are of a *judicatory nature.* (Madison, 5 Elliot's Debates, 483.) Id. § 85a, 100. *[Has the court jurisdiction of every case or question? 195.]*

Not to all questions by which an AMBASSADOR may be affected. Id. See Stanbery's arguments in the Mississippi and Georgia Injunction cases, against the President and others, reported in 4 Wallace. See the United States v. Ferreira, 13 How. 40.

"ORIGINAL JURISDICTION" is the right to take original cognizance of the case or controversy, and to hear and determine it in the first instance. It is that in which something is demanded in the first instance by the institution of process, or the commencement of a suit. Curtis' Com. § 107; Story's Const. § 1703, 1704. *[What is original jurisdiction?]*

The residue of the original jurisdiction remains to be vested by Congress in any inferior tribunals which it may see fit to create. (Martin v. Hunter, 1 Wheat. 304, 307; Osborn v. The Bank of the United States, 9 Wheat. 738, 820; Cohens v. Virginia, 6 Wheat. 395; Story's Const. § 1698.) Curtis' Com. § 111. *[Where is the residue of the original jurisdiction?]*

Original jurisdiction, so far as the Constitution gives a rule, is coextensive with the judicial power. (Osborn v. Bank of United States, 9 Wheat. 820.) Curtis' Com. § 159. And it would seem to follow that in cases where the Constitution itself has vested original jurisdiction in the Supreme Court, that investiture must operate as an exception to the general authority to Congress to vest original jurisdiction according to its discretion. Id. And there is doubt whether in such cases jurisdiction of the Supreme Court is not both original and exclusive. (United States v. Ortega, 11 Wheat. 467; See Story's Const. § 1699; 1 Kent's Com. Lect. XV. p. 315.) Curtis' Com. 160. But there are decisions the other way. United States v. Ravara, 2 Dall. 297; and see also Chisholm v. Georgia, 2 Dall. 419, 431, 436; Act of 28 Feb. 1839 (5 St. 32); Curtis' Com. § 161–164; Schooner Exchange v. McFaddin, 2 Cr. 117. *[What is the extent of the original jurisdiction?]*

Jurisdiction is the power to hear and determine a cause. It is *coram judice*, whenever a case is presented, which brings this power into action. If the petitioner states such a case in his petition, that on a demurrer, the court would render judgment in his *[What is jurisdiction? 195.]*

9*

favor. it is an undoubted case of jurisdiction. (United States v. Arredondo, 6 Pet. 709.) Banton v. Wilson, 4 Tex. 403, 404.

It is the power to hear and determine the subject-matter in controversy between the parties to a suit; to adjudicate or to exercise judicial power over them, the question is, whether on a cause before a court, their action is judicial or extrajudicial; with or without authority of law to render a judgment or decree upon the rights of the litigant parties. If the law confer the power to render a judgment or decree, then the court has jurisdiction. (Rhode Island v. Massachusetts, 12 Pet. 718.) Banton v. Wilson, 4 Tex. 404.

**Has a State court cognizance of consuls?** A State court has no jurisdiction of a suit against a consul; and whenever this defect of jurisdiction is suggested, the court will quash the proceeding. It is not necessary that it should be by plea before general imparlance. Mannhardt v. Soderstrom, 1 Binn. 138; Davis v. Packard, 6 Pet. 41; Commonwealth v. Kosloff, 5 S. & R. 545; Griffin v. Dominguez, 2 Duer, 656. A consul may, however, be summoned as a garnishee in an attachment from a State court. Kidderlin v. Meyer, 2 Miles, 242. The circuit courts have no jurisdiction of a cause in which a State is a party. Gale v. Babcock, 4 Wash. C. C. 199; S. C. Id. 344; Cohens v. Virginia,

**When is there original and appellate jurisdiction?** 181, 182, 202. already cited. In those cases in which original jurisdiction is given to the Supreme Court, founded on the character of the parties, the judicial power of the United States cannot be exercised in its appellate form. Osborn v. United States Bank, 9 Wheat. 820. But if a case draws in question the laws, Constitution, or treaties of the United States, though a State be a party, the jurisdiction of the federal courts is appellate; for in such case the jurisdiction is founded, not upon the character of the parties, but upon the nature of the controversy. Cohens v. Virginia, 6 Wheat. 392; Martin v. Hunter's Lessee, 1 Wheat. 337. Congress has no power to confer original jurisdiction on the Supreme Court in other cases than those enumerated in this section. Marbury v. Madison, 1 Cr. 137; In the matter of Metzger, 5 How. 176, 191-2; In re Kaine, 14 How. 119. See 1 St. 80, § 13; 1 Brightly's Dig. 861, 862, and notes.

And it seems that the original jurisdiction is exclusive. (Marbury v. Madison, 1 Cr. 137.) Curtis' Com. § 108; Osborn v. Bank of United States, 9 Wheat. 738, 820, 821; Story's Const. § 1697-1699.

Where the character of the cause gives appellate jurisdiction, and the character of the party (as an ambassador or State) gives original jurisdiction, the appellate jurisdiction is not thereby ousted. (Cohens v. Virginia, 6 Wheat, 392 et seq.; Martin v. Hunter, 1 Wheat. 337.) Curtis' Com. § 109; Story's Const. § 1706-1721.

The original jurisdiction of the Supreme Court can only include cases enumerated in the Constitution. (Marbury v. Madison, 1 Cr. 137.)

**What is appellate jurisdiction?** **211.** "IN ALL OTHER CASES BEFORE MENTIONED, THE SUPREME COURT SHALL HAVE APPELLATE JURISDICTION," &c.—It is the essential criterion of appellate jurisdiction, that it revises and corrects the proceedings in a cause already instituted, and does not create that cause. Marbury v. Madison, 1 Cr. 138; Curtis' Com. § 110, 113.

The Supreme Court possesses no appellate power in any case, *How must* unless conferred upon it by act of Congress, nor can it, when con- *it be con-* ferred, be exercised in any other mode of proceeding than that *ferred?* . which the law prescribes. Barry v. Mercein, 5 How. 119.

The appellate powers are not given by the judicial act, but by the Constitution. They are limited and regulated by the judicial act, and by such other acts as have been passed upon the subject. Durousseau v. The United States, 6 Cr. 313. Curtis' Com. § 112.

Congress may prescribe the mode of exercising this appellate jurisdiction. Marbury v. Madison, 1 Cr. 137; Weston v. Charleston, 2 Pet. 449; United States v. Hamilton, 3 Dall. 17; *Ex parte* Bollman, 4 Cr. 75; *Ex parte* Kearney, 7 Wheat. 38; *Ex parte* Crane, 5 Pet. 190; Story's Const. § 1755, 1756; Curtis' Com. § 113.

By the 22d section of the judiciary act, the controversy must *What does* be concerning a thing of money value; the judgment must be *the act* final; and the matter in controversy must exceed the sum of two *require* thousand dollars. By the 25th section, the right to re-examine does not depend on the money value of the thing in controversy, but upon the character of the right in dispute, and the judgment which the State court has pronounced upon it; and it is altogether immaterial whether the right in controversy can or can not be measured by a money standard. (1 St. 84–86; § 22, 25. Barry v. Mercein, 5 How. 120. See Wilson v. Daniel, 3 Dall. 401; 3 Cond. 185; Course v. Stead, 4 Dall. 22; 1 Cond. 217; United States v. Brig Union, 4 Cr. 216; 2 Cond. 91; Smith v. Henry, 3 Pet. 469; Gordon v. Ogden, Id. 33; Hagan v. Foison, 10 Pet. 160; Oliver v. Alexander, 6 Pet. 143; Scott v. Lunt, 6 Pet. 349; Wallen v. Williams, 7 Cr. 278; Fisher v. Cockrell, 5 Pet. 248; Martin v. Hunter, 1 Wheat. 304; 3 Cond. 575; Williams v. Norris, 12 Wheat. 117; 6 Cond. 462.) Bank of United States v. Daniel, 12 How. 52. Rector v. Ashley, U. S. C. C. Dic. T., 1867; 6 Wall. 000.

To give appellate jurisdiction under the 25th section, it must appear:—

First—That some one of the questions stated in the section did *What gives* arise in the court below; and Secondly, that a decision was *appellate* actually made thereon by the same court, in the manner required *jurisdic-* by the section. (Shoemaker v. Randell, 10 Pet. 394.) McKinney *tion?* v. Carroll, 12 How. 70.

That is, that the question was made and the decision given by the court below on the very point; or that it must have been given in order to have arrived at the judgment. (Owings v. Norwood, 5 Cr. 344; Smith v. The State, 6 Cr. 281; Martin v. Hunter, 5 Wheat. 305, 355; Inglee v. Coolidge, 4 Cond. 155; Miller v. Nicholls, 4 Wheat. 311, 315; 4 Cond. 465; Williams v. Norris, 12 Wheat. 117, 124; 6 Cond. 462; Fisher v. Cockerill, 5 Pet. 255, 258; Wilson v. Blackbird Creek Marsh Company, 2 Pet. 245; Satterlee v. Mathewson, 2 Pet. 380, 410; Craig v. Missouri, 4 Pet.

410; Davis v Packard, 6 Pet. 41, 48; Mayor of New Orleans v. De Armas. 4 Pet. 234.) Crowell v. Randell, 10 Pet. 394-398.

**Give the four requisites?** After this full review, these propositions were stated:—1. That some one of the questions (stated in the 25th section) did arise in the State court: 2. That the question was decided by the State court as required in the same section; 3. It is not necessary that the question should appear on the record to have been raised, and the decision made in direct and positive terms *ipsissimis verbis*; but that it is sufficient if it appear by clear and necessary intendment, that the question must have been raised, and must have been decided in order to have induced the judgment. 4. That it is not sufficient to show that a question might have arisen and been applicable to the case; unless it is further shown on the record, that it did arise, and was applied by the State court in the case. Crowell v. Randell, 10 Pet. 398. Affirmed, Choteam v. Marguerite, 12 How. 510; McKinney v. Carroll, 12 How. 70. See Brightly's Digest, Tit. " ERRORS AND APPEALS," pp. 257-261, and voluminous notes thereon.

**Define law and fact? 270-272.** "LAW AND FACT."—Since the seventh amendment, Congress can not confer upon the Supreme Court authority to grant a new trial by a re-examination of the facts, and tried by a jury, except to redress errors of law. (Parsons v. Bedford, 3 Pet. 447, 449. See Bank of Hamilton v. Dudley, 2 Pet. 492). Curtis' Com. § 114.

**What gives the appellate jurisdiction?** It is the "*case*" and not the *court* which gives the appellate jurisdiction. (Martin v. Hunter, 1 Wheat. 394). Curtis' Com. § 115. Therefore, if the question or the parties give federal jurisdiction, it may be reached by appeal. Id.; Cohens v. Virginia, 6 Wh. 413. The objects of appeal, not the tribunals from which it is to be made, are alone contemplated. Id. 416; Curtis' Com. § 116. And see Osborn v. Bank of United States, 9 Wheat. 820, 821; Story's Const. § 1701.

If the objects can be attained without excluding the concurrent jurisdiction of the State courts, over cases which existed before, it would seem to be necessary to adopt such a construction as will sustain their concurrent powers. (Teal v. Felton, 12 How. 284, 292.) Curtis' Com. § 121, 123, 124. As to when original jurisdiction is exclusive, see same author, § 129-135, and Martin v. Hunter; Houston v. Moore, 5 Wheat. 1, 12.

**What jurisdiction can Congress confer?** Congress can not confer jurisdiction upon any courts, but such as exist under the Constitution and laws of the United States, although the State courts may exercise jurisdiction in cases authorized by the laws of the State, and not prohibited by the exclusive jurisdiction of the federal courts. Houston v. Moore, 5 Wheat. 24-28, § 135, p. 178. And wherever the law of Congress furnishes the offense, the State law can only be enforced by the authority of Congress, or unless the power remain concurrent. Id.

If the jurisdiction be concurrent, the sentence of either court may be pleaded in law. Houston v. Moore, 5 Wheat. 40; 1 Curtis' Com. p. 180.

**Can the States superadd any thing?** Where Congress has exercised a power over a particular subject given them by the Constitution, it is not competent for State legislation to add to the provisions of Congress upon that subject.

The action by Congress seems to exclude State legislation.
(Houston v. Moore, 5 Wheat. 1, 22, 23 ; Prigg v. Pennsylvania,
16 Pet. 608.)  Story's Const. 3d ed. p. 615.

"WHERE A STATE SHALL BE A PARTY."—That is: 1. Where one **In what** **three cases** State is plaintiff, and another State is defendant ;  2. Where a **may a State** State is plaintiff, and an individual, whether a citizen of some other **be a party ?** State or an alien, is defendant.  3. Where a foreign State is plaintiff against one of the United States as defendant.  Curtis' Com.
§ 153–157.  See Rhode Island v. Massachusetts, 12 Pet. 657 ; New
Jersey v. New York, 5 Pet. 283 ; Pennsylvania v. The Wheeling
& Belmont Bridge Co. 13 Howard, 528 ; Cherokee Nation v.
Georgia, 5 Pet. 1 ; Ex parte Juan Madrazo, 7 Pet. 627.

[3.] The trial of all crimes, except in cases of im- **How and** **where must** peachment, shall be by jury; and such trial shall be **trials be** **had ?** held in the State where the said crimes shall have been committed; but when not committed within any State, the trial shall be at such place or places as the Congress may by law have directed.

**212.** "THE TRIAL." (L. Lat. *trialio. Exactissima litis contestatæ,* **Define** *coram judice, per duodecem virale exagititio.* SPELMAN.)—The term **trial ?** means here, the examination before a competent tribunal, according to the laws of the land, of the *facts* put in issue upon the indictment or presentment, for the purpose of determining the truth of such issues.  United States v. Curtis, 4 Mason, 232 ; Co. Litt.
124b.  And see Burrill's Law Dic., TRIAL.; Magna Charta, ch. 29
(9 Henry III.); 2 Inst. 45 ; 3 Black. Com. 379–381 ; 4 Black.
Com. 349, 350 ; 2 Kent's Com. Lect. 24, pp. 1–9 ; 3 Elliot's
Debates, 331, 339 ; De Lolme, B. 1, ch. 13, B. 2, ch. 16 ; Paley,
B. 6, ch. 8 ; 2 Wilson's Law Lect. P. 2, ch. 6, p. 305 ; Story's
Const. § 1778–1794.

"The trial" *per pais,* or by the country, is the trial by a jury,
who are called the peers of the party accused, being of the like
condition and equality in the State. (Magna Charta.) Story's Const.
§ 1779.

"OF ALL CRIMES EXCEPT IN CASES OF IMPEACHMENT."—See **What means** "CRIME" defined, notes 193, 194.  Here it means treason, piracy, **"crimes"** **here ?** felony, or some offense against the law of nations or an act of the Congress of the United States.  And this clause is to be taken **39.** subject to the exceptions, in the fifth amendment, as to trials in the land and naval service.  The term "crime" here doubtless embraces misdemeanor.

In the case of the United States v. Hudson & Goodwin (7
Cranch, 32), it was held that "the legislative authority must first
make an act a crime, affix a punishment to it, and declare the
court that shall have jurisdiction of the offense," before the courts
of the United States can exercise jurisdiction over it.  This doctrine was affirmed by the case of the United States v. Coolidge *et
al.* (1 Wheaton, 415), and Chief-Justice Marshall, in delivering the
opinion of the court in *Ex parte* Bollman & Swartwout (4 Cranch,

95), said: "Courts which originate in the common law possess a jurisdiction which must be regulated by the common law, until some statute shall change their established principles; but courts which are created by written law, and whose jurisdiction is defined by written law, can not transcend that jurisdiction." And it was in following these cases that Justice McLean held, in United States v. Lancaster (2 McLean's R. 433), that "the federal government has no jurisdiction of offenses at common law. Even in civil cases the federal government follows the rule of the common law as adopted by the States, respectively. It can exercise no criminal jurisdiction which is not given by statute, nor punish any act, criminally, except as the statute provides." The same doctrine is followed in Kitchen v. Strawbridge, 1 Wash. C. C. R., 84; United States v. New Bedford Bridge, 1 Wood & Minot 401: *Ex parte* Sullivan, 3 Howard, 103; 12 Peters, 654; 4 Dallas, 10, and note; 1 Kent's Com. 354; Sedgwick on Statutory and Constitutional Law, 17; and Wharton, in reviewing this question, says: "However this may be on the merits, the line of recent decisions puts it beyond doubt that the federal courts will not take jurisdiction over any crimes which have not been placed directly under their control by act of Congress." (Am. Criminal Law, 174.) Report on the Impeachment of the President, 75, 76.

**Define jury?**

**260.**

"BY A JURY" is generally understood to mean, *ex vi termini*, a trial by a jury of *twelve* men, impartially selected (in accordance with law), who must *unanimously* concur in the guilt of the accused before a conviction can be had. Any law, therefore, dispensing with any of these requisites, may be considered unconstitutional. (Work v. The State, 2 Ohio St. R. 296; The State v. Cox, 3 English, 436; The State v. The People, 2 Parker C. C. 322, 329, 402, 562; 2 Leading Criminal Cases, 327, and note.) Story's Const. 3d edition, § 1779.

**Does it make the jury the judges of the law?**

This does not constitute them judges of the law in criminal cases. United States v. Morris, 1 Curt. C. C. 23, 49; United States v. Shive, Bald. 510; United States v. Battiste, 2 Sumn. 240. And see Townsend v. The State, 2 Blackf. (Ind.), 152; Pierce v. The State, 13 N. H. 536; Commonwealth v. Porter, 10 Met. 263; Commonwealth v. Sherry, Wharton on Homicides, 481. It only embraces those crimes which by former laws and customs had been tried by jury. United States v. Duane, Wall. 106. It did not secure to the conspirators who assassinated the President in Washington city during the war, and while martial law existed in Washington city, the right to trial by jury. The Trial of the Conspirators.

**231-237.**

This section compared with the fourth, fifth, and sixth amendments. *Ex parte* Milligan, 4 Wallace, 119; Story's Const. § 1782. The first of these secures a presentment or indictment by a grand jury before there can be a trial by a jury. Id. And for the reason of these amendments in the shape of a Bill of Rights, see 2 Elliot's Debates, 331, 380-427; 1 Id. 119-122; 3 Id. 139-153, 300.

**Why in the State where committed?**

**213.** IN STATES WHERE COMMITTED.—This was to prevent the defendant from being dragged into a distant State. (2 Elliot's

Debates, 399, 400, 407, 420 ; 2 Hale's P. C. ch. 24, pp. 260, 264 ;
Hawk P. C. ch. 25, § 34 ; 3 Bl. Com. 383.)

Many of the States are divided into two or more districts (circuits) defined by law ; and the rule of trying the accused in such district is believed to be now strictly adhered to.

**214.** "BUT WHEN NOT COMMITTED WITHIN ANY STATE, THE Where are
TRIAL SHALL BE AT SUCH PLACE OR PLACES AS CONGRESS MAY BY offenders
LAW HAVE DIRECTED."—The offenses committed in the District of tried?
Columbia have always been tried in the District, under the "exclusive legislation;" those in the organized territories have been tried
there by the local courts of the territories; those committed by
whites, or by Indians against whites (to a limited extent), have been
tried in the States to whose federal courts jurisdiction had been
committed by the laws to regulate trade and intercourse with the
Indian tribes; those committed in forts and arsenals, over which
jurisdiction had been ceded by the States, have been tried in the
United States District or Circuit Courts in that State; those upon
the high seas in the State where the vessel first arrives.

So that "NOT COMMITTED IN ANY STATE," may be defined to be
offenses committed in the District of Columbia, in forts or arsenals
to which jurisdiction has been ceded by the States; in the territories of the United States; in the Indian country; upon the
high seas, and everywhere, when against the law of nations.

SEC. III.—[1.] Treason against the United States Define
shall consist only in levying war against them, or in treason?
adhering to their enemies, giving them aid and com- 192,
fort. No person shall be convicted of treason, unless By how
on the testimony of two witnesses to the same overt witnesses?
act, or on confession in open court.

**215.** "TREASON."—[Law Lat. *Proditio.* L. Fr. *Treson,* from Define
*treer, trehir, trahir,* to betray.] Burrill's Law Dic., TREASON. treason at
The word "ONLY" was used to exclude from the criminal juris- law?
prudence of the new republic the odious doctrines of constructive Define
treason. Its use, however, while limiting the definition to plain "only"?
overt acts, brings these acts into conspicuous relief, as being
always, and in essence, treasonable.

War, therefore, levied against the United States by citizens of
the republic, under the pretended authority of the new State
government of North Carolina, or the new central government
which assumed the title of the "Confederate States," was treason
against the United States. Chief-Justice Chase in Shortridge v.
Macon (North Carolina), 16th June, 1867.

In the prize cases the Supreme Court simply asserted the right 117,
of the United States to treat the insurgents as belligerents, and to
claim from foreign nations the performance of neutral duties under ·
the penalties known to international law. The decision recognized,
also, the fact of the exercise and concession of belligerent rights,
and affirmed, as a necessary consequence, the proposition that

What were during the war all the inhabitants of the country controlled by
the relations the rebellion and all the inhabitants of the country loyal to the
of the inhab- Union were enemies reciprocally each of the other.   But there is
itants of the
rebel States nothing in that opinion which gives countenance to the doctrine
to those loy- which counsel endeavor to deduce from it : that the insurgent
al to the
Union? States, by the act of rebellion, and by levying war against the
nation, became foreign States, and their inhabitants alien enemies.
United States v. Shortridge.  Id.

What is the      Held, that the enforced payment of a debt under the confederate
effect of se- sequestration laws, was no protection.  It was denied that the
questration?
"Confederate States" was a *de facto* government.

For the enumeration of the acts of treason in England, see 4
Steph. Com. 185–193; 4 Bl. Com. 76–84; Wharton's American
Crim. Law, B. 7, ch. 1, § 2715–2777.  Burrill's Law Dic., TREASON.

What war is      There must be an actual levying of war ; a conspiracy to subvert
necessary? the government by force is not treason; nor is the mere enlistment of men, who are not assembled, a levying of war.  *Ex parte*
Bollman, 4 Cr. 75; United States v. Hanway, 2 Wall. Jr. 140; Id.
136; 4 Am. L. J. 83.  And no man can be convicted of treason,
who was not present when the war was levied.  2 Burr's Trial,
401, 439; and see the same case, Appendix to 4 Cranch, 469–508.
See United States v. Willberger, 5 Wheat. 97.

From        The whole definition is copied from the statute of 25 Ed. III., ch.
whence 2; 1 Hale's Pleas of the Crown, 259 ; Judge Marshall's charge in
copied?
Burr's Trial; Story's Const. § 1799.  See 3 Wilson's Law Lect.,
ch. 5, pp. 95, 96; Montesquieu Spirit of Laws, B. 12, ch. 7 ; 4 Bl.
Com. 75–84.  The definition admits of no *constructive* treasons.
Federalist, No. 43; Story's Const. § 1798; Jefferson's Correspondence, 72–103.

What is a      If war be actually levied, that is, if a body of men be actually
levying of assembled for the purpose of effecting by force a treasonable pur-
war?
pose, all who perform any part, however minute, or however
remote from the scene of action, and who are actually leagued
in the general conspiracy, are to be considered as traitors.  But
there must be an actual assemblage of men for the treasonable
purpose, to constitute a levy of war.  (*Ex parte* Bollman, 4 Cr. 126;
United States v. Burr, 4 Cr. 469–508; Sergts. Const. ch. 30 [32];
People v. Lynch, 1 John. 553.)

And further, for the definition of treason, see United States v.
Hoxie, 1 Paine, 265; United States v. Hanway, 2 Wallace, Jr.
139; Regina v. Frost, 9 C. & P. 129; 2 Bishop on Cr. Law, § 1032.

Treason is a breach of allegiance, and can be committed by him
only, who owes allegiance either perpetual or temporary.  United
States v. Willberger, 5 Wheat. 97.

To what      **216.** TWO WITNESSES.—The evidence, it seems, refers to the
trial does it proofs on trial, and not to the preliminary hearing before the com-
refer?
mitting magistrate, or the proceeding before the grand inquest.
United States v. Hanway, 2 Wall. Jr. 138; 1 Burr's Trial, 196.
But see Fries's Trial, 14 Whart. St. Tr. 480, and the same in 2
pamphlet, 171.

There must be, as there should be, the concurrence of two witnesses to the same overt act, that is, open act of treason, who are

above all reasonable exception.  (United States v. Burr, 4 Cr. 469, 496, 503, 505, 506, 607; Greenleaf's Ev. § 237.)

[2.] The Congress shall have power to declare the punishment of treason, but no attainder of treason shall work corruption of blood, or forfeiture, except during the life of the person attainted. *What is the limitation on the punishment?*

**217.** PUNISHMENT OF TREASON.—Punishment is the penalty of the law, inflicted after judgment or sentence. For the English punishment of treason, see Story's Const. § 1298, and notes. *Define punishment?*

The punishment was first declared by Congress to be death by hanging.  Act of 30th April, 1790, ch. 36, 1 St. 112, § 1, note (a). It is now death or imprisonment.  Act of 17th January, 1862, 12 St. 589, 590.  See 1 Brightly's Digest, 201, § 1, notes a to h; Wharton's Criminal Laws, § 1117-1120; Id. 2719-2736; 2 Brightly, 100, 101.

ATTAINDER OF TREASON.—See Bill of Attainder, note 142.    *142.*

"CORRUPTION OF BLOOD."—By corruption of blood all inheritable qualities are destroyed; so that an attainted person can neither inherit lands nor other hereditaments from his ancestors, nor retain those he is already in possession of, nor transmit them to any heir.  Story's Const. § 1299, 1300; 4 Bl. Com. 381-388. *Define corruption of blood?*

The power of punishing treason against the United States is exclusively in Congress. (The People v. Lynch, 11 Johns. 553; Rawle's Const. ch. 11, pp. 140-143; Id. ch. 21, p. 207; Sergeant's Const. ch. 30 [ch. 32.]; Story's Const. § 1301.

## ARTICLE IV.

SEC. I.—Full faith and credit shall be given in each State to the public acts, records, and judicial proceedings of every other State. And the Congress may by general laws, prescribe the manner in which such acts, records, and proceedings shall be proved, and the effect thereof. *What credit shall be given to what acts, &c.? Who may prescribe the proofs?*

**218.** "FULL FAITH AND CREDIT," as the cases cited will show, means that credit, which the State itself gives, not to the mode of proof, but to the acts when proven. *Define full faith?*

"PUBLIC ACTS."—This has reference to the legislative acts and resolves; that is, to the laws of the State. *Public acts?*

"RECORDS" are the registration of deeds or the civil law records of titles, as in Louisiana, the registration of wills, public documents, archives, legislative journals; and, in fact, all acts, legislative, executive, judicial, and ministerial, which constitute the public records of a State.  McGrew v. Watrous, 16 Tex. 509, 512; White v. Burnley, 20 How. 250; Paschal's Annotated Digest, Art. 3710, note 835. *Records?*

JUDICIAL PROCEEDINGS are the proceedings and judgments which appertain to courts of record. *Define judicial proceedings?*

**What is the rule where jurisdiction has attached?**

Where the jurisdiction has attached, the judgment is conclusive for all purposes, and is not open to any inquiry upon the merits. (Bissell v. Briggs, 9 Massachusetts, 462; United States Bank v. Merchants' Bank, 7 Gill, 430.) Christmas v. Russel, 5 Wall. 302. " If a judgment is conclusive in the State where it was pronounced, it is equally conclusive everywhere " in the courts of the United States. (Story's Const. § 1313, 3d ed.) Id. 302. By that statute (of Mississippi) it was enacted that " no action shall be maintained on any judgment or decree rendered by any court without this State, against any person who, at the time of the commencement of the action in which such judgment or decree was or shall be rendered, was or shall be a resident of this State, in any case where the cause of action would have been barred by any act of limitation of this State, if such suit had been brought therein." (Mississippi Code, 400.) This act was unconstitutional. Christmas v. Russel, 5 Wall. 299, 302. Had it been an act merely limiting the time within which the suit should be brought, it would have been constitutional. (McElmoyle v. Cohen, 13 Pet. 312.) Id. 300.

**What is the effect of a judgment?**

A judgment of a State court has the same credit, validity, and effect in every other court within the United States, which it had in the State where it was rendered. Hampton v. McConnell, 3 Wh. 234; Sarchet v. The Davis, Crabbe, 185. And it matters not that it was commenced by an attachment of property, if the defendant afterward appeared and took defense. Mayhew v. Thatcher, 6 Wh. 129. Nor that the service was illegal. Houston v. Dunn, 13 Tex. 480. Such judgments, as far as the court rendering them had jurisdiction, are to have, in all courts, full faith and credit; and the merits of the judgment are never put in issue, with the qualification, that it must appear by the record that the party had notice. Benton v. Bergot, 10 S. & R. 242. They have not, however, by the act of Congress, full power and conclusive effect, but only *such* effect as they possessed in the State where the judgment was rendered. Green v. Sarmiento, 3 Wash. C. C. 17; Bank of the State of Alabama v. Dalton, 9 How. 528. And therefore, whatever pleas would be good therein, in such State, and none others, can be pleaded in any other court within the United States. Hampton v. McConnell, 3 Wh. 234; Mills v. Duryee, 7 Cr. 484. Thus, it would be competent to show that the judgment was obtained by fraud, or that the court rendering it had no jurisdiction. Warren Manufacturing Co. v. Etna Insurance Co. 2 Paine. 502; Steele v. Smith, 7 W. & S. 447; Drinkard v. Ingram, 21 Tex. 653. This has been denied as to fraud between parties and privies. Christmas v. Russel, 5 Wall. 505–508. But not to litigate the merits of the judgment. Ingram v. Drinkard. 14 Tex. 352. When the judgment of a sister State is produced, which was rendered by a court of general jurisdiction, the presumption is in favor of the power and jurisdiction until the contrary appears. (Scott v. Coleman, 5 Littel. 350; Mills v. Martin, 19 Johns. 33; 3 Wend. 267; 4 Cow. 282; 6 Wend. 447; 8 Cow. 311; Phillips's Evid., Cow. & Hill's Notes, vol. 5, p. 896, note 639.) And the plaintiff need not aver and prove the jurisdiction. Reid v. Boyd, 13 Tex. 242. Where the writ was a *capias ad respondendum,* and the return was, "executed personally," it was *prima facie* evidence of service. Reid v. Boyd, 13 Tex. 242, 243. If there has been no personal service, and if the defendant has not appeared and taken defense, the judgment of a sister State will not support an action. Notice or appearance is essential to the jurisdiction. Webster v. Reid, 11 How. 460; Nations v. Johnson, 24 How. 208. Notice by publication is not sufficient. Boswell's Lessee v. Otis, 9 How. 350; Oakley v. Aspinwall, 4 Comst. 135; Mills v. Duryee, 7 Cr. 481; McElmoyle v. Cohen, 13 Pet. 330. And see the notes in American Leading Cases, vol. 2, p. 551; 3 Phillips's Ev., Cow. & Hill's Notes, p. 353, note 636.

If a court of any State should render judgment against a man not within the State, nor bound by its laws, nor amenable to the jurisdiction of the court, if that judgment should be produced in another State, against the defendant, the jurisdiction of the court might be inquired into; and if a want of jurisdiction appeared, no credit would be given to the judgment. Bissell v. Briggs, 9 Mass. 462; Green v. Sarmiento, 1 Pet. C. C. 20; Hall v. Williams, 6 Pick. 232; Woodward v. Tremere, 9 Pick. 355; Schaffer v. Yates, 2 Mon. 253; Batwick v. Hopkins, 4 Ga. 48; Towns (Gov.) v. Springer, 9 Ga. 132; The Central Bank of Georgia v. Gibson, 11 Ga. 455; Darcy v. Ketchum, 11 How. 165. And the judgment may be shown to be void, collaterally, for want of personal service. Webster v. Reid, 11 How. 460; Gleason v. Dodd, 4 Met. 333; Lincoln v. Trevor, 2 McLean, 473. Where the original process was attachment and publication, and no personal service, and judgment was rendered in California, and suit brought upon this judgment in Texas the California judgment was rightly held to be void. Green v. Custard, 23 How. 486. But where a suit was brought in chancery, in Mississippi, and the defendants were served with process, and appeared and answered, and the chancellor rendered a decree dismissing the bill; and two years afterward, a writ of error was prosecuted to the Supreme Court, and an affidavit filed that the defendants were not within the jurisdiction, and had no counsel within the jurisdiction, and citation to appear and defend the writ of error was published in a newspaper; after which the Supreme Court reversed the judgment, and rendered a decree against the defendants, which judgment was perfected by the chancellor; and upon this judgment suit was brought in the United States District Court of Texas: Held, that the judgment or decree was not a nullity, as it would have been had there been no original service. Nations v. Johnson, 24 How 203 Some of the courts have strongly intimated that a law which should make a judgment, obtained without personal service, the foundation of an action, would be unconstitutional and void. And some of them go much further, and lay down the rule as applicable to the inception of the suit, that notice by publication is insufficient to support the judgment in any jurisdiction, except in the courts of the State where it was rendered. (Boswell's Lessee v. Otis, 9 How. 350; Oakley v. Aspinwall, 4 Comst. 513.) Nations v. Johnson, 24 How. 203. The publication in the Supreme Court will be held to be constructive service, provided the defendant was served with original process in the lower court, and appeared and

*Marginal note:* What is the effect of want of jurisdiction?

took defense. Nations v. Johnson, 24 How. 203. A decree of a court of chancery is within this article and the act of Congress for authentication. Patrick v. Gibbs, 17 Tex. 277. And this court will not look to the formula of the decree, if the parties, and the final result be certain, so that it is a final judgment which could be enforced in the sister State from which it came. (Whiting v. The Bank, 13 Pet. 6; Ordinary v. McClure, 1 Bailey, 7.) Patrick v.

**How may judgments of a foreign country be proved?** Owens, 17 Tex. 278. Judgments of foreign countries may be proved:—1. By an exemplification under the great seal; 2. By a copy proved to be correct; 3. By the certificate of an officer authorized by law, which certificate must, of itself, be properly authenticated. (Church v. Hubert, 2 Cr. 187.) Phillips v. Lyons, 1 Tex. 394.

**Define the great seal?** The "Great Seal" means the seal of the nation, whether the country be a monarchy or a republic. Phillips v. Lyons, 1 Tex. 394. The seal of one of the States of the American Union, is not the "Great Seal." Id.; Wellborn v. Carr, Id. 469.

**What is the limitation upon judgments?** In a suit upon a judgment obtained in courts other than the courts of the State, the limitation prescribed by the law of the forum will bar the action, although the period be shorter than that prescribed for judgments of the State where the suit was brought. McElmoyle v. Cohen, 13 Pet. 312; Story's Conflict of Laws, § 582; Robinson v. Peyton, 4 Tex. 278; Pryor v. Moore, 8 Tex. 252; Bacon v. Howard, 20 How. 23. First, that the statute of limitations of Georgia can be pleaded to an action in that State, founded upon a judgment rendered in the State of South Carolina; and, secondly, that in the administration of assets in Georgia, a judgment rendered in South Carolina, upon a promissory note against the intestate when in life, should not be paid in preference to simple contract debts. Mills v. Duryee; McElmoyle v. Cohen, 13 Pet. 330. Affirmed in a Texas case. Bacon v. Howard, 20 How. 25. There is no clause in the Constitution which restrains this right in each State to legislate upon the remedy in suits on judgment of other States, exclusive of all interference with their merits. Id. The act of the congress of Texas, of 25th June, 1845, which prescribed the time within which suits on judgments rendered in foreign States should be brought, having been passed before annexation, was not subject to this provision of the Constitution of the United States; but if it had been, the law would not have been unconstitutional. Robinson v. Peyton, 4 Tex. 278; Pryor v. Moore, 8 Tex. 250; Bacon v. Howard, 20 How. 22. It has been held, under the Texas statute of limitations, that the same rule applies to a judgment of a sister State as to a judgment of this State. (Clay v. Clay, 13 Tex. 195; Allison v. Nash, 16 Id. 560.) Spann v. Crummerford, 20 Tex. 220.

**Are the judgments prima facie or conclusive?** Judgments of another State are not *prima facie*, but conclusive evidence of debt. They can be impeached on such grounds only as would be good against a judgment of a sister State. Clay v. Clay, 13 Tex. 204. The judgments rendered before a justice of the peace of a sister State, are not judgments of courts of record within this article, unless it be averred and proved that the State law had made them so. Beal v. Smith, 14 Tex. 309. The opinion reviews the authorities in Cowen & Hill's Notes to Phillips's Evidence, Part 2, note 58. And see Grant v. Bledsoe, 20 Tex. 458; Thomas v. Robinson, 3 Wend. 267.

The legislation of Congress amounts to this: that the judgment *What does* of another State shall be record evidence of the demand; and that *the legisla-* the defendant, when sued on the judgment, cannot go behind it and *to?* controvert the contract or other cause of action on which the judgment is founded; that it is evidence of an established demand, which, standing alone, is conclusive between the parties to it. (Bank of the State of Alabama v. Dalton, 9 How. 528.) Norwood v. Cobb, 20 Tex. 594.

They certainly are not foreign judgments; nor are they domestic *Are the* judgments in every sense, because they are not the proper founda- *judgments* tion of final process, except in the State where they were rendered. *domestic?* Besides, they are open to inquiry as to the jurisdiction of the court and notice to the defendant; but in all other respects they have the same faith and credit as domestic judgments.

Subject to those qualifications, the judgment of a State court is conclusive in the courts of all the other States wherever the same matter is brought in controversy. The established rule is, that so long as the judgment remains in force it is of itself conclusive of the right of the plaintiff to the thing adjudged in his favor, and gives him a right to process, mesne or final, as the case may be, to execute the judgment. D'Arcy v. Ketchum *et al.* 11 Howard, 165; Webster v. Reid, Id. 437; Voorhees v. United States Bank, 10 Peters, 449; Huff v Hutchingson, 14 Howard, 558; Christmas v. Russel, 5 Wall. 305; Benton v. Bargot, 10 Sergt. & Rawle, 240.

To render a defense, or plea to the judgment of another State good, it must go sufficiently far to negative the reasonable intendment which exists, *prima facie*, in favor of the jurisdiction, and of the regularity of the proceedings. (Shumway v. Stillman, 4 Cow. 296; 6 Wend. 447; Holt v. Alloway, 2 Blackford, 108; Welch v. Sykes, 3 Gil. 197; Moreland v. Trenton Ins. Co. 4 Zabriskie, 222; Latterett v. Cooke, 1 Clarke, 1; Black v. Black, 4 Brad. 174; Bissell v. Wheelock, 11 Cush. 277; Buchanan v. Post, 5 Ind. 264.) 1 Smith's Leading Cases, Part 2, pp. 1026, 1027.

It is now well settled that judgments of one State of the Union *On what* may be controverted in another, on the ground that the court *ground may* which pronounced them did not obtain jurisdiction over the parties *be con-* by due service of process or notice. (Reed v. Wright, 2 Iowa, 15; *trolled?* 2 Am. Leading Cases, 798, 4th ed.; Price v. Ward, 1 Dutcher, 225; Smith v. Smith, 17 Ill. 482; Rape v. Heaton, 9 Wis. 328; Black v. Black, 4 Brad. 174; Wright v. Boynton, 37 N. H. 9; Judkins v. Union Life Ins. Co. Id. 470; McLaurine v. Monroe, 30 Mo. 462.) 1 Smith's Leading Cases, Part 2, p. 1025. This may be not only proven in opposition to the record, but also against its averments. Id. Baltzell v. Nosler, 1 Clarke, 588; Gleason v. Dodd, 4 Met. 335; Carleton v. Bickford, 13 Gray, 591; Norwood v. Cobb, 15 Tex. 500; S. C. 24 Tex. 551; Brinder v. Dawson, 1 Scammon, 541. But, *contra*, see Pritchet v. Clark. 5 Harrington, 63; Westcott v. Brown, 15 Ind. 83; Rowe v. Hackett, 2 Bosworth.

10

579; Lapham v. Briggs, 1 Williams, 29; Bank of North America v. Wheeler, 24 Conn. 433.

**219.** CONGRESS MAY PRESCRIBE THE MANNER OF PROVING.— The mode of proof prescribed under this clause has been as follows:—

"The acts of the legislatures of the several States shall be authenticated by having the seal of their respective States affixed thereto : That the records and judicial proceedings of the courts of any State shall be proved or admitted in any other court within the United States, by the attestation of the clerk, and the seal of the court annexed, if there be a seal, together with a certificate of the judge, chief-justice, or presiding magistrate, as the case may be, that the said attestation is in due form. And the said records and judicial proceedings, authenticated as aforesaid, shall have such faith and credit given to them, in every court within the United States, as they have, by law or usage, in the courts of the State from whence the said records are or shall be taken." Paschal's Annotated Dig., Art. 3709.

The seal of the State imports absolute verity. The United States v. Amedy, 11 Wheat. 407; The United States v. Johns, 4 Dall. 416. And is *prima facie* evidence that the officer who used it had competent authority to act. No other authentication is necessary than the seal of the State. Id. The usual attestation of the enactment and signature is not necessary. United States v. Amedy, 11 Wheat. 408. It is sufficient that their existence and time of enactment is shown. Id. It must be certified under the seal of the State. Craig v. Brown, Pet. C. C. 354. The laws of a State may be thus certified and proved. But private laws, and special proceedings of a judicial character, are matters of fact, and must be proven in the ordinary manner. Leland v. Wilkinson, 6 Pet. 317, 322. A statute book of a State, in the State Department at Washington, may be read as evidence of the law. The Commercial & Farmers' Bank of Baltimore v. Patterson, 2 Cr. C. C. 347.

Under the Constitution and this section, a judgment recovered in any State of the Union, before a court of competent jurisdiction, upon due notice to the defendant, is not to be regarded in any other State as a *foreign*, but as a *domestic* judgment, throughout the United States, so far as to give it the same effect in every other State. Baxley v. Dinah, 27 Penn. State R. (4 Harris), 242, 247. And the State court will take notice of the local laws, upon which the judgment was rendered, in the same manner as the Supreme Court of the United States does. (7 Cr. 408; 3 Wheat. 234; Baxley v. Dinah, 27 Penn. State R. (4 Harris), 243.) State of Ohio v. Hinchman, 27 Penn. State R. (4 Harris), 483; Rogers v. Burns, Id. 526. And if the certificate state that it is in "due form," it matters not that the judge and the clerk of the probate court were the same person. Id. But as a surrogate acts as a clerk, in certifying his proceedings, and as he also acts in the capacity of judge, he must certify as to the authentication. (Catlin v Underhill, 4 McLean, 190.) Ohio v. Hinchman, 27 Penn. State R. 484. So that it results that when the judgment of a court of record is *proved* under

---

*Marginal notes:*

How are acts of the legislature authenticated?
Act of May 26, 1790, 1 St. 122.

Judicial proceedings?

What does the seal of State import?
218.

How are judgments proved?
218.

Who must certify the clerk's signature?

the act of Congress, the court where it is produced will take the same notice of the laws of the State from which it comes, that the court which rendered the judgment, or the Supreme Court of the United States would take. Id. This rule seems only to apply to courts of general jurisdiction. 1 Greenl. Ev. § 506. It does not apply to judgments rendered before a justice of the peace, when not courts of record. (Cow. & Hill's Notes to Phillips's Ev. Part 2, note 58.) Beal v. Smith, 14 Tex. 309; Grant v. Bledsoe, 20 Tex; 458; Snyder v. Wyse, 10 Barr, 157; Warren v. Flagg, 2 Pick. 448; Robinson v. Prescott, 4 N. H. 450; Mahuren v. Blackford, 6 N. H. 567; Silver Lake Bank v. Harding, 5 Ohio, 545; Thomas v. Robinson, 3 Wend. 267. Unless they be courts of record. Bissell v. Edwards, 5 Day, 363; Blodget v. Jordan, 6 Verm. 580; Starkweather v. Loomis, 2 Verm. 573; Scott v. Cleveland, 3 Monr. 62. But the proceedings of courts of chancery and probate, as well as of common law, may be thus proved. State of Ohio v. Hinchman, 27 Penn. State R. (4 Harris), 243; Scott v. Blanchard, 8 Mart. (N. S.) 106; Balfour v. Chew, 5 Id. 517; Johnson v. Runnells, 6 Id. 621; Ripple v. Ripple, 1 Rawle, 381; Craig v. Brown, Pet. C. C. 352; Hunt v. Lyle, 8 Yerg. 142; Barbour v. Watts, 2 A. K. Marsh, 290, 293. Other judicial proceedings besides judgments are included. Hopkins v. Ludlow, Phila. R. 272. *How may chancery proceedings be proved?*

"OF ANY STATE," does not apply to the records of the courts of the United States. Mason v. Lawrence, 1 Cr. C. C. 190. But the same rule of proof is applicable to these courts. Tucker v. Thompson, 3 McLean, 94. And may be proved by like certificates. Buford v. Hickman, Hemp. 232. This method of proof is not exclusive of any other which the States may prescribe. Ohio v. Hinchman, 24 Penn. State R. 485; Kean v. Rice, 12 S. & R. 203, 208; Raynham v. Canton, 3 Pick. 293; The State v. Stade, 1 D. Chipm. 303; Biddle v. James, 6 Binn. 321; *Ex parte* Poval, 3 Leigh, 816; Elmore v. Mills, 1 Hayw. 359; Baker v. Jenkins, 2 Johns. Cases, 119. The clerk who certifies the record, must be the clerk of the same court, or of its successor; the certificate of his under clerk, in his absence, or the clerk of any other court or tribunal, is insufficient. Sampson v. Overton, 4 Bibb, 409; Lathorp v. Blake, 3 Barr, 405; Donahoo v. Brannon, 1 Overton, 328; Schnertzell v. Young, 3 H. & McHen. 502. Where the clerk certified under the seal of the court, that he was clerk; and the judge certified that his attestation was in due form, no other evidence of the usual form of attestation can be received. Harper v. Nichol, 13 Tex. 161. When the court has no seal, the fact should be certified by the court or the judge. Craig v. Brown, Pet. C. C. 353. The seal must be annexed to the record itself; not to the judge's certificate. Turner v. Waddington, 3 W. C. C. 126. The certificate to the clerk's attestation must be given by the *judge*, if there be but one; or if there be more than one, then by the *chief-justice or presiding judge or magistrate* of the court from whence the record comes; and he must possess that character at the time he gives the certificate. A certificate that he is the judge who presided at the time of the trial, or that he is the senior judge of the courts of law in the State, is deemed insufficient. Lathorp v. Blake, 3 Barr, 496; Stephenson v. Bannister, 3 Bibb, 369; Kirkland v. Smith, 2 Mart. *What means "of any State?"*

*What judge must certify?*

**What must the certificate of the judge state?**

(N. S.) 407. And so is the certificate of the judge, styling himself "one of the judges of the court." Stewart v. Gray, Hemp. 94; Catlin v. Underhill, 4 McLean, 199. The certificate of the judge must state that the attestation of the clerk is in due form. Wigg v. Conway, Hemp. 538. Which means, the form of attestation used in the State from whence the record comes. Craig v. Brown, Pet. C. C. 354. And such certificate of the judge is indispensable and conclusive. Ferguson v. Harwood. 7 C. R. 408; Tooker v. Thompson, 3 McLean, 33; Taylor v. Carpenter, 2 W. & M. 4. That the "signature is in the clerk's handwriting," is not sufficient. Craig v. Brown, Pet. C. C. 352. Where, however, the record of a judgment of a State court is offered in evidence in a circuit court sitting in the same State, the certificate of the clerk, and seal of the court, is a sufficient authentication. Mewster v. Spaulding, 6 McLean, 24.

**What validity has the judgment? 218.**

A judgment of a State court has the same validity, credit, and effect, in every other court within the United States, that it had in the State wherein it was recovered; and whatever pleas would be good in a suit thereon, and none others, can be pleaded in any other court within the United States. Hampton v. McConnell, 3 Wheat. 234; Mills v. Duryee, 7 Cranch, 481; Westerwelt v. Lewis, 2 McLean, 511; Warren Manuf. Co. v. Ætna Ins. Co. 2 Paine, 502; 2 Am. Leading Cases, 774. But the State may enact statutes of limitation, barring such judgment in their courts. McElmoyle v. Cohen, 13 Pet. 312; Bank State of Ala. v. Dalton, 9 How. 522. There must have been personal appearance, or service of process. D'Arcy v. Ketcham, 11 How. 165; Rogers v. Burns, 24 Penn. State R. (3 Casey), 525. Where judgment was rendered in a sister State against an ancillary administrator, it is no foundation for an action, in Texas, against the administrator or heir of the same estate. (Story's Conflict of Laws, 3d ed. § 522; Lightfoot v. Birkley, 2 Rawle, 431, 436–7.) Jones

**What faith and credit?**

v. Jones, 15 Tex. 464. The record, when duly authenticated, shall have in every other court of the United States the same faith and credit as it has in the State court from whence it was taken." (Mills v. Duryee, 7 Cr. 483) Christmas v. Russell, 5 Wall. 302.

**Is nil debet a good plea?**

Nil debet is not a good plea to such a judgment. Id. 304. Nor is fraud as to the promise on which the judgment was obtained; nor the manner of obtaining it. (Bank of Australasia v. Nias, 4 Eng. Law and Eq. 252.) Id.; Granger v. Clark, 22 Maine, 130; Anderson v. Anderson, 8 Ohio, 108. They cannot be attacked collaterally by the parties and privies to the record. B. & W. Railroad v. Sparhawk, 1 Allen, 448; Homer v. Fish, 1 Pickering, 435; McRae v. Mattoon, 13 Pickering, 57; Atkinsons v. Allen, 12 Vermont, 624; Christmas v. Russel, 5 Wall. 306. That is where it appears that the court had jurisdiction of the cause, and that the defendant was duly served with process, or appeared and made defense (Hampton v. McConnel, 3 Wheaton, 332; Nations et al. v. Johnson et al. 24 Howard, 203; D'Arcy v. Ketchum, 11 Id. 165; Webster v. Reid, Id. 460.) 5 Wall. 302. The rule is undeniable that the judgment or decree of a court possessing competent jurisdiction is final, not only as to the subject thereby de-

termined, but as to every other matter which the parties might
have litigated in the cause, and which they might have had decided. (Dobson v. Pearce, 2 Kernan, 165. Hollister v. Abbott,
11 Foster, 448; Rathbone v. Terry, 1 Rhode Island, 77; Topp v.
The Bank, 2 Swan, 188; Wall v. Wall, 28 Mississippi, 413.)
Christmas v. Russell, 5 Wall. 307.

"1. From and after the passage of this act, all records and ex- Act of
emplifications of office books, which are or may be kept in any March 27,
public office of any State, not appertaining to a court, shall be 208. 2 Stat.
proved or admitted in any other court or office in any other State,
by the attestation of the keeper of the said records or books, and
the seal of his office thereto annexed, if there be a seal, together What is the
with a certificate of the presiding justice of the court of the county mode of
or district, as the case may be, in which such office is or may be proving
kept; or of the governor, the secretary of State, the chancellor, judicial
or the keeper of the great seal of the State, that the said attes- records?
tation is in due form, and by the proper officer; and the said certificate, if given by the presiding justice of a court, shall be
further authenticated by the clerk or prothonotary of the said
court, who shall certify, under his hand and the seal of his office,
that the said presiding justice is duly commissioned and qualified;
or if the said certificate be given by the governor, the secretary of
State, the chancellor or keeper of the great seal, it shall be under
the great seal of the State in which the said certificate is made.
And the said records and exemplifications, authenticated as aforesaid, shall have such faith and credit given to them in every court
and office within the United States, as they have by law or usage,
in the courts or offices of the State from whence the same are or
shall be taken." Paschal's Annotated Digest, Art. 3710; 1 Brightly's Dig. p. 266.

Where a conveyance to lands in Texas was dated on the 14th How are
April, 1838, and executed and recorded before a notary public of civil law
the city of New Orleans, La., in accordance with the laws of Louis- proved?
iana, a copy of which was certified by the notary's successor,
on the 6th March, 1851; to which was appended the certificate of
the judge of the district court of New Orleans, that the certificate
was in due form, and by the proper officer; and the official certificate of the clerk of that court, that the judge was such, the
authentication was in accordance with this act. Watrous v.
McGrew, 16 Tex. 509, 512. See Paschal's Annotated Digest, note
508. By that article (Ord. of 22d January, 1836) and the act
of the provisional government of Texas, we take judicial notice
of the civil code and Code of Practice of Louisiana. Watrous v.
McGrew (16 Tex. 512), reviewed and affirmed. White v. Burnley, 20 How. 250. It was a civil law conveyance, made in a
notary's book, and a copy furnished to the grantee, as a second
original. Id. Sworn copies of records in a foreign country can
be given in evidence when better evidence cannot be procured.
But that they are records, must be shown by other evidence.
Bryant v. Kelton, 1 Tex. 435, 436. The laws authorizing the
record of bills of sale in a foreign country (as Georgia was before
annexation), and showing who was the keeper of the records,

should also be proven. Id. So where the record of a marriage, solemnized by a justice of the peace in Missouri, was certified under this act, the statute which authorized the justice to solemnize the marriage, should also have been proven; as also the statute authorizing the registration. Smith v. Smith, 1 Tex.

**Can records be proved by secondary evidence?**
625, 626. The records are among the public writings recognized by the common law invested with an official character, and therefore susceptible of proof by secondary means, but which are not of the nature of judicial records or judgments; such as acts and orders of the executive of a State; legislative acts and journals; registers kept in public offices; books which contain the official proceedings of corporations, if the public at large are concerned with them; parish registers, and the like. Snyder v. Wise, 10 Barr, 158. The certificate must state that the attestation is in due form, and by the proper officer. Drummond v. McGruder, 9 Cr. 122; 1 Burr's Trial, 98.

**Act of March 27, 1804, 2 S. C. 208.**
"2. All the provisions of this act, and the act to which this is a supplement, shall apply, as well to the public acts, records, office books, judicial proceedings, courts, and officers of the respective territories of the United States, and countries subject to the jurisdiction of the United States, as to the public acts, records, office books, judicial proceedings, courts, and offices of the several States." Paschal's Annotated Dig. Art. 3711.

This extension is a constitutional exercise of the legislative powers of Congress. Hughes v. Davis, 8 Maryland, 271.

**What are the privileges of citizens?**

SEC. II.—[1.] The citizens of each State shall be entitled to all privileges and immunities of citizens in the several States.

**Who are citizens? 274, 17, 18.**
**220.** "THE CITIZENS OF EACH STATE."—See Confederation, *ante*, Art. IV. p. 10. "I find no definition, no authoritative establishment of the meaning of the phrase (citizen of the United States), neither by a course of judicial decisions in our courts, nor by the continued and consentaneous action of the different branches of our political government." Bates on Citizenship, 3.

**How many classes of citizens of the U. S.? 169.**
It may be deduced from the previous definitions and all the authorities, that the following classification of "CITIZENS" may satisfy most students:

**What is the rule as to colonists of 1776? 274. 277.**
1. All *white* persons, or persons of European descent, who were born in any of the colonies, or resided and had been adopted there before 1776, and who adhered to the cause of independence up to the fourth of July, 1776. Paschal's Annotated Digest, notes 147, 148, 238, 240, 350; United States v. Ritchie, 17 How. 538; Orson v. Hoag, 3 Hill (N. Y.), 80–85; Jackson v. White, 20 John, 313; Inglis v. The Trustees of the Sailors' Snug Harbor, 3 Pet. 99; Kelly v. Harrison, 20 Johns. Cases, 29; Dawson v. Godfrey, 4 Cr. 321; Fairfax v. Hunter, 7 Cr. 603; Orr v. Hodgson, 4 Wheat. 453. The males of these are eligible to the Presidency.

**Who of the native born?**
2. All the descendants of such persons, who have since been born in any of those thirteen States, or in any new State or Territory of the United States, or in the District of Columbia, or abroad,

since the enabling acts of Congress (Indians not taxed or tribal Indians excepted). That is, all free white persons born within the jurisdiction of the United States, and all born abroad, whose parents are citizens absent on business. Paschal's Annotated Digest, Art. 5410, Act of 10th Feb. 1855; 10 St. 604.

3. All the free white or European inhabitants of Louisiana, and the Creoles of native birth, residing there at the time of the purchase from Napoleon the First, by the treaty of 30th April, 1803, and who remained in and adhered to the United States, and the descendants of all such. 6 St. Art. III. p. 202. *Who of the Louisiana territory?*

4. All the inhabitants of Florida, at the date of the treaty of cession of 24th October, 1819, who adhered to the United States, and remained in the country. Treaty with Spain, 8 St. p. 256, Art. VI. This included those who had left their native domiciles, and were on their way to Florida at the time of the exchange of flags. Levy's (Yulee's) Case. This treaty is the law of the land, and admits the inhabitants of Florida to the enjoyment of the privileges, rights, and immunities of citizens of the United States. (American Insurance Company v. Carter, 1 Pet. 542, 543; and see United States v. Gratiot [4 Pet. 526]; Cross v. Harrison, 16 How. 189); S. C., Whiting, 332. *What of the inhabitants of Florida?*

*19.*

*220.*

5. All the free inhabitants of Texas at the date of the annexation of that republic (29th December, 1845), descendants of Africans and Indian tribes excluded. 9 St. 108; Paschal's Annotated Digest, p. 46, note 159; Calkin v. Cocke, 14 How. 227. *Who became citizens by the annexation of Texas?*

When the Congress of the United States, under the authority to admit new States, receives a foreign nation into the confederacy, the laws of these respective nations, in relation to the naturalization of individual immigrants, have no application to the respective citizens of each. By the very act of union, the citizens of each become citizens of the government or governments formed by this union. Cryer v. Andrews, 11 Tex. 105. See Sabariego v. McKinney, 18 How. 240; Paschal's Annotated Digest, notes 148, 237–240. *What was the effect of annexation of Texas upon citizenship?*

*229, 93.*

6. All the inhabitants of California and other territory acquired by the treaty of Guadalupe Hidalgo, on the 2d February, 1848 (St. 929, Art. VIII.), who remained and adhered to the United States. Sabariego v. McKinney, 18 Howard, 289; Paschal's Annotated Digest, p. 39, note 147. *Who of the inhabitants of California became citizens?*

By the plan of Iguala, adopted by the revolutionary government of Mexico, 24th Feb., 1821, it is declared that "all inhabitants of New Spain, without distinction, whether Europeans, Africans, or Indians, are citizens of this monarchy, with a right to be employed in any post, according to their merit and virtues;" and that " the person and property of every citizen will be respected and protected by the government." We are also referred to the treaty of Cordova, of 24th August, 1821, and the declaration of independence of the 28th September, 1821, reaffirming the principles of the plan of Iguala. Also to the decree of the 24th February, 1822, by which " the sovereign Congress declares the equality of civil rights to all free inhabitants of the empire, whatever may be their origin in the four quarters of the earth." Also to the decree of the 9th *Who were citizens of Mexico?*

April, 1823, which reaffirms the three guaranties of the plan of Iguala, viz.:—1. Independence; 2. The Catholic religion; 3. Union of all Mexicans of whatever race. The United States v Ritchie, 17 How. 538. The decree of the 17th September, 1822, with a view to give effect to the 12th article of the plan of Iguala, declared that classification of the inhabitants, with regard to their origin, shall be omitted. Id. The foregoing solemn declarations of the political power of the government, had the effect, necessarily, to invest the Indians with the privilege of citizenship, as effectually as had the declaration of independence of the United States of 1776, to invest all those persons with these privileges, residing in the country at the time, and who adhered to the interests of the colonies. (Inglis v. Sailors' Snug Harbor, 3 Pet. 99, 121.) Id. 540. Under the Constitution and laws of Mexico, as a race, no distinction was made between the Indians, as to rights of citizenship and the privileges belonging to it, and the European or Spanish blood. Id.; Paschal's Annotated Digest, note 350. Therefore, all these inhabitants, without distinction of race or color, seem to have been made citizens of the United States.

**Who of Arizona?**
7. All the inhabitants (Mexican citizens) of Arizona, at the date of the Gadsden treaty (1854), who adhered to and remained in the United States. 10th St. 1035, Art. V.

**Are there any by special enactments?**
8. A few who have been naturalized by special enactments, as La Fayette.

**Who of the former slaves and free persons of color?**

**6, 18.**
9. All the slaves, who, by the laws of war, the proclamations of the Presidents, the oaths of amnesty and allegiance required by President Johnson, the thirteenth amendment of the Constitution of the United States, and the various amendments of the Constitutions of the fifteen slave States, the treaties with the Indians, the Civil Rights Bill, and the fourteenth (?) constitutional amendment, have become citizens of the United States. 14 St. 358 (Treaties), pp. 72, 85, 102, 117; Paschal's Annotated Digest, Art. 5382; note 144, p. 37; note 120, p. 24; note 1062, p. 786; note 1174, p. 930.

**Who by naturalization?**

**93.**
10. All persons naturalized according to "uniform rule." 2 St. 153, 292, 811; 3 St. 53, 259; 4 St. 69, 310; 9 St. 240; 10 St. 604; 13 St. 957; Paschal's Annotated Digest, Arts. 5392–5412, notes 1168–1172, pp. 919–925; Story's Const. § 1806.

**What rule as to women?**
And "any woman who might be lawfully naturalized under the existing laws, married, or who shall be married, to a citizen of the United States, shall be deemed and taken to be a citizen." 10 St. 604, § 2; Paschal's Annotated Digest, Art. 5411.

**Who of the Indian tribes?**

**21, 91, 92.**

**274.**
11. All such Indians as have ceased their tribal relations, and been declared citizens of the United States by treaties or acts of Congress: as the Choctaws, who remained citizens of Mississippi and Alabama, under the treaty of 1833; Wilson v. Waul, U. S. C., December 7, 1867, 6 Wall. 000. The Ottawas, by treaty of June 24 and July 28, 1862, to take effect five years from the ratification thereof, 12 St. 315; and 24th June, 1862, 12 St. 1237, Art. I; the Wyandottes, 31st Jan. 1855, 10 St. 1159, Art. 1; Ottawas and Chippewas, of Michigan, 11 St. 621, Art. 5; Chippewas, 2d Aug. 1855, 11 St. 633, Art. 6; Pottawattomies, 15th Nov. 1861, 12

St. 1191, Art. 3; Kickapoos, 28th June, 1862, 13 St. 623, Art. 3; Delawares, 4th July, 1866, 14 St. 109.

12. Whether a corporation is "a citizen," within the meaning of this clause does not seem to be clearly determined. Bank of United States v. Devaux, 5 Cr. 61; Bank of Augusta v. Earle, 13 Pet. 586; Slocomb v. Bank of Vicksburg, 14 Pet. 60; Louisville Railroad Co. v. Letson, 2 How. 556; People v. Islay, 20 Barb. 68; Warren Manufacturing Co. v. Ætna Ins. Co. 2 Paine, 502; Holmes v. Nelson, Phila. R. 218, 219.

*Is a corporation a citizen? 205a.*

As they are citizens of a State who may sue citizens of another State; as they are artificial persons; and as the guaranty secures the rights, whether the citizen of a State ever goes into another State or not, it is difficult to see why the rule will not apply, that the private corporation shall have all the privileges and immunities which like corporations have in the State where the right is asserted, not where the artificial person is created. See Mills v. The State, 23 Tex. 295, 302, 306; Paschal's Annotated Digest, notes 202, 203, 639.

It will thus be seen that all citizens of the United States are either native born or naturalized. The native born, who owe allegiance to the United States from the moment of their birth, *ought* to be citizens; and about it there never would have been any dispute, but for color and the extreme doctrines of States Rights, which maintained that there was no national citizenship. The adopted or naturalized citizens have been made so by treaties, statutes, and uniform rule of naturalization.

**221.** "PRIVILEGES AND IMMUNITIES."—And the words *rights, privileges,* and *immunities,* are abusively used, as if they were synonymous. The word "rights" is generic, common, embracing whatever may be lawfully claimed. Bates on Citizenship, 22.

*Define privileges and immunities. 220, 274.*

*Privileges* are special rights belonging to the individual or class, and not the mass. Properly an exemption from some duty, an immunity from some general burden or obligation; a right peculiar to some individual or body. *Ex parte* Coupland, 26 Tex. 420. *Immunities* are rights of exemption only—freedom from what otherwise would be a duty or burden. Bates on Citizenship, 22.

"In my opinion the meaning is, that in a given State, every citizen of every other State shall have the same privileges and immunities—that is, the same rights—which the citizens of that State possess. They are not subject to the disabilities of alienage; they can hold property by the same titles by which every other citizen may hold it, and no other; discriminating legislation against them would be unlawful." Lemmon v. The People (Denio, J.), 20 N. Y. R. 608.

But the clause has nothing to do with the distinctions founded on domicile. The citizen cannot carry the legal institutions of his native State with him. The privileges and immunities are not limited by time, but are permanent and absolute. Any law which should deny ingress or egress to citizens would be void. Id.

The States possess the power to forbid the introduction into their territory of paupers, criminals, or fugitive slaves. (Moore v. Illinois, 14 How. 13.) Lemmon v. The People, 20 N. Y. R. 610.

10*

**How far can the State determine the *status* of persons?** The State may determine the *status* of persons within its jurisdiction, except so far as it has been modified or restrained by the Constitution of the United States. (Groves v. Slaughter, 15 Pet. 419; Moore v. Illinois, 14 How. 13; City of New York v. Miln, 11 Pet. 131, 139.) Lemmon v. The People, 20 N. Y. R. 693. See Articles of Confederation, *ante*, p. 10, Art. IV., Federalist, Nos. 42, 80; Story's Const. § 1098, 1804–1809.

**What are the privileges and immunities here guaranteed?** This is confined to those privileges and immunities which are, in their nature *fundamental;* which belong, of right, to the citizens of all free governments; and which have, at all times, been enjoyed by the citizens of the several States which compose this Union, from the time of their becoming free, independent, and sovereign. They may be all comprehended under the following general heads :—Protection by the government; the enjoyment of life and liberty, with the right to acquire and possess property of every kind, and to pursue and to obtain happiness and safety,—subject, nevertheless, to such restraints as the government may justly prescribe for the general good of the whole. The right of a citizen of one State, to pass through or to reside in any other State, for purposes of trade, agriculture, professional pursuits, or otherwise; to claim the benefit of the writ of *habeas corpus;* to institute and maintain actions of any kind in the courts of the State; to take, hold, and dispose of property, either real or personal; and an exemption from higher taxes or impositions than are paid by the other citizens of the State, may be mentioned as some of the particular privileges and immunities of citizens, which are clearly embraced by the general description of privileges deemed to be fundamental; to which may be added, the elective franchise, as regulated and established by the laws or Constitution of the State in which it is to be exercised. Corfield v. Coryell, 4 Wash. C. C. 380–1; Smith v. Moody, 26 Ind. 302. And to this clause of the Constitution, it seems, may be properly referred the right which, it has been asserted, is possessed by a citizen of one State to pass freely with his slaves through the territory of another State, in which the institution of slavery is not recognized. United States v. Williamson, 4 Am. L. R. 19; see The People v. Lemmon, 5 Law Rep. 486. It does not embrace privileges conferred by the local laws of a State. Conner v. Elliott, 18 How. 591. Such as the rights of representation or election. Murray v. McCarty, 2 Munf. 393. And see the questions fully discussed in Scott v. Sandford, 19 How. 399.

**Can a State make a citizen of the United States?** Since the adoption of the Constitution no State can, by any subsequent law, make a foreigner, or any description of persons, citizens of the United States, nor entitle them to the rights and privileges secured to citizens by that instrument. Scott v. Sandford, 19 How. 393.

**Negroes?** Negroes are not " citizens " intended to be included in the Constitution, and can therefore claim none of the rights and privileges which that instrument provides for and secures to citizens of the United States. Id. 404. We must not

**National citizenship?** confound the rights of citizenship which a State may confer within its own limits, and the rights of citizenship as a member of the Union. Id. 405. He may have all the rights and privileges of the citizen of a State, and yet not be entitled to the rights and

privileges of a citizen in any other State. Id. Nor have the        6.
States surrendered the power and privilege of conferring the rights
and privileges of citizens, by adopting the Constitution of the
United States. Each State may still confer them upon an alien, or  Can a State
any one it thinks proper, or upon any class or description of       make citi-
persons; yet he would not be a citizen in the sense in which the   zens of the
word is used in the Constitution of the United States, nor entitled States?
to sue as such in one of its courts, nor to the privileges and immunities of a citizen in the other States. Id. The State cannot
make a man a member of the community of the United States by
making him a member of its own. Id. 406.

"I fully concur in the statement that the description, *citizen of the* 19, 30, 35, 63
*United States,* used in the Constitution, has the same meaning that 69, 170.
it has in the several acts of Congress passed under the authority
of the Constitution." (William Wirt, Attorney-General, 1 Op. 7th
Nov. 1821, vol. 1, p. 506.) Bates on Citizenship, pp. 17, 18.

But it means in them all the simple expression of the political
*status* of the person in connection with the nation—that he is a
member of the body politic. Id. 18.

It is said in the opinion that "the allegiance which the free man  Was a free
of color owes to the State of Virginia, is no evidence of citizenship, negro a
for he owes it not in consequence of an oath of allegiance." (1 Op. citizen of
506, Wirt.) "This proposition surprises me; perhaps I do not       Virginia?
understand it. The oath of allegiance is not the cause but the      93.
consequence of citizenship. Upon the whole I am of the opinion
that free persons of color *in Virginia* are not citizens of the United
States, within the intent and meaning of the acts regulating the
coasting and foreign trade." (1 Op. 510, Wirt.) Bates on Citizenship, 19. As an authority this opinion is rebutted by the opinion
of Attorney-General Legaré, of 15th March, 1843. (4 Op. 147.)
Bates, Id. He held that a colored man was a citizen of the
United States, entitled to a pre-emption. Id.

"If this be so (that is, if they be negroes), they are not citizens Were free
of the United States," entitled to passports under the act of 18th  negroes in
August, 1856, which restricts the right to *citizens.* (William L.   any State
Marcy, Sec'y of State, 4th Nov. 1856.) Bates on Citizenship, 20.  entitled
But see the certificate offered, which is equivalent to a passport.  to all the
Id. The citizens here spoken of are those who are entitled to "all  privileges?
the privileges and immunities of citizens." But free negroes, by
whatever appellation we call them, were never *in any of the States*
entitled to all the privileges and immunities of citizens, and consequently were not intended to be included when this word was
used in the Consitution. (The State of Tennessee v. Ambrose, 1
Meigs, 331.) Bates on Citizenship, 21.

The meaning of the language is that no privilege by, or immunity Construe the
allowed to the most favored class of citizens in said State shall be language?
withheld from a citizen of any other State. (Tennessee v.
Ambrose, 1 Meigs, 331.) Bates on Citizenship. Either a free
negro is not a citizen in the sense of the Constitution, or, if a
citizen, he is entitled to all the privileges and immunities of the
most favored class of *citizens.* But this latter consequence will be
contended for by no one. It must then follow that they are not

**How does the Constitution speak of citizens?**
**221.**

citizens. (Tennessee v. Ambrose. 1 Meigs, 331.) Bates on Citizenship. But the Constitution speaks of *citizens* only, without any reference to their rank, grade, or class, or to the number or magnitude of their rights and immunities—*citizens* simply, without an adjective to qualify their rights. Id.

Scott v. Sandford, 19 How. 393, reviewed. Id. 24. It is shown

**274.**

that it only determines that persons of African descent, whose ancestors were of pure African blood, who have been *brought* to this country and sold, are not citizens of Missouri *in* the sense in which that word is used in the Constitution. Bates on Citizenship.

Indeed the exclusive right of the State of Missouri to determine and regulate the *status* of persons within her territory was the only point in judgment in the Dred Scott case, and all beyond this was *obiter* (*Ex parte* Simmons, 4 Wash. C. C. R. 396; Groves v. Slaughter, 15 Pet. 508; Strader v. Graham, 10 How. 92.) Lemmon v. The People, 20 N. Y. (6 Smith), 624.

**What was the intention of the guaranty?**

The intention of this clause was to confer on the citizens of each State all the privileges and immunities which the citizens of the same would be entitled to under the like circumstances. (Story's Const. § 1806.) Smith v. Moody, 26 Ind. 301. Among which privileges and immunities is the right to become a citizen of any one of the several States, by becoming a resident thereof. Id.

A citizen of the United States residing in any State of the Union, is a citizen of that State. (Gassies v. Ballou, 6 Peters, 761.) Smith v. Moody, 26 Ind. 301.

The thirteenth article of the Constitution of Indiana denies these rights to all persons of African descent. Id.

The case of Scott v. Sandford, 19 How. 417, 422, 423, quoted. Id. The opinions of Attorneys-General Bates and Legaré, *ante*, quoted. Id. 303.

**Is Scott v. Sandford law?**

The opinion in Scott v. Sandford, though never formally overruled, is now disregarded by every department of the government. Id. 304. Passports are granted to free men of color; Congress declares them to be citizens; the Supreme Court of the United States admits them to its bar. Id.

**6.**
**274.**

At the time of the adoption of the Constitution, all free native-born inhabitants of the States of New Hampshire, Massachusetts, New York, New Jersey, and North Carolina, though descended from *African* slaves, were not only citizens of those States, but

**18.**

such of them as had the other necessary qualifications possessed the franchise of electors on equal terms with other citizens. (The State v. Manuel, 4 Dev. Bat. 20.) Smith v. Moody, 26 Indiana, 304.

**Who were meant by citizens of the several States?**
**144, 221, 206.**
**221.**

**222.** "OF CITIZENS IN THE SEVERAL STATES."—This was intended to secure to the citizens of every State, within every other, the privileges and immunities (whatever they might be) accorded in each to its own citizens, and no others. Lemmon v. The People, 20 N. Y. (6 Smith), 627. See Confederation, Art. IV. *ante*, p. 10.

It did not mean that the citizens of Virginia, who were entitled to hold slaves there, could bring those slaves into New York and hold them as such, in accordance with the laws of Virginia. Lemmon v. People, 20 N. Y. (6 Smith), 627.   Jackson v. Bulloch, 12 Conn. 38.

As a general principle, the slaves who were carried from slave to free States, with the permission of their masters, and permitted to reside there, obtained their freedom; and the owners could not resume their control over them as slaves upon the return of such slaves to such slave States.   Harry v. Lyles, 4 H. & McHen. 215; Baptiste v. Volundrum. 5 H. & Johns. 86; Davis v. Jaquin, Id. 100, 107: Respublica v. Blackmore, 2 Yates, 234; C. S., Addis. 284; David v. Porter, 4 H. & McHen. 418; Gilmer v. Fanny Gilmer, Id. 143; Lewis v. Fullerton, 1 Rand. 15; Butler v. Hopper, 1 Wash. C. C. 499; Vincent v. Duncan, 2 Missouri, 214; Milly v. Smith, Id. 36; Winney v. Whitesides, 1 Id. 472; Julia v. McKinney, 3 Id. 270; Nat. v. Ruddie, Id. 400; Vincent v. Duncan, 2 Id. 214; Rankin v. Lydia, 2 A. K. Marshall, 467.   See the cases fully collected in Wheeler's Law of Slavery. 335-388 ; Cobb on Slavery. *[right margin: What was the effect of carrying slaves from a slave to a free State?]*

The result of the cases seems to be that the citizen of one State does not carry the local laws of his State, which are repugnant to the laws of his new domicile into that State.   But when he goes into a State, he is entitled to all the rights and privileges of the citizens of that State, no more, no less.   He is not entitled to vote, as one of his privileges, until the Constitution or laws of that State give him the *power*.   See Story's Confl. Laws, § 321-327. *[right margin: 221. 13, 226-223.]*

It is fresh in the memory of all that the Southern school occupied the ground that this was not the law as to the Territories, but that the citizen might carry his slave there, and hold him as a slave, despite any law of Congress or the Territories, until a State Constitution was formed for admission into the Union.

The opposite extreme held, that neither Congress nor the Territorial legislature, nor both combined, could legalize slavery in the "common territory ;" but that it could only be legalized by a State Constitution, when the people were about to apply for admission into the Union.   A subject which led to such opposite absurdities, might well be called a very *obscuring* one.   See Cobb on Slavery ; *passim*, Douglas's Speeches for ten years ; the Debates in Congress from 1848 to 1860 ; Benton's Thirty Years, and the political platforms everywhere.   Scott v. Sandford, 19 How. 393. *[right margin: 226-223.]*

This "GUARANTY" applies to the people of the United States, whether existing in States complete, or in inchoate States called Territories.   6 Op. 304. *[right margin: 226.]*

The fourth article of the Confederation quoted (*ante*, p. 10).   Congress refused to insert the word "*white*."   Id.   It is clear that under the Confederation, and at the time of the adoption of the Constitution, free colored persons of *African* descent might be, and by reason of their citizenship in certain States were, citizens of the United States.   Smith v. Moody, 26 Ind. 305 ; Bates on Citizenship. *[right margin: p. 9.]*

[2.] A person charged in any State with treason, felony, or other crime, who shall flee from justice, and be found in another State, shall, on demand of the executive authority of the State from which he fled, *[right margin: What are the obligations as to fugitives from justice?]*

be delivered up, to be removed to the State having jurisdiction of the crime.

**What does "person" mean?**
16, 20, 21, 22, 24, 35, 46, 144, 169, 220, 226, 228, 215, 192, 194, 110–116.
**For what crimes?**

**223.** "A PERSON," in practice, has been held to extend to free and slave; naturalized and not naturalized; white, Indian, and colored; male and female; in fact, not only to the "people," the "numbers," or "inhabitants;" the "citizens," "aliens," and "all others;" but to every manner of "PERSON," whether resident, or not, who is "CHARGED IN ANY STATE WITH TREASON, FELONY, OR OTHER CRIME."

213, 193, 194.
It is not necessary that the crime charged should constitute an offense at the common law. In the matter of William Fetter, 3 Zabr. 311. It is enough that it is a crime against the laws of the State from which he fled. Johnson v. Riley, 13 Ga. 97; In the matter of Clark, 9 Wend. 221; Commonwealth v. Daniels, 6 Penn. L. J. 428; Hayward's Case, 1 Am. L. J. 231. The words embrace every act made punishable by the laws of the State. Kentucky v. Ohio, 24 How. 99. Misdemeanors as well as treason. Id. 100, 102. By the act of 12th Feb. 1793, 1 St. 302, provision is made to carry into practical effect this provision of the Constitution. Johnson v. Riley, 13 Ga. 133. All that is required is to produce the copy of an indictment found, or an affidavit made, before a magistrate of such State, charging the person so demanded with having committed a crime against the governor. Id.

**8.**
**What is "to flee"?**

**224.** "WHO SHALL FLEE FROM JUSTICE AND BE FOUND IN ANOTHER STATE."—To FLEE is to run away, as from danger or evil; as "the wicked flee when no man pursueth." Webster's Dic., FLEE. Here, to be "found in another State" is sufficient without any actual flight.

**Upon what may the fugitive be arrested?**
A fugitive from justice may be arrested and detained until a formal requisition can be made by the proper authority. Commonwealth v. Deacon, 10 S. & R. 135; Dow's Case, 6 Harr. 39; In the matter of William Fetter, 3 Zabr. 311; The State v. Buzine, 4 Harring. 572; In the matter of Clark. 9 Wend. 221; Goodhue's Case, 1 City Hall Recorder, 153; Gardner's Case, 2 Johns. 477; Commonwealth v. Wilson, Phila. R. 80. The executive upon whom the demand is made, cannot go behind the demand and accompanying charge of the governor demanding, to determine whether, by the laws of his own State, the offense charged is a crime. Each State, as a sovereign, must determine for itself, what is a crime. Johnson v. Riley, 13 Ga. 133–4. And see the case of McGoffin, Governor of Kentucky v. Dennison, Governor of Ohio, 24 How. 99, 100, 106. The duty of the executive on whom the demand is made, is merely ministerial. Id. This article was substantially copied from an article of the Confederation, which required the demand to be made upon the executive. The same rule was intended. Id. 102–3; *ante*, Art. III. p. 10. The right to demand is absolute; and the duty to deliver, correlative. Id. 103. The proceedings should correspond to the act of 12th February, 1793. Id. The governor on whom the demand is made, cannot look to the sufficiency of the indictment. Id 106–7. While the act of Congress declares that it is the "duty" of the governor to comply with the

**Is the Indictment conclusive?**

demand, there is no power in the Supreme Court of the United States to enforce the performance of this moral duty. Kentucky v. Ohio, 24 How. 107–8.

The relator insists on his discharge, on the ground of insufficiency and illegality of the warrant; in this, that it does not show by recital, that the representation and demand of the governor of the State of Arkansas, was accompanied with a copy of an indictment found, or an affidavit made, before some magistrate of the State of Arkansas, certified to by said executive as being duly authenticated, and charging the relator with having committed the crime of forgery within the said State; and we are of opinion, that, on the ground set forth, he is entitled to his discharge. *Ex parte* Thornton, 9 Tex. 614–5. The chief-justice quoted the foregoing clause of the Constitution and the act of 1793, and concluded the things necessary are:—1. A copy of the indictment found, or affidavit made, charging the alleged fugitive with having committed the crime. 2. The certificate of the executive of Arkansas, that such copy was authentic. (*Ex parte* Clark, 9 Wend. 222, cited.) The counsel for Thornton had relied upon this case, and Buckner v. Finley, 2 Pet. 586; *Ex parte* Holmes, 12 Vt. 631; Case of Jose Ferriara de los Santos, 2 Brock. 493; The matter of Short, 10 S. & R. 125; Holmes v. Jennison, 14 Pet. 540; Warden v. Abell, 2 Wash. Va. 359, 380. The alleged crime must have been committed in the State from which the party is claimed to be a fugitive; and he must be actually a fugitive from that State. *Ex parte* Joseph Smith, 3 McLean, 133; Hayward's Case, 1 Am. L. J. 231; In the matter of William Fetter, 3 Zabr. 311. The affidavit, when that form of evidence is adopted, must be at least so explicit and certain that, if it were laid before a magistrate, it would justify him in committing the accused to answer the charge. 6 Penn. L. J. 414, 418. It must state positively that the alleged crime was committed in the State from which the party is alleged to be a fugitive, and that the party is actually a fugitive from the State. *Ex parte* Smith, 3 McLean, 121, 132; Fetter's Case, 3 Zabr. 311; In the matter of Hayward, 1 Sandf. S. C. 701; Degant v. Michael, 3 Cart. 396.

For the general principles, as an international question, see 1 Kent's Com. Lect. 2, p. 36; Matter of Washburn, 4 John. Ch. R. 106; Rex v. Bull, 1 Am. Jurist, 297; Vattel, B. 2, § 76, 77; Rutherforth Inst. B. 2, ch. 9, § 12; Commonwealth v. Deacon, 10 Serg. & R. 125; 1 Am. Jur. 297; Commonwealth v. Green, 17 Mass. 515, 546–548; In re Fetter, 3 Zabr. 311; Executive Document of 1840, 1 Sess. 26 Cong. No. 99.

**225.** "SHALL ON DEMAND, ETC., BE DELIVERED UP."—A precept by the governor of a State, appointing an agent to receive a fugitive from justice, reciting that he had made a requisition, agreeably to the Constitution and laws of the United States, upon the governor of the State into which the fugitive was alleged to have escaped, is *prima facie* evidence, for the protection of the agent, of the truth of the recitals. Commonwealth v. Hall, 9 Gray (Mass.), 267. A *prima facie* case is all that is necessary. Somerset's Case, 20 State Trials 79 · Story's Const. § 1812.

And a warrant issued by the governor on whom the demand is made, to "take and receive into custody" a fugitive from justice, authorizes him to arrest such fugitive; and is not repugnant to the Constitution and laws of this State or of the United States. Commonwealth v. Hall, 9 Gray (Mass.), 267. The foreign extradition jurisdiction is purely political; and does not properly belong to the judiciary, but to the executive. (*In re* Kaine, 14 How. 103.) Curtis' Com. § 94, 95. And see Holmes v. Jennison, 14 Pet. 540; S. C., Curtis' Com. § 218, note 1. The governor may mean the "executive authority of a State," under the U. S. statute of Feb. 12, 1793. (1 St. 302; 1 Brightly's Dig. 293.) Commonwealth v. Hall,

*223.*   9 Gray (Mass.), 262. Where the warrant is issued, the courts cannot go behind it; the only question they can entertain is as to the identity of the alleged fugitive. Pennsylvania v. Daniels, 6 Penn. L. J. 417, note; The State v. Buzine, 4 Harring. 572.

*Suppose the fugitive has been convicted and pardoned?*   Where a defendant is brought into a State as a fugitive from justice, after acquittal, or conviction and pardon, he cannot be surrendered to the authorities of another State as a fugitive, but must be allowed an opportunity to return to the State in which he is domiciled. Daniels' Case, cited in Binn's Justice, 267. The agent appointed under the second section of the act of 12th Feb., 1793 (1 Stat. 302), is not liable to an action for false imprisonment by reason of any irregularity in the warrant of arrest. Johnston v. Vanamringe, 2 Blackwood, 311.

*What are the obligations as to persons held to service?*   [3.] No person held to service or labor in one State, under the laws thereof, escaping into another, shall, in consequence of any law or regulation therein, be discharged from such service or labor, but shall be delivered up on claim of the party to whom such service or labor may be due.

*What is a person?*   **226.** "A PERSON," here is limited, in practice, to apprentices and fugitive slaves; but there is no sound reason why it should not apply to all the domestic relations, where the party is "held

*227, 224.*   to service or labor." See Act of 12th Feb., 1793, 1 Stat. 302; Act of 18th Sept., 1850, 9 Stat. 462; 1 Brightly's Dig. 294, 295; 6 Op. 309; 3 Black. Com. 4.

*What means in a State?*   "IN ONE STATE."—This extends to the Territories, District of Columbia, and the Indian Territory. See 6 Op. 302–306; 3 Op. 370. The word "State," in both clauses of this article is *pari mate-*

*225, 226, 2.*   *riá,* and it possesses, in some of its relations, a meaning broader than its apparent or usual signification. 6 Op. 304, which fully discusses the whole subject.

*What means escaping?*   **227.** "UNDER THE LAWS THEREOF ESCAPING INTO ANOTHER."—"Escaping," here is not so comprehensive as "fleeing," in the last

*222.*   clause, since if the slave be carried by his master into another State, and there left, he obtains his freedom. See note 222; Webster's Dictionary, ESCAPE.

*226.*   This includes apprentices. Boaler v. Cummins, 1 Am. L. R. 654. It does not extend to the case of a slave voluntarily carried by his master into another State, and there leaving him, under the Did it apply to slaves who were allowed to go voluntarily into a free State? protection of some law declaring him free. Butler v. Hopper, 1 Wash. C. C. 499; Vaughan v. Williams, 3 McLean, 530; Pierce's Case, 1 Western Leg. Ob. 14; Kauffman v. Oliver, 10 Barr, 517; Strader v. Graham, 10 How. 82; Miller v. McQuerry, 5 McLean, 469; In the matter of Perkins, 2 Cal. 424; Commonwealth v. Alberti, 2 Par. 505. Slavery is a municipal regulation; is local; and cannot exist without authority of law. Miller v. McQuerry, 5 McLean, 469. But the question, whether slaves are made free by going into a State in which slavery is not tolerated, with the permission of their master, is purely one of local law, and to be determined by the courts of the State in which they may be found. Strader v. Graham, 10 How. 82; Scott v. Sandford, 19 How. 396. See In the matter of Perkins, 2 Cal. 424.

It was formerly held that the President had no power to cause As to slaves in Indian country? fugitive slaves, who had taken refuge among the Indian tribes, to be apprehended and delivered up to their owners. 3 Opin. 370. But this has been since overruled, and it is now held that such fugitive in the Indian territory, being there unlawfully, and as an intruder, is subject to arrest by the executive authority of the United States; and if in such territory there be no commissioner of the United States to act, the claimant may proceed by recapture without judicial process. 6 Opin. 302.

The owner of a slave is clothed with full authority, in every What were the owner's power over his slaves? State of the Union, to seize and recapture his slave, whenever he can do it without a breach of the peace, or any illegal violence. Prigg v. Pennsylvania, 16 Pet. 539; Norris v. Newton, 5 McLean, 92; Johnson v. Tompkins, Bald. 571; Commonwealth v. Taylor, 2 Am. L. J. 253; Van Metre v. Mitchell, 7 Penn. L. J. 115. But it is under the Constitution and acts of Congress only, that the owner of a slave has the right to claim him in a State where slavery does not exist. There is no principle in the common law, in the law of nations, or of nature, which authorizes such a recapture. Giltner v. Gorham, 4 McLean, 402. The Constitution, however, recognizes slaves as property, and pledges the federal government to protect it. Scott v. Sandford, 19 How. 395. A statute which punishes the harboring or secreting a fugitive slave, is not in conflict with the Constitution or laws of the United States. Moore v. Illinois, 14 How. 13. Nor does the Constitution exempt fugitive slaves from the penal laws of any State in which they may happen to be. Commonwealth v. Holloway, 3 S. & R. 4.

The Constitution confers on Congress an exclusive power to Is the power of Congress exclusive? 141. legislate concerning fugitive slaves; and the act of 1793 was constitutional and valid. Prigg v. Pennsylvania, 16 Pet. 539; In the matter of Martin, 2 Paine, 348; Jones v. Vanzandt, 2 McLean, 612; In the matter of Susan, 2 Wheat. Cr. Cases, 594.

The Constitution and laws do not confer, but secure, the right to reclaim fugitive slaves against State legislation. Johnson v. Tompkins, Bald. 571; Giltner v. Gorham, 4 McLean, 402. The act of 18th Sept. 1850, was constitutional and valid. Ableman v. Booth, 21 How. 526; Sims' Case, 7 Cush. 285; Long's Case, 3 Am. L. J. 201; 1 Blatch. 685; 6 Op. 713.

Was "slave" used in the original Constitution? 226, 21.

The term "slave" is not used in the Constitution, and if "person" means "slave," then the Constitution treats slaves as persons, and not as property, and it acts upon them as persons and not as property, though the latter character may be given to them by the laws of the States in which slavery is tolerated.  Lemmon v. People, 20 N. Y. (6 Smith), 624.

By what character of proceeding is the delivery enforced? 225.

Through the State or the Federal laws?

**228.** "SHALL BE DELIVERED UP."—This contemplates summary and informal proceedings (not a suit), and a *prima facie* case of ownership only. (Somerset's Case, 20 State Trials, 79.)  Story's Const. § 1812; Jack v. Martin, 12 Wend. 511; Prigg v. Pennsylvania, 16 Pet. 667; Sims' Case, 7 Cush. 731; 2 Story's Const. (3d ed.) pp. 622, 625; Wright v. Deacon, 5 S. & R. 62.  The delivery is to be through the congressional enactments of Congress; and is not obligatory upon the States, through their executives or authorities.  Prigg v. Pennsylvania, 16 Pet. 608; affirmed in Jones v. Vanzandt, 5 How. 225; Moore v. Illinois, 14 How. 13.  The student, who may wish to calmly survey this irritating subject, which served chiefly to prepare the public mind for the effort to destroy the Union, but which has ceased to be a matter of agitation since the destruction of slavery, is recommended to read attentively the last-named cases (which are also carefully reported in Story's Const. § 1812a, 1812b), and Glen v. Hodges, 9 Johns. 62; Wright v. Deacon, 5 Serg. & R. 62; Commonwealth v. Griffith, 2 Pick. 211; Jack v. Martin, 12 Wend. 311; S. C. 12 Wend. 507; Wheeler's Law of Slavery; Cobb on Slavery; The Debates of 1850, 1860, and 1861; The Report of the Committee of Thirty-one in 1861, and the authorities cited in these notes.

What resemblance did this clause bear to a treaty?

This clause of the Constitution was, in character, precisely a treaty.  It was a solemn compact, entered into by the delegates of States then sovereign and independent, and free to remain so, on great deliberation, and on the highest considerations of justice and policy, and reciprocal benefit, and in order to secure the peace and prosperity of all the States.  (Sims' Case, 7 Cushing (Mass.) 285.)  Story's Const. (3d ed.) § 1812b, note 1, pp. 615, 616.  And see Miller v. McQuerry, 5 McLean, 469; Henry v. Lowell, 16 Barbour; Commonwealth v. Griffith, 2 Pick. 11; Wright v. Deacon, 5 Sergt. & Rawle, 62.

For what was this clause designed?

This clause was designed to provide a practicable and peaceable mode, by which such fugitive, upon the claim of the person to whom such labor or service should be due, might be delivered up.  Sims' Case, 7 Cush. 288.  The law of 1793 (7 St. 302), for delivering up without trial, was constitutional.  Commonwealth v. Griffith, 2 Pick. 11; Wright v. Deacon, 5 S. & R. 62; Jack v. Martin, 12 Wend. 311; Hill v. Low, 4 Wash. C. C. 327; Prigg v. Pennsylvania, 16 Pet. 539; Johnson v. Tompkins, Baldwin, 371; Jones v. Vanzandt, 5 How. 215, 229.  The fugitive must not only have owed service or labor in another State, but he must have escaped from it. (Commonwealth v. Fitzgerald, 7 Law Reports, 379, Commonwealth v. Avis, 18 Pick. 193.)  Sims' Case, 7 Cush. 728.

How may new States be admitted?

SEC. III.—[1.] New States may be admitted by the Congress into this Union, but no new State shall be formed or erected within the jurisdiction of any other **With what restrictions?** State; nor any State be formed by the junction of two or more States, or parts of States, without the consent **229.** of the legislatures of the States concerned, as well as of the Congress.

**229.** "NEW STATES" are others than those which formed the **What is a State?** Constitution. "States" is here used in a broader sense than in **226, 28.** the second and third sections of this article. Out of whatever territory such States may be created, it seems to be settled that it belongs to Congress to determine when a State shall be added to the Union; and when admitted, the State becomes an equal in the Union.

For a history of the subject, see Confederation, *ante*, Art. XI., p. 19; Scott v. Sandford, 19 How. 395; Journals of Convention, p. 222. 305–311; 2 Pitk. Hist ch. 11, pp. 19, 36; 1 Kent's Com. Lect. 10. pp. 197, 198: 1 Secret Journals of Congress in 1775, 368–386, 433–446; 1 Tuck. Black. Com. App. 383, 386; 6 Journal of Congress, 10th Oct., 1780, p. 213; 7 Id. 1st March, 1781, pp. 43–48; Land Laws U. S. Int. chap; Story's Const. § 1316. These give the history and the early legislation in regard to the crown lands. And see Federalist, Nos. 38, 42, 43; Am. Ins. Company v. Canter, 1 Pet. 511, 542; The Ordinance of the 13th July, 1787; 3 Story's Laws, App. 2073; 1 Tuck. Black. Com. App. 278, 282; 1 St. And for a very full discussion, see Scott v. Sandford, 19 How. 395. Much of this "Dred Scott" opinion is also given in Story's Const. § 1318, note 1, pp. 193–226. As an historical review, the opinions, and the vast range of discussion which they called forth, are valuable. And see Webster's Speeches, &c., 360–364. From so vast a range, which filled the whole political literature of the country and formed the platforms of political parties, it would be useless to make citations.

This clause enabled Congress to admit new States; it refers to **What terri-** and includes new States to be formed out of this territory, expected **tory did the** to be thereafter ceded by North Carolina and Georgia, as well as **clause** new States to be formed out of territory northwest of the Ohio, **include?** which then had been ceded by Virginia. Scott v. Sandford (Justice Curtis), 19 How. 611, 612; 2 Story's Const. 3 ed. p. 212.

The Constitution confers absolutely on the government of the **117, 118, 178.** Union the powers of making war and treaties; consequently the power of acquiring territory either by conquest or treaty. (American Insurance Company v. Canter, 1 Pet. 542; see Cerre v. Portot, 6 Cr. 336.) Scott v. Sandford, 19 How. 395; 2 Story's Const. 3d ed. p. 213; Cross v. Harrison, 16 How. 189. And see Fleming v. Page, 9 How. 614.

The Confederate States Constitution imposed this restriction upon **What re-** the admission of new States into the Confederacy: "Other States **striction** may be admitted into the Confederacy by a vote of two-thirds of **did the** the whole House of Representatives, and two-thirds of the Senate **Confederate** —the Senate voting by States." Paschal's Annotated Digest, p. 93, **States** Art. IV., sec. 3, cl. 1. **impose?**

**What is the power of Territorial governments as to forming new States?**

The territorial legislatures cannot, without permission from Congress, pass laws authorizing the formation of Constitutions and State governments. All measures commenced and prosecuted with a design to subvert the territorial government, and to establish and put in force in its place a new government, without the consent of Congress, are unlawful. But the people of any Territory may peaceably meet together in primary assemblies, or in conventions chosen by such assemblies, for the purpose of petitioning Congress to abrogate the territorial government, and to admit them into the Union as an independent State; and if they accompany their petition with a Constitution framed and agreed on by their primary assemblies, or by a convention of delegates chosen by such assemblies, there is no objection to their power to do so, nor to any measures which may be taken to collect the sense of the people in respect to it: provided such measures be prosecuted in a peaceable manner, in subordination to the existing government, and in subserviency to the power of Congress to adopt, reject, or disregard them at their pleasure. 2 Opin. 726. And see the practice in the admission of Maine, Vermont, Tennessee, Kentucky, and all the States since, including West Virginia; from the differences in which it would appear that there is no uniform rule for the admission of new States. Hickey's Const. ch. 8, p.

**What new States have been admitted, and when? Vt. & Ky.?**

**230.** Under this section the following States have been admitted:—

VERMONT, formed from part of New York, by act of Feb. 18, 1791, which took effect March 4, 1791. 1 Stat. 191; Brightly's Dig. 894. KENTUCKY, formed from part of Virginia; by act of Feb. 4, 1791, which took effect June 1, 1792. 1 Stat. 189; Brightly's

**Tennessee?** Dig. 455. TENNESSEE, formed from territory ceded to the U. S. by North Carolina, by act of June 1, 1796, which took effect from

**Ohio?** date. 1 Stat. 491; Brightly's Dig. 863. OHIO, formed from territory ceded to the U. S. by Virginia, by act of Feb. 19, 1803, which took effect from date. 2 Stat. 201; Brightly's Dig. 708.

**Louisiana?** LOUISIANA, formed from part of the territory purchased of France, by treaty of April 30, 1803; by act of April 8, 1812, which took

**Indiana?** effect from date. 2 Stat. 701; Brightly's Dig. 582. INDIANA, formed of part of territory ceded to the U. S. by Virginia, by act of Dec. 11, 1816, which took effect from date. 3 Stat. 399; Bright-

**Mississippi?** ly's Dig. 416. MISSISSIPPI, formed from part of the territory ceded to U. S. by Georgia and South Carolina, by act of Dec. 10, 1817, which took effect from date. 3 Stat. 472; Brightly's Dig. 640. IL-

**Illinois?** LINOIS, formed from part of the territory ceded to U. S. by Virginia, by act of Dec. 3, 1818, which took effect from date. 3 Stat. 536;

**Alabama?** Brightly's Dig. 310. ALABAMA, formed from part of the territory ceded to United States by Georgia and South Carolina, by act of Dec. 14, 1819, which took effect from date. 3 Stat. 608; Brightly's

**Maine?** Dig. 29. MAINE, formed from part of Massachusetts, by act of March 3, 1820, which took effect March 15, 1820. 3 Stat. 544;

**Missouri?** Brightly's Dig. 590. MISSOURI, formed from part of the "Louisiana Purchase," by act of March 2, 1821; which took effect Aug. 10,

**Arkansas?** 1821. 3 Stat. 645; Brightly's Dig. 617. ARKANSAS, formed from part of the "Louisiana Purchase," by act of June 15, 1836, which took effect from date. 5 Stat. 50; Brightly's Dig. 45. MICHIGAN, formed from part of the territory ceded to United States Michigan? by Virginia, by act of June 15, 1836, which took effect from date. 5 Stat. 49; Brightly's Dig. 614. FLORIDA, formed from territory Florida? purchased from Spain under treaty of Feb. 22, 1819, by act of March 3, 1845, which took effect from date. § 1, 5 Stat. 742; Brightly's Dig. 288. IOWA, by act of March 3, 1845, which took Iowa? effect from date. 5 Stat. 742; boundaries readjusted, Aug. 4, 1846. § 1, 9 Stat. 52. Readmitted Dec. 28, 1846. 9 Stat. 117, § 1; Brightly's Dig. 442, 444. TEXAS, an independent republic, annexed Texas? Dec. 29, 1845, by act of that date. 9 Stat. 1; Brightly's Dig. 872; Calkin v. Cocke, 14 How. 227; Paschal's Dig. 46, note 159. WIS- Wisconsin? CONSIN, by act of May 29, 1848, which took effect from date. 9 Stat. 57; Brightly's Dig. 906. CALIFORNIA, formed from part of the ter- California? ritory ceded to U. S. by Mexico, by treaty of Hidalgo, Feb. 3, 1848; by act of Sept. 9, 1850. 9 Stat. 452; Brightly's Dig. 105. MINNESOTA, Minnesota? formed from part of the "Louisiana Purchase," by act of May 11, 1858, which took effect from date. 11 Stat. 285; 2 Brightly's Dig. 301. OREGON, see Treaties of the U. S. with France, of April 30, Oregon? 1803, with Spain, Feb. 22, 1819; with Great Britain, June 15, 1846; admitted by act of Feb. 14, 1859. 11 Stat. 383; Brightly's Dig. 349. KANSAS, formed from part of the "Louisiana Purchase," by act of Kansas? Jan. 29, 1861, which took effect from date. 12 Stat. 126; Brightly's Dig. 278. WEST VIRGINIA, formed of certain counties of Virginia, West Va.? by act of Dec. 31, 1862. 12 Stat. 633; admitted by same act, to date from June 20, 1863, by proclamation of the President. Appendix, 12 Stat. ii. NEVADA, formed from part of California. Nevada? by act of March 21, 1864. 13 Stat. 32. To take effect, Oct. 31, 1864, the date of proclamation of the President. Appendix, 13 Stat. ii. NEBRASKA, formed from part of the "Louisiana Pur- Nebraska? chase," by act of Feb. 9, 1867, which took effect from date. 14 Stat. 391.

For the enabling acts and manner of admission, see Hickey's Constitution, chap. 10, pp. 405–449. And see Cross v. Harrison, 16 How. 189.

All Congress intended (by the enabling act of 1811), was to What is the declare in advance to the people of the territory, the fundamental object of an principles which their Constitution should contain; this was very act? enabling proper under the circumstances; the instrument having been duly formed and presented, it was in the national legislature to judge whether it contained the proper principles, and to accept it if it did, or reject it if it did not. Having accepted the Constitution and ad- What is the mitted the State, "on an equal footing with the original States," in effect of the all respects whatever in express terms, by the act of 1812, Con- acceptance of the Con- gress was concluded from assuming that the instructions contain- stitution? ed in the act of 1811, had not been complied with. No funda- mental principles could be added by way of amendment, as this would have been making part of the State Constitution. If Congress could make it in part, it might, in form of amendment, make it entire. Permoli v. First Municipality, 1 How. 610. But see the act of Con- gress of 9th Feb., 1867, requiring the agreement by the legislature 17, 18.

of Nebraska, to the fundamental principle, that there should be no distinction, as to the right of suffrage, on account of color.  14 St. 392, and Id. App. iv.

**What is the power over the territory and other public property of the United States?**

[2.] The Congress shall have power to dispose of and make all needful rules and regulations respecting the territory or other property belonging to the United States; and nothing in this Constitution shall be so construed as to prejudice any claims of the United States, or of any particular State.

**What is "to dispose of"?**

**231.** "To Dispose of."—In other words, to make sale of the lands, or to raise money from them.  Scott v. Sandford, 19 How. 615; S. C. 2 Story's Const. 3 ed. p. 196.

**How limited?**

The power of Congress to 'dispose of'' the public lands, is not limited to making sales; they may be leased.  United States v. Gratiot, 1 McLean, 454; 14 Pet. 526; 4 Opin. 487.  But no property belonging to the United States can be disposed of except by the authority of an act of Congress.  United States v. Nicol, 1 Paine, 646.

**Define "needful rules and regulations"?**
**138.**

"And make all needful Rules and Regulations."—"*Needful*," here may well be compared with "*necessary and proper*," in the 18th clause of Art. I. Sec. 8.  And as Congress can only authorize dispositions by legislative enactments, so the "needful rules," must mean the appropriate legislation touching the subject-matter.  See Justice Curtis in Scott v. Sandford, 19 How. 615; 2 Story's Const. 3d ed. p. 213.

**28, 29, 129.**

The words "RULES AND REGULATIONS," are usually employed in the Constitution in speaking of some particular specified power which it means to confer on the government, and not, as we have seen, when granting general powers of legislation.  As to make

**85, 93, 99, 100.**

"rules" for the government and regulation of the land and naval forces; to "*regulate* commerce;" "to establish an uniform *rule* of naturalization;" "to coin money and *regulate* the value thereof."

**211.**

In all these, as in respect to the Territories, the words are used in a restricted sense.  (Scott v. Sandford, 19 How. 437.)  2 Story's Const. 3d ed. pp. 196, 213.

**Define "territory"?**
**222-223.**

"Respecting the Territory."—Territory.  [Fr. *Territoire*; It. and Sp. *Territorio*; Lat. *Territorium*; from *terra*, land.]  1. The extent, or compass of land within the bounds, or belonging to the jurisdiction, of any State, city, or other body.  2. A tract of land belonging to or under the dominion of a prince or State, at a distance from the parent country or the seat of government, &c.  Webster's Dic., TERRITORY.  Called by Pomponius in the Digests, the whole amount of the lands within the limits of any State (*universitas agrorum intra fines cujusque civitatis*).  (Dig. 50, 16, 239, 8.)  Burrill's Law Dic., TERRITORIUM; United States v Bevans, 3 Wheat. 386; Justice Curtis in Scott v. Sandford, 19 How. 615; 2 Story's Const. p. 211.  It applied only to the "*property*" which the States held in common at that time, and had no reference whatever to any "territory," or other property which the new sovereignty might afterward itself acquire.  Scott v. Sandford, 19 How. 615; S. C. 2 Story's Const. 3d ed. p. 196.  The term "territory," as here used, *To what is* is merely descriptive of one kind of property, and is equivalent to *the word* the word "lands."  United States v. Gratiot, 14 Pet. 537.  This *equivalent?* clause applies only to territory within the chartered limits of some one of the States, when they were colonies of Great Britain.  It does not apply to territory acquired by the present federal government, by treaty or conquest, from a foreign nation.  Scott v. Sandford, 19 How. 395; S. C., Story's Const. § 1318, 3d ed. p. 193. But see Justice Curtis' Opinion, 2 Story, 3d ed. p. 211.

It does not speak of *any territory*, nor of *territories*, but uses language which, according to its legitimate meaning, points to a particular thing.  The power is given in relation only to *the* territory of the United States, that is, to territory then in existence, and then known or claimed as the territory of the United States. Scott v. Sandford, 19 How. 436; S. C. 2 Story's Const. 3d ed. p. 196.

The power of governing a territory belonging to the United *Does the* States, which has not, by becoming a State, acquired the means of *power to* self-government, has been said to result necessarily from the facts *govern re-* that it is not within the jurisdiction of any particular State, and *the power to* is within the power and jurisdiction of the United States.  The *acquire?* power to govern seems to be the inevitable consequence of the      *233.* right to acquire territory.  American Insurance Co. v. Canter, 1 Pet. 542–3; United States v. Gratiot. 14 Id. 537; Cross v. Harrison. 16 How. 194; Whiting, 331.  Congress has the constitutional power to pass laws punishing Indians (within their territory) for crimes and offenses committed against the United States.  The Indian tribes are not so far independent nations as to be exempt from this kind of legislation.  United States v. Cha-to-kah-na-pe-sha, Hemp. 27.  The United States, under the present Constitution, cannot acquire territory to be held as a colony, to be governed at its will and pleasure.  But it may acquire territory which, at the time, has not the population that fits it to become a State, and may govern it as a territory until it has a population which, in the judgment of Congress, entitles it to be admitted as a State of the Union.  During the time it remains a territory, Congress *220–223.* may legislate over it within the scope of its constitutional powers, in relation to citizens of the United States, and may establish a territorial government; and the form of this local government must be regulated by the discretion of Congress. but with power not exceeding those which Congress itself. by the Constitution, is authorized to exercise over citizens of the United States, in respect to their rights of person or rights of property.  The territory thus acquired, is acquired by the people of the United States, for their common and equal benefit; and every citizen has a right to take with him into the territory any article of property, including his slaves, which the Constitution recognizes as property, and pledges the federal government for its protection.  Scott v. Sandford, 19 How. 395.  The country dedicated to Indian purposes still re- *What is the* mains a part of the territory of the United States, subject to its *power over* laws.  The United States v. Rogers, 4 How. 567.  And the power *the Indian* exists to punish crimes committed in that country, whether perpe- *territory?* trated by Indians or whites.  Id.  And see 6 Op.

What is the general rule?

It will be seen that the principle stated by Chief-Justice Taney, in United States v. Rogers, 4 How. 567, recognizes the plenary power of Congress to legislate for the Territories—that is, as stated in the American Insurance Co. v. Canter, 1 Pet. 542, all the powers which both Congress and the State legislatures combined, possess in the States. But in the Dred Scott Case he limits the power, and confines its exercise to the country ceded before the adoption of the Constitution. But in the case of the United States v. Rogers, 4 How. 567, the territory under discussion was part of that acquired from Louisiana. In reference to this territory, as well as that acquired from Georgia, Spain, Mexico, and Russia, there has been no distinction in regard to the character of legislation. Congress has exercised *power* both as to crimes and civil and political rights. The organized territorial governments have been treated as inchoate States for some purposes. Slavery has been tolerated or prohibited, according to circumstances. And now that the agitating question of slavery is out of the way, the author would venture to suggest that the country will settle down upon the principle that organized "Territory" carries along the idea of power and jurisdiction; and that Congress has the right to organize governments there, "making rules" which shall not be inconsistent with the Constitution of the United States; and exercising all the power over the inhabitants, no more, no less, which may be exercised over the States; not exclusive legislation as in the District, and forts, and arsenals; but all the legislation which may be necessary

138, 221, 222. and proper to guarantee the principles of republican government; and to insure the erection and admission of new States, with those principles. The failure has been in observing, that an organized territorial government is for all purposes of municipal legislation, a State, and has been so recognized in many ways. And the supervision of Congress over such legislation is no greater than the national supervision over unconstitutional legislation by the States. The only difference is in the mode of revision and redress. See Scott v. Sandford, 19 How. 395–633; 2 Story's Const. pp. 205, 214–218.

Define "all" and "needful"?

In Scott v. Sandford, Mr. Justice Curtis insisted that "ALL" meant *all*; that Congress alone could judge of what was "NEEDFUL." But the majority denied that "ALL" included the right to make a rule excluding slavery; or rather, it was denied that a cession of territory cedes the legislative jurisdiction for any other purpose than to dispose of the property in the land. See 19 How. pp. 615, 616; Story's Const. 3d ed. p. 214. The difference of opinion cannot be more strongly stated than in these words :—
"I construe this clause, as if it read : Congress shall have power to make all needful rules and regulations respecting those tracts of country out of the limits of the several States, which the United States have acquired, or may hereafter acquire, by cessions, as well of the jurisdiction as of the soil, so far as the soil may be the property of the party making the cession, at the time of making it." Justice Curtis, 2 Story's Const. 3d ed. p. 213. The opposite view was expressed in these words :—
" 2. The Congress shall have power to dispose of and make all

needful rules and regulations concerning the property of the Confederate States, including the lands thereof.

3. The Confederate States may acquire **new territory, and Congress shall have power to legislate and provide governments for the inhabitants of all territory belonging to the Confederate States, lying without the limits of the several States, and may permit them, at such times and in such manner as it may by law provide, to form States to be admitted into the Confederacy. In all such territory the institution of negro slavery, as it now exists in the Confederate States, shall be recognized and protected by Congress, and by the territorial government; and the inhabitants of the several Confederate States and Territories shall have the right to take to such Territory any slaves lawfully held by them, in any of the States or Territories of the Confederate States." Paschal's Annotated Digest, p. 93, Art. IV., Sec. III., Cl. 2, 3.

This was making the Constitution precisely what this school contended the Dred Scott decision had settled that it was. The power to acquire and govern territory seems to grow out of the war power and to rest upon constitutional principles. Fleming v. Page, 9 How. 614; Cross v. Harrison, 16 How. 189.

*How did the Confederate Constitution differ from this?*

**232.** " OR OTHER PROPERTY BELONGING TO THE UNITED STATES." —" PROPERTY " (*Proprietas, proprius*) is the most comprehensive word of dominion or ownership. See Webster's Dic., PROPERTY. It is the right to dispose of the substance of a thing in every legal way, to possess it, to use it, and to exclude every one else from interfering with it. (Mackeld Civil Law, 269, § 259; Bell's Dict.; Taylor's Civil Law, 476; 2 Bl. Com. 15.) Burrill's Law Dic., PROPERTY.

*What is property?*

And the same power of making needful rules respecting the territory is, in precisely the same language, applied to the *other* property belonging to the United States—associating the power over the territory in this respect with the power over movable or personal property—that is, the ships, arms, and munitions of war, which then belonged in common to the State sovereignties. And it will hardly be said, that this power, in relation to the last-mentioned objects, was deemed necessary to be thus specially given to the new government, in order to authorize it to make needful rules and regulations respecting the ships it might itself build, or arms and munitions of war it might itself manufacture or provide for the public service. (Scott v. Sandford, 19 How. 436.)  2 Story's Const. 3d ed. p. 196, and § 1324, 1325.

By this conquest (the acquisition of New Mexico, in 1846), this substitution of a new supremacy, although the former political relations of the inhabitants were dissolved, their private relations, their rights, vested under the government of their former allegiance, or those arising from contract or usage, remained in full force and unchanged, except so far as they were in their nature and character found to be in conflict with the Constitution and laws of the United States, or with any regulation which the conquering power, and occupying authority should ordain. Leitensdorfer v. Webb, 20 How. 336.

11

To what did the saving clause refer?

"AND NOTHING IN THIS CONSTITUTION SHALL BE SO CONSTRUED AS TO PREJUDICE THE CLAIMS OF THE UNITED STATES OR OF ANY PARTICULAR STATE."—This member of the clause applied to the claims of North Carolina and Georgia, and could apply to nothing else. Scott v. Sandford, 19 How. 437; 2 Story's Const. 3d ed. p. 197. It was to exclude the conclusion that either party would surrender their rights. Id. and p. 212.

How is republican form of government &c., guaranteed?

SEC. IV.—The United States shall guarantee to every State in this Union a republican form of government, and shall protect each of them against invasion; and on application of the legislature, or of the executive (when the legislature cannot be convened), against domestic violence.

Why "the United States"?

**233.** "THE UNITED STATES."—This is the only instance in the Constitution where the government, by its corporate name, has covenanted for any duty. The "*powers*" of the government are vested in the respective departments thereof; and, as to the

14, 15, 165, 195.

"necessary and proper" legislation, that is specially conferred upon Congress. Here the obligation is from the "United States" to the "States;" but whether to be exercised by Congress or the

138, 275-279.

President, is one of the questions which has grown out of the reconstruction measures.

One of the grounds of impeachment alleged against the President was the usurpation of this power. The Report on Impeachment of the President, 55. In the case of Luther v. Borden, 7 How. 42. Chief-Justice Taney said: "It rests with Congress to decide what govern

What department is to decide such political questions?

ment is the established one in a State. For, as the United States guarantee to each State a republican government, Congress must necessarily decide what government is established in the State before it can determine whether it is republican or not. And when the senators and representatives of a State are admitted into the councils

195.

of the Union, the authority of the government under which they are appointed, as well as its republican character, is recognized by the proper constitutional authority. And its decision is binding on every other department of the government, and could not be questioned in a judicial tribunal." Quoted and approved. *Ex parte* Coupland, 26 Tex. 434; Federalist, No. 21, p. 112.

Define "to guarantee"?

"SHALL GUARANTEE."—[L. Lat. *guarrantar, guarrantisare.*]—To become responsible for; to warrant; to undertake for another, that, if that other does not do the thing, the party guaranteeing will himself do it. The obligation of a guaranty is essentially in the alternative. Britton, chap. 75; 3 Kent's Com. 121; Story on Contracts, § 852; Fell on Guaranties, 1. The word seems to be essentially the same with warranty. Id. Burrill's Law Dic.,

220-233, 226, 229-232.

GUARANTY, or GUARANTEE. For a technical and limited signification, see Parker v. Culvertson, 1 Wall. Jr. Ct. Ct. 149, 153.

"TO EVERY STATE IN THIS UNION."—State here also means as well the States which agreed to the Constitution, as also the inchoate States or organized territories, and the new States, since admitted, or hereafter to be admitted. A "State" (for the purpose of the judicial power) must be a member of the Union. It is not enough to be an organized political body within the limits of the Union. Scott v. Jones, 5 How. 343, 377; Cherokee Nation v. Georgia, 5 Pet. 18. But this is not so, as to the guaranty of a republican form of government. That is in favor of the people—the citizens—as well as the States.  **205.**

"A REPUBLICAN FORM OF GOVERNMENT."—A government of the people; it is usually put in opposition to a monarchical or aristocratic government. This clause supposes a government already established, and this is the form of government the United States have undertaken to guarantee. (Story's Const. § 1807.) Burrill's Law Dic., REPUBLICAN GOVERNMENT.  *What is a republican form of government?*

This term has of course received no practical authoritative definition. It supposes a pre-existing government of the form which is to be guaranteed. As long, therefore, as the existing republican forms are continued by the States, they are guaranteed by the federal Constitution. Whenever the States may choose to establish other republican forms, they have a right to do so, and to claim the federal guaranty for the latter. The only restriction imposed on them is, that they will not exchange republican for anti-republican constitutions; a restriction which it is presumed will hardly be considered as a grievance. (Federalist, No. 21; see Montesquieu, B. 9, chap. 1, 2; 1 Tuck. Black. App. 366, 367.) Story's Const. § 1817; Federalist, No. 43, pp. 214, 215. But this still leaves the term undefined, except so far as the description may be derived from the character of the State governments when they formed this Constitution. The restrictions which they had imposed upon themselves, and to which they agreed when they made this Constitution the supreme law; and the rights of the citizens secured by the amendments, which constitute a Bill of Rights. The first guaranty is the elective principle. But upon whom the elective franchise shall be conferred is not defined, and must be controlled by circumstances. The right need not be universal; and must not be too restricted. The next is, the model, upon which all our governments are based, legislative, executive, and judicial. Certainly the guaranty is to enforce upon the States the restrictions imposed upon them in the federal Constitution; that is, the States shall not exercise the prohibited powers, nor the powers which have been granted to and exercised by Congress. And now, practically, we have the great examples, that where States deny the obligation of the federal Constitution, and form a confederation among themselves upon the same model, although they may retain the same forms and constitutions of the State governments, yet the United States have regarded it as an occasion for the exercise of this power; have declared such existing State governments as in fact not republican; have annulled them, and have required new Constitutions to be formed, based upon the organic change, which had destroyed slavery, and thus settled that it was no longer a republican institution. About the *right* to exercise this power, there has been no dispute. Unfortunately, the controversy has been, as to what department of the government of the United States  *To what does the guaranty extend?* *What is the restriction?* *238–241. 245–275. 16–18.* *How is it affected by the elective principle?* *16–18.* *275–278. 139–143.* *71–138. What has been the effect of the rebellion?* *274–276, 279.*

shall judge of the necessity and apply the remedy, and what shall
be the extent of the organic changes in the States? If the practice and common understanding in the admission of new States,
and the precedent of Luther v. Borden, 7 How. 1, are to control,
then the question would seem to be settled in favor of the power
of Congress to determine when a State government is republican
in form and in practice.—[EDITOR. See President Lincoln's proclamation of 1st Jan., 1863, and the amnesty proclamations, and the
proclamations of President Johnson, appointing provisional governors; his directions declaring what the State conventions shall
do, and declaring civil government restored. See also his messages and veto messages upon the subject; the debates of the
thirty-ninth and fortieth Congresses everywhere; the President's
Message to the second session of the fortieth Congress, Dec. 3,
1867; the reports of the joint committee upon reconstruction;
the reconstruction acts; the majority and minority reports of the
committee on judiciary upon the impeachment of the President,
and the debates of the thirty-ninth and fortieth Congresses thereon.
McPherson's Manual, and Paschal's Annotated Digest, note 1174.

275-277.

" I take it that the States would not be allowed to establish pri-
mogeniture; to abolish the trial by jury *in all cases;* to unite the
Church and State; nor in any way to violate the great cardinal
principles of liberty secured by the national Bill of Rights, and which
the fourteenth amendment seeks to extend to the States. I
cannot subscribe to the omnipotence of a State legislature, or
that it is absolute and without control, although its authority should
not be restrained by the Constitution or fundamental law of the
State. The nature and end of legislative power will limit the exercise of it. This fundamental principle flows from the very nature
of our free republican governments, that no man should be compelled to do what the law does not require, *nor refrain from doing
that which the law permits.* There are certain vital principles in
our free republican governments, which will determine and over-
rule an apparent flagrant abuse of legislative power, such as to
authorize manifest injustice by a positive law, or to take away that
security for personal liberty or private property, for the protection
whereof government was established." (Calder v. Bull, 3 Dall. 386.)
Wynehamer v. The People, 13 N. Y. (3 Kern.), 391, 392. The
cases of *ex post facto* law; impairing contracts; making a man
accuse himself; taking A's property to give to B, punishing inno-
cence as guilt, and violating property, cited. (Calder v. Bull, 3
Dall. 386; Fletcher v. Peck, 3 Cranch, 385; Dash v. Van Kleek, 7
Johns. 477; Taylor v. Porter, 4 Hill, 146; Goshen v. Stonington, 4
Conn. 225.) Wynehamer v. The People, 13 N. Y. 391, 392. See
Wilkinson v. Leland, 2 Pet. 653; Harding v. Goodlet, 3 Yerg. 41;
2 Kent's Com. 11th ed. p. 339, and notes.

That State must not boast of its civilization, nor of its progress
in the principles of civil liberty, where the legislature has power
to provide that a man may be condemned unheard. Oakley v. Aspinwall, 4 Comstock, 522.

What laws would infract the principles of a republican form of government?

143, 156-161.

What is invasion?

**234.** "AND SHALL PROTECT EACH OF THEM AGAINST INVA-
SION."—Invasion has been defined in note 133. The means to be

employed are the whole powers of declaring war and its incidents.
See Act of 12th Jan. 1862, 12 St. 589, 590.   The latitude of expres- 117-133.
sion here used, secures each State not only against foreign hostility,
but against ambitious or vindictive enterprises of its more powerful neighbors.   Story's Const. § 1818; Federalist, No. 43, p. 215.

**235.** "AND ON THE APPLICATION OF THE LEGISLATURE, OR OF Who are
THE EXECUTIVE (WHEN THE LEGISLATURE CANNOT BE CONVENED), the Legisla-
AGAINST DOMESTIC VIOLENCE."—The President must determine ture? 233, 234.
what body of men constitute the legislature, and who is the gov-
ernor; which is the government and which party is unlawfully
arrayed against it, before he can act.   Luther v. Borden, 7 How.
43-45.   The history of the rebellion affords us these examples: 1.
The case of Virginia.   A large majority of the legislature of the
State adhered to the rebellion, and after an ordinance of secession Give the
Virginia became one of the "Confederate States of America." But example of
Congress recognized the minority of the legislature assembled at Virginia?
Wheeling as the legislature of Virginia, with authority to consent 229, 230.
to the creation of the new State of West Virginia, which was admitted into the Union.   2. In the case of Missouri.   The majority Of Mis-
of the legislature and the governor adhered to the rebellion; and, souri?
after the commencement of hostilities, passed an ordinance of secession; and the legislature elected senators, and a minority of the
people elected representatives to the Confederate Congress at
Richmond.   This was in accordance with an enabling act of that
Congress, and the State was admitted as a member of the "Confederate States," and continued to be represented until the over-
throw of the rebellion.   On the other hand, Missouri retained
its place in the Union through the agency of a convention elected
by the authority of an act of the legislature passed in 1860, which
convention, having refused to pass an ordinance of secession, was
reconvened upon the call of its president, and was recognized as
the lawful authority of Missouri by the government of the United
States.   3. In the case of Kentucky.   The legislature refused to Of Ken-
call a convention or to pass an ordinance of secession.   But a con- tucky?
vention of rebels did assemble and pass an ordinance of secession;
and senators and representatives were elected to the Congress of
the "Confederate States," who served until the close of the rebellion.   4. Louisiana.   This was one of the seven original seceded Of Louisi-
States which adopted the Confederate Constitution ordained at ana?
Montgomery, Alabama, in 1861.   After the occupation of Louisiana by the federal troops, a quorum of the rebel legislature could
not be obtained.   But it was solemnly decided by the Supreme
Court of Louisiana, that so long as a single parish remained loyal
to the Confederacy, such parish, or minority of the people, should
be regarded as the State of Louisiana; and that the conquered districts of the State were lost to it, and would so remain until re-
conquered or restored by a treaty of peace.   5. Arkansas and Ten- Arkansas
nessee had the same history as Louisiana.   And yet all these prac- and Tennes-
tically dissolved corporations and their exiled governors continued see?
to be recognized by the Confederate government as the lawful authorities of those States.   6. Maryland.   The majority of the legis- Of Mary-
lators being known to side with the rebellion, the assemblage of land?

**What is the doctrine upon which the country is estopped?** that body was prevented by the military power of the United States. Therefore, the country seems to be *estopped* upon the doctrine, that when the exigencies of the republic require it, the government of a State, whether regular or irregular, majority or minority, which adheres to the Union and acknowledges the supremacy of the federal Constitution, will be recognized and treated as the lawful legislature and executive entitled to the guaranty to be protected.

"AGAINST DOMESTIC VIOLENCE."—By the first act of Congress to secure this guaranty (28th Feb., 1795, 1 Stat. 424), it is provided, that " in case of an insurrection in any State against the government thereof, it shall be lawful for the President of the United States, on application of the legislature of such State, or of the executive (when the legislature cannot be convened), to call forth such number of the militia of any State, or States, as may be applied for, as he may judge sufficient to suppress such insurrection." Luther v. Borden, 7 How. 43; Brightly's Digest, p. 440, § 1-4.

**What is "domestic violence"?** If there be an armed conflict, it is a case of "domestic violence," and one of the parties must be in insurrection against the lawful government. As the law gives a discretionary power to the President, to be exercised by him upon his own opinion of certain facts, he is the sole and exclusive judge of the existence of those facts. If he err, Congress may apply the proper remedy. But the courts must administer the law as they find it. (Martin v. Mott, 12 Wheat. 29-31.) Luther v. Borden, 7 How. 44, 45. And see Act of 12th July, 1861. 12 St. 257; 2 Brightly's Dig. 1231, Tit. INSURRECTION; United States v. One hundred packages, 11 Am. L. R. 419; Kulp v Ricketts, 20 Leg. Int. 228; Vallandigham's Trial, 259; Hodgson v. Millwood, 20 Leg. Int. 60, 164; Ohio v. Bliss, 10 Pittsburgh L. J. 304. The acts upon "INSURRECTION" are fully collected in 2 Brightly's Dig. p. 1230-1239. The framers of the Constitution seemed to have looked to the possibility of domestic violence by the slaves. Federalist, No. 43, p. 246.

## ARTICLE V.

**How are amendments to be made?**

**139, 144, 145.**

The Congress, whenever two-thirds of both houses shall deem it necessary, shall propose amendments to this Constitution, or, on the application of the legislatures of two-thirds of the several States, shall call a convention for proposing amendments, which, in either case, shall be valid to all intents and purposes, as part of this Constitution, when ratified by the legislatures of three-fourths of the several States, or by conventions in three-fourths thereof, as the one or the other mode of ratification may be proposed by the Congress;

provided, that no amendment, which may be made prior to the year one thousand eight hundred and eight, shall in any manner affect the first and fourth clauses in the ninth section of the first article; and that no State, without its consent, shall be deprived of its equal suffrage in the Senate.

**236.** CONGRESS MAY PROPOSE AMENDMENTS, &c.—These terms need no definition. Upon a call of Congress in regard to the submission of the fourteenth amendment to the legislatures of the States, President Johnson more than intimated an opinion, that the resolution proposing the amendment ought to be submitted to the President's approval. But the practice has been otherwise; and as the reason for such a rule is superseded by the "two-thirds" vote, the rule itself ought to cease. It has been held that the approval of the President is not necessary. Hollingsworth v. Virginia, 3 Dall. 378. All the amendments have been proposed to the legislatures; none to conventions of the States. See Federalist, No. 43; Story's Const. § 1826–1831; 1 Tucker's Black. Com. App. 371, 372. The amendments when made are binding upon the States.

*Is the President's approval necessary?*

*66–70.*
*275–277.*
*244, 274, 275.*

*242*

### ARTICLE VI.

[1.] All debts contracted, and engagements entered into, before the adoption of this Constitution, shall be as valid against the United States, under this Constitution, as under the Confederation.

*What debts did the United States assume?*

**237.** UNITED STATES TO PAY THE DEBTS OF THE CONFEDERATION.—This was but asserting a principle of moral obligation, which always applies to revolutions. See Story's Const. § 1832–1835; Journal of Convention, 291; Jackson v. Lunn, 3 Johns. Cases, 109; Kelly v. Harrison, 2 Id. 29; Terrett v. Taylor, 9 Cr. 50; Rutherford Inst. B. 2, ch. 9, § 1, 2; ch. 10, § 14, 15; Vattel, Prelim. Dis. ch. 1, § 1; ch. 5, § 64; ch. 14, § 214–216; Grotius, B. 2, ch. 9, § 8, 9; Federalist, Nos. 43, 84; 1 Tuck. Black. Com. App. 368; Confederation, Art. XII. *ante*, p. 19.

The principle is, that revolution ought to have no effect whatsoever upon private rights and contracts, or upon the public obligations of nations. Terrett v. Taylor, 9 Cr. 50.

[2.] This Constitution, and the laws of the United States which shall be made in pursuance thereof, and all treaties made, or which shall be made, under the authority of the United States, shall be the supreme law of the land; and the judges in every State shall

*What is the supreme law of the land?*

be bound thereby, any thing in the Constitution or laws of any State to the contrary notwithstanding.

**What is the Constitution?**
2.
195, 242.
2, 67, 68.

**238.** This Constitution creates the government. Of course it stands paramount. And if any law of Congress, treaty, or State law, be found to be a plain infraction of this Constitution, they will be held to be void. The object was to establish a government which, to the extent of its powers, is supreme. Story's Const. § 1837; Ableman v. Booth, 21 How. 517, 520. A law, by the very meaning of the term, includes supremacy. Story's Const. § 1837.

179, 245.
195-198.

And the government must be strong enough to execute its own laws, by its own tribunals. Ableman v. Booth, 21 How. 517. The supremacy could not peacefully be maintained unless clothed with judicial power. Id. 518, 519. This clause fully compared with the judicial power. Id.

**What is a law?**

246.

195, 203.

211.
138.

**239.** "And all Laws of the United States which shall be made in pursuance thereof."—A law is a solemn expression of legislative will. Louisiana Civil Code, Art. I. It is a rule of action. It is a rule of civil conduct prescribed by the "supreme" power in a State. 1 Bl. Com. 44; 1 Kent's Com., Lect. XX. p. 447. It includes supremacy. Story's Const. § 1738. See Federalist, Nos. 33, 64; Gibbons v. Ogden, 9 Wh. 210, 211; McCulloch v. Maryland, 4 Wh. 405, 406. All such laws, made by the general government, upon the rights, duties, and subjects specially enumerated and confided to their jurisdiction, are necessarily exclusive and supreme, as well by express provision as by necessary implication. Sims' Case, 7 Cush. 729 And the general government has the power to cause such laws to be carried into full execution, by its own powers, without dependence upon State authority, without any let or restraint imposed by it. Id.

A law is made in pursuance of the Constitution, whenever it is enacted by a constitutional quorum of Congress and approved by the President; or, being returned with his objections, is passed over the veto by the necessary two-thirds vote. It then becomes the supreme law; and is generally regarded as binding until decided to be unconstitutional by the Supreme Court of the United States, in a proper case arising upon the law.

After grave consideration, cases might arise where, after the laws had been passed, with all constitutional forms and time, and placed on statute books, it would be the duty of the executive to refuse to carry them out, regardless of consequences. This would be involving the country in a justifiable civil war. President Johnson's Message, 3d Dec., 1867. The editor cannot give this sentiment without expressing his disbelief in its correctness.

The sovereignty to be created was to be limited in its powers of legislation, and if it passed a law not authorized by its enumerated powers, it was not to be regarded as the supreme law of the land, nor were the State judges bound to carry it into execution. And as the courts of a State, and the courts of the United States, might, and certainly would, often differ as to the extent of the powers conferred by the government, it was manifest that serious controversies would arise between the authorities of the United States and of the

States, which must be settled by force of arms, unless some tribunal **138.**
was created to decide between them finally and without appeal.
Ableman v. Booth, 21 How. 519, 520. The Supreme Court of the
United States shown to be that tribunal. Id. 520–526.

And no power is more clearly conferred by the Constitution
and laws of the United States, than the power of this court to decide, ultimately and finally, all cases arising under such Constitution
and laws, &c. Id. 525.

**240.** A TREATY is a solemn agreement between nations. Fos- Define a
ter v. Neilson, 2 Pet. 314. treaty?

Whenever a right grows out of, or is protected by, a treaty, it is **173.**
sanctioned against all the laws and judicial decisions of the States; What is the
and whoever may have this right, it is to be protected. Owing v. rule as to
Norwood's Lessee, 5 Cr. 348; People v. Gerke, 4 Am. L. R. 604; treaties?
6 Opin. 291. But though a treaty is a law of the land, and its pro- **195.**
visions must be regarded by the courts as equivalent to an act of
the legislature when it operates directly on a subject, yet, if it be
merely a stipulation for future legislation by Congress it addresses
itself to the political and not to the judicial department, and the
latter must await the action of the former. Foster v. Neilson, 2
Pet. 253. "Shall be confirmed," was construed to act presently on
the perfect Spanish grants. Id. A treaty ratified with proper
formalities, is, by the Constitution, the supreme law of the land,
and the courts have no power to examine into the authority of the
persons by whom it was entered into on behalf of the foreign nation. Doe v. Braden, 16 How. 635. Though a treaty is the law
of the land, under the Constitution, Congress may repeal it, so far
as it is municipal law, provided its subject-matter be within the
legislative power. Taylor v. Morton, 2 Curt. C. C. 454; Talbot v.
Seaman, 1 Cr. 1; Ware v. Hylton, 3 Dall. 361; Story's Const.
§ 1838.

A treaty concluded by the President and Senate binds the nation, What is the
in the aggregate, and all its subordinate authorities, and its citizens obligation
as individuals, to the observance of the stipulations contained in it. of a treaty?
(Ware v. Hylton, 3 Dall. 199; Worcester v. Georgia, 6 Pet. 575.)
Fellows v. Dennison, 23 N. Y. R. (9 Smith), 427.

"SUPREME LAW OF THE LAND."—The highest law; that which What is the
binds all the people of the nation, and cannot be abrogated by the supreme
States. It was intended to declare that, to the extent of its pow- law?
ers, the Constitution, laws, and treaties of the United States, are 2, 6, 233.
prescribed by the "supreme power of the State." and are supreme.
This power of the government can be exercised by Congress, or,
to the extent of the treaty-making power, by the President and
Senate. The national rule of action then is: 1. The Constitution; What is the
2. Acts of Congress; 3. Treaties; 4. The judicial decisions as national rule
precedents. The State constitutions, laws, and decisions on, are of action?
subordinate to these. See Ableman v. Booth, 21 How. 525;
Story's Const., § 1836–1841, Federalist, No. 33; Gibbons v. Ogden, 9 Wheat. 210, 211; McCulloch v. Maryland, 4 Wheat. 405,
406; Letter of Congress, 13th April, 1787; 12 Journal of Congress, 32–36; 1 Wirt's State Papers, 45, 47, 71, 81, 145; Sergt's
Const. ch. 21, pp. 212, 219; ch. 34, pp. 406, 407; Ware v. Hylton,

11*

How is a treaty to be regulated?

195.

3 Dall. 270–277; Journal of Convention, 222, 282, 283, 293; Federalist, Nos. 44, 64; Debates on the British Treaty of 1794; Journal of the H. of Reps., 6th April, 1796; Marshali's Life of Washington, ch. 8, pp. 650–659. Sergt's Const. 3d edition, ch. 34, p. 410; 1 Debates on British Treaty, by Bache (1796), pp. 374–386; 4 Elliot's Debates, 244–248. A treaty is to be regarded by courts of justice as equivalent to an act of the legislature whenever it operates itself without the aid of any legislative provision. Foster v. Neilson, 2 Pet. 314.

What was Jefferson's opinion?

See Jefferson's Opinion in Washington's Cabinet, that a treaty was a law of a superior order (Greek Treaty of 1796), and could not be repealed by a future one; and see a different view, 4 Jefferson's Corresp. 497, 498; Wheaton's Life of Pinckney, p. 517.

139, 154–161, 203, 210, 211, 215, 219, 226, 223.

**241.** The Constitution or laws of any State to the contrary notwithstanding. It matters not whether the action of a State is organic, and in its Constitution, or any ordinance; or whether it be in a statute, if it violate the Constitution, laws, or treaty of the United States, it is simply void, and "the judges of every State" are bound by the supreme law, and not by the State law. Marbury v. Madison, 1 Cr. 137, 176; Calder v. Bull, 3 Dall. 386; Satterlee v. Matthewson, 2 Pet. 380, 413; Ex parte Garland, 4 Wall. 399; Cummings v. Missouri, 5 Wall. 277, 329.

142, 143.

239.

All courts will declare State Constitutions and laws, which clearly violate the Constitution, laws, or treaties of the United States, void. But only in clear cases. Id. See particularly Ableman v. Booth, 21 How. 507–526.

Who shall be bound by the oath of office?

19, 35, 46, 174, 182.

Any religious test required?

[3.] The senators and representatives before mentioned, and the members o the several State legislatures, and all executive and judicial officers, both of the United States and of the several States, shall be bound, by oath or affirmation, to support this Constitution; but no religious test shall ever be required as a qualification to any office or public trust under the United States.

What officers are embraced? 229–231. 241–242.

274–285.

**242.** "THE SENATORS," &c.—The classification embraces all the legislative, executive, and judicial officers of the United States, and of the States. The practice has also been to embrace all the ministerial and militia officers of the country. The object doubtless was to procure solemn recognitions of the preceding clause. Story's Const. § 1844–1846. Especial attention is invited to the fourteenth amendment. The disqualification for participation in rebellion seems to be based upon the higher obligation to observe this oath.

The act of 1st June, 1789, prescribed the following oath:—

What was the oath?

"I, A. B., do solemnly swear, or affirm (as the case may be), that I will support the Constitution of the United States." 1 Stat. 23; 1 Brightly's Dig. 706.

No other oath is required. "yet he would be charged with insanity who would contend that the legislature might not superadd to the oath directed by the Constitution such other oath of office as its wisdom might suggest." (McCulloch v. Maryland, 4 Wheat. 416·) The United States v. Rhodes (by Justice Swayne, in Kentucky, October T. 1867).

This is the last and closing clause of the Constitution, and inserted when the whole framework of the government had been adopted by the convention. It binds the citizens and the States. And certainly no faith could be more deliberately and solemnly pledged than that which every State has pledged to the other States to support the Constitution as it is, in all its provisions, until they shall be altered in the manner which the Constitution itself prescribes. In the emphatic language of the pledge required, it is to *support this Constitution.* Ableman v. Booth, 21 How. 524, 525. [174, 182] [236.]

The act of Congress of 2d July, 1862, 12 Stat. 502, § 1, requires all federal officers to take the following oath:—"I, A. B., do solemnly swear (or affirm), that I have never voluntarily borne arms against the United States since I have been a citizen thereof; that I have voluntarily given no aid, countenance, counsel, or encouragement to persons engaged in armed hostility thereto; that I have neither sought nor accepted, nor attempted to exercise the functions of any office whatever, under any authority or pretended authority in hostility to the United States; that I have not yielded a voluntary support to any pretended government, authority, power, or Constitution within the United States, hostile or inimical thereto. And I do further swear (or affirm) that, to the best of my knowledge and ability, I will support and defend the Constitution of the United States, against all enemies, foreign and domestic; that I will bear true faith and allegiance to the same; that I take this obligation freely, without any mental reservation or purpose of evasion, and that I will well and faithfully discharge the duties of the office on which I am about to enter, so help me God." [What is the test oath?]

The oath may be taken before any State officer authorized to administer oaths. If it be falsely taken, or if it be subsequently violated, it is perjury. The oath is required of all attorneys practicing in the federal courts, and before any of the departments of government, and of all captains of vessels. 2 Brightly's Dig. p. 348 and p. 50; 12 St. 610. It was held by Judge Busteed, of the United States District Court of Alabama, that, as to lawyers, this test oath was unconstitutional. [142, 143.]

The statute has been held to be unconstitutional as to attorneys of the Supreme Court of the United States who were such before the rebellion, and who could not take the oath because of their participation in it. Garland's Case, 4 Wall. 381. [How far unconstitutional?]

"No Religious Test" was doubtless used in the sense of the statute of 25 Charles II., which required an oath and declaration against transubstantiation, which all officers, civil and military, were formerly obliged to take within six months after their admission. See Webster's Dic., Test. The object was to cut off all pretense of alliance between Church and State. Story's Const. § 184, [What is a religious oath?] [245.] [235.]

754; 4 Black. Com. 44, 53–57; 2 Kent's Com. Lect. 24, 34, 35; Rawle's Const. ch. 10, p. 121.

## ARTICLE VII.

*By how many States to be ratified?*　The ratification of the conventions of nine States shall be sufficient for the establishment of this Constitution between the States so ratifying the same.

Done in Convention, by the unanimous consent of the States present, the seventeenth day of September, in the year of our Lord one thousand seven hundred and eighty-seven, and of the independence of the United States of America the twelfth. In witness whereof, we have hereunto subscribed our names.

### GEORGE WASHINGTON, *Presid't,*

And deputy from Virginia.

*New Hampshire.*
JOHN LANGDON,
NICHOLAS GILMAN.
*Massachusetts.*
NATHANIEL GORHAM,
RUFUS KING.
*New Jersey.*
WIL: LIVINGSTON,
DAVID BREARLY,
WM. PATERSON,
JONA: DAYTON.
*Pennsylvania.*
B. FRANKLIN,
THOMAS MIFFLIN,
ROBERT MORRIS,
GEO: CLYMER,
THO: FITZSIMONS,
JARED INGERSOLL,
JAMES WILSON,
GOUV: MORRIS.
*Delaware.*
GEO: READ,
GUNNING BEDFORD, JUN'R,
JOHN DICKINSON,
RICHARD BASSETT,
JACO: BROOM.

*Connecticut.*
WM. SAML. JOHNSON,
ROGER SHERMAN.
*New York.*
ALEXANDER HAMILTON
*Maryland.*
JAMES M'HENRY,
DAN: OF ST. THOS. JENIFER,
DANL. CARROLL.
*Virginia.*
JOHN BLAIR,
JAMES MADISON, JR.
*North Carolina.*
WM. BLOUNT,
RICH'D DOBBS SPAIGHT,
HU. WILLIAMSON.
*South Carolina.*
JOHN RUTLEDGE,
CHARLES COTESWORTH PINCKNEY,
CHARLES PINCKNEY,
PIERCE BUTLER.
*Georgia.*
WILLIAM FEW,
ABRAHAM BALDWIN.

*Attest:* WILLIAM JACKSON, *Secretary.*

**243.** "Ratification" [*Ratificare*; from *ratus*, valid, and *facere*, Define to make. Litt. Sec. 515. Equivalent to "*confirmare*."]—Co. Litt. ratification? 295*b*. A confirmation of a previous act done either by the party 46. himself or by another. (Story on Agency, § 250, 251; 2 Kent's Com. 237.) Burrill's Law Dic., Ratification.

"Of the Conventions of nine States."—This was intended to leave the action to the people, as the legislatures could only make a league or treaty between the parties. Federalist, No. 43. See Story's Const. § 1850–1856, and 621.

"Between the States ratifying the same."—"States" is In what here used in the sense of independent governments, which could sense is not act, however, through their legislatures; but only through the here used? conventions of the people. But *when*, is not declared. That the 6. rejection by a convention was no estoppel upon a State, is proved by the case of North Carolina, whose first convention rejected the Constitution. The condition of the non-ratifying States is not defined; but the principles of self-preservation were strongly set forth at that day. Federalist, 43; No. 2 Kent's Com. Lect. 24, 30–36; Rawle's Const. ch. 10, p. 121; Story's Const. § 1851, 1852.

"Establishment," is here used in the same sense as the verb 1–13, 243. in the preamble: the putting the government created by the Constitution into operation.

Ratifying extends beyond a literal definition of the term. For To what although the "new States," and the independent nation (Texas) does ratify- which have since been admitted into the Union, cannot be said to ing extend? have *ratified* the Constitution in the sense of agreeing to the act 229–292. done by themselves or another for them; yet in theory and in practice, they have agreed to all its obligations; and because of this agreement, every citizen for himself, and each State in its 205, 271. sovereign or corporate capacity, is bound by all the obligations which the Constitution and the amendments impose. See the able opinions in Chisholm v. Georgia, 2 Dall. 474. See Preface, p. v.

Thus we see that from the first word in the preamble to the end 6. of this stupendous work, there is a constant recurring necessity to carefully weigh every word and phrase; to arrive at the definitions by consulting the whole context, and interpreting each part by the ordinary rules of interpreting other great laws and compacts among men; that is by the words of the instrument, its context, its reason and spirit, the old law, the mischiefs and the remedies intended to be applied; always bearing in mind the great principle, that the compact must strengthen rather than perish.

The Constitution was adopted on the 17th September, 1787, by When was the convention appointed in pursuance of the resolution of the the Consti- Congress of the Confederation, of the 21st February, 1787, and tution rati- was ratified by the conventions of the several States, as follows, States? viz.:—Of Delaware, on the 7th December, 1787; Pennsylvania, 12th Dec., 1787; New Jersey, 18th Dec., 1787; Georgia, 2d Jan., 229, 230. 1788; Connecticut, 9th Jan., 1788; Massachusetts, 6th Feb., 1788; Maryland, 28th April, 1788; South Carolina, 23d May, 1788; New Hampshire, 21st June, 1788; Virginia, 26th June, 1788; New York, 26th July, 1788; North Carolina, 21st Nov. 1789; Rhode Island, 29th May, 1790. North Carolina rejected it at its first convention. Story's Const. § 1851.

**When were the amendments proposed?**

**244.** AMENDMENTS TO THE CONSTITUTION.—These thirteen articles proposed by Congress, in addition to, and amendment of the Constitution of the United States, having been ratified by the legislatures of the requisite number of the States, have become parts of the Constitution. The first ten amendments were proposed by Congress at its first session, in 1789. The eleventh was proposed in 1794, the twelfth in 1803, and the thirteenth and fourteenth (in note 275), as explained in notes 274, 275-285. Brightly's Dig. p. 12, note (a).

For the reasons which led to these amendments, see 2 Elliot's Debates, 331, 380-427; 1 Id. 119-122; 3 Id. 139, 140, 149, 153; Story's Const. § 1857-1868; 2 American Museum, 423, 425; Id. 534; Id. 540-546; Id. 553; 2 Kent's Com. Lect. 24; Federalist, No. 84; 1 Lloyd's Debates, 414, 420, 430-447. And see the History of the Rebellion for the 13th and 14th.

**What was the object of the amendments?**

The whole object seems to have been to limit the powers of the government by the prohibitory power of a bill of rights, notwithstanding the government was one of limited powers, and contained many restrictions in the shape of a bill of rights.   Story's Const. § 1857-1862.

## ARTICLE I.

**What restrictions as to religion, speech, the press, and right of petition?**

Congress shall make no law respecting an establishment of religion, or prohibiting the free exercise thereof; or abridging the freedom of speech, or of the press; or the right of the people peaceably to assemble, and to petition the government for a redress of grievances.

**Define "establishment"? 93, 104, 243.**

**245.** "ESTABLISHMENT."—Here it means a system of religion recognized and supported by the State; as the Establishment or Established Church of England.  Worcester's Dictionary, ESTABLISHMENT; Story's Const. § 1871.

**What is religion?**

"OF RELIGION."—[Lat. Religio, from re and ligo to bind.]—An acknowledgment of our obligation to God as our creator, with a feeling of reverence and love, and consequent duty of obedience to him, &c.   Here a particular system of faith or worship.   Worcester's Dic., RELIGION.   Webster, Id. for a more comprehensive definition.

**What was the object?**

**242.**

The real object of the amendment was, not to countenance, much less to advance Mahometanism, or Judaism, or infidelity, by prostrating Christianity; but to exclude all rivalry among Christian sects, and to prevent any national ecclesiastical establishment which would give to a hierarchy the exclusive patronage of the national government.   Story's Const. § 1877; 2 Lloyd's Debates, 195-197.   For a discussion of the subject, see 2 Kent's Com. (11 ed.) Lect. 24, pp. 35-37, notes 1, a, b, c, d.  Rawle's Const. ch. 10, pp. 12', 122; Montesq. Spirit of Laws, B. 24, ch. 3, 5; 1 Tuck. Black. Com. App. 296; 2 Id. note G, pp. 10, 11; 4 Black. Com. 41-59; Lord King's Life of Locke, 373; Jefferson's Notes on Virginia, 264–270; Story's Const. § 1870–1879; People v. Ruggles, 8 Johns. 160; Vidal v. Girard's Executors, 2 How. 127.

This, and the clause in the VIth Article, that "no religious test shall ever be required for office," are the only provisions in the federal Constitution upon the subject.    *Ex parte* Gurland, 4 Wallace, 397.

No restraint is placed on the action of the States; but the whole power over the subject of religion is left exclusively to the State governments. (Story's Const. § 1878.)    *Ex parte* Garland, Id.    <sub>Is the restraint upon the action of the States? 243–245.</sub>

This makes no provision for protecting the citizens of the respective States in their religious liberties; that is left to the State constitutions; nor is there any inhibition imposed by the Constitution of the United States in this respect on the States. (Permoli v. First Municipality, 3 How. 589, 609; *Ex parte* Garland, 4 Wall. 399.

This court now holds the provision in the Constitution of Missouri void, on the ground that the federal Constitution forbids it. (Such as a test oath to priests.)    *Ex parte* Garland, 4 Wallace, 398.    See the subject fully discussed in 1 Kent's Com. 11th edition, Part IV. sec. XXIV. p. 633; Story's Const. § 1870–1879; Andrew v. The Bible, &c., Society, 4 Sandf. N. Y. 156; Ayers v. M. E. Church, 3 Id. 351.    <sub>17.</sub>    <sub>142, 143.</sub>

Christianity is not a part of the municipal law.    Andrew v. N. Y. & P. B. Society, 4 Sandf. N. Y. R. 182.    With us, all religions are tolerated, and none is established; each has an equal right to the protection of the law.    Ayers v. The Methodist Church, 3 Sandf. 377.    It must be understood to extend equally to all sects, whether they believed in Christianity or not, and whether they were Jews or Infidels. (Updegraff v. The Commonwealth, 11 Sergt. & Rawle, 394.)    Vidal v. Girard's Executors, 2 How. 198.    <sub>Is Christianity a part of the common law?</sub>    <sub>What is the extent of our toleration?</sub>

This declaration (to the same effect in the Constitution of the republic of Texas) reduced the Roman Catholic Church from the high privilege of being the only national church, to a level and an equality with every other denomination of Christians.    Blair v. Odin, 3 Tex. 300; Wheeler v. Moody, 9 Tex. 376.    After this fundamental change, assessments and contributions could not be levied for the purpose of creating such edifices and supporting ecclesiastics, on the ground that the previous system had destined such contributions. (Antoines v. Esclava, 9 Porter, 527; Terrett v. Taylor, 9 Cr. 43.) Paschal's Annotated Digest, note 154; Blair v. Odin, 3 Tex. 300.    <sub>What is the revolutionary effect of such declarations?</sub>

So far as they (the acts of Congress organizing the territories) conferred political rights, and secured civil and religious liberties (which are political rights), the laws of Congress were all superseded by the State Constitution; nor are any part of them in force, unless they were adopted by the Constitution of Louisiana, as laws of the State.    Permoli v. First Municipality, 3 How. 610.    <sub>229, 231.</sub>

**246.** "FREEDOM OF SPEECH" [from *freo*, free, and *dom*, jurisdiction].—Liberty; exemption from servitude.    Syn.    Freedom and liberty, as applied to nations, are often used synonymously. *Freedom* is personal and private; *liberty* public.    Worcester's Dic., FREEDOM.    <sub>What is freedom?</sub>

**Define "freedom of the press"?**    **247.** "AND OF THE PRESS."—This language imports no more than that every man shall have a right to speak, write, and publish his opinions upon any subject whatsoever, without any prior restraint, so, always, that he does not injure any person in his rights, person, or reputation; and so always that he does not thereby disturb nor attempt to subvert the government. (Rawle's Const. ch. 10, pp. 123, 124; 2 Kent's Com. Lect. 24, pp. 16–26; De Lolme, B. 2, ch. 12, 13; 2 Lloyd's Debates, 197, 198.) Story's Const. § 1880–1885; Paschal's Annotated Digest, note 161, p. 47; 1 Black. Com. 152, 153; Rex v. Burdett, 4 Barn & Ald. 95; De Lolme, B. 2, ch. 12, 291–297.

**6, 16, 251.**    **248.** "THE PEOPLE" here is used in the broad sense of the preamble; and a broader sense than "electors." It was never understood to apply to slaves.

**Define the "right to petition'?**    "RIGHT TO PETITION."—This right is incident to a republican government. Story's Const. § 1994, 1995. The only question is as to the "GRIEVANCES" to be redressed. That must always be determined by the power of the "government" to give the redress asked. See the discussions on the 21st rule of the House of Representatives in 1838, and the debates thereon until 1846.

It is to be observed that the right is to petition the "GOVERNMENT." This must mean to address the petition to the appropriate department: to Congress, the executive, or the judiciary, according to their respective jurisdictions, as prescribed by the Constitution and laws. The questions of jurisdiction and of right must always determine whether the redress sought can be granted.

## ARTICLE II.

**What is the right to bear arms?**    A well-regulated militia being necessary to the security of a free State, the right of the people to keep and bear arms shall not be infringed.

**249, 130, 175, 238, 240.**    **249.** This clause has reference to a free government, and is based on the idea, that the people cannot be oppressed or enslaved, who are not first disarmed. Cockrum v. The State, 24 Tex. 401. See Tucker's Black. Com. upon the Militia, App. 300; Black. Com. 143, 144; Rawle's Const. ch. 10, pp. 126, 127; 2 Lloyd's Debates, 23.

The President, by order, disbanded the volunteer companies of the District of Columbia, in November, 1867. His right to do so has been denied.

## ARTICLE III.

No soldier shall, in time of peace, be quartered in any house without the consent of the owner; nor in time of war, but in a manner to be prescribed by law.

**What is a soldier?**    **250.** "NO SOLDIER."—SOLDIER, a man engaged in military service; one whose occupation is military; a man enlisted for

service in an army; a private or one in the ranks.     Webster's
Dic., SOLDIER.

"SHALL BE QUARTERED IN ANY HOUSE."—TO QUARTER is to
station soldiers for lodging.     Webster's Dic., QUARTER.

The object is to secure the perfect enjoyment of that great right
of the common law, that a man's house shall be his own castle,
privileged against all civil and military intrusion.     Story's Const.
§ 1900.

"THE OWNER" here means the occupant in possession.

## ARTICLE IV.

The right of the people to be secure in their persons, Warrants?
houses, papers, and effects, against unreasonable
searches and seizures, shall not be violated ; and no
warrants shall issue, but upon probable cause, supported by oath or affirmation, and particularly describing the place to be searched, and the persons or things
to be seized.

**251.** "THE PEOPLE" is here used in as comprehensive a sense Who are the
as in the preamble, and perhaps in a more enlarged sense than people?
there or elsewhere.     It embraces all the inhabitants—citizens and
aliens—who are entitled to the protection of the law.     The slaves 6, 16, 93, 220,
were never treated as a part of this "people."     The provision 221, 243, 253.
is indispensable to the full enjoyment of the rights of personal
security, personal liberty, and private property.     Story's Const.
§ 1902.

"SEARCHES AND SEIZURES," are always unreasonable when they When un-
are without authority of law.     It was intended to prevent domi- reasonable?
ciliary visits and arbitrary arrests, which are the natural fruits of
unrestricted power.

**252.** "AND NO WARRANT," &c.—[O. Fr. *guarent;* Lomb. *warens.*] What is a
—An authority to do some judicial act; a power derived from warrant?
a court, to take some person or property.     Burrill's Law Dic.,
WARRANT.

This refers only to process issued under authority of the United To what
States.     Smith v. Maryland, 18 How. 71.     And it has no applica- confined?
tion to proceedings for the recovery of debts, as a treasury distress     257.
warrant.     Murray's Lessee v. Hoboken Land & Improvement Co.
Id. 272.     See *Ex parte* Burford, 3 Cr. 448 ; Wakely v. Hart, 6
Binn. 316 ; 1 Opin. 229 ; 2 Id. 266.     See *Ex parte* Milligan, 4 Wall.
119.     It was caused by the practice of issuing general warrants.
Story's Const. § 1902.     See Moody v. Beach, 3 Burr. 1743 ; 4
Black. Com. 291, 292 ; 15 Hansard's Parliamentary History, 1398–
1419 (1764); Bell v. Clapp, 10 Johns. 263; Sailley v. Smith, 11
Johns. 500 ; Report and Resolutions of the Virginia Legislature,
25th Feb. 1799 ; 4 Jefferson's Correspondence, justifying arrests
by Wilkinson, 75–136 ; Story's Const. § 1902, note 2.

## ARTICLE V.

**What is necessary to charge a capital or infamous crime?**

No person shall be held to answer for a capital or otherwise infamous crime, unless on a presentment or indictment of a grand jury, except in cases arising in the land or naval forces, or in the militia, when in actual service, in time of war or public danger; nor

**What of the rights of property?**

shall any person be subject for the same offense to be twice put in jeopardy of life or limb; nor shall be compelled, in any criminal case, to be witness against himself; nor be deprived of life, liberty, or property, without due process of law; nor shall private property be taken for public use without just compensation.

**What is a "person"?**
**19, 35, 159.**

**253.** PERSON.—Practically the slaves and people of color were never considered as embraced in this amendment, as they were often proceeded against without indictment. It meant a free white.

**What is a capital or infamous crime?**
**40, 99, 110–116, 142, 191–194.**

"CAPITAL OR OTHERWISE INFAMOUS CRIME."—This must mean treason, piracy, or felony ("high crime"), as contradistinguished from "misdemeanor." Story's Const. § 1784.

In England, it formerly incapacitated the party committing it from giving evidence as a witness; such as treason, *præmunire*, felony, and every species of *crimen falsi*, as perjury, forgery, and the like. Roscoe's Criminal Evidence, 135. Usually, in this country, it means such as are punished with death, or imprisonment in a State prison or penitentiary. Id.

**What is a presentment?**
**252, 260.**

But the "PRESENTMENT OR INDICTMENT" is used in all offenses against the United States. "*Presentment*" is the notice taken by a grand jury of any offense, from their own knowledge or observation, without any bill of indictment laid before them, upon which the officer of the court must afterward frame an indictment, before the party presented can be put to answer for it. 4 Black. Com. 301.

*Presentment* (information) is not synonymous with "indictment." An indictment must be found by a grand jury; an information may be preferred by an officer of court. Clepper v. The State, 4 Tex. 244; Paschal's Annotated Digest, notes 162, 163, p. 48. It has never yet been authorized by act of Congress. Story's Const. § 1785.

**What is an indictment?**
**252, 260.**

An "INDICTMENT" is a written accusation of one or more persons of a crime or misdemeanor, preferred to and presented on oath by a grand jury. (4 Bl. Com. 302; 4 Stephens' Com. 69, Arch. Cr. Pl. 1.) Burrill's Law Dic., INDICTMENT. See Paschal's Annotated Digest, Art. 2863, notes 720–721.

**What is a grand jury?**

A "GRAND JURY" is a body of men varying from not less than twelve to not more than twenty-three, who, in secret, hear the evidence offered by the government only, and find or ignore bills of in-

dictment presented to them. (4 Bl. Com. 302, 303; 4 Stephens    260.
Com. 369, 370.) Burrill's Law Dic., GRAND JURY; Story's Const.
§ 1784; The King v. Marsh, 6 Adolph. & Ell., 236; 1 Nev. &
Perry, 187; People v. King, 2 Caines' Cases, 98; Commonwealth
v. Wood, 2 Cush. 149. The subject of grand juries is regulated
by Act of Congress. 9 St. 72; 4 St. 188; 1 Brightly's Dig. 223,
232.

**254.** "EXCEPT IN CASES ARISING IN THE LAND OR NAVAL    What is the
FORCES, OR THE MILITIA WHEN IN ACTUAL SERVICE IN TIME OF    exception?
WAR OR PUBLIC DANGER."—This article, compared with the eighth    117, 130.
section of the first article, "to provide and maintain a navy;" "to    127–129, 260.
make rules for the government of the land and naval forces."
Under these provisions Congress has the power to provide for the
trial and punishment of military and naval offenses in the manner    What is the
then and now practiced by civilized nations; and the power to do    jurisdiction
so is given without any connection between it and the third article    in a military
of the Constitution defining the judicial power of the United States.    trial?
Indeed, the two powers are entirely independent of each other.
Dynes v. Hoover, 20 How. 78.

And if the sentence be confirmed, it becomes final, and must be
executed, unless the President pardon the offenders. When confirmed, it is beyond the jurisdiction of any civil tribunal whatever,
unless it should be in a case where the court had not jurisdiction
over the subject-matter of the charge. Dynes v. Hoover, 20 How.
81; 3 Whiting, 335.

If the court-martial had no jurisdiction, or should inflict a punish-    Suppose the
ment forbidden by the law, although the sentence be approved,    court-
civil courts may, on an action by a party aggrieved, inquire into    martial has
the want of jurisdiction and give redress. (Harman v. Tuppenden,    tion?
1 East, 555; Marshall's Case, 10 Cr. 76; Morrison v. Sloper, Willes,
30; Parton v. Williams, B. & A. 330.) Dynes v. Hoover, 20
How. 82; S C. 3 Whiting, 336.

**255.** "FOR THE SAME OFFENSE TO BE PUT TWICE IN JEOPARDY    What
OF LIFE OR LIMB."—The meaning of this phrase is, that a party    means
shall not be tried a second time for the same offense, after he has    twice in
once been acquitted or convicted, unless the judgment has been    jeopardy?
arrested or a new trial granted on motion of the party. But it    260.
does not relate to a mis-trial. (United States v. Haskell, 4 Wash.
C. C. 402, 410.) United States v. Perez, 9 Wheat, 579. The court
may discharge a jury from giving a verdict, in a capital case, without the consent of the prisoner, whenever, in their opinion, there
is a manifest necessity for such an act, or the ends of justice would
be otherwise defeated. United States v. Perez, 9 Wh. 579. See
United States v. Haskell, 4 Wash. C. C. 402; United States v. Gilbert,
2 Sumn. 19; Story's Const. § 1787. See the cases fully collected
and the distinctions nicely stated in 2 Graham & Waterman on
New Trials, ch. 2, pp. 51–135. Paschal's Annotated Digest, note
113

**256.** "WITNESS AGAINST HIMSELF."—To make a man a witness    Why not
against himself would be contrary to the principles of a republi-    a witness
can government. Wynehamer v. The People, 13 N. Y. 391, 392.    against himself?

| | |
|---|---|
| Is the inhibition confined to criminal cases? | This must have reference to criminal proceedings, since the practice of discovery in civil cases is universal. See 4 Bl. Com. 326; 3 Wilson's Law Lect. 154–159; Cicero pro Sulla, 28. Rutherford's Inst. B. 1, ch. 18, § 5. Such a practice in criminal cases is conceived in a spirit of torture. Story's Const. § 1788. |
| 233. | |

What is due process of law?

260.

**257.** "WITHOUT DUE PROCESS OF LAW."—By the "due course of law," is meant all the guaranties set forth in the sixth amendment. Jones v. Montes, 15 Tex. 353; James v. Reynolds, 2 Tex. 251. In *Magna Charta* it probably meant the established law of the kingdom, in opposition to the Civil or Roman law. James v. Reynolds, 2 Tex. 251; Paschal's Annotated Digest, note 155.

Repeat Magna Charta?

251.

*Nec super eum ibimus, nec super eum mittimus, nisi per legale judicium parium suorum, vel per legem terræ.* Neither will we pass upon him, or condemn him, but by the lawful judgment of his peers or the law of the land. Magna Charta; Story's Const. § 1789. See the question examined. Murray's Lessee v. Hoboken Land & Improvement Company, 18 How. 272.

It conveys the same meaning as "law of the land," in *Magna Charta.* (2 Inst. 50.) Id. 276.

What is due course of law?

260.

" DUE PROCESS OF LAW."—This means that the right of the citizen to his property, as well as life or liberty, could be taken away only upon an open, public, and fair trial before a judicial tribunal, according to the forms prescribed by the laws of the land for the investigation of such subjects. 9th Op. 200. An executive officer cannot make an order to violate this principle. Id. Property and life are put upon the same footing. Id.

Define the right of a citizen?

253.

The true interpretation of these constitutional phrases is, that where rights are acquired by the citizen under the existing law, there is no power in any branch of the government to take them away; but where they are held contrary to existing law, or are forfeited by its violation, then they may be taken from him—not by an act of the legislature, but in the due administration of the law itself, before the judicial tribunals of the State. Wynehamer v. People, 13 N. Y. R. 393; Taylor v. Porter, 4 Hill, 145. That is by indictment or presentment of good and lawful men. (2 Kent's Com. 13; Story's Const. § 1782; 2 Coke's Inst. 45–50.) Wynehamer v. People, 13 N. Y. R. 395; Jones v. Montes, 15 Tex. 352; Paschal's Annotated Digest, note 155; 2 Inst. 50, 51; 2 Kent's Com. Lect. 24, p. 10; Story's Const. § 1789.

What is law?

239.

What law? Undoubtedly a pre-existing rule of conduct, not an *ex post facto* law, rescript, or decree made for the occasion—the purpose of working the wrong. (Norman v. Heist, 5 Watts & Sergt. 193; Taylor v. Porter, 4 Hill, 145; Hoke v. Henderson, 4 Dev. 15.) Wynehamer v. People, 13 N. Y. R. 393, 394. See full citations, 2 Kent's Com. 11th ed. 339, 240, and notes.

Does the rule apply to the collection of revenue?

This is intended to secure the citizen the right to a trial, according to the forms of law. Parsons v. Russel, 11 Mich. 113. But it does not apply to proceedings to collect the public revenue. Ames v. Port Huron, &c., Co. 11 Mich. 139. See that question exhaustively investigated. Taylor's Lessee v. Hoboken Land & Improvement Company, 18 How. 272.

For though "due process of law" generally implies and includes

*actor, reus, judex,* regular allegations, opportunity to answer, and a
trial according to some settled course of judicial proceeding, yet
this is not universally true. (2 Inst. 47, 50; Hoke v. Henderson,
4 Dev. N. C. R. 15; Taylor v. Porter, 4 Hill, 146; Van Zandt v.
Waddel, 2 Yerg. 260; State Bank v. Cooper; Id. 599; Jones v.
Heirs of Perry, 10 Id. 59; Greene v. Briggs, 1 Curtis, 311.) Murray v. Hoboken L. & I. Co., 18 How. 280.

The article is a restraint on the legislative as well as on the executive and judicial branches of the government, and cannot be so construed as to leave Congress free to make any process "due process of law." Id. 276.   We must examine the Constitution itself, to see whether the process be in conflict with any of its provisions.   Id. 277.   Summary process to collect revenue was always allowed.   Id.   Authorities exhausted.   Id. *Does the article restrain the legislature?*

The law of New York, which authorizes a person to be committed as an inebriate to the lunatic asylum upon an *ex parte* affidavit, without being heard, violates this guaranty.   In matter of Jones, 30 How. Pr. 446. *Exemplify a violation of this clause?*

**258.** "PRIVATE PROPERTY FOR PUBLIC USE WITHOUT JUST COMPENSATION.—"PRIVATE PROPERTY" is the sacred right of individual dominion.   It is one of the great absolute rights of every citizen to have his property protected.   And the government has no right to deprive the citizen of his property, except for the use of the public; nor then, without compensation.   Story's Const. § 1790. *What is private property?* 231, 233, 144, 72.

This phrase includes all private property.   United States v.
Harding, 1 Wall. Jr. 127; 2 Opin. 655.   See Murray's Lessee v.
Hoboken Land & Improvement Company, 18 How. 276.   This last
clause refers solely to the exercise by the State of the right of
eminent domain. (The People v. The Mayor of Brooklyn, 4 Comst.
419.)   Gilman v. The City of Sheboygan, 2 Blackf. 513.   This provision is only a limitation of the power of the general government;
it has no application to the legislation of the several States.   Barron v. Mayor of Baltimore, 7 Pet. 243–7; Bonaparte v. Camden &
Amboy R. R. Co., Bald. 220.   It is now settled that the amendments to the Constitution do not extend to the States.   Livingston's
Lessee v. Moore, 7 Pet. 551; Boring v. Williams, 17 Ala. 516.
They are exclusively restrictions upon federal power, intended to
prevent interference with the rights of the States, and of their
citizens.   Fox v. Ohio, 5 How. 434; James v. Commonwealth, 12
S. & R. 221; Barker v. The People, 3 Cow. 686.   It is a great
principle of the common law, which existed anterior to the Constitution and to *magna charta*, and which was embodied in the 29th
article of that great charter:—"No freeman shall be taken, or imprisoned, or disseized of his freehold, or liberties, or otherwise
destroyed, but by lawful judgment of his peers, or by the law of
the land.".   Young v. McKenzie, 3 Ga. 42.   This is an affirmance
of a great doctrine established by the *common law* for the protection of private property.   It is founded on natural equity, and laid
down by jurists as a principle of universal law. (Story's Const.
§ 1790; Bradshaw v. Rogers, 2 Johns. 106; Louisville, Cincinnati
& Charleston Railroad Co. v. Chappell, Rice, 387; Doe v. The *What says Magna Charta?*

Georgia R. R. & B. Co., 1 Kelley, 524; 1 Bl. Com. 139, 140.) Young v. McKenzie, 3 Ga. 40–44; 2 Kent's Com. Lect. 24, pp. 275, 276; 3 Wilson's Law Lect. 203; Ware v. Hylton. 3 Dall. 194, 235. In the absence of any such declaration in the Constitution of Georgia, we refer to this amendment as a plain, simple declaration of a great constitutional principle, of universal application, as asserted and declared in the Constitution of the United States. Young v. McKenzie, 3 Ga. 45. The true principle from this case would seem to be, that the Constitution of the United States, and the amendments, enter into and form parts of the State Constitutions—paramount *pro tanto.*—ED. Some of these amendments were *declaratory;* some *restrictive* of the powers of the federal government. The latter clause of this article is only declaratory. Young v. McKenzie, 3 Ga. 44.

A "public use" means a use concerning the whole community, as distinguished from particular individuals, though each and every member of society need not be equally interested in such use. Gilmer v. Line Point, 18 Cal. 229. And see Honeyman v. Blake, 19 Cal. 579. See People v. Kerr, 3 Barb. N. Y. 357. The right of the owners of town lots to the adjoining street, is as much property as the lot itself. Lackland v. North Missouri R. R. Co. 31 Mo. 180.

**What is just compensation?**    **259.** "JUST COMPENSATION."—Although we may hold that "compensation" is not altogether synonymous with "payment," yet the means of payment must not be doubtful. The making of compensation must be as absolutely certain as that the property is taken. (Carr v. Ga. R. R. & B. Co., 1 Kelley, 524; Young v. Harrison, 6 Ga. 130; Bloodgood v. M & H. R. R. Co., 18 Wend. 9; 2 Kent's Com. 339.) B. B., Brazos & Colorado Railroad Co. v. Ferris, 26 Tex. 602. (See 2 Kent's Com. 3d ed. notes f, and 7; Miller v. Craig, 3 Stockt. N. J. 106.)

**In what must be the payment?**    The payment must be in money, the constitutional currency. Id. The advantages to the land not taken cannot be estimated against the intrinsic value of the land actually taken. (Jacob v. The City of Louisville, 9 Dana, 114; The People v. The Mayor of Brooklyn, 6 Barb. 309; Rogers v. R. R. Co. 3 Maine, 310; State v Miller, 3 Zab. 383; Hatch v. R. R. 25 Vt. 49; Moale v. Baltimore, 5 Md. 314.) B. B., Brazos & Colo. R. R. Co. v. Ferris, 26 Tex. 603, 604; Paschal's Annotated Dig. note 168.

**What provision for payment must be made?**    Under an act which authorizes a work, but does not provide for compensation for private property, which it will be necessary to take, such property cannot be taken without the owner's consent. Carson v. Coleman, 3 Stockt. N. J. 106. The consequential injury occasioned by the grading of a street, is not a taking of private property for public use within the meaning of the prohibition of the Constitution. Macy v. Indianapolis, 17 Ind. 267.

The question is not judicial, but one of political sovereignty, to be exerted as the legislature directs. Ford v. Chicago, &c., R. R. Co. 14 Wis. 609.

**For what purpose cannot a railroad condemn?**    A railroad company cannot condemn a site for erecting a manufactory of railroad cars. Eldridge v. Smith, 34 Vermont (5 Shaw), 484. Nor dwelling-houses for employees. Id. Otherwise as to

wood and lumber used on the road. Id. There must be a con-
demnation, or an agreement consummated.    Id. ; Whitman v.
Boston, &c., 3 Allen (Mass.), 133. The condemnation may be within
the liberal construction of the charter. Fall River, &c., Co. v. Old
Colony, &c., R. R. Co. 5 Allen (Mass.), 221. And see Wadhams v.
Lackawana, &c., R. R. Co., 42 Penn. State R. 303 ; Vicksburg, &c.,
R. R. Co., 15 La. Ann. 507.

The actual occupant of vacant public lands is entitled to damages, To what<br>title does it<br>extend?
even where the land is taken under an act of Congress. California,
&c., R. R. Co. v. Gould, 21 Cal. 254. A statute fixing the minimum
of fees for defending criminals is not taking private property for
public use.  Samuels v. Dubuque, 13 Iowa (5 With.), 536.

The law of New York, which forbade the sale of spirituous State the<br>principle<br>of the<br>liquor laws?
liquors, "*deprived*" the owners of their property; and violated this
guaranty.  Wynehamer v. The People, 13 N. Y. R. 395, 396, 397.
When a law annihilates the value of property, and strips it of its
attributes, by which, alone, it is distinguished as property, the
owner is deprived of it according to the plainest interpretation, and
certainly within the spirit of the constitutional provision intended
expressly to shield private rights from the exercise of power.
Wynehamer v. People, 13 N. Y. R. 398.  These views do not interfere with the license laws, which have been held to be constitutional : nor with the laws which merely affect the value of property,
or render its destruction necessary as a means of safety. (Story's
Const. § 1790; Radcliff's Executors v. The Mayor of Brooklyn,
4 Comst. 195; 2 Kent, 330; Russel v. The Mayor, &c., of New
York, 2 Denio, 461.)  Wynehamer v. The People, 13 N. Y. R. 402;
Mitchell v. Harmony, 13 How. 115; The License Cases, 5 Howard,
504 : Lorocco v. Geary, 3 Cal. 69; Am. Print Works v. Lawrence,
1 Zabr. 248.

A law prohibiting the indiscriminate traffic in intoxicating What con-<br>trol has the<br>legislature<br>over the<br>liquor<br>trade?
liquors, and placing the trade under public regulation to prevent
abuse in their sale and use, violates no constitutional restraints.
It deprives no one of his liberty or property.  Metropolitan Board
of Excise v. Barrie, 34 N. Y. R. 667.

No one legislature can curtail the power of its successors to Can a<br>legislature<br>control its<br>successors?
make such laws as they may deem proper in matters of police.
(Alger v. Weston, 14 Johns. 231 ; People v. Morris, 13 Wend. 329;
State v. Holmes, 38 New Hamp. 225 : Calder v. Kirby, 5 Gray,
59"; Hun v. The State, 1 Ohio, 15; Wynehamer v The People,
3 Kern. (13 N. Y. R.) 378 : License Cases, 5 How. 504; Butler v.
Pennsylvania, 10 How. 416; Coates v. The Mayor, 7 Cow. 587;
2 Parsons on Cont. 538; 3 Id. 5th ed. 556.) Metropolitan Board v.
Barrie, 34 N. Y. R. 668.  Some of the dicta in Wynehamer v. The
People have misled. Id.

## ARTICLE VI.

In all criminal prosecutions, the accused shall enjoy What are<br>the rights of<br>defendants<br>in criminal<br>cases?
the right to a speedy and public trial, by an impartial
jury of the State and district wherein the crime shall
have been committed, which district shall have been 16, 35, 46.

previously ascertained by law, and to be informed of the nature and cause of the accusation ; to be confronted with the witnesses against him ; to have compulsory process for obtaining witnesses in his favor ; and to have the assistance of counsel for his defense.

**258, 263.**
**12, 212, 245.**

**260.** "THE ACCUSED," here means the "person" presented or indicted. The "him" does not limit the accused to sex. Because the amendments did not apply to the States, the slaves and free persons of color were often deprived of a trial by jury.

**263.**

This is only to be intended of those crimes which, by our former laws and customs, had been tried by jury. United States v. Duane, (Penn.) Wall. 106. The conspirators who assassinated the President of the United States, while the country was in a state of war, and while the city of Washington was under martial law, were triable by military commission under the act of Congress, and not entitled to a trial by jury. The Trial of the Conspirators. Any person charged with a crime in the courts of the United States, has a right, before as well as after indictment, to the process of the court to compel the attendance of his witnesses. 1 Burr's Trial, 179–80.

**212, 251–259.**

This section compared with Art. III., Sec. II., clause 3, and the third, fourth, and fifth amendments. *Ex parte* Milligan, 4 Wallace, 119, 120, 139. The history of these guaranties. Id.

What is the Constitution of the United States? 2, 8, 117.

The Constitution of the United States is a law for rulers and people, equally in war and in peace, and covers with the shield of its protection all classes of men, at all times and under all circumstances. *Ex parte* Milligan, 4 Wallace, 120, 121. But see the war

What is the power of a military commission?

power discussed. Id. 138, 139. A military commission could exercise no judicial power over a citizen of Indiana during the rebellion. Id. The laws and usages of war could not be applied to citizens in States which have upheld the authority of the government, and

To whom is jury trial secured? 254. 253, 254.

where the courts are open and their process unobstructed. *Ex parte* Milligan, Id. 121. This right of trial by jury is preserved to every one accused of crime, who is not attached to the army or navy, or militia in actual service. Id. See dissentient opinion, p. 139. The fifth amendment recognizes the necessity of an indictment or presentment, before any one can be held to answer for high crimes, with the exception therein stated ; by which it was meant to limit the right of trial by jury, in this sixth amendment, to those persons who were subject to indictment or presentment

What are the exceptions? 254.

in the fifth. *Ex parte* Milligan, 4 Wallace, 123. Those connected with military or naval service are amenable to the jurisdiction which Congress has created for their government, and, while thus serving, they surrender their right to be tried by the civil courts. Id.

How are the citizens to be tried? What of martial law? 140, 141.

*All other persons,* citizens of States where the courts are open, if charged with crime, are guarantied trial by jury. Id. Civil liberty and martial law (at the will of the commander) cannot endure together ; the antagonism is irreconcilable. Id. Neither Congress nor the President can disturb one of these guaranties of liberty, except the one concerning the writ of *habeas corpus.* Id. But the suspension of the writ and of investigation does not give the power of trial otherwise than by the course of the common law. Id. 125, 126. Martial law cannot arise from *threatened* invasion. The necessity must be actual and present; the invasion real, such as effectually closes the courts and deposes the civil administration. Id. 127. *Then* it may exist, until the restoration of civil authority, but no longer. Id. Why martial law cannot be tolerated. (McConnell v. Hampden, 12 Johns. 257; Smith v. Shaw. Id. 234.) *Ex parte* Milligan, 4 Wallace, 129. The case of Luther v. Borden, 7 Howard, 1, explained. Id. It was not a case arising under the federal Constitution. Id. 129, 130. As the applicant was a citizen of the United States residing in Indiana, he could not be treated as a prisoner of war. Id. 131, 134. Chief-Justice Chase and Justices Wayne, Swayne, and Miller concurred in the judgment of, but disagreed as to the powers of Congress over the subjects of MILITARY LAW, which they divided into the articles of war for the government of the national forces, military government superseding, as far as may be deemed expedient, the local law, and exercised by the military commander under the direction of the President; and MARTIAL LAW PROPER, which is called into action by Congress, or temporarily, when the action of Congress cannot be invoked, and in the case of justifying or excusing peril, by the President, in times of insurrection or invasion, or of civil or foreign war, within districts or localities where ordinary law no longer adequately secures public safety and private rights.

*Marginal notes:* What is the effect of suspending the habeas corpus? 257. — What justifies martial law? — 233. — Can a citizen be treated as a prisoner of war? — What is the military law and how divided? — 118, 119.

This was intended as a constitutional safeguard in the trial of those cases for which it was stipulated that the courts shall remain open, and wherein a party shall have his remedy by due course of law. (Beekman v. Saratoga & Schenectady Railroad Company, 3 Paige, 45; Bonaparte v. C. & A. Railway, Bald. C. C. R. 205; Bloodgood v. M. & H. Railway, 14 Wend. 51; S. C. 18 Wend. 9; Stevens v. Middlesex Canal, 12 Mass. 466; Wheelock v. Young, 4 Wend. 650; Stowel v. Flagg, 11 Mass. 364; Mason v. Kennebec & Portland Railroad Company, 31 Maine, 215; Aldrich v. The Cheshire Railroad Company, 1 Foster, N. H. 350.) B. B., Brazos & C. R. R. Co. v. Ferris, 26 Tex. 599; Paschal's Annotated Dig. note 166.

*Marginal note:* What was the intention of this guaranty? 257.

These decisions are generally made upon similar provisions in the State Constitutions. This provision of the Constitution of the United States applies only to the general government, and not to the States. Withers v. Buckley, 20 How. 84.

*Marginal note:* 276, 277.

"THE ACCUSATION" means a copy of the presentment or indictment. All of these rights have been regulated by acts of Congress. 1 St. 88; 1 Brightly's Dig. 221–224, and exhaustive notes thereon.

*Marginal note:* 253.

**261.** "COMPULSORY PROCESS," means forcible process, such as attachment. The principle grew out of the oppressive one which denied witnesses to the accused. See 4 Black. Com. 359, 360; Rawle's Const. ch. 10, pp. 128, 129; 3 Wilson's Law Lect. 170, 171; Hawk. P. C. ch. 46, § 160, 2 Hale P. C. 283. Upon affidavit of inability, the accused can have his witnesses at the expense of the United States. 9 St. 72, § 11; 1 Brightly's Dig. 223, § 116.

*Marginal note:* What is the meaning of "compulsory process"?

12

**262.** "ASSISTANCE OF COUNSEL."—When this was adopted the accused were not allowed the assistance of counsel in England. That defect has been cured by an act in 1836.  4 Black. Com. 355, 356, note 9; Story's Const. § 1793–1795.

For the power of the court to assign counsel in cases of treason, see act of 30th April, 1790, 1 St. 117, § 29; 1 Brightly's Dig. 221, § 104.

## ARTICLE VII.

*Trials in civil cases?*

In suits at common law, where the value in controversy shall exceed twenty dollars, the right of trial by jury shall be preserved; and no fact tried by a jury, shall be otherwise re-examined in any court of the United States than according to the rules of the common law.

*What are suits at common law?*

**263.** This includes not merely the modes of proceeding known to the common law, but all suits not of equity or admiralty jurisdiction, in which legal rights are settled and determined.  Parsons v. Bedford, 3 Pet. 433; United States v. La Vengeance, 3 Dall. 297; Webster v. Reid, 11 How. 437; Bains v. The Schooner James & Catherine, Bald. 544; Smith's Const. 552, 554; 2 Graham & Waterman, 30.  It does not apply to an examination as to the claim for services under the fugitive slave law. Miller v. McQuerry, 5 McLean, 469; In the matter of Martin, 2 Paine, 348. Nor to a motion for summary relief. Banning v. Taylor, 12 Harr. 289.

*What is the common law?*

The phrase "COMMON LAW," as used in this section, is used in contradistinction to equity, and admiralty, and maritime jurisprudence.  Parsons v. Bedford, 3 Pet. 446; Story's Const. § 1769; Smith's Const. 552.  It is reconcilable with the 3d article, and the several acts of Congress about jury trials. Id. 446.  Neither this article, nor the act of 1824, gives to the Supreme Court the right to revise the verdict of the jury upon the facts. Id. 446, 447.  The common law, or *lex non scripta*, means those immemorial customs of England, whereof the memory of man runneth not to the contrary. 1 Bl. Com. 62.

*For whose benefit is the trial by jury?*

The right to trial by jury is for the benefit of the parties litigating, and may be waived by them.  United States v. Rathbone, 2 Paine, 578.  But the circuit courts have no power to order a peremptory nonsuit against the will of the plaintiff.  Elmore v. Grymes, 1 Pet. 469; D'Wolf v. Rabaud, Id. 476; Crane v. Lessee of Morris, 6 Id. 598; Thompson v. Campbell, Hemp. 8.  The common law here alluded to, is not the common law of any individual State, but the common law of England; according to which, facts once tried by a jury are never re-examined, unless a new trial be granted, in the discretion of the court before which the suit is depending, for good cause shown; or unless the judgment of such court be reversed by a superior tribunal on a writ of error, and a *venire facias de novo* awarded.  United States v. Wonson, 1 Gall. 20.  The government is as much bound by this provision as any other party who may desire to collect a debt.  9 Op. 200.

It has been well settled, that the amendments to the Constitution 277·279.
of the United States were never intended to control the proceedings
of the State courts. (Wood v. Wood, 2 Cowen, 819, *note;* Murphy
v. The People, 2 Cowen, 815; Livingston v. Mayor of New York,
8 Wend. 85, 100; Warren v. Mayor of Baltimore, 7 Peters, 250;
Livingston v. Moore, 7 Peters, 551; Colt v. Evers, 12 Conn. 243;
In the matter of Smith, 10 Wend. Rep. 449; Lea v. Tillotson, 24
Wend. 337.) 2 Graham & Waterman's New Trials, p. 31, *note.*

**264.** AND NO FACT TRIED BY JURY SHALL BE RE-EXAMINED,
&c.—See a discussion on the original Constitution (prior to this
amendment), which gave appellate jurisdiction "*both as to law and
fact.*" Story's Const. § 1763-1770, and notes to third edition;
Federalist, Nos. 81, 83.  And see 1 Elliot's Debates, 121, 122; 2 Id.
346, 380-410; Id. 413-427; 3 Elliot's Debates, 139-157; 2
American Museum, 425, 534, 540, 548, 553; 3 Id. 318, 347, 419,
420.

The amendment struck down the objection; and has secured the    21L
trial by jury in civil cases in the fullest latitude of the common law.
(1 Tucker's Bl. Com. App. 351; Rawle's Const. ch. 10, p. 135;
Bank of Hamilton v. Dudley, 2 Pet. 492, 525.) Story's Const.
§ 1568.

This is a prohibition to the courts of the United States to re-examine any facts tried by a jury, in any other manner. (Parsons v.
Bedford, 3 Pet. 447.) Story's Const. § 1770. It is denied that
the judiciary act of 1789, ch. 20, § 17, 22, 24; or the act of 1824,
has given the right to the Supreme Court to grant a new trial, on
the mere facts. It was intimated that if Congress had attempted
to confer such power, the act would be unconstitutional. Id.

**265.** RE-EXAMINED AFTER VERDICT.—Sec. 5 of the act of 3d    264.
March, 1863 (13 St. 756), so far as it authorizes the removal of
certain causes after verdict, and a trial and determination of the
facts and the law, is in violation of this amendment. (14 Mass.
412.) Patrie v. Murray, 29 How. Pr. R. 312; S. C. 43 Barb. 323;
Benjamin v. Murray, 28 How. N. Y. R. 193.  And see The People
v. Murray, 5 Park. Cr. 577.

And see Spencer v. Lapsley, 20 How. 267; Martin Insurance
Co. v. Hodgson, 6 Cr. 206; Sims v. Hundley, 6 How. 1.

## ARTICLE VIII.

Excessive bail shall not be required, nor excessive
fines imposed, nor cruel and unusual punishments inflicted.

What is the
rule about
bail, fines,
and punish-
ments?

**266.** "EXCESSIVE BAIL."—Bail is a delivery from custody on
security. Burrill's Law Dic., BAIL. The meaning is, that the sum
required shall not be too large. Bail should not be fixed in criminal cases at a sum so large as purposely to prevent the prisoner
from giving bail. United States v. Lawrence, 4 Cr. 518.

What is
bail?

**267.** "NOR EXCESSIVE FINES, IMPOSED."—The offense charged
was the keeping and maintaining, without license, a tenement for

Give an
example of
usual pun-
ishment?
the illegal sale and il'egal keeping of intoxicating liquors. It appears from the record that the fine and punishment in the case before us was fifty dollars, and imprisonment at hard labor in the
house of correction for three months. We perceive nothing excessive, or cruel, or unusual in this. The object of the law was to
protect the community against the manifold evils of intemperance.
The mode adopted. of prohibiting under penalties the sale and
233.          keeping for sale of intoxicating liquors, without license, is the
usual mode adopted in many, perhaps all, of the States. It is
wholly within the discretion of State legislatures. Pervear v. The
Commonwealth, 5 Wall. 480. The amendment is an exact transcript of a clause in the English Bill of Rights of 1688. It was
intended to warn our government against such violent proceedings.
See 5 Cobbett's Parl. Hist. 110; 2 Elliot's Debates, 345; 3 Id.
345; 2 Lloyd's Debates, 225, 226; Rawle's Const. ch. 10, pp. 130,
131; Story's Const. § 1903, 1904.

This amendment does not apply to the States, but only restricts
the national government. (Barker v. The People, 3 Cow. 686
James v. Commonwealth, 12 Sergt. and Rawle, 220; Barron v.
The Mayor of Baltimore, 7 Pet. 243.) Story's Const. § 1904; Pervear v. The Commonwealth, 5 Wall. 480.

"CRUEL AND UNUSUAL PUNISHMENTS."—The disfranchisement of
a citizen is not an unusual punishment. Barber v. The People, 20
Johns. 459. The punishments of whipping and standing in the
pillory are abolished by act 28th February, 1839, § 5, Stat. 322.
See James v. Commonwealth, 12 S. & R. 220.

## ARTICLE IX.

What of the
reserved
rights?
The enumeration in the Constitution of certain
rights, shall not be construed to deny or disparage
others retained by the people.

What is
enumera-
tion?
71, 138.
**268.** "ENUMERATION."—[Lat. *Enumero.*]—The counting or
telling by numbers. Webster's Dic., ENUMERATION.

"OF CERTAIN RIGHTS."—This has reference to the several
general and special POWERS granted, surrendered, or delegated to
the different departments of the government. It was intended to
For what
was the
amendment
intended?
prevent any perverse or ingenious misapplication of the maxims.
that an affirmation in particular cases implied a negation in all
others; and, *e converso*, that a negation in particular cases implies
an affirmation in all others. (Federalist, Nos. 83, 84; No. 83 is
reprinted in Story's Const. § 1768, 3d ed. pp. 574–582). Story's
Const. § 1905. See also Id. § 448.

Define
"deny"?
"DENY."—[Lat. *denego.*]—To contradict; gainsay; disown; reject. Webster's Dic, DENY.

Define "dis-
parage"?
"DISPARAGE"—[Norman, *desperegar*].—This word is strangely
used here. It literally means to dishonor by an unequal match or
marriage; to match unequally; to dishonor or injure by comparison
with something of less value or excellence; to *undervalue*. Webster's Dic., DISPARAGE.

"RETAINED BY THE PEOPLE."—"PEOPLE" here must be used in
the sense of "WE THE PEOPLE" in the preamble, and in the
tenth amendment. To illustrate the right of appeal "upon the law
and facts," was given to the Supreme Court. It had been objected,
that this denied or disparaged the right of trial by jury, as understood at common law. Hence the sixth amendment. Federalist,
No. 83. And hence the declaration of the same general principle
in this amendment.

*Sidenote: 6, 269, 251, 250. 260–262, 276–277.*

## ARTICLE X.

The powers not delegated to the United States
by the Constitution, nor prohibited by it to the
States, are reserved to the States respectively or to
the people.

*Sidenote: How are the powers not delegated reserved?*

**269.** "THE POWERS" of course mean all those which had been
committed to the different departments of the government.

"DELEGATED."—[Lat. *Delego*].—To intrust; to commit; to deliver
to another's care and exercise. Webster's Dic., DELEGATE.

The secessionists laid great stress upon the word "delegate,"
and attached to it the meaning that the States had, in fact, *surrendered* none of their sovereignty; but only created a common
agency with certain powers, in trust, which each State, for itself,
had the right to resume at pleasure. The "nor prohibited to the
States," could have little force with those holding such doctrines.
It has been so fashionable to interpolate, "expressly," that many
believe the participle "delegated" is so qualified. But such a
qualification was moved in Congress and rejected. 2 Lloyd's Debates, 234, 243, 244; McCulloch v. Maryland, 4 Wheat. 404; Martin v. Hunter, 1 Wheat. 325; Houston v. Moore, 5 Wheat. 49;
Anderson v. Dunn, 6 Wheat. 225, 226; 2 Article of Confederation,
*ante*, p. 9. See Ableman v. Booth, 21 How. 596.

All powers not delegated (not all not *expressly* delegated) and
not prohibited are reserved. (McCulloch v. Maryland, 4 Wheat.
406, 407.) Story's Const. § 1908.

See United States v. Bailey, 1 McLean, 234. The same reservation, in substance, was contained in the second article of the Articles of Confederation, except that the word "expressly" was there
placed before the word "delegated." Metropolitan Bank v. Van
Dyck, 27 N. Y. Rep. 416; McCulloch v. Maryland, 4 Wh. 327.
See *ante*, p. 9. This amendment compared with the 9th section
of the 1st article. They contain no inhibition upon Congress to
legislate upon legal tenders. Metropolitan Bank v. Van Dyck, 27
N. Y. Rep. 418.

*Sidenote: What are the delegated powers? 71–138, 162, and every note. 6.*

*Sidenote: 133, 155.*

## ARTICLE XI.

The judicial power of the United States shall not
be construed to extend to any suit in law or equity
commenced or prosecuted against one of the United

*Sidenote: What is the limitation of judicial power?*

States, by citizens of another State, or by citizens or subjects of any foreign State.

**What caused this amendment?**
195, 199, 200, 205a, 210, 271.

**270.** "THE JUDICIAL POWER," and "ANY SUITS IN LAW OR EQUITY," are to be taken as an amendment of the first section of the third article, so as to take away the jurisdiction of suits against States by individuals. The amendment was caused by the decision in Chisholm v. Georgia, 2 Dallas, 419, 475; S. C. 2 Cond. 635; 1 Kent's Com. Lect. 14, p. 278; Cohens v. Virginia, 6 Wheat. 381, 406.

This decision held that the original Constitution embraced suits *by* as well as *against* States. Story's Const. § 1683. See Federalist, Nos. 80, 81; 2 Elliot's Debates, 300, 301, 401, 405; Curtis' Com. § 61.

**What is now the rule?**

The suits against the States were principally for money sequestrated or confiscated in the hands of the debtors of the British loyalists. The amendment was held to extend to all pending suits, and they were dismissed. Hollingsworth v. Virginia, 3 Dall. 378; Cohens v. Virginia, 6 Wheat. 294; Georgia v. Brailsford, 2 Dall. 402; S. C. 3 Dall. 1.

So that now no suit lies by citizen or alien against a State, in the courts of the United States.

**In what character must the State sue?**
205.

**271.** "AGAINST ONE OF THE UNITED STATES."—Where the State is sued, and made a party on the record in its political capacity, this amendment applies; and the State may be considered as a party on the record when its chief magistrate is sued, not by his name, but by his style of office, and the claim made upon him is entirely in his official character. (The Governor of Georgia v. Madrazo, 1 Pet. 110, 123, 124.) Curtis' Com. § 67–70.

**What suits did the amendment include?**

This amendment was construed to include suits then pending, as well as suits to be commenced thereafter; and accordingly, all the suits then pending were dismissed without any further adjudication. (Hollingsworth v. Virginia, 3 Dall. 378.) Story's Const. § 1683. For a history of the amendment, see Cohens v. Virginia, 6 Wheat. 406.

The amendment only applies to original suits; not to appeals or writs of error for revision. (Cohens v. Virginia, 6 Wheat. 264.) Story's Const. § 1864.

**272.** "BY CITIZENS OR SUBJECTS OF ANY FOREIGN STATE."— The power of these to sue the State was simply taken away by the amendment.

**Does the suit apply to admiralty cases?**

It does not extend to suits of admiralty or maritime jurisdiction. Olmstead's Case, Brightly, 9. See *Ex parte* Madrazo, 1 Pet. 127. If the State be not necessarily a defendant, though its interest may be affected by the decision, the courts of the United States are bound to exercise jurisdiction. Louisville R. R. Co. v. Letson, 2 How. 550; United States v. Peters, 5 Cr. 115. For the history of this amendment, see Chisholm v. Georgia, 2 Dall. 471, 475. A State, by becoming interested with others in a banking or trading corporation, or by owning all the capital stock, does not impart to that corporation any of its privileges or prerogatives; it lays down its sovereignty, so far as respects the transactions of the corpora-

**205a**

tion, and exercises no power or privilege in respect to those transactions not derived from the charter. Bank of the United States v. Planter's Bank of Georgia. 9 Wh. 904 ; Bank of Kentucky v. Wiston, 3 Pet. 431 ; Briscoe v. Bank of Kentucky, 11 Id. 324 ; Louisville R. R. Co. v. Letson, 2 How. 497 ; Darrington v. Bank of Alabama, 13 How. 12 ; Curran v. Arkansas, 15 Id. 309. And see Cohens v. Virginia, 6 Wh. 264. Where a State sues in its own courts, and obtains a judgment against a citizen, the defendant may prosecute a writ of error in the Supreme Court, and test the constitutionality of a State law. Craig v. Missouri, 4 Pet. 410 ; and the Arkansas, Kentucky, and Alabama cases above cited.

The State is not a party unless it appears on the record as such, 205, 271. either as plaintiff or defendant. It is not sufficient that it may have an interest in the cause, or that the parties before the court are sued for acts done as agents of the State. (Fowler v. Lindsay, 3 Dall. 411 ; State of New York v. Connecticut, 3 Dall. 1–6 ; United States v. Peters, 5 Cr. 115–139 ; 1 Kent's Com. Lect. 15, p. 302 ; Osborn v. Bank of United States, 9 Wheat. 846.) Story's Const. § 1865, notes 1, 2.

## ARTICLE XII.

**273.** See Art. II., Sec. 3, pp. 164–166, notes 168, 168a, 168b, for this amendment. It was considered proper by the editor to transfer it to its appropriate place. It does not disturb the arrangement in the original Constitution, nor in the analysis and index. See *ante*, p. 46.

## ARTICLE XIII.

1. Neither slavery nor involuntary servitude, except How was slavery as a punishment for crime, whereof the party shall abolished? have been duly convicted, shall exist within the United States, or any place subject to their jurisdiction.

2. Congress shall have power to enforce this article The power? by appropriate legislation.

**274.** The following is the proclamation which declared the 13th When did amendment in force :— this article take effect?
WILLIAM H. SEWARD, Secretary of State of the United States, to all to whom these presents may come, greeting :

Know ye, that whereas the Congress of the United States, on the 1st of February last, passed a resolution which is in the words following, namely :—

" *A Resolution submitting to the Legislatures of the several States a proposition to amend the Constitution of the United States.*

" *Resolved by the Senate and House of Representatives of the United States of America in Congress assembled (two-thirds of both houses concurring*), That the following article be proposed to the legislatures of the several States as an amendment to the Constitution of the United States, which, when ratified by three-fourths of said legislatures, shall be valid, to all intents and purposes, as a part of the said Constitution, namely:"—[Here follows the amendment.]

And whereas it appears from official documents on file in this department that the amendment to the Constitution of the United States proposed, as aforesaid, has been ratified by the legislatures of the States of Illinois, Rhode Island, Michigan, Maryland, New York, West Virginia, Maine, Kansas, Massachusetts, Pennsylvania, Virginia, Ohio, Missouri, Nevada, Indiana, Louisiana, Minnesota, Wisconsin, Vermont, Tennessee, Arkansas, Connecticut, New Hampshire, South Carolina, Alabama, North Carolina, and Georgia; in all twenty-seven States:

And whereas the whole number of States in the United States is thirty-six; and whereas the before specially-named States, whose legislatures have ratified the said proposed amendment, constitute three-fourths of the whole number of States in the United States:

Now, therefore, be it known that I, WILLIAM H. SEWARD, Secretary of State of the United States, by virtue and in pursuance of the second section of the act of Congress, approved the twentieth of April, eighteen hundred and eighteen, entitled "An act to provide for the publication of the laws of the United States and for other purposes," do hereby certify that the amendment aforesaid has become valid, to all intents and purposes, as a part of the Constitution of the United States.

In testimony whereof, I have hereunto set my hand, and caused the seal of the Department of State to be affixed.

Done at the city of Washington, this eighteenth day of December, in the year of our Lord one thousand eight hundred and sixty-five, and of the independence of the United States of America, the ninetieth.

    [L. S.]               WILLIAM H. SEWARD,
                                  *Secretary of State.*

**17, 275.**      This proclamation is given to show the views of the executive, that the seceded States had a right to vote upon the amendment, and did in fact, make up the number necessary to put it into operation. The President had previously given notice, that no State would be regarded as restored until it adopted this amendment. Seward's dispatch to the governor of Florida.

List of States which have ratified the amendment to the Constitution prohibiting slavery, &c., and given official notice thereof, with the respective dates of ratification :—

In 1865.—Illinois, Feb. 1; Rhode Island, Feb. 2; Michigan, Feb. 2; Maryland, Feb. 1, 3,; New York, Feb. 2, 3,; West Virginia, Feb. 3; Maine, Feb. 7; Kansas, Feb. 7; Massachusetts, Feb. 8, Pennsylvania, Feb. 8; Virginia, Feb. 9; Ohio, Feb. 10; Missouri, Feb. 10; Nevada, Feb. 16; Indiana, Feb. 16; Louisiana, Feb. 17; Minnesota, Feb. 8, 23; Wisconsin, March 1; Vermont, March 9; Tennessee, April 5,7; Arkansas, April 20; Connecticut, May 5;

New Hampshire, July 1, South Carolina, Nov. 13; Alabama, Dec. 2; North Carolina, Dec. 4; Georgia, Dec. 9; Oregon, Dec. 11; California, Dec 20; Florida, Dec. 28  In 1866.—New Jersey, Jan. 23; Iowa, Jan. 24.

It will thus be seen that the States which have not ratified the amendment are Delaware, Kentucky, Mississippi, and Texas. Delaware alone, of these, gave notice through the governor, of the rejection. Governor Parker of New Jersey, gave notice of rejection on the first of December, 1865; but the same State afterward ratified it.

Because of this amendment Congress had the right to pass the Civil Rights Bill to secure the citizenship of the negro.    Smith v. Moody, 26 Ind. 307.

In the matter of Elizabeth Turner, on *Habeas Corpus*, by Chief-Justice Chase (Maryland, 1867).    And because of the Civil Rights Bill, the United States Circuit Court had jurisdiction of a *Habeas* 6, 18, 220. *Corpus* case, to relieve a child of color from an apprenticeship, under the laws of Maryland, which were in conflict with that law.    Id.

The apprenticeship, among other things, allowed the assignment of the apprentice's services by the master, with the sanction of the orphan's court.    The Chief-Justice said: "The following propositions seem to me to be sound law, and they decide the case: First. The first clause of the thirteenth amendment to the Constitution of the United States interdicts slavery and involuntary servitude, except as a punishment for crime, and establishes freedom as the constitutional right of all persons in the United States.    Second. The alleged apprenticeship in the present case is involuntary servitude within the meaning of these words in the amendment."    Id.

This amendment is the last one made.    It treuches directly upon the power of the States and of the people of the States.    It is the first and only instance of a change of this character in the organic law.    United States v. Rhodes (by Justice Swayne, Kentucky, Oct. T. 1867).

The act of Congress (the Civil Rights Bill) confers citizenship. Who are The Constitution uses the words "citizen" and "natural born citizens of citizen;" but neither that instrument nor any act of Congress of the has attempted to define their meaning.    In Johnson's Dictionary, States? "citizen" is thus defined:    "(1) A freeman of a city; not a 18, 19, 35, 46, foreigner; not a slave; (2) a townsman, a man of trade; not a 93, 169, 205a, gentleman; (3) an inhabitant; a dweller in any place."    In 206, 220–222 Jacob's Law Dictionary (edition of 1783) the only definition given is as follows:    "Citizens (*cives*) of London are either freemen or such as reside and keep a family in the city, &c.; and some are citizens and freemen, and some are not, who have not so great privileges as others.    The citizens of London may prescribe against a statute because their liberties are re-enforced by statute.    (1 Roll. 105.)"    Id.

"The word *civis*, taken in the strictest sense, extends only to him that is entitled to the privileges of a city of which he is a member, and in that sense there is a distinction between a citizen and an inhabitant within the same city, for every inhabitant there is not a citizen."    (Scott *qui tam* v. Swartz, Com. Rep. 68.)    Id.

"A citizen is a freeman who has kept a family in a city."    (Roy v. Hanger, 1 Roll. Rep. 138, 149.)    Id.

12*

"The term citizen, as understood in our law, is precisely analogous to the term subject in the common law; and the change of phrase has entirely resulted from the change of government. The sovereignty has been changed from one man to the collective body of the people, and he who before was *a subject of the king is now a citizen of the State.*" (The State v. Manuel, 4 Dev. & Batt. 26.) Id.

**What was the effect of the American Revolution upon citizenship? 220.** "During the war each party claimed the allegiance of the natives of the colonies as due exclusively to itself. The Americans insisted upon the allegiance of all born within the States, respectively; and Great Britain asserted an equally exclusive claim. The treaty of 1783 acted upon the state of things as it existed at that period. It took the actual state of things as its basis. All those, whether natives or otherwise, who then adhered to the American States, were virtually absolved from their allegiance to the British crown, and those who then adhered to the British crown were deemed and held subjects of that crown. The treaty of peace was a treaty operating between the States on each side, and the inhabitants thereof: in the language of the seventh article, it was a 'firm and perpetual peace between his British majesty and the said States, *and between the subjects of the one and the citizens of the other.*' Who then were *subjects* or *citizens* was to be decided by the state of facts. If they were originally subjects of Great Britain and then adhered to her, and were claimed by her as subjects, the treaty deemed them such; if they were originally British subjects, but then adhering to the states, the treaty deemed them citizens." (Shanks v. Dupont, 3 Pet. 247.) United States v. Rhodes (Justice Swayne).

All persons born in the allegiance of the king are natural born subjects, and all persons born in the allegiance of the United States are natural born citizens. Birth and allegiance go together. Such is the rule of the common law, and it is the common law of this country as well as of England. There are two exceptions, and only two, to the universality of its application. The children of ambassadors are, in theory, born in the allegiance of the powers the ambassadors represent, and slaves, in legal contemplation, are property, and not persons. (2 Kent's Com. 3d ed. 1; Calvin's Case, 7 Coke, 1; 1 Black. Com. 366; Lynch v. Clark, 1 Sandf. Ch. Rep. 139.)

The common law has made no distinction on account of race or color. None is now made in England nor in any other Christian country of Europe. The fourth of the articles of confederation, (*ante,* p. 10) quoted; also Scott v. Sandford, 19 How. 575. Id. When the Constitution was adopted, free men of color were clothed with the franchise of voting in at least five States, and were a part of the people whose sanction breathed into it the breath of life. (Scott v. Sandford, 19 How. 573: The State v. Manuel, 2 Dev. & Batt. 24, 25.) United States v. Rhodes.

"Citizens under our Constitution and laws mean free inhabitants born within the United States or naturalized under the laws of Congress." (1 Kent's Com. 292, note.) It is further said in the note in 1st Kent's Commentaries, before referred to: "If a slave born in the United States be manumitted or otherwise lawfully discharged from bondage, or if a black man born in the United States become free, he becomes thenceforward a citizen, but under such disabilities as the laws of the several States may deem it expedient to prescribe to persons of color." Id

In the case of the State v. Manuel it was remarked: "It has been 18, 220. said that, by the Constitution of the United States, the power of naturalization has been conferred exclusively upon Congress, and therefore it cannot be competent for any State by its municipal regulations to make a citizen. But what is *naturalization?* It is the removal of the *disabilities* of *alienage.* Emancipation is the removal of the *incapacity* of slavery. The latter depends wholly upon the internal regulations of the State. The former belongs to the government of the United States. It would be dangerous to confound them." (The State v. Manuel, 2 Dev. & Batt. 25; The State v. Newcomb, 5 Iredell, 253.) Id.

We cannot deny the assent of our judgment to the soundness of the proposition. that the emancipation of a native-born slave by removing the disability of slavery made him a citizen. If these views be correct, the provision in the act of Congress conferring citizenship was unnecessary and is inoperative. Granting this to be so, it was well, if Congress had the power, to insert it. in order to prevent doubts and differences of opinion which might otherwise have existed upon the subject. We are aware that a majority of the court in the case of Scott v. Sandford, arrived at conclusions different from those we have expressed. But in our judgment these points were not before them. They decided that the whole case, including the agreed facts, was open to their examination, and that Scott was a slave. This central and controlling fact excluded all other questions, and what was said upon them by those of the majority, with whatever learning and ability the argument was conducted, is no more binding upon this court as authority than the views of the minority upon the same subjects. (Carroll v. Carroll, 16 How. 287.) Id.

Citizenship has no necessary connection with the franchise of voting, eligibility to office, or indeed with any other rights,civil or political. Women, minors, and persons *non compos* are citizens. and not the less so on account of their disabilities. In England, not to advert to the various local regulations, the new reform bill gives the right to the various local regulations, the new reform bill gives the right of voting for members of Parliament to about eight hundred thousand persons from whom it was before withheld. There, the subject is wholly within the control of Parliament. Here, until the 13th amendment was adopted, the power belonged entirely to the States, and they exercised it without question from any quarter, as absolutely as if they were not members of the Union. Id. *[margin: What is the effect of citizenship upon suffrage? 18, 220.]*

Our attention has been called to several treaties by which Indians were made citizens; to those by which Louisiana, Florida, and California were acquired, and to the act passed in relation to Texas. 220, 230, 117. All this was done under the war and treaty-making powers of the Constitution, and those which authorize the national government to regulate the territory and other property of the United States, and to admit new States into the Union. (American Ins. Co. v. Canter, 1 Pet. 511; Cross v. Harrison, 16 How. 164; 2 Story's Const 158.) Id.

Congress has power "to establish an uniform rule of naturalization." Art. 1, Sec. 8. After considerable fluctuation of judicial opinion it was finally settled, by the Supreme Court, that this power is vested exclusively in Congress. (Collet v. Collet, 2 Dall. 294; United States v. Velati, 2 Dall. 370; Golden v. Prince, 3 Wash. C. C. 313; Chirac v. Chirac, 2 Wheat. 259; Houston v. Moore, 2 Wheat. 49; Federalist, No. 32.) United States v. Rhodes. Id. An alien naturalized is "to all intents and purposes a natural born subject." (Co. Litt. 129.) Id. "Naturalization takes effect from birth; denization from the date of the patent." (Vin. Ab. Tit. Alien, D.) Id.

The form under the English act of Parliament appears in Godfrey v. Dickson, Cro. Jac. 539, c. 7. Under the late act, a resident alien may accomplish the object by a petition to the Secretary of State for the Home Department Id.

**93.**　　The power is applicable only to those of foreign birth. Alienage is an indispensable element in the process. To make one of domestic birth a citizen, is not naturalization, and cannot be brought within the exercise of that power. There is an universal agreement of opinion upon this subject. (Scott v. Sandford, 19 How. p. 578; 2 Story's Const. 44.) Id. It was well remarked by one of the dissenting judges, in Scott v. Sandford, 19 Howard, 586, in regard to the African race: "The Constitution has not excluded them, and since that has conferred on Congress the power to naturalize colored aliens, it certainly shows that color is not a necessary

**267.**　　qualification for citizenship under the Constitution of the United States." Id. The Constitution, 10th amendment, and clause 2 of Sec. 2, Art. IV., and generally the notes thereon (*ante*, notes 220, 221), quoted. Id.

**220-223.**　　What the several States under the original Constitution only could have done, the nation has done by the thirteenth amendment. An occasion for the exercise of this power by the States may not, perhaps cannot, hereafter arise. United States v. Rhodes.

The thirteenth amendment quoted, and the same rules of interpretation applied to "APPROPRIATE LEGISLATION." That is, "*appropriate*" is equivalent to "necessary and proper." (McCulloch v. Maryland, 4 Wheat. 421–423.) Id. The rule in the United

**188.**　　States v. Coombs, 12 Pet. 72; United States v. Holliday, 3 Wall. 407; United States v. Beavan, 3 Wheat. 390; Prigg v. Pennsylvania, 16 Pet. 60; quoted and applied as to the general power. Id. [Out of its place it may be noted, that under the power to

**85.**　　regulate commerce, it has recently been ruled, that the power extends to commerce on land, carried on by railroads which are parts of lines of inter-State communication, as well as to commerce carried on by vessels, and such railroads may be regulated by Congress as well as steamboats. By Associate Justice Miller, in Gray v. Clinton Bridge, American Law Register (January, 1868), pp. 149–

**69.**　　154. The power to regulate commerce is the power to regulate the instruments of commerce. (Cooley v. The Board of Wardens, 12 How. 316.) Id. And it extends to railroads as well as steamboats. Id.]

**195.**　　Since the organization of the Supreme Court, but three acts of Congress have been pronounced by that body void for unconstitutionality. (Marbury v. Madison, 1 Cr. 137; Scott v. Sandford, 19 How. 393; Ex parte Garland, 4 Wall. 334.) United States v. Rhodes.

The present effect of the amendment was to abolish slavery

wherever it existed within the jurisdiction of the United States. In the future it throws its protection over every one, of every race, color, and condition, within that jurisdiction, and guards them against the recurrence of the evil.  Id.

The history of slavery, and the State legislation which followed its destruction given.  The Civil Rights law is an "appropriate" means of carrying out the object of the first section of the amendment.  Id.

It would be a remarkable anomaly if the national government, without this amendment, could confer citizenship on aliens of every race or color, and citizenship, with civil and political rights, on the 13, 220. "inhabitants" of Louisiana and Florida, without reference to race or color, and cannot, with the help of the amendment, confer on those of the African race, who have been born and always lived within the United States, all that this law seeks to give them.

It was passed by the Congress succeeding the one which proposed the amendment.  Many of the members of both Houses were the same.  This fact is not without weight and significance. (McCulloch v. Maryland, 4 Wheat. 401.)  Id.

The amendment reversed and annulled the original policy of the Constitution, which left it to each State to decide exclusively for itself whether slavery should or should not exist as a local institution, and what disabilities should attach to those of the servile race within its limits.  The whites needed no relief nor protection, and they are practically unaffected by the amendment.  The emancipation which it wrought was an act of great national grace, and was doubtless intended to reach further in its effects, as to every one within its scope, than the consequences of manumission by a private individual.  We entertain no doubt of the constitutionality of the act in all its provisions.  It gives only certain civil rights. We are not unmindful of the opinion of the Court of Appeals of Kentucky, in the case of Brown v. The Commonwealth.  With all our respect for the eminent tribunal from which it proceeded, we have found ourselves unable to concur in its conclusions.  The constitutionality of the act is sustained by the Supreme Court of Indiana and the Chief-Justice of the Court of Appeals of Maryland, in able and well-considered opinions. (Smith v. Moody, 26 Ind. 307; In re A. II. Somers.)  United States v. Rhodes.  Id.

The nisi prius courts of several of the Southern States have decided against the constitutionality of the Civil Rights law on various grounds; but the editor regrets that he has not preserved the newspaper reports of their decisions.

Where an obligation was given to pay £7,800 sterling for a transfer of the vendor's claim to the services of 153 apprentices (who had been slaves), but before the installments fell due, the slaves were declared free and obtained their freedom, under an ordinance of Berbice, in British Guiana, in pursuance of the act of 3 and 4 W. IV., c. 73, S. 10, whereby the defendant lost the services, so that the covenant of warranty of title failed; held, that the plaintiff was entitled to the last two installments, though the legislature had determined the apprenticeship before they became due.  Mittelhozezer v. Fullarton, 6 Adolph. & Ellis, 989, 990.

*What effect had such a law upon contracts?*

Lord Denman : "My brother Wightman asked what would have been the result if, at the end of the year, the services had been determined by the act of God. And to this no sufficient answer was given." Id. 1018. The plaintiff's right vested when the bargain was made; the subsequent interference of the colonial legislature does not prevent his recovering what was then stipulated. Id. The whole question is, who shall bear the losses occasioned by a *vis major*. And that depends upon the question, who was the proprietor when that loss was occasioned. Id.

The question was whether the defendants were liable for the value of slaves purchased in Texas in September, 1863. "I have always regarded the proclamation of the President, issued on the 1st January, 1863, declaring the negroes free, as a war measure. The President did not base his right to issue that proclamation upon any clause of the Constitution, or even any act of Congress. It was justified by the necessities of the war, and, as commander-in-chief of the army and navy of the United States, he resorted to it, as he himself declared, as a *war measure*. Its operation and effect depended wholly upon the success of the national arms. The negroes were set free, not by the mere declaration of the President that they were so, but by force of arms. Hence, I have always supposed that slaves who occupied certain sections of the country, say in Virginia and Tennessee, and who first fell under the armed control of the Union, were free sooner than those in Texas or the extreme South. If the proclamation of the President, of itself, made slaves free persons, then every negro held in bondage after the 1st January, 1863, is now entitled to sue not only for the value of his services subsequent to that time, and for damages on account of being unlawfully deprived of his liberty, but could also subject their former owners to criminal prosecutions for false imprisonment. Not believing that such an effect should be, or was intended to be given to the Proclamation, I must sustain the demurrer of the plaintiff." Connett v. Williams, United States Circuit Court (Texas), Jan. T., 1866, by Judge Thomas H. Duval. There have been State decisions to the effect that contracts made for the purchase of negroes, even before the war, but which matured after their emancipation, cannot be enforced; but the editor has not preserved the newspaper reports of them. He supposes the correct principle to be, as stated by the English bench, " Who owned the negroes when they obtained their freedom?" If they were property when sold, the purchaser must sustain the loss.

[CONCURRENT RESOLUTION, RECEIVED AT DEPARTMENT OF STATE JUNE 16, 1866.]

## JOINT RESOLUTION PROPOSING AN AMENDMENT TO THE CONSTITUTION OF THE UNITED STATES.

Who are citizens of the United States ?

*Be it resolved by the Senate and House of Representatives of the United States of America in Congress assembled (two-thirds of both Houses concurring)*

That the following article be proposed to the legis- 6, 18, 220. latures of the several States as an amendment to the Constitution of the United States, which, when ratified by three-fourths of said legislatures, shall be valid as part of the Constitution, namely:

## ARTICLE XIV.

SEC. 1. All persons born or naturalized in the United States, and subject to the jurisdiction thereof, are citizens of the United States and of the State wherein they reside. No State shall make or enforce any law which shall abridge the privileges or immunities of citizens of the United States; nor shall any State deprive any person of life, liberty, or property, without due process of law, nor deny to any person within its jurisdiction the equal protection of the laws.

SEC. 2. Representatives shall be apportioned among How are representa-the several States according to their respective tives appor-numbers, counting the whole number of persons in each tioned? State, excluding Indians not taxed. But when the right to vote at any election for the choice of electors for President and Vice-President of the United States, representatives in Congress, the executive and judicial officers of a State, or the members of the legislature thereof, is denied to any of the male inhabitants of such State, being twenty-one years of age, and citizens of the United States, or in any way abridged, except for participation in rebellion or other crime, the basis How is the of representation therein shall be reduced in the pro- reduced? portion which the number of such male citizens shall bear to the whole number of male citizens twenty-one years of age in such State.

SEC. 3. No person shall be a senator or repre- Who are dis-sentative in Congress, or elector of President and Vice- from hold-President, or hold any office, civil or military, under ing office? the United States, or under any State, who, having previously taken an oath, as a member of Congress, or as any officer of the United States, or as a member of any State legislature, or as an executive or judicial officer of any State, to support the Constitution of the United States, shall have engaged in insurrection or rebellion against the same, or given aid or comfort to the enemies thereof. But Congress may, by a vote of two-thirds of each House, remove such disability.

How restored?

SEC. 4. The validity of the public debt of the United States, authorized by law, including debts incurred for payment of pensions and bounties for services in suppressing insurrection or rebellion, shall not be questioned. But neither the United States nor any State shall assume or pay any debt or obligation incurred in aid of insurrection or rebellion against the United States, or any claim for the loss or emancipation of any slave; but all such debts, obligations, and claims shall be held illegal and void.

How is the public debt guaranteed?

The rebel debt, how repudiated?

SEC. 5. The Congress shall have power to enforce, by appropriate legislation, the provisions of this article.

236.

**275.** This amendment was never submitted to the President for his approval or veto. In a message to Congress, he said, that the sending it to the States was not to be construed into an approval of its provisions. Nevertheless, it was sent by the Secretary of State to all the States.

In a letter of transmission to the editor, on the 29th October, 1867, the Secretary of State remarks: "I also send an accurate copy (of the fourteenth amendment) as proposed by Congress, but as this amendment has not yet been ratified by a sufficient number of the States, through their legislatures, agreeably to the requirements of the Constitution, it is not deemed expedient in this case to promulgate any official data in relation thereto."

Application was then made to the clerk of the House of Representatives who politely furnished the following:—

Dates of the ratification of the XIVth constitutional amendment. 1866: Connecticut, June 30; New Hampshire, July 7; Tennessee, July 19; New Jersey, September 11; Oregon, September 19; Vermont, November 7  1867 New York, January 10; Ohio, January 11 (withdrawn Jan. 1868); Nevada, January 11 and 22; Illinois, January 15; West Virginia, January 16; Kansas, January 18; Missouri, January 26; Indiana, January 29; Minnesota, February 1; Rhode Island, February 7; Pennsylvania, February 13;

Wisconsin, February 13; Michigan, February 15, Massachusetts, March 15 and 20; Nebraska, June 15. Rejected by Delaware, Maryland, Kentucky, Virginia, North Carolina, South Carolina, Georgia, Florida, Alabama, Louisiana, Mississippi, Arkansas, Texas. Not acted: California, Iowa.

Ratified by 22 States; rejected by 13; not acted on by 2. When submitted there were 36 States; Nebraska added, makes 37. Three-fourths of all were 27, now 28. If we deduct the ten rebel States, 19 would be sufficient.

In the case of Mississippi v. Johnson, 4 Wall. 475, it was sought to enjoin the operation of these laws upon the ground of their unconstitutionality. The arguments are fully reported; but the court limited the inquiry to the single point, Can the President be restrained by injunction from carrying into effect an act of Congress alleged to be unconstitutional? After reviewing Marbury v. Madison, 1 Cr. 137, and Kendall v. Stockton & Stokes, 12 Pet. 527, it was said: "The Congress is the legislative depart- 14, 165. ment of the government; the President is the executive depart- 195. ment. Neither can be restrained in its action by the judicial department; though the acts of both, when performed, are, in proper cases, subject to its cognizance." Mississippi v. Johnson, 4 Wall. 500. The rule was denied. Id. 501.

There are many persons whose opinions are entitled to respect, 236. who maintain that the ratification is complete without the concurrence of the non-reconstructed States. (See Farrar's Const. § 448, note 1.) If this view be correct, then the ratification is already accomplished, and the fourteenth amendment stands as a part of the Constitution. But if it be not correct, the editor doubts not but the amendment will be adopted within the present year, by enough of those ten States (*unless prevented by civil war*), to insure its ratification, after the same manner that the thirteenth amend- 274. ment was ratified. It has therefore been printed, to prevent future confusion, in the index, and stereotyped pages. Should it never go into practical operation, the constitutional student will reject the propositions which it embraces. It has been seen that the Secretary of State discards the notion that the amendment is yet complete. It is also painfully true, that in a message to the Senate, and in other public declarations, the President questioned the ex- 236. pediency, if he did not deny the power of Congress to submit this amendment, while a portion of the States were not represented and allowed to vote upon such submission. But this argument 274. would also go to the thirteenth amendment, unless, indeed, there 117, 118. be a distinction between the rights of States of the Union, when engaged in actual war against the United States, and after that 46. resistance has been conquered and such rebellious peoples have sent back their representatives to Congress.

**276.** It has been seen that the President imposed upon these same States the condition of adopting the thirteenth amendment, and thus forever destroyed slavery within the jurisdiction of the 274. United States. This was claimed in virtue of the war power, and for the general welfare of the whole Union. The thing has been 11, 79, 80. done, and the complete change of organic law has gone into history.

**236.** The country accepted the act, and there were those who thought this enough But Congress, adopting the view that further amendments were necessary; and, either holding that the ratification of three-fourths of all the States was required; or else wishing to test the fact, that these States so lately in rebellion, had given evidence of loyalty and submission, and claiming for Congress the power to impose further conditions than the President had demanded, with a view to secure liberty and equal political rights to all, and to compel those States to ratify the amendment, enacted the following series of laws:—

*Act of March 2, 1867.*

*Preamble?*

" *An Act to provide for the more efficient Government of the Rebel States.*

" WHEREAS no legal State governments or adequate protection for life or property now exists in the rebel States of Virginia, North Carolina, South Carolina, Georgia, Mississippi, Alabama, Louisiana, Florida, Texas, and Arkansas; and whereas it is necessary that peace and good order should be enforced in said States, until loyal and republican State governments can be legally established; therefore,

*How are certain rebel States to be divided, and subjected to military authority?*

" *Be it enacted, &c.*, That said rebel States shall be divided into military districts, and made subject to the military authority of the United States as hereinafter pre cribed, and for that purpose Virginia shall constitute the first district; North Carolina and South Carolina, the second district; Georgia, Alabama, and Florida, the third district; Mississippi and Arkansas, the fourth district; and Louisiana and Texas, the fifth district.

*Is the President to assign an army officer to command each district?*

*Military force to be detailed?*

" 2. It shall be the duty of the President to assign to the command of each of said districts, an officer of the army, not below the rank of brigadier-general, and to detail a sufficient military force to enable such officer to perform his duties, and enforce his authority within the district to which he is assigned.

*What are the duties of commanders of districts? Local civil tribunals? State interference declared null?*

" 3. It shall be the duty of each officer assigned as aforesaid, to protect all persons in their rights of person and property, to suppress insurrection, disorder, and violence, and to punish, or cause to be punished, all disturbers of the public peace and criminals; and to this end he may allow local civil tribunals to take jurisdiction of and to try offenders, or, when in his judgment it may be necessary for the trial of offenders, he shall have power to organize military commissions or tribunals for that purpose, and all interference under color of State authority with the exercise of military authority under this act, shall be null and void.

*Persons under military arrest to be speedily tried?*

*What rule of punishment?*

*How are sentences of military tribunals to be executed?*

" 4. All persons put under military arrest by virtue of this act shall be tried without unnecessary delay, and no cruel or unusual punishment shall be inflicted, and no sentence of any military commission or tribunal hereby authorized, affecting the life or liberty of any person, shall be executed until it is approved by the officer in command of the district, and the laws and regulations for the government of the army shall not be affected by this act, except in so far as they conflict with its provisions: *Provided*, That no sentence of death under the provisions of this act shall be carried into effect without the approval of the President.

"5. When the people of any one of said rebel States shall have formed a constitution of government in conformity with the Constitution of the United States in all respects, framed by a convention of delegates elected by the male citizens of said State, twenty-one years old and upward, of whatever race, color, or previous condition, who have been resident in said State for one year previous to the day of such election, except such as may be disfranchised for participation in the rebellion, or for felony at common law, and when such Constitution shall provide that the elective franchise shall be enjoyed by all such persons as have the qualifications herein stated for electors of delegates, and when such Constitution shall be ratified by a majority of the persons voting on the question of ratification who are qualified as electors for delegates, and when such Constitution shall have been submitted to Congress for examination and approval, and Congress shall have approved the same, and when said State, by a vote of its legislature elected under said Constitution, shall have adopted the amendment to the Constitution of the United States, proposed by the Thirty-ninth Congress, and known as article fourteen, and when said article shall have become a part of the Constitution of the United States, said State shall be declared entitled to representation in Congress, and senators and representatives shall be admitted therefrom on their taking the oath prescribed by law, and then and thereafter the preceding sections of this act shall be inoperative in said State : *Provided*, That no person excluded from the privilege of holding office by said proposed amendment to the Constitution of the United States, shall be eligible to election as a member of the convention to frame a Constitution for any of said rebel States, nor shall any such person vote for members of such convention.

*Upon what conditions are States entitled to representation in Congress? Delegates to conventions, by whom elected? What is the elective franchise? The State to adopt the amendment to the Constitution? What qualifications of senators and representatives?*

"6. Until the people of said rebel States shall be by law admitted to representation in the Congress of the United States, any civil governments which may exist therein shall be deemed provisional only, and in all respects subject to the paramount authority of the United States at any time to abolish, modify, control, or supersede the same ; and in all elections to any office under such provisional governments all persons shall be entitled to vote, and none others, who are entitled to vote, under the provisions of the fifth section of this act ; and no person shall be eligible to any office under any such provisional governments who would be disqualified from holding office under the provisions of the third article of said constitutional amendment."

*What are the civil governments of such States? Who may vote in elections?*

This act was passed over the President's veto, March 2, 1867.

" AN ACT supplementary to an act entitled 'An act to provide for the more efficient government of the rebel States,' passed March second, eighteen hundred and sixty-seven, and to facilitate restoration.

*Act of March 23, 1867.*

" *Be it enacted, &c.*, That before the first day of September, eighteen hundred and sixty-seven, the commanding general in each district defined by an act entitled 'An act to provide for the more efficient government of the rebel States,' passed March second, eighteen hundred and sixty-seven, shall cause a registration to be made of

*Who are entitled to be registered as voters?*

the male citizens of the United States, twenty-one years of age and upwards, resident in each county or parish in the State or States included in his district, which registration shall include only those persons who are qualified to vote for delegates by the act aforesaid, and who shall have taken and subscribed the following oath or affirmation: 'I, ——, do solemnly swear (or affirm), in the presence of Almighty God, that I am a citizen of the State of ——; that I have resided in said State for —— months next preceding this day, and now reside in the county of ——, or the parish of ——, in said State (as the case may be); that I am twenty-one years old; that I have not been disfranchised for participation in any rebellion or civil war against the United States, nor for felony committed against the laws of any State or of the United States; that I have never been a member of any State legislature, nor held any executive or judicial office in any State and afterward engaged in insurrection or rebellion against the United States, or given aid or comfort to the enemies thereof; that I have never taken an oath as a member of Congress of the United States, or as an officer of the United States, or as a member of any State legislature, or as an executive or judicial officer of any State, to support the Constitution of the United States, and afterward engaged in insurrection or rebellion against the United States, or given aid or comfort to the enemies thereof; that I will faithfully support the Constitution and obey the laws of the United States, and will, to the best of my ability, encourage others so to do, so help me God;' which oath or affirmation may be administered by any registering officer.

"2. After the completion of the registration hereby provided for in any State, at such time and places therein as the commanding general shall appoint and direct, of which at least thirty days' public notice shall be given, an election shall be held of [for] delegates to a convention for the purpose of establishing a Constitution and civil government for such State loyal to the Union, said convention in each State, except Virginia, to consist of the same number of members as the most numerous branch of the State legislature of such State in the year eighteen hundred and sixty, to be apportioned among the several districts, counties, or parishes of such State by the commanding general, giving to each representation in the ratio of voters registered as aforesaid as nearly as may be. The convention in Virginia shall consist of the same number of members as represented the territory now constituting Virginia in the most numerous branch of the legislature of said State in the year eighteen hundred and sixty, to be apportioned as aforesaid.

"3. At said election the registered voters of each State shall vote for or against a convention to form a Constitution therefor under this act. Those voting in favor of such a convention shall have written or printed on the ballots by which they vote for delegates, as aforesaid, the words 'For a convention;' and those voting against such a convention shall have written or printed on such ballots the words 'Against a convention.' The persons appointed to superintend said election, and to make return of the votes given thereat, as herein provided, shall count and make return of the votes given for and against a convention; and the commanding general to whom the same shall have been returned shall ascertain and declare the

---

*Side notes:*

What oath of the voters?

282.

242.

When and by whose order is the election to be held?

How to vote for or against a convention?

total vote in each State for and against a convention. If a majority of the votes given on that question shall be for a convention, then such convention shall be held as hereinafter provided; but if a majority of said votes shall be against a convention, then no such convention shall be held under this act: *Provided*, That such convention shall not be held unless a majority of all such registered voters shall have voted on the question of holding such convention.

"4. The commanding general of each district shall appoint as many boards of registration as may be necessary, consisting of three loyal officers or persons, to make and complete the registration, superintend the election, and make return to him of the votes, list of voters, and of the persons elected as delegates by a plurality of the votes cast at said election; and upon receiving said returns he shall open the same, ascertain the persons elected as delegates, according to the returns of the officers who conducted said election, and make proclamation thereof; and if a majority of the votes given on that question shall be for a convention, the commanding general, within sixty days from the date of election, shall notify the delegates to assemble in convention, at a time and place to be mentioned in the notification, and said convention, when organized, shall proceed to frame a Constitution and civil government according to the provisions of this act, and the act to which it is supplementary; and when the same shall have been so framed, said Constitution shall be submitted by the convention for ratification to the persons registered under the provisions of this act at an election to be conducted by the officers or persons appointed, or to be appointed, by the commanding general, as hereinbefore provided, and to be held after the expiration of thirty days from the date of notice thereof, to be given by said convention; and the returns thereof shall be made to the commanding general of the district. *How are boards of registration to be appointed?*

"5. If, according to said returns, the Constitution shall be ratified by a majority of the votes of the registered electors qualified as herein specified, cast at said election, at least one-half of all the registered voters voting upon the question of such ratification, the president of the convention shall transmit a copy of the same, duly certified, to the President of the United States, who shall forthwith transmit the same to Congress, if then in session, and if not in session, then immediately upon its next assembling; and if it shall moreover appear to Congress that the election was one at which all the registered and qualified electors in the State had an opportunity to vote freely and without restraint, fear, or the influence of fraud, and if the Congress shall be satisfied that such Constitution meets the approval of a majority of all the qualified electors in the State, and if the said Constitution shall be declared by Congress to be in conformity with the provisions of the act to which this is supplementary, and the other provisions of said act shall have been complied with, and the said Constitution shall be approved by Congress, the State shall be declared entitled to representation, and senators and representatives shall be admitted therefrom as therein provided. *What to be done with the Constitution?*

"6. All elections in the States mentioned in the said 'Act to provide for the more efficient government of the rebel States.' shall, *How are the votes to be cast?*

during the operation of said act, be by ballot; and all officers making the said registration of voters and conducting said elections shall, before entering upon the discharge of their duties, take and subscribe the oath prescribed by the act approved July second, eighteen hundred and sixty-two, entitled 'An act to prescribe an oath of office:' *Provided.* That if any person shall knowingly and falsely take and subscribe any oath in this act prescribed, such person so offending, and being thereof duly convicted, shall be subject to the pains, penalties, and disabilities which by law are provided for the punishment of the crime of willful and corrupt perjury.

**What is the penalty of false swearing?**

"7. All expenses incurred by the several commanding generals, or by virtue of any orders issued, or appointments made, by them, under or by virtue of this act, shall be paid out of any moneys in the treasury not otherwise appropriated.

**How are the expenses to be paid?**

"8. The convention for each State shall prescribe the fees, salary, and compensation to be paid to all delegates and other officers and agents herein authorized or necessary to carry into effect the purposes of this act not herein otherwise provided for and shall provide for the levy and collection of such taxes on the property in such State as may be necessary to pay the same.

**How are the salaries &c., to be paid?**

"9. The word 'article,' in the sixth section of the act to which this is supplementary, shall be construed to mean 'section.'"

Passed over the President's veto, March 23, 1867.

**Act of July 19, 1867.**

"AN ACT supplementary to an act entitled 'An act to provide for the more efficient government of the rebel States,' passed on the second day of March, eighteen hundred and sixty-seven, and the act supplementary thereto, passed on the twenty-third day of March, eighteen hundred and sixty-seven.

**What are the governments of the States declared to be?**

"*Be it enacted, &c.,* That it is hereby declared to have been the true intent and meaning of the act of the second day of March, one thousand eight hundred and sixty-seven, entitled 'An act to provide for the more efficient government of the rebel States,' and of the act supplementary thereto, passed on the twenty-third day of March, in the year one thousand eight hundred and sixty-seven, that the governments then existing in the rebel States of Virginia, North Carolina, South Carolina, Georgia, Mississippi, Alabama, Louisiana, Florida, Texas, and Arkansas were not legal State governments; and that thereafter said governments, if continued, were to be continued subject in all respects to the military commanders of the respective districts, and to the paramount authority of Congress.

**What is the power of removal?**

"2. The commander of any district named in said act shall have power, subject to the disapproval of the general of the army of the United States, and to have effect till disapproved, whenever in the opinion of such commander the proper administration of said act shall require it, to suspend or remove from office, or from the performance of official duties and the exercise of official powers, any officer or person holding or exercising, or professing to hold or exercise, any civil or military office or duty in such district, under any power, election, appointment or authority derived from, or granted by, or claimed under, any so-called

State or the government thereof, or any municipal or other division thereof, and upon such suspension or removal, such commander, subject to the disapproval of the general as aforesaid, shall have power to provide from time to time for the performance of the said duties of such officer or person so suspended or removed, by the detail of some competent officer or soldier of the army, or by the appointment of some other person, to perform the same, and to fill vacancies occasioned by death, resignation, or otherwise.

" 3. The general of the army of the United States shall be invested with all the powers of suspension removal, appointment, and detail granted in the preceding section to district commanders. *What are the powers of the General as to removals?*

" 4. The acts of the officers of the army already done in removing in said districts persons exercising the functions of civil officers, and appointing others in their stead, are hereby confirmed : *Provided,* That any person heretofore or hereafter appointed by any district commander to exercise the functions of any civil office, may be removed either by the military officer in command of the district, or by the general of the army. And it shall be the duty of such commander to remove from office as aforesaid all persons who are disloyal to the government of the United States, or who use their official influence in any manner to hinder, delay, prevent, or obstruct the due and proper administration of this act and the acts to which it is supplementary.

" 5. The boards of registration provided for in the act entitled 'An act supplementary to an act entitled "An act to provide for the more efficient government of the rebel States," passed March two, eighteen hundred and sixty-seven, and to facilitate restoration,' passed March twenty-three, eighteen hundred and sixty-seven, shall have power, and it shall be their duty, before allowing the registration of any person, to ascertain, upon such facts or information as they can obtain, whether such person is entitled to be registered under said act; and the oath required by said act shall not be conclusive on such question, and no person shall be registered unless such board shall decide that he is entitled thereto ; and such board shall also have power to examine, under oath (to be administered by any member of such board), any one touching the qualification of any person claiming registration ; but in every case of refusal by the board to register an applicant, and in every case of striking his name from the list as hereinafter provided, the board shall make a note or memorandum, which shall be returned with the registration list to the commanding general of the district setting forth the grounds of such refusal or such striking from the list: *Provided,* That no person shall be disqualified as member of any board of registration by reason of race or color. *What are the duties of the board of registration?*

" 6. The true intent and meaning of the oath prescribed in said supplementary act is (among other things), that no person who has been a member of the legislature of any State, or who has held any executive or judicial office in any State, whether he has taken an oath to support the Constitution of the United States or not, and whether he was holding such office at the commencement of the rebellion, or had held it before, and who has afterwards engaged in insurrection or rebellion against the United States, or *What is the extent of the disqualification?*

given aid or comfort to the enemies thereof, is entitled to be registered or to vote; and the words 'executive or judicial office in any State' in said oath mentioned shall be construed to include all civil offices created by law for the administration of any general law of a State, or for the administration of justice.

**To what time is the registration extended?**
"7. The time for completing the original registration provided for in said act may, in the discretion of the commander of any district, be extended to the first day of October, eighteen hundred and sixty-seven; and the boards of registration shall have power, and it shall be their duty, commencing fourteen days prior to any election under said act, and upon reasonable public notice of the time and place thereof, to revise, for a period of five days, the registration lists, and upon being satisfied that any person not entitled thereto has been registered, to strike the name of such person from the list, and such person shall not be allowed to vote. And such board shall also, during the same period, add to such registry the names of all persons who at that same time possess the qualifications required by said act who have not been already registered; and no person shall, at any time, be entitled to be registered, or to vote, by reason of any executive pardon or amnesty, for any act or thing which, without such pardon or amnesty, would disqualify him from registration or voting.

**What are the powers of the commanding general?**
"8. Section four of said last-named act shall be construed to authorize the commanding general named therein, whenever he shall deem it needful, to remove any member of a board of registration, and to appoint another in his stead, and to fill any vacancy in such board.

**What oath is required of the board?**
"9. All members of said boards of registration and all persons hereafter elected or appointed to office in said military districts, under any so-called State or municipal authority, or by detail or appointment of the district commanders, shall be required to take and to subscribe the oath of office prescribed by law for officers of the United States.

**By whose opinions are the district commanders bound?**
"10. No district commander or member of the board of registration, or any of the officers or appointees acting under them, shall be bound in his action by any opinion of any civil officer of the United States.

"11. All the provisions of this act, and of the acts to which this is supplementary, shall be construed liberally to the end that all the intents thereof may be fully and perfectly carried out."
Passed over the President's veto, 19th July, 1867.

"JOINT RESOLUTION to carry into effect the several acts providing for the more efficient government of the rebel States.

"*Be it resolved, &c.,* That, for the purpose of carrying into effect the above named acts, there be appropriated, out of any money in the treasury not otherwise appropriated, the sum of one million dollars."
Passed over the President's veto, 19th July, 1867.

**What meant the second section of the amendment?**
**277.** It will be seen that the second section of the fourteenth amendment only contemplated the rejection from the basis of representation of the "numbers," whose male representative men should be denied the elective franchise. This applied especially to the free

persons of color. Upon the estimate of four and a half mil- 21, 23.
lions of those, very few of whom are allowed to vote, unless the
rule of suffrage should be changed, nearly one-eighth of the whole
representation would have to be deducted. Nearly all of this
would, in fact, fall upon the late slave States, and the greater part
upon the remaining ten rebel States. The reconstruction acts ad- What is the
vance one step further. They still recognize the principle that the effect of
States may determine for themselves who of their inhabitants may to the
vote; but, as in the case of Nebraska, it is imposed "as a funda- negroes?
mental condition of admission" that these States shall make no 17.
distinction, as to the right of suffrage, on account of color. While,
then, it was intended to enforce the adoption of the constitutional
amendment, if the law imposed the burden of negro suffrage, it
also secured to the unwilling whites the benefit of the increased
representation which would have been lost without this principle. 275.
While the means adopted have been denounced as onerous, and the
executive and judicial departments of the government have been
appealed to to arrest them, the candid historian will have to record,
that the object of this legislation has been to secure the fourteenth
amendment to the Constitution. And, viewed as a revolution in
organic law, superinduced by the mighty events which preceded,
the friends and the opponents of the measure will have to be judged, By what
as they are being judged in regard to the thirteenth amendment, rule will
by the question of whether it was right, expedient and wise thus the friends
to secure the fruits of the victory which prevented the destruction nents have
of the Union? If the end shall be approved, the severities of the to be
war and the great loss of property, in the one case, and the com- judged?
plaints of the unfortunate men, who fought against a beneficent 275.
government, in the other, will be forgotten.

**278.** Under these laws the voters registered have been as fol- Compare the
lows: black and
white vote?

|  | Whites. | Blacks. | Total. |
|---|---|---|---|
| Alabama | 72,746 | 93,543 | 166,289 |
| Arkansas | 43,170 | 23,146 | 66,316 |
| Florida | 11,151 | 15,541 | 26,692 |
| Georgia | 96,262 | 95,973 | 192,235 |
| Louisiana | 45,169 | 83,249 | 128,418 |
| Mississippi | 47,434 | 62,091 | 109,525 |
| North Carolina | 103,060 | 71,657 | 174,717 |
| South Carolina | 46,676 | 80,714 | 127,390 |
| Texas | 56,666 | 47,430 | 104,096 |
| Virginia | 120,101 | 105,832 | 225,933 |
| Aggregates | 642,435 | 679,176 | 1,321,611 |

—*The World* Almanac, pp. 102–106.

In 1860, the white vote of the same States was about 652,000.
But it is estimated that 300,000, who would have been voters, lost
their lives by the civil war. Probably 100,000 were either excluded, under the acts of Congress, or else failed to register. And
yet there seems to be a falling off of less than 10,000. The vote
of West Virginia is also to be deducted from the vote of Virginia.
The conventions have been carried and delegates elected in all the

States except Texas. In that State an election has been ordered to take place on the 10th, 11th, 12th, 13th and 14th of February, 1868.

**17.**  The conventions of Alabama, Virginia, North Carolina, Georgia, Florida, and Arkansas have adopted the principle of suffrage for whites and blacks alike.

The new Constitutions will be submitted to the people for their ratification; and a bill has passed the House of Representatives, and may become a law, to secure the ratification by a simple majority of the votes cast; and to elect members of Congress at the same time. Should the Constitutions be ratified, and State officers elected under them, the contest may possibly then arise between the new governments thus organized and the governments intended to be superseded. But whatever form the controversy may assume, no candid mind should ever lose sight of the fact, that the great issue is, Shall the fourteenth amendment be ratified by those States not now allowed representation or not?

What do the amendments propose? The first?
6, 19, 25, 28, 93, 163, 169, 220-223.

**279.**  In view of so important an issue, it may be well for every reader to consider carefully what this amendment proposes or has done? This may be answered thus :—

Sec. 1.  Defines national citizenship, and thus makes organic what had already been declared law by the first section of the Civil Rights Bill. Paschal's Annotated Digest, Art. 5382. See Farrar's Const. § 448.

220-225, 245-274.
260, 264.

All else in this section has already been guarantied in the second and fourth sections of the fourth article; and in the thirteen amendments. The new feature declared is that the general principles, which had been construed to apply only to the national government, are thus imposed upon the States. Most of the States, in general terms, had adopted the same bill of rights in their own constitutions.

The second?
21-24, 276.
17, 18, 220, 221.
What is the effect of curtailment of suffrage?
18.
16-18.
173, 174, 269.

**280.**  The second section amends the third clause of the second section of the first article, so as to make representation depend upon voters as well as numbers. It thus more clearly defines who of those " persons," now "citizens," shall be counted in the basis of representation. Curtailment of representation will follow curtailment of suffrage. But the rights of the States to determine who of their inhabitants shall vote seems still to be left unimpaired. This view, however, has been denied; and there are those of great weight, who claim that Congress has the power to prescribe an universal rule of suffrage for all the States. Putting it upon the ground of a right still retained by the States and people, it is not probable that any State would long exclude a large class of voters at the expense of its weight of representation in the national assembly and the electoral college. The prejudice against caste would be overcome by the necessity for strength.

The third?
242, 276.
921, 222, 215.

**281.**  The third section contains a decree of exclusion from office, against all, everywhere, and for the past as well as future, who, having previously taken an oath as a member of Congress, or as an officer of the United States, or as a member of any State legislature, or as an executive or judicial officer of any State, to support the Constitution of the United States, shall have engaged in insurrection or rebellion against the same, or given aid or comfort to the enemies thereof.

One of the complaints against the reconstruction laws has been, that this same disqualification has been extended to the right to vote upon all the measures of reconstruction; and that so large a class has thus been excluded that "negro supremacy" has been established in all those ten States. It is no part of this book to defend or denounce any policy. The truth is, that the disqualification did not and could not reach any voter under twenty-seven years of age; it could reach comparatively few below thirty-five; and in no community is there an alarming number above fifty years of age. Neither by statistical possibility nor by count, has it been found fairly to extend to one-tenth part of the population. Upon Attorney-General Staubery's interpretation, one-twentieth would be much nearer the number. (Opinions upon the Reconstruction Laws, 1861.) It does, however, reach a class; and the disqualification would extend to future as well as to past rebellions, and the *power* of holding office, or *disability* could only be removed by a two-thirds vote of each house of Congress.

And as the country seems to have settled down into the notion, that the elective franchise and the qualification for office are *powers*, which always require something superadded to mere citizenship, the disqualification as an organic rule for the future becomes one of wisdom and sound policy. I say nothing of the argument that it is a punishment for past offenses against the efficacy of executive pardon. As the number of participants in past rebellions will daily decrease, let us hope that the love of office, the very strongest in the restless, ambitious spirits, who always control popular sentiment, may render it almost impossible that ever the section shall extend to others who shall hereafter engage in insurrection or rebellion against the United States.

"STATE" in this section would doubtless be interpreted, as in the fugitive clauses, to extend to the District of Columbia and the Territories, and, indeed, to all who owed allegiance to the United States, and had held an office within the category of those defined. And "PERSON" would receive the most comprehensive definition.

**282.** The fourth section declares, that "the validity of the public debt of the United States, authorized by law, including debts incurred for the payment of pensions and bounties for services in suppressing insurrection or rebellion shall not be questioned." While this has been supposed to relate to the debt contracted in the suppression of the late rebellion, it is, in fact, an organic pledge for all debts contracted in the past and for the future. The debt is not only not to be repudiated, but "not questioned."

While so large a debt is thus intended to be secured, the section further stipulates: "But neither the United States nor any State shall assume or pay any debt or obligation incurred in aid of insurrection or rebellion against the United States, or any claim for the loss or emancipation of any slave; but all such debts, obligations, and claims shall be held illegal and void."

The debt of the Confederate States could not have been less than two thousand millions of dollars; and the value of the slaves

*Marginal notes:*
What is the effect of the disqualification?

What percentage could it possibly reach?

277.

242.

16-18, 220-223.

16-19, 35, 46, 93, 169-171.

142, 143

117

226, 215, 242.

What is the fourth section?

What debts does it embrace? 78, 82.

What debts are stipulated not to be paid?

What are the probable amounts?

emancipated exceeded that sum. The debts incurrred by States, counties, corporations, and individuals in aid of insurrection or rebellion against the United States, probably amount to a thousand millions more, to say nothing of pensions and "bounties for services," if one clause of the article is to be consulted in expounding the other. The terms of reconstruction prescribed by President Johnson required the States to repudiate their war debts. This has been done to a more or less limited extent in the constitutions and ordinances of the reconstruction conventions. But this is only **78, 82.** for the protection of the States. Every one will judge for himself of the influence of such a debt, combined with the danger of having so large a national debt "questioned" or repudiated.

The problem of allowing the representations from States withdrawn from Congress and incurring such enormous debts of their own, while fighting the United States, an equal voice in reference to debts incurred by the nation in conquering them, is one of no small difficulty. Viewed from the stand-point of extraneous influences upon Congress, no one can now fully comprehend its danger. The organic guaranty is only an additional security.

**The fifth?**  **283.** The fifth section is little more than a repetition of the **138.** general powers of legislation. It is precisely the same expressed in the thirteenth amendment.

"The Congress shall have power to enforce, by appropriate **274.** legislation, the provisions of this article." The appropriate legislation which would arise under this article, would be governed by time and circumstances, just as all the other powers of Congress have been.

**What is the** **284.** Whether this constitutional amendment has become, or **importance** shall become, a part of the organic law, as covenant for the great **of the** future, is a matter for the serious contemplation of the whole **subject?** country. In the late very able message of the President, he re- **274.** commends Congress to retrace the measures of the past. This cannot be understood to recommend the annulment of the thirteenth constitutional amendment. He is very explicit in opposing the reconstruction laws ; and therefore he may be construed as recommending the repeal of the Civil Rights Bill, and opposing this whole fourteenth amendment, with no other recommendation in its stead, than to allow the representation from the States elected since the **46, 242.** acts of reconstruction, directed by the President himself. Few, if any, of these persons, could take the test oath now required of all. But whether this is to be repealed or to be regarded as obsolete, has not been very distinctly avowed by those who demand the admission of members from those States.

**What may** **285.** It may not be out of place to observe, that, as the third **be the effect** section disqualifies a class from office, the principle of *inclusio unius,* **of the third** *exclusio alterius,* may remove the disability caused by the test oath **section upon** as to all not in that section enumerated. If this be so, those en- **the test** gaged in the late rebellion would gain rather than lose by the adop- **oath?** tion of the amendment. Many leaders in that movement are not **242.** disqualified.

The question of what are the constitutional rights of men, regardless of the past, is always one of serious import. Such an issue, at such a time, is well calculated to awaken the most painful apprehensions. The issues involved are:—1. Does freedom to the slave mean equal liberty to the citizen? 2. Have they been made citizens, and if so, what is the extent of their rights? 3. Shall the governments of the States lately in rebellion be left to those only who controlled it; or shall all participate regardless of color or previous condition? 4. Shall the ratio of representation remain, thus superadding two-fifths to the slave States without one-half of the citizens having any greater participation in the government than the slaves had; or shall the ratio be changed so as to represent votes as well as numbers? 5. Shall any one for the past or the future be disqualified from holding office because of participation in insurrection or rebellion against the United States? 6. Shall there be an organic guaranty in respect to the national debt; or shall there be such guaranty against the rebel debt and the claim for slaves? *What are the real issues involved? 220, 274, 23, 24.*

See Farrar upon the Fourteenth Amendment, § 448, 449.

As to the speculative question, What is to be the future of the negroes? an opinion would be as hazardous as would have been an uninspired prophecy as to the future of the Jews the day they crossed the Red Sea.

**286.** The editor of the foregoing notes cannot dismiss the subject without a few general remarks, which have suggested themselves during the years of study necessary to the preparation of such a work. These reflections will be confined to the changes in the organism of the government, silent and conventional. The first reflection is, that in the choice of President the expectations of the framers of the Constitution have been disappointed. The choice was intended to be left to the electoral colleges uninfluenced by a previous canvass. It was probably expected that a failure to agree would be the rule—not the exception—and that the choice would devolve upon the House, and be made by States as co-equals. The first disagreement led to a change of principle. The convention system of nominations has destroyed the influence of the small States, and transferred the selection of candidates to the large States. The contest is really directly for the candidates, and the electors are but *conduit* pipes, fearfully responsible to their direct constituents to whom they stand pledged. *1-278. What are the general reflections of the editor? What as to the choice President 167.*

The next noticeable fact has been the increase, and now the curtailment, of the President's power and patronage. The appointing to office was always a prerogative of the crown. The power to remove officers at pleasure, at first doubtfully exercised, has become a fearful engine of party. The tenure-of-office law has attempted to check the exercise of the power without reaching the root of the evil. But the mischief lies not so much in the constitutional powers of the President, as the too common error that the administration is the government. Upon this fallacy of not living "under Lincoln rule," the Southern heart was fired unto resistance and civil war; the same popular fallacy has controlled in the same section in the contest between the President and Congress. So that whether the *184-186. 184. What is the too common error as to the power of the President?*

executive sympathies are against or for us, we overrate his powers
for evil or good.   Like all other magistrates, the President is
obliged to be controlled by the Constitution and the laws of the
land.

**What of the judicial power?**
**195, 275.**
The third noticeable fact is, that the judicial jurisdiction and
influence have been rather increased and enlarged than diminished.
The reports of this branch of the government stand as vast monu-
ments of learning.   They are more permanently and generally
accessible to the people than the expositions of the other departments.   In a country where the legal profession exert so mighty
an influence, they are regarded as more authoritative than other
precedents, because the exact demarcations of judicial power are
not clearly understood.

**What revo-
lutions have
marked the
history of
the govern-
ment?**
**229-232.**
The revolutions which have marked the history of the government will be found in the several constitutional amendments, in
the acquisition of foreign territory, the annexation of Texas, the
history of the rebellion and the consequences which have followed.
The acquisition of territory led to the creation of "colonial governments," or "inchoate States" (generally confused under the undefined title of "Territories"), and a series of legislation for which
no direct constitutional grant could be found; and which consequently caused a rapid concentration of central power.   Each new
revolutionary fact has excused an exercise of the supposed "neces-
**133.** sary and proper" legislation.   These were incidents of national
sovereignty which, perforce, revolutionized the public ideas of
the country.   The same may be said of the practical necessity
which crushed the theory of secession.   Sundry express powers
were specially granted in the Constitution.   To protect and shield
these for the benefit of the whole people, all of the incidental neces-
**133.** sary powers had to be exerted.   And, in such a contest, the leading actors can never nicely discriminate.   So that if it should be-
**233-235.** come necessary to revolutionize States or change State boundaries
and organizations, for safety, hereafter, we have the living precedents.

And yet the candid student must admit that our Constitution
and Union still stand as the same glorious fabric, with the powers
of departments clearly defined; with whole bills of rights unimpaired; with new guaranties for liberty; with human slavery
stricken out of the instrument; and with a continuing struggle to
protect the political equality of all.   The nation is mighty and
glorious among the great powers of the earth, and may it be perpetual.   If I shall have contributed any thing to the study of
this great fabric, my prayers will have been answered.

                                    GEO. W PASCHAL.
JAN. 1, 1868.

# ANALYTICAL INDEX.

*The texts of the Constitution are arranged analytically and alphabetically. The Articles, Sections, and Clauses are shown both as to the Constitution noted and not noted. The Preface, Declaration of Independence, Articles of Confederation and the author's notes are likewise copiously indexed.*

13*

# INDEX. 299

Art. sec. cl.    pp.

304 INDEX.

# 306 INDEX.

|  | Art. | sec. | cl. | pp. |
|---|---|---|---|---|
| Of weights, n. 202, p. 118. A ton, n. 102, pp. 116, 118. The spirit measure, n. 102, p. 116. |  |  |  |  |
| To provide for the punishment of counterfeiting the securities and current coin of the United States.................... | 1 | 8 | 6 | 29, 118 |
| To establish post-offices and post-roads...................... | 1 | 8 | 7 | 29, 119 |
| To establish, defined and compared with the word elsewhere, n. 104; as in notes 8, 13, 93, 94, 95, 195, 243, 245. Post-offices defined, and their history and present standing given, n. 106. Post-roads defined, n. 106. |  |  |  |  |
| To promote the progress of science and useful arts, by securing, for limited times, to authors and inventors, the exclusive right to their respective writings and discoveries....................................... | 1 | 8 | 8 | 29, 121 |
| To promote, and every word and phrase, defined, n. 107, pp. 121, 122. Inventors defined, and the law discussed, n. 108. |  |  |  |  |
| To constitute tribunals inferior to the Supreme Court........ | 1 | 8 | 9 | 29, 124 |
| To constitute, and tribunals, defined, and doctrine stated, n. 109. When bound by State decisions, Id. |  |  |  |  |
| To define and punish piracies and felonies committed on the high seas, and offenses against the law of nations......... | 1 | 8 | 10 | 29, 124 |
| "To define" defined, n. 110. To punish defined, and death punishment stated, n. 111. Piracy and pirate defined, n. 112. Felony defined and discussed, n. 113. High seas defined, n. 114. Offenses against the law of nations defined and discussed, n. 115. Law of nations defined, n. 116. |  |  |  |  |
| To declare war, grant letters of marque and reprisal, and make rules concerning captures on land and water ....... | 1 | 8 | 11 | 29, 127 |
| War, civil war, and our forms of declaring, defined and given, n. 117. Gives the right to acquire territory, n. 118. Citizens of the countries at war are personally at war, n. 118. Their disabilities, n. 118. The effects of the late rebellion, n. 118. Marauders and bushwhackers not protected, n. 118, p. 128. Allegiance during civil war, n. 118, p. 129. Gives the right of conscription, notes 118, 121, 124. Marque and reprisal defined, notes 119, 120, 121. The power under the Confederation, Arts. VI., VII., VIII., pp. 11–18. |  |  |  |  |
| To raise and support armies; but no appropriation of money to that use shall be for a longer term than two years...... | 1 | 8 | 12 | 29, 130 |
| This power did not exist in Congress under the Confederation, n. 122. To raise and support, and armies, defined, 123, 124, 125. (See Armies.) |  |  |  |  |
| To provide and maintain a navy ........................... | 1 | 8 | 13 | 29, 132 |
| This power defined and discussed, n. 127. The sovereign rights on public ships, n. 127, p. 133. Ranks in the navy, Id. The right of Habeas Corpus over enlistments, n. 141, p. 145. |  |  |  |  |
| To make rules for the government and regulation of the land and naval forces......... ........ ........ | 1 | 8 | 14 | 29, 133 |
| For where these rules are to be found, see n. 129. |  |  |  |  |
| To provide for calling forth the militia to execute the laws of the Union, suppress insurrections, and repel invasions ... | 1 | 8 | 15 | 29, 133 |
| Militia defined, n. 130, and the laws in relation to calling them out, n. 130. The laws to be executed, notes 131, 238, 240. Insurrection defined and discussed, notes 132, 234, 235. Invasion, the law about, n. 133. |  |  |  |  |
| To provide for organizing, arming, and disciplining the militia, and for governing such part of them as may be employed in the service of the United States, reserving to the States, respectively, the appointment of the officers, and the authority of training the militia according to the discipline prescribed by Congress ................................. | 1 | 8 | 16 | 29, 135 |
| This power defined and discussed, n. 134. The subject of conscription, n. 134. |  |  |  |  |
| To exercise exclusive legislation, in all cases whatsoever, over such district (not exceeding ten miles square) as may, by |  |  |  |  |

# 314

INDEX.

316 INDEX.

14*

| | Art. | sec. | cl. | pp. |
|---|---|---|---|---|

Art. sec. cl. pp.

The several acts and decisions thereon, which have been prescribed under this clause, n. 219.

GENERAL welfare. The Constitution established to promote the general welfare. Preamble ...... .......... ....... | | | | 22, 53
This clause defined, n. 10. Was stricken out of the Confederate Constitution, n. 5.

GENERAL welfare. Congress shall have power to provide for the general welfare.................. .................. | 1 | 8 | 1 | 28, 91
Judge Story's reading of this clause, n. 80. Mr. Jefferson's construction, n. 80.

GEORGIA. Signed the Dec. of Ind. p. 8; the Articles of Confederation, pp. 9, 21; and the Constitution of the United States, pp. 43, 252. Qualifications for voters in, n. 17, p. 60.

GEORGIA. Entitled to three representatives in the first Congress. | 1 | 2 | 3 | 28, 67
Seven representatives by the census of 1860. n. 24, p. 69. Population through each decade, n. 24, pp. 69, 70. Did not vote in the presidential election of 1864, n. 167. Assigned to fifth judicial circuit, n. 197, p. 192. Ceded Alabama and Mississippi, notes 230, 231, 232. Ratified the 13th constitutional amendment, n. 274, and rejected the 14th, n. 275. Declared one of the rebel States, n. 276, p. 282. Civil government subject to military control, n. 274, p. 286, § 1. Held convention, 277. Registered voters in, Id.

GERRY, ELBRIDGE, of Mass. Signed the Dec. of Ind., p. 7; and Articles of Confederation, p. 21. Vice-President, n. 37.

GILMAN, NICHOLAS. Deputy from New Hampshire. Signed this Constitution, pp. 42, 252.

GOD, ALMIGHTY. (See *Almighty God*, n. 5.)

GOD, the act of, not to affect the termination of services, n. 274.

GOLD and silver coin. No State shall make any thing but gold and silver coin a tender in payment of debts................. | 1 | 10 | 1 | 31, 153
Remark upon this, n. 152. But Congress may make paper a legal tender, notes 83, 97, 98, 99, 100, 155. This denied, notes 97-100. Examples of paper legal tenders, n. 83. The first legal-tender act was in favor of foreign coin, n. 155.

GOOD behavior. The judges, both of the Supreme and inferior courts, shall hold their offices during good behavior ...... | 3 | 1 | 1 | 36, 189
That is for life or until impeachment, notes 191, 192, 193, 194, 197. The precedents of impeachment for want of, n. 194.

GORHAM, NATHANIEL, of Mass. Signed the Constitution, pp. 41, 252.

GOVERNING the militia. Congress shall have power to provide for governing such part of the militia as may be employed in the service of the United States,...................... | 1 | 8 | 16 | 29, 135
This power defined, n. 134. Power of the President over, notes 134, 135.

GOVERNMENT. The Constitution created a, not a mere compact, Pref. p. viii. notes 2, 4. Cannot take the rights of the citizen away, except by due course of law, n. 257. Grand juries hear the evidence of the government only, n. 283. Reasons for the exclusive in the District of Columbia, n. 136. How it is changed by abolishing slavery, n. 274. Changes in the, silent and conventional, n. 286, p. 293. The fallacy that the President is the government, Id. The decisions and influence of the judicial department of, Id. 294. The revolutions which have marked the history will be found where, Id. p. 294.

GOVERNMENT. Congress shall have power to make rules for the government and regulation of the land and naval forces... | 1 | 8 | 14 | 29, 135
These rules, how made and where found, n. 129.

GOVERNMENT of the United States. Congress shall have power to make all laws which shall be necessary and proper for carrying into execution the foregoing powers, and all other powers vested by this Constitution in the government of the United States, or in any department or office thereof.................................................. | 1 | 8 | 18 | 80, 153
(See power discussed, notes 71, 128.) Does not mean abso-

15

# INDEX. 341

# 350

# INDEX.

# 354 INDEX.

|  | Art. | sec. | cl. | pp. |
|---|---|---|---|---|
| maritime contracts wherever made, n. 203. As for material, &c., Id. | | | | |
| MARQUE. This power under the Confederation, Art. IX. p. 14. | | | | |
| MARQUE and reprisal. Congress shall have power to grant letters of marque and reprisal. | 1 | 8 | 11 | 29, 127 |
| These terms defined, notes 119, 120, 121. | | | | |
| MARQUE and reprisal. No State shall grant letters of marque and reprisal. | 1 | 10 | 1 | 31, 153 |
| Because it is a national power, n. 152. | | | | |
| MARRIAGE. Used in connection with definition of disparage, n. 268. | | | | |
| MARSHAL of the United States. R. C. Parsons, the present, n. 197, p. 192. | | | | |
| MARTIAL law. Cannot exist with civil liberty, n. 260. Defined and distinguished from other military law. n. 260, p. 265. | | | | |
| MARTIAL law, or military law, defined and explained, n. 262, p. 265. | | | | |
| MARYLAND. Signed the Dec. of Ind. p. 7. One of the Confederation, p. 9. Signed the Articles of Confederation, p. 21; the Constitution of the United States, pp. 41, 252. Qualification of voters, n. 17, p. 61. | | | | |
| MARYLAND. Entitled to six representatives in the first Congress. | 1 | 2 | 3 | 23, 67 |
| Five representatives by census of 1860, n. 24. p. 69. The number of inhabitants through each decade, n. 24, pp. 69, 70. Assigned to the fourth judicial circuit, n. 197, p 192. Ratified the 13th constitutional amendment, n. 274 and rejected the 14th, n. 275. | | | | |
| MASSACHUSETTS. Signed the Dec. of Ind. p. 7. One of the Confederation, p. 9. Signed the Articles of Confederation, p. 21. Signed the Constitution of the United States, p. 41. Qualification of voters, n. 17, p. 61. Eight representatives in first Congress. Ten representatives in 1860, n. 24, p. 69. Number of inhabitants through each decade, n. 24, pp. 69, 70. Assigned to the first judicial circuit, n. 197, p. 192. | 1 | 2 | 3 | 23, 67 |
| MASTERS of vessels cannot be required to pay a passenger tax, n. 88. | | | | |
| MASTERS. Might seize and recapture their slaves, n. 227, p. 233. The slaves to be delivered up to them, n. 228. Can assign their apprentices in Maryland, n. 274. p. 273. | | | | |
| MATERIALS for ships under admiralty jurisdiction, n. 203. | | | | |
| MEASURES. The President shall, from time to time, recommend to the consideration of Congress such measures as he shall judge necessary and expedient, | 2 | 3 | 1 | 36, 183 |
| MEASURES. Congress has power to fix the standard of weights and measures | 1 | 8 | 5 | 29, 114 |
| To fix defined, n. 101. Weights and measures of the metric system made lawful, n. 102, p 117, § 1. And contracts therein rendered valid, Id. Tables for, established, Id. § 2. Measures of length, Id. Of surface, Id. Of capacity, Id., p. 118. | | | | |
| MEETING of Congress. The census to be taken within three years of the first meeting of Congress | 1 | 2 | 3 | 23, 67 |
| MEETING. The Congress shall assemble at least once in every year, and such meeting shall be on the first Monday in December, unless they shall by law appoint a different day | 1 | 4 | 2 | 25, 83 |
| When the constitutional term expires, n. 43. The meetings as now prescribed by law, n. 45. Three of each Congress, Id. | | | | |
| MEMBERS of House of Representatives. (See *Representatives*.) | | | | |
| MEMBERS of the Senate. (See *Senators*.) | | | | |
| MICHIGAN. Qualifications for suffrage in, n. 17. Number of representatives, n. 24. Population in each decade, n. 24, pp. 69, 70. Assigned to sixth judicial circuit, n. 197. Admitted into the Union, n. 280. Ratified the 13th amendment, n. 274; the 14th, n. 275. | | | | |
| MIDDLETON, ARTHUR, of South Carolina. Signed Dec. of Ind. p. 8. | | | | |

16

16*

www.ingramcontent.com/pod-product-compliance
Lightning Source LLC
Chambersburg PA
CBHW032303280326
41932CB00009B/678